Morrison, Robert

A parting memorial, consisting of Miscellaneous Discourses

Morrison, Robert

A parting memorial, consisting of Miscellaneous Discourses

Inktank publishing, 2018

www.inktank-publishing.com

ISBN/EAN: 9783747703847

A

PARTING MEMORIAL;

CONSISTING OF

MISCELLANEOUS DISCOURSES,

WRITTEN AND PREACHED

IN CHINA; AT SINGAPORE; ON BOARD SHIP AT SEA, IN THE INDIAN OCEAN; AT THE CAPE OF GOOD HOPE; AND IN ENGLAND.

WITH

REMARKS ON MISSIONS,

&c. &c.

BY

ROBERT MORRISON, D.D.F.R.S.M.R.A.S.

PRESIDENT OF THE ANGLO-CHINESE COLLEGE;
MEMBER OF THE SOCIETE ASIATIQUE OF PARIS; AUTHOR OF A CHINESE DICTIONARY
TRANSLATOR OF THE SACRED SCRIPTURES,
&c.

"*Behold! these shall come from afar; And lo! these from the north and the west; And these from the land of* Sinim."—ISAIAH.

LONDON:

PRINTED FOR W. SIMPKIN AND R. MARSHALL,

STATIONERS' HALL COURT, LUDGATE STREET.

1826.

TO

HIS PERSONAL FRIENDS,

THROUGHOUT THE UNITED KINGDOM,

AND TO

THE FRIENDS OF THAT CAUSE

TO WHICH HE HAS DEVOTED HIS LIFE,

THE FOLLOWING

MEMORIAL

IS AFFECTIONATELY AND RESPECTFULLY

INSCRIBED,

BY

THE AUTHOR.

5, GROVE, HACKNEY,
Jan. 5, 1826.

PREFACE.

DURING the year of our Lord 1824, whilst travelling in England, Ireland, and Scotland, the Author of the following Discourses received much attention, and many civilities from zealous Christian Friends, in every part of the United Kingdom, to whom he had no introduction but his public character. His having resided many years in a distant heathen, populous country, for the purpose of transfusing into its language the Holy Scriptures, excited on his behalf an interest which, under other circumstances, could not have been felt.

Having had the satisfaction, during his stay in England, to see originated a public attention to the language of China, he is now about to revisit that country; and therefore, in accordance with a principle he has often advocated, he avails himself of

THE PRESS,

to leave with his Friends, and the Public, this Volume, as a

PARTING MEMORIAL.

Although he does not assume that these discourses possess, irrespective of the circumstances connected with them, intrinsic excellence, sufficient to call for their being published; he still thinks, that they may prove instructive to some individuals, and not an unedifying memorial to many among whom he has travelled, occasionally preaching the Gospel.

On the means to be employed for the propagation of the Christian Religion throughout the world, the same ideas will frequently recur, but perhaps in a varied connexion, that will, on the whole, strengthen the argument.

He has used great plainness of speech, without effort or design, in his natural, unassumed manner; not with malevolence or intentional asperity, but with a frankness which is spontaneous; and, if he knows his own heart, affectionate, though seemingly severe.

He humbly prays that the Almighty Father's blessing, and the "Power of Christ," may rest on all Christian Churches; and that the Holy Spirit's influences may be abundantly shed down from on high upon all men; to the end that all the nations may be turned from darkness to light, and from dumb idols to the living God;—that Truth and Righteousness, Holiness and Happiness, may fill the whole Earth.

5, GROVE, HACKNEY,
March 11, 1826.

CONTENTS.

c

A

PARTING MEMORIAL,

&c. &c.

DISCOURSE I.

INTRODUCTION.

The city of Canton in China is situated on the banks of a river about one hundred miles from the sea. The river is in this part of its progress called *Chookeang*, "The Pearl River," from the circumstance of its once having contained pearl oysters.

Between the walls of the city and the river, on the south west corner, is the residence of Europeans and Americans, who visit China for commercial purposes. In this neighbourhood also are situated the counting-houses, warehouses, and shops, of those natives who are concerned in European commerce. These native warehouses are in Chinese called *Hongs*, or "*Walks*," from their extent.

On Saturday, the 2d of Nov. 1822, a fire, which broke out the preceding night, about half a mile to the north of the British Factories, extended southward and westward, with tremendous fierceness; and, impelled by a strong gale, overpowered all human efforts to resist its progress, till factories, hongs, and shops, were involved in flames, and consumed in one general conflagration. Thousands of houses, and millions of property were entirely destroyed. About a hundred lives were lost, partly by the fire, and partly by attacking or defending property. The governor of Canton, and all the local magistrates, attended.

B

On Sunday, the 3d, the first Bethel Flag ever hoisted on the rivers of China, was to have appeared at the mast-head of the Ship Pacific, of Philadelphia; and whilst preparing a discourse to the sailors, on the evening of Friday, the writer of this was called away to assist at the fire-engines. Friday night, Saturday, Saturday night, and Sunday, were all spent in sleepless anxiety, and unavailing efforts to extinguish the fire. It burnt till it arrived at the river's brink, and found no more materials to feed the flames.

The following Sunday, the sermon to sailors was preached at the anchorage called Whampoa, about eleven miles from Canton; and on Nov. 16th, the following discourse was delivered in an unconsumed native warehouse, called after its owner, *Consequa's Hong*. To the end of this building the fire of Canton extended, but being saved, it became a temporary dwelling for the English whose habitations were consumed. The congregation consisted of commercial agents, British and American Captains, Officers, Surgeons and others. The service commenced by reading the Prayers of the English Church.

THE WAY OF SALVATION.

ACTS XVI. 30.

"What must I do to be saved?"

THESE words were originally spoken under very extraordinary circumstances. St. Paul and his companions, whilst deliberating whither they should go to preach the Gospel, having been forbidden of the Holy Ghost to preach the word at that time in Lesser Asia; saw a vision, which directed them to pass, for the first time, into Europe. A man of Macedonia appeared in this vision, and prayed St. Paul, saying, "Come over into Macedonia and help us." The Apostle deemed that this was a divine intimation, and proceeded thither accordingly. There was at that time a Roman Colony at Philippi, and the place was governed by Roman laws. The religious customs were of course made up partly of the Paganism of Greece, and partly of that of Rome. Divinations, sorcery, and fortune-telling, were practised. Sometimes those who pretended to sorcery, magic, &c. were impostors; and, sometimes, there is every reason to believe, they were actuated by Satan, the father of lies and of false miracles, and of lying prophecies.

At Philippi there was a certain damsel possessed with a spirit of divination, which brought her masters much gain by soothsaying. This young woman followed Paul and his companions for several days, crying out aloud, "These men are the servants of the most high God, which shew unto us the way of salvation." This statement was consistent with the real fact; but it is supposed the design of Satan, in suggesting this assertion, was insidiously to identify the sorceress and satanic influences with the apostles and the divine inspiration, which, blending the two, would hinder the truth amongst the Pagans, by leading them to say, "our religion is from the same source as yours;" and would hinder it likewise amongst the Jews, who resided at Philippi, and who hated sorcery and divination, in which they were fully justified by divine command.

Paul was therefore grieved; and eventually, in the name of our Saviour, commanded the demon, or false spirit, to abandon the woman. It was done, and she was silenced. The false prophetess was struck dumb, and could no longer utter the responses, which she had been accustomed to do, for money paid to her masters. The proper effect of this would have been, for them to acknowledge the superiority of the Apostles, and that theirs was the true inspiration. They, however, actuated by a mercenary spirit, seeing that their gains were gone, seized Paul and Silas, dragged them before the magistrates, and accused them of being Jews, who exceedingly troubled their city; teaching customs, not lawful for those who were Romans to observe. And these magistrates, to satisfy the multitude, tore the raiment off Paul and Silas, laid many stripes upon them, and cast them into prison. The jailer, zealous in this bad cause, thrust them into the *inner* prison, and made their feet fast in the stocks. This jailer was the man (whether a Roman or a Greek does not appear) who, that very night, came trembling, and falling prostrate before Paul and Silas, said, "Sirs, *What must I do to be saved?*" An earthquake, which shook the prison, opened the gates, and loosened every prisoner's bonds, alarmed him, and at the same time convinced him, that these men were indeed the *servants of the most high God, who shewed the true way of salvation.* The jailer received no upbraidings for his gratuitous severity to the Apostle; but was readily and kindly answered, "Believe in the Lord Jesus Christ, and thou shalt be saved." The apostolic party further spake to the jailer the word of the Lord; he believed, was baptized, and rejoiced. His heart was changed—he was another man—a new creature. The jailer washed the prisoners' wounds, brought them into his house, and set meat before them, rejoicing and believing in God, with all his house.

From this interesting portion of sacred Scripture we infer,

I. The *necessity* of salvation.

II. The *way* of obtaining it; and,

III. The *effects* of being saved.—As this is a subject which, in the New Testament, is addressed to, and concerns all mankind, we shall gather our illustrations from all the nations, and not from our own country alone.

I. To *save*, and *salvation*, in sacred Scripture, imply *deliverance* from evil, whether natural or moral.

The salvation of which we would this day speak is salvation from sin, and from everlasting punishment. And is there a necessity for this? Is man a sinner, one who has violated the divine law; and is the just retribution of sin eternal death? Is this the state of some men only? or is it the fallen condition of all men, those in power, and those out of power; high and low; rich and poor; learned and ignorant. If this be the truth, the *necessity* of salvation is self-evident. And to prove that this is the truth, we argue thus: The prevalence of much vice and misery in the world is universally allowed; and that man is prone to evil, and has often sinned, is admitted by every breast; the confessions of the penitent, and the admonitions of the moralist, and the complaints of most men, in every land, prove that man is depraved and sinful. But man's *sense* of moral evil is confined, chiefly, to offences against the social duties—against himself, *in fact;* of the offences against high heaven, and the great God who there reigns, the perception of sinful man is blunted, or perverted, or lost. The revolt of our nature, and man's rebellion against God, the supreme Sovereign, has induced in every mind, even in the midst of abounding impiety, and practical atheism, a self-justifying spirit. Therefore man's opinion of sin is very far from being equal to the truth; it by no means comes up to the strong delineation derived from heaven, and contained in the Holy Bible. For example, take the sin of idolatry; that of changing the glory of the incorruptible God, into an image made like to corruptible man, or to birds, or four-footed beasts, or creeping reptiles, or stocks, or stones. Intellectual spiritual man abandons the worship of Jehovah, and falls prostrate to these. Yet in India, and China, do we Christians, who should feel the deepest regret that God is so dishonoured, and our fellow creatures in such an apostate, low, degraded state, generally look upon idolatry with the utmost indifference; and still more, in the face of the strongest abhorrence against this abominable sin, expressed in the sacred page by the mouth of God's holy prophets, there are those who palliate, or excuse, or even justify it.

And, which strengthens our argument, the idolater himself, always, instead of considering his idolatry a sin, the more enthusiastic and mad he is after his idols, he deems himself by so much the more meritorious. "A deceived heart hath turned him aside," and he has not spiritual perception of the truth sufficient to detect the lie that is in his right hand. Man always finds an excuse for his besetting, prevailing sin; and so far is this carried, that some immoralities, which, by persons not concerned, are universally condemned, are often thought excusable by the parties implicated. The pirate and the assassin, still suppose they may attain to heaven, and will keep up some forms of religion, or superstition. But is it reasonable that the opinions of sinful depraved mortals, concerning the demerits of sin, shall be more just and true than the revealed decision of the righteous and holy God? Ought we not, in the exercise of common sense, to relinquish all apologies and excuses for sin, and receive with reverence the divine sentence concerning it. What saith the Scripture? "Cursed is every one that continueth not in all things written in the book of the law to do them," (Galatians iii. 10.) "There is no man that sinneth not," (1 Kings viii. 46.) "If we say we have no sin, we deceive ourselves," (1 John i. 8—10.) "If we say we have not sinned, we make God a liar;" we give the lie to heaven, from whence it is declared, "There is none righteous, no not one," (Rom. iii. 10.) "Men together have become unprofitable, destruction and misery are in their ways." The holy law considers every mouth stopped, every cavilling tongue silenced, and the whole world become guilty before God, and inexcusably so. "For the invisible things of God, from the creation of the world, are clearly seen," God having shewn them to men; but "when they knew God, they glorified him not as God; neither were thankful, but became vain in their imaginations, and their foolish hearts were darkened:" man is self-ruined, and, if heaven may be believed, he is without excuse. Now, it is further declared that "the wrath of God is revealed from heaven against all unrighteousness and ungodliness of men. The wages of sin is death: the wicked shall be cast into hell, and all the nations that forget God;" they shall be cast into outer darkness; shall be immersed in a lake of fire, fire that shall never be quenched, the gnawing worm that torments shall never die; in that place "shall be weeping, and wailing, and gnashing of teeth;" in that place there shall be punishment everlasting.

Whatever interpretation is put on these awful declarations of the sacred Scriptures, they fully confirm our argument, that salvation is necessary to all men: for all men have sinned; all are liable to the eternal punishment of sin; and hence it becomes an infinitely important question, to be put by every human being, "*What shall* I *do to be saved?*" Suppose that no answer could be given to this question; that there was no salvation—no hope; nothing but a fearful looking for of judgment and fiery indignation to consume the wicked. What would be the feelings of a convinced sinner? Oh, how indescribable the anguish! And the day is coming, when to many this will really be the case; when it must be said, Now there is no salvation—now all hope is for ever fled. Oh, then, that none of us may defer a satisfactory answer to this question till it be too late; for happily it can *still* be said, "*Now* is the accepted time, *now* is the day of salvation." To every convinced and anxious penitent it is, by the divine word, said, "Believe in the Lord Jesus Christ, and *thou* shalt be saved."—This brings us to the second division of our discourse, viz.

II. *The way* of salvation.

Salvation, in common use, is very generally restricted to deliverance from future misery, anticipated as the punishment of sin: but salvation, in the sense of sacred Scripture, is not confined to that, but includes also a deliverance from the tyranny of Satan, and from the dominion of sinful propensities in this life.

Although there be many in every country who seem to give themselves no concern about future happiness or misery, there is a large proportion of our species, whose minds are ill at ease on this subject; and there are a few, who are very anxious about it. But there are various mistaken or false ways suggested; some more, and others less distantly removed from the true one. We sometimes suppose that, in religious matters, the false must be diametrically opposite to the true. But Satan, who goes about seeking whom he may *deceive*, as well as whom he may devour, like all tempters, cheats, and counterfeits, often endeavours to make the false resemble the true. On this principle it is, that false religion and superstition prevail so much in the world. Man's conscience is not easy without some religion, some object of worship; and the arch-apostate gains his malicious purpose by inducing men to be satisfied with the mere form of religion for the reality; and sometimes, to worship devils or demons, instead of God.

In order to be saved, to be forgiven, and made happy hereafter, the human mind has suggested sometimes things cruel, sometimes frivolous, and sometimes, seeming to us, not altogether irrational; but yet all different from the heaven-revealed way of salvation. It is to save himself, or to have merit to transfer for the salvation of others, that the devotee subjects himself to almost incredible austerities; it is to save herself infallibly, and her deceased kindred, (as well as from grief and affection,) that the Hindoo widow submits to be burned to death in the fire which consumes the corpse of her deceased husband. Man's anxious mind has led him to say, "Shall I give my first-born for my transgression; the fruit of my body for the sin of my soul!"

The philosophists, both Christian and Pagan, for the most part make a mock at the idea of sin, and it would be in vain for a serious awakened sinner, to ask them what he must do to be saved. The religionists of all kinds have more humanity in this respect. Many of these, however, suggest things which cannot profit—such as the reciting of certain *formularies* of words, which cannot often, with any propriety, be called *prayers;* because, as in China for example, they consist of words which are unintelligible to the person pronouncing them. The incessant repetition of the name Amidah Budh! Amidah Budh! is a certain means of the remission of sin; but there is no reason, no plausible theory adduced, why it should be so. Four prostrations towards the south on the day of every new moon will procure the forgiveness of millions of sins. Others prescribe the lighting of candles, the burning of incense, the saying of masses for the salvation of the soul. These are examples of the false ways which may be denominated superstitious or frivolous.

Those ways of obtaining salvation which appear more reasonable, are the performance of meritorious deeds, or works of righteousness, charity, or almsgiving. The Chinese have a table of vices and of virtues, stated in exact numbers, and direct that the one be balanced against the other, by the sinner himself, that he may thence calculate whether his virtues are sufficient in number to make amends for his vices: and there are many persons amongst Christians, who deem that the sicknesses and other trials of this life merit a reward in the next; and some, with seeming reason, say, repentance and amendment of life constitute the meritorious ground of salvation.

But, according to the Scriptures, all these ways of being saved, proceed upon the erroneous supposition that austerities, ceremonies, and obedience to the law in some things, will make amends for disobedience in others; that man can atone for his own sin; that he can be saved by his own doings; that he can save himself; that he needs no Saviour. Not only does man's foolish heart dream of this capability to save himself; but it, in some parts of the world, imagines, that by austerities, mortifications, abstractions, &c. man can raise himself to be a divine person—a god; thereby perpetuating the foolish suggestion of the serpent in paradise, that eating the interdicted fruit would make the parents of mankind become as gods.

Self-salvation is, perhaps, not more unscriptural than self-deification. The just sentence of condemnation, pronounced by the divine law, is not so easily removed; deliverance from the captivity of Satan is not so easily effected; emancipation from the slavery of sin is not so easily procured, as the above-mentioned false ways of salvation seem to suppose.

"The redemption of the soul is precious, and would cease for ever," if left to man. He can neither save himself, nor redeem his brother. Salvation must come to man from a power beyond himself, and greater than his own. He is a brand fit only for the burning, and cannot pluck himself out of the fire. Falling, sinking, drowning, he cannot save himself.

But the sacred Scriptures reveal to us *One who is mighty to save*—"able to save to the uttermost all who come to him." He is more than man—more than angel. Him all the angels of God worship. He is "God manifest in the flesh." "Help was laid upon Him." He undertook to crush the serpent's head; He was, from the beginning, (before Abraham's days,) the object of the sinner's hope. God so loved the world, and compassionated guilty man, as to constitute his beloved Son our surety—our Redeemer. He suffered for us; he gave himself to be a sacrifice; he became a propitiation; he died, "the just for the unjust." The Son of God is the author of salvation; in him the Father is well pleased. The Spirit of God that strives with man, is, through him, become the regenerator; and thus God himself, Father, Son, and Spirit, has become our salvation; and in the Bible he says, "*Look unto me and be ye saved, all the ends of the earth*; for I am God, and beside me there is no Saviour." Now, then, salvation is to be sought for *out* of ourselves, and not from works of righteousness that we can do. The glad tidings, the gospel of salvation, is promulgated to guilty man, and commanded to be preached to every human creature. He that avails himself of it *shall be saved;* he that will not avail himself of it shall be condemned. Whosoever avails himself of this salvation shall not perish, but have eternal life. And how in the nature of things can a man avail himself of it, but by *believing* the testimony of God our Saviour concerning the whole of this important subject? and hence the answer given by the Apostle to the jailer, "*Believe* in the Lord Jesus Christ, and thou shalt be saved."

Therefore the true *way of salvation* is by *faith in Christ;* and by *faith alone;* without the deeds of the law; the works prescribed by any law, either ceremonial or moral. But the act of faith is not a meritorious thing, for which salvation is granted to us as a reward. It resembles somewhat the act of a beggar's stretching out his open hand to receive an alms; only the one is a physical act, the other a mental operation. It resembles a drowning man's grasping the outstretched arm of a humane friend, who is anxious to save him from death. It resembles the act of a man's running from imminent destruction to a place of refuge and of safety. But the alms are *gratuitous*, not given *because* the beggar stretched his hand out. The attempt to save the drowning man was generous humanity, that preceded the grasp of the sinking person; and though the offer would have been unavailing had he not caught hold of the saving arm, still his salvation from temporal death was not the *reward* of any act of his. And so of every other illustration of this subject; they all shew, that whilst salvation is by faith in God our Saviour it is not the *reward* of faith. Salvation is by the free grace of God; it is perfectly gratuitous, and excludes from the creature every imaginable ground of boasting. Salvation is granted—by what law? asks the Apostle, by the law of works?—nay, but by the law of faith; for if salvation be by works, it is no more of grace, but of debt: but it is by faith, that it might be by grace. Therefore, in the language of St. Paul, we conclude, that a man is justified by faith without the works of the law. Not by works of righteousness which we have done, but according to His mercy he saved us.

To understand this subject aright, the object of faith, or things to be believed, must be particularly considered: these are not any human creed, any saint's ideas of Christianity, expressed in his own words, or words attributed to him; not any thing that people can justly call mysterious, unintelligible dogmas, for the believing of which men will be rewarded with salvation. Such a representation is a caricature, drawn by ignorance, and prejudice, or malice, of the doctrine of salvation by faith. The thing to be believed is, *the testimony of God*, contained in the book of divine revelation, and chiefly concerning the guilt and depravity of mankind; their just subjection to many natural evils now, and their just liability to punishment after death, of a nature and degree more awful than any language can describe. Human depravity and guilt form the ground-work of the whole structure of Christianity; and it being admitted, hence follows the importance of the divine revelation of an almighty and gracious Saviour; belief in whom always implies belief in the preceding fundamental truths; and faith, or believing in the Saviour, is simply our availing ourselves of the deliverance from sin and misery, which he can and does afford; whence follows, our duty to avail ourselves also of his instruction, his direction, his protection and government in this life, and of the eternal happiness he has to bestow in the next. It never can be supposed that the divine Saviour died to save men from the guilt and punishment of sin, and at the same time procured a licentious liberty for them still to go on to sin. The disciple who imagines this, does, as far as in him lies, by every reiterated transgression, crucify the Son of God afresh, and tramples the Saviour's blood under his feet. The real believer in Christ does not view sin, and its punishment, and deliverance therefrom, such light matters as to trifle with them.

Those who think that their rites, or ceremonies, or penance, or alms, or public benevolence, or masses, or prayers for the dead, can wash away sin, may, and do make light of sin; but not so he, who believes the awful truths expressed and implied by the humiliation and crucifixion of the Son of God. No man who ever really believes God's testimony, that sin is justly punished by everlasting destruction; that he, as an individual, has himself deserved that punishment; but by an amazing, never-to-be-expected effort of divine beneficence, he is now delivered from it, can make light of sin, and go on wilfully, and with a quiet conscience, to commit sin. It is therefore a mistake, or it is a calumny, that the doctrine of salvation, by faith in Christ alone tends to licentiousness. But further, the believer's mind is restored to a proper apprehension of the just authority of God; and he obeys him because he ought —because of the excellence and bliss-conferring nature of all God's commandments, and because it is his true interest and real happiness so to do. He has high sentiments of the infinite goodness and loving-kindness of *Jehovah*, and he obeys from gratitude and love. He now, first of all, yields *any proper* obedience, or, indeed, does *any good work;* for love to God is the great and *first* commandment, without which there is no true, no acceptable obedience; and further, the truly repentant believer resists and strives against sin; he crucifies the flesh, with its affections and lusts; he denies himself, and takes up his cross and follows Christ; and, in this sense, works out his own salvation with fear and trembling, and gives all diligence to "make his calling and election sure."

Is not this state of mind, and these motives, then, as powerful to produce good morals, as the opinion that salvation is easily obtained by some doings of our own, such as that, if poor we have only to repent, and reform a little before we die, or steadily adhere to some sect or hierarchy; or be staunch in reciting, or in contemning some prayers; and in observing or in avoiding some festivals; or, if we be rich, we have only to give money to the poor, or leave money to say masses, or erect an hospital, or build a temple, or make an idol-god, or an image of the Virgin, or beautify a church; if we have power, we can persecute heretics, or infidels, or Christians, according to the country in which we live, and so defend the faith, and the national religion; and then, as a *reward* for these, and other similar good works, our sins will be forgiven, and we shall be saved? Yes, the doctrine of the cross furnishes more powerful motives to live a good life than any of these; for all these, and such-like, proceed upon the supposition that sin against God is really not a matter of much moment.

But should not faith and works be united? Assuredly; faith is the root, good works are the fruit—they are the *consequence* or *effect* of salvation by faith; which is the

Third topic to be noticed. The humane behaviour of the jailer was *subsequent* to his faith in the doctrine of the Lord. Faith without works is dead, being alone; if the fruit does not appear, the inference is, that the root of the matter is not there. In that case, the supposed faith is either unreal, or the things believed are not the truths revealed and taught in God's holy word; but something different or contrary. If many who say they believe the

Christian religion, and who attend to its forms, and who yet live vicious lives, were asked, "And pray what is it that you do believe?" they would not be able to give any other answer than, generally, they believed the Christian religion to be the true one; or, they believed what the particular church, the Greek or Romish, English or Scotch, or any other church in which they were born and educated, taught. In such cases there is no distinct perception of the truths of the Bible, and there is nothing that can be properly called faith; for a person cannot believe a proposition, the existence of which he does not know; nor can he believe a proposition, the *terms* of which he does not comprehend; although he often believes propositions which state things *beyond* his comprehension. For example, take this short proposition, "God is omniscient." An unlettered person, who did not know what "omniscient" meant, could not be said to believe the proposition, although he might repeat it as his creed, his church-going, solemn belief, all his life long; nor would it at all influence his moral conduct. But he who does understand the terms of the proposition, and does fully believe the important truth contained therein, is, I imagine, still unable to comprehend *how* the Deity knows all things, throughout eternal duration and infinite space. Therefore, when I say that a man cannot believe what he does not comprehend, my meaning is very different from that of those persons, who sometimes use a similar phrase, to denote that they will not believe any thing is really true, the *mode* or *manner* of which *they* cannot comprehend.

A man's faith may be unproductive of good works, not only from the vagueness and indistinct perception of divine truth, commonly arising from wilful disregard of the means of better information; for how few, after all, study the Bible or religious books; but if, instead of believing the testimony of our Lord, they believe something different from, or contrary to divine truth, their faith will not only be dead, but mischievous. St. Paul, at one time, verily *believed* that he ought to do many things contrary to Jesus of Nazareth. The faith of the Gospel is faith in God, and in our Lord Jesus Christ, and in what the Almighty caused to be made known to us by the mouths of all his holy prophets, and the apostles of our Lord.

The different effects produced upon men's minds by their faith, is not from any metaphysical difference in the *act* of believing; but solely from the different ideas or propositions which they do believe. For example, the Bible says, "The wrath of God is revealed from heaven against all *ungodliness* and unrighteousness of men." A man conscious of being *ungodly* and unrighteous, believes this, and he flees for refuge from divine wrath to the hope set before him in the Gospel, and henceforward he walks with God.

Another person, it may be a professing Christian, laughs at the godly, and shuns every thing that can lead him to godliness, and declares his belief to be, that, as long as a man is honest and upright in his dealings, and is not worse than his neighbours, however ungodly they may be, he sees no reason to apprehend the wrath of God; and he consequently neglects and disregards the Gospel, its refuge, its Saviour, and its hope; he lives without God, and without Christ in the world. Again, the Bible says, "The Lord searcheth the hearts of the children of men." Many, on the contrary, believe that he is too great to regard the little concerns of men, and they say in their hearts, in reference to their wickedness, "God hath forgotten—he hideth his face; he will never see it—he will not require it." Must not the effect be very different in the tempers and conduct of him who believes the divine testimony; and of him who, contrary to it, believes rather the suggestions of the devil and of his own wicked mind; and this will account for the very little moral or religious efficacy of the faith of many, who fancy they believe Christianity; and who, whilst impious and vicious, yet continue attached, and even bigotted, to some particular church or sect.

But this lamentable fact does not prove that the faith of the Gospel of God our Saviour, by which we are saved, is unproductive of good works; on the contrary, it may be fully proved that this faith worketh by love to God and man; operates benevolence, and produces a virtuous life. These are some of its proper effects; joy is another. Religion, or rather a mistaken idea concerning it, sometimes produces melancholy and gloom; but the religion of Jesus, rightly understood and sincerely believed, is productive of joy. The jailer was full of joy; he rejoiced in God his Saviour, with all his house. *Holy living* and *a cheerful heart* are the genuine *effects* of faith in Christ, by which we are saved.

And since the belief of any proposition, on the mind's discerning its truth clearly, is instantaneous, when the mind actually does believe, so the effects follow at once. The jailer's was a sudden conversion, against which some people declaim. He, being concerned about his salvation, was no sooner informed of the truth, and *convinced* that Jesus was willing and able to save him, than he *believed;* and the effects *immediately followed* the cause. Benevolence and joy shewed themselves. Undecided characters are those who still halt between two opinions, who really do not believe the truths of the Bible, or the doctrines of Christ crucified, although they have some conviction that Christianity, on the whole, is true.

It is confessed, that to man's wicked, weak, and beclouded mind, there are in the world many things to bewilder, and which will afford an excuse for scepticism to those who desire to avail themselves of them; but, on the other hand, it is maintained that many of these difficulties are magnified by objectors; that there is carelessness of a most criminal nature in not searching for the truth. Truth is indeed difficult to be found in this deluded and deceitful world, but in matters that concern our salvation, it is not unattainable to the humble, industrious inquirer.

When we look at all the nations of the world, we see that there are "gods many,"—false gods without number; yet still there is *One true God.* So also, as Jesus said, Many will come in my name, saying, "I am Christ." There are indeed many false Christs, false Saviours, false miracles, lying wonders; but there is also a true Saviour and true miracles, and signs and wonders were performed by Him. There are also, in different countries, and in China (this country) pretensions to miraculous conceptions, and divine incarnations, and to revelations sent down from the gods above; some persons have hastily concluded that the proper inference from these facts is, that all these pretensions are *equally false*; but this inference, which is put into the mouths of philosophers, seems as inconclusive and unphilosophical an inference as that put into the mouths of the vulgar, that these pretensions are all *equally true*. The fair inference, in my humble opinion, is, that one God, one Saviour, one divine revelation, one way of salvation is true, and all the rest are imitations or counterfeits.

But what! says the feeling doubting mind, shall we suppose that all the millions of human beings around us, in pagan lands, who know not the true way of salvation, cannot possibly be saved! I affirm it not; I deny not the possibility of salvation to any nation. The Judge of all the earth will do right; justice and judgment are the habitation of his throne, *mercy* and *truth* are ever before his face. The principle which suggests that to whom much is given, of them much will be required, is equally true conversely; to whom little is given, of them will little be required.

It is not our duty to govern and judge the world; that must be left to God. And it is unreasonable for any sinful man to reject the salvation of God, because he is *ignorant* whether God will save or condemn others; or because he is ignorant *how* God will convey salvation to those who have not had the same full exposition of the way of salvation that he has had. In a cavilling spirit, similar to this, probably it was, that, as is recorded in the New Testament, a man said to Jesus, "Are there *many* that be saved?" to which question he received no direct answer, but one that deeply concerned himself, "Strive to enter in at the strait gate." Do thou, instead of speculating about the probabilities of others being saved, be in good earnest to avail thyself of the salvation which is provided for, and made known to thee. They that come to the Saviour, he will in no wise cast out.

And finally, my brethren, let me now say, "to you is the word of this salvation sent," and it is your duty to receive it with joy, to exhibit its effects in a virtuous and pious life, and *to promulgate it to others.* Yes! promulgate it to others—Eat not your spiritual morsel alone, live not secluded from the world, studying only your own edification and comfort; but since you have freely received, freely give. Even Chinese moralists inculcate the duty which requires every one who loves and practices good morals, to diffuse the principles of those morals amongst their kindred, and neighbours, and mankind. And to effect this end, some of them advise and exhort people, when they think them wrong; and print, at their own expense, what they consider good books, and give them away. They pronounce heaven's displeasure on those who omit the diffusion of good principles. And this sentiment of theirs, suggested by the remaining light of the divine law written on man's heart, is perfectly in accordance with the second table of God's law, "Love thy neighbour as thyself," and it condemns the selfishness of many seemingly pious Christians, whose practice evinces a regard only to their own spiritual improvement, and an almost total neglect of their neighbours' instruction and salvation. Oh, that while we look to Jesus alone for justification, our eyes may be fixed on the law of God as a constant rule of life; and may we ever seek excellence and bliss in an entire conformity to that eternal rule.

DISCOURSE II.

DELIVERED TO AN EUROPEAN AUDIENCE, IN THE WAREHOUSE OF A PAGAN CHINESE, NOVEMBER 23, 1822.

ROM. VII. 14.

"The Law is Spiritual."

A LAW is a rule of action, given by power, or by a just authority. The law of which we shall to-day speak, is the law given by the great Creator to human creatures. When he formed the vast universe, he gave laws to matter and to motion, to things animate and inanimate, to the incalculable variety of organized beings which fill the earth, the sea, the air; he gave laws to suns and to systems of starry worlds; to angels and to man. The preservation of the order and harmony of the vast universe, depends on obedience or conformity to those laws. In the physical world, the law was impressed upon matter; and in the moral world, the law of God was written upon man's heart. But man, by transgression, fell, and the heart became depraved, and the letters of God's law scarcely legible; the adversary of mankind induced a disregard of, and a disobedience to the law, with a perversion of the reasoning faculty, and beclouded the perception of truth; in consequence of which, the law of God was misinterpreted, and wrested, so as to be made to sanction things it really and originally did not. To restore the knowledge of the divine law in our world, heaven was pleased, at different times, and in divers manners, to grant reiterated elucidations of the law of God to man by direct revelation; and this revelation, in the usual way of the diffusion of knowledge, by

C 2

tradition and books, has preserved that portion of acquaintance with the divine law, which is possessed, in different degrees, amongst the several nations of mankind.

Now, reason, honestly exercised, can ascertain much of the original law, and man, having what we call the light of nature, is by no means left without law; still no system of morality or ethics, merely reasoned out by the human mind, can ever be set up as of equal authority with the divinely revealed law, contained in the Jewish and Christian Scriptures, nor does any other code of morals contain so clear and so accurate a preceptive rule of human duty.

Of the right of any one to make laws, that of our Creator is most indisputable. That his laws are designed for man's happiness, is most surely inferred from the divine benignity; God is love: His tender mercies are over all his works. That God's laws, had they been obeyed by man, would have ensured the happiness designed, is certain, from the infinite wisdom of the Law-giver. He must have made the means adequate to the end. These propositions require not any laboured proof; it is self-evident that the Almighty Creator *has a right* to prescribe laws to his creatures, and that his laws must be "holy, just, and good."

The point which our text requires us to illustrate and enforce is, that "the law is *spiritual.*" The word *spiritual* denotes that which has a relation to spirit, to the Divine Being, and to the soul of man; to angels and the heavenly world. The word itself, apart from its connexion, does not denote either moral good or evil; for bad angels, or devils, as well as good angels, are *spirits;* but they are unclean spirits, and their deeds constitute *spiritual* wickedness. *Spiritual* is understood in contradistinction to what is *material,* the acts of the *mind* in contradistinction from the acts of the *body.* The *faculties* of the mind, or soul, the will, the affections, and so on, in contradistinction from the *organs* of the body, the senses, the touch, the taste, and so forth. Thus also *spiritual* and *carnal, flesh* and *spirit,* are opposite terms; resembling which distinction is the "*Heavenly* principle and *human* passion" of Chinese moralists.

Human laws can take cognizance only for the *actions* of men; of theft, of murder, of fraud, of rebellion. Whenever they attempt to legislate for the operations of mind, they quit their proper sphere, and are ever liable to err. They cannot detect, and therefore cannot punish malice, so long as there is no overt act. An implacable enmity and desire to murder may exist in a human breast; but so long as no attempt is made to kill, human laws cannot apply; for spirit, or mind, is beyond their cognizance.

In contradistinction from such laws, it is said in our text, that the *law*, viz. the law which God has given as the rule by which man must be judged, *is spiritual*. This law also indeed commands what is right in action, and forbids what is wrong; but it does much more, it is a rule for the "thoughts and intents of the heart;" its precepts reach to the will, directing what man ought to choose, and what he ought not; to the affections, what man should love and what he should hate, what he should desire and what he should abhor, what he should reverence and what he should despise; and it reaches to man's motives, and requires not only rectitude of conduct, but also rectitude of principle and intention; not only the honest action, but also the purely honest design; not only the charitable deed, but likewise the benevolent heart.

Moreover, one half of that law, of which we speak, refers solely to spiritual things, to spiritual vice or spiritual virtue; to man's duty to his Maker, who is the Great Spirit, the Father of Spirits, and from whom the human spirit is derived. In this class of man's duties, merely "bodily service," the bended knee, the serious look, the solemn accents of audible prayer, profit nothing; unless the soul, the spirit, be there, the spiritual law is violated, and it condemns the transgressor. Let us take the Decalogue, and look over its precepts, remembering that the law is spiritual, and the subject will thereby be illustrated. And to begin, take the

First commandment, "Thou shalt have no other gods

before me." This precept does not only mean that man shall not nominate the sun, moon, or stars, or any imaginary beings, gods, and go and offer worship to them; but it also denotes, that the reverence, submission, and awe—the gratitude, esteem, and admiration, which constitute worship—the affection, love, devotedness, and the trust, hope, and dependance, which are due from man to God, shall not be given to any other object whatever; whether to the distinctions and honours of the ambitious, the pride of life, the pomps and vanities of this world, or the hoards of the covetous—riches, and all their attendant luxuries and attractions; or inordinate affection to any human creature—such as the devotion of the impassioned lover, or a parent's excessive attachment to a favourite child; for, in the estimation of the heart, all must be subordinated to the Great Supreme. The spiritual law says, "Thou shalt love the Lord thy God, with all thy heart, and soul, and strength, and mind; this is the first and great commandment. He whose *heart departs* from the living God, who *trusts* in any creature, any power, instead of the Almighty arm, who does not, at all times, and in all circumstances, cherish supreme love, with all the workings of mind that the divine perfections deserve—gratitude, esteem, and adoration—has violated the spiritual law, and is condemned thereby, as a transgressor of the first commandment, first in order, and first in dignity and importance; the great commandment, which has, indeed, been violated by the whole human race.

Again, although a man does not carve a graven-image, and set it up to worship, he may set up an idol in his heart; although he does not curse and swear, he may want that reverence for the Divine Name, which the third commandment implies; and in these cases, he is convicted, by the spiritual law, of having broken the second and the third commandments.

The Sabbath-day is not only a rest from bodily labour, but is designed as a spiritual rest from secular concerns and worldly pursuits, that the eternal interests of the soul may be attended to, and that man may not forget his relation to the world of spirits. Hence the law says, "Thou shalt not do thine own pleasure on my holy day, but shalt call the Sabbath a delight, the holy of the Lord, honourable, and shall honour him, not doing thine own ways, not finding thine own pleasure, not speaking thine own words."

"The Lord blessed the Sabbath-day and hallowed it," as a memorial of the wonderful works of creation; and the Lord's day, observed by Christians, is in commemoration of the resurrection of the Saviour, and the wonders of redemption; on that day, therefore, the mind should be turned to the study of the divine perfections, as displayed in creation, providence, and redemption, in the public and private exercises of devotion, and in the perusal of the Bible, or of religious books, otherwise the spiritual import of the fourth commandment is violated. Further,

None can ever imagine that the precept, "honour thy father and thy mother," is obeyed by merely external acts of respect. Even the Chinese, (who indeed place filial duty at the head of all the virtues,) inculcate the spiritual meaning of the law, and teach that the most complete attention to external forms of respect, and the most abundant supply of bodily comforts, is still not a fulfilling of the law, unless the heart of the child honour, and be deeply interested in the parent. But they err egregiously in not subordinating duly, filial piety, towards an earthly parent, to what all owe to the great Parent of mankind, our Father in heaven; for the law requires that in the performance of the social duties we should still have a supreme reference to the Divine Being; and not only so, but whether we eat or drink, or whatever we do, we should do all to the glory of God.

The same principle of spiritual obedience applies to the remaining precepts of the Decalogue, in a manner similar to the cases which have been exemplified. Actual murder is happily not often committed; but divine revelation so expounds the law as to declare, "He that *hateth* his brother *is a murderer*." (1 John iii. 15.) And thus he who maliciously harbours in his breast a spirit of hatred and enmity against another man, although he may not have actually injured his person, or destroyed his life, has violated the sixth commandment.

And so of the seventh, "Thou shalt not commit adultery," it is so explained by the Saviour and his apostles, as to include a prohibition of every form and degree of lewdness and impurity of the mind; and "he that looketh with licentious desire, hath committed adultery already in his heart."

The sins forbidden in the eighth commandment, "Thou shalt not steal," are not only "Theft, robbery, and man-stealing, but also receiving any thing that is stolen, fraudulent dealing, false weights and measures, removing land-marks, injustice and unfaithfulness in contracts between man and man, or in matters of trust, extortion, engrossing commodities to enhance the price, and all other unjust or sinful ways of taking, or withholding from our neighbour what belongs to him; or of enriching ourselves;" and (which is more strictly a spiritual violation of the law) all "envying at the prosperity of others, and secretly wishing their downfal."

The ninth precept of the Decalogue, which forbids malicious falsehoods injurious to our neighbour, should not be confined to evidence given before a magistrate; the spirit of the law is violated by all slander and defamation, or rejoicing in the disgrace and infamy of others.

Discontentment with our own estate or condition in life, envying and grieving at the good of our neighbour, together with all inordinate motions and affections of the mind to any thing that is his, constitute a violation of the tenth and last precept of the Decalogue; and the duties required, as well as sins forbidden in it, are all solely of a spiritual nature.

Now the spirituality of the divine law being established, it follows of course that its penalties are spiritual, that the punishment of violations of this law are not confined to temporal and bodily calamities, but affect the immortal spirit after its separation from the body.

And it should be remembered, that he who administers this law, and judges of offences against it, is the Searcher of hearts, "from whom no secret is hid," but before whom all thoughts and imaginations are naked and open; from whose sight the darkness is no covering, and to whose all-seeing eye, night and day are the same.

Now if God enter into judgment with us, and we be tried by his holy and spiritual law, who can stand acquitted? even we ourselves being judges, who of us is not self-condemned? Yes! by the law, is ONLY the knowledge of sin, it can only serve to convict and to condemn; it never can justify; we can never be acquitted if judged by it; the obedience of the best man on earth, since the first fatal sin was committed, has not come up to its requirements; and he who goes about to establish his own righteousness, or to seek salvation by the works of the law, by pleading before Heaven his well-spent life, or other similar pleas, shews only his own gross ignorance of God's righteousness, and of the spirituality of the divine law.

The fact is, the more we know of the law the more we shall be convinced of our own guilt; and therefore the law is now a "Schoolmaster," (as St. Paul says,) a preceptor, to lead or point us to Christ, the surety and the Saviour of men; and the design is that we may become dead to the law, abandon it as to any idea of ever being acquitted and justified by it, and seek for salvation only by the faith of the gospel. For, even defective as our illustration has now been, it is sufficient to shew every heart, that its obedience to the spiritual law is imperfect, even when in its very *best* state, and how much more when in its *worst*. When the mind, as the Bible says, is "carnal, sold under sin," as a willing slave to a diabolical profligate master, at "enmity against God;" and yielding the bodily members "servants to uncleanness and to iniquity," fallen man, having a hard and impenitent heart, filled with all unrighteousness, fornication, wickedness, covetousness, maliciousness, full of envy, murder, debate, deceit, malignity, being haters of God, despiteful, proud, boasters, inventors of evil things, without natural affection, disobedient to parents, implacable, unmerciful; and still more, men knowing the judgment of God, that they who commit such things are worthy of death; not only do the same, but take pleasure in those who do them.

This description of human nature is drawn by St. Paul, the same inspired person who in our text stated the holy and spiritual requirements of the divine law.

But some say, "Jesus died that he might *mitigate* the strictness of the law;" however, of this there is no evidence; the evidence is all on the other side. His exposition of the law *increases*, instead of *mitigating* its *strictness*, and exalts its sublime spiritual import. The Bible says, he died to *magnify* the law, and to *make it honourable;* but to *mitigate* its requirements would, by assuming its originally excessive strictness, and by consequence its injustice, degrade it and dishonour it, as well as its Author. The Scripture doctrine is, that sooner may heaven and earth pass away, than one jot or tittle of the law fail; that ere forgiveness could be granted to sinful man, it was necessary that God, manifest in the flesh, must obey and suffer the penalty of the law, as a substitute. Herein is the mystery of redemption; it honours all the divine perfections; *justice* and *mercy*, though seemingly opposed to each other, there meet together; the law is honoured and magnified, and yet the sinner is saved. This is the wonderful subject into which the angels desire to look; for they see in the Church of Christ, in the assembly of the redeemed, the manifold wisdom of God; they see a grand and full display of all the attributes of Deity.

Thus it will appear, that the Scripture doctrine of justification by faith, or salvation only by a complete relinquishment of all claims on account of man's righteousness, and a humble, sincere application to the Saviour, to be clothed by his righteousness, to be "*found in him*," so far from making void the law, in fact establishes it. For the argument runs thus:

The holy spiritual law of God, framed by the divine and infinite wisdom, is a standard to which no man, since the fall, can come up. And this law knows nothing of forgiveness; it says, "Do this and live," if not, *suffer the penalty*. Nor is it judged right by Heaven to mitigate its requirements, or lower the purity, spirituality, and strictness of the standard.

But then, the case being thus, man must perish, for he has not only once violated the law, not only often transgressed it; but it may be safely affirmed, that no man, in any instance, now FULFILS the law; he does not love God and love his neighbour to the *degree* that the law *requires*.

Thus the hope of salvation by our own doings, by works of righteousness, which we think we have done or can do, is excluded. Man is "shut up" to the faith of Christ. There is no door of hope open, but the door of faith. He who knew no sin; Jesus, the Messiah, the Son of God, was made a sin-offering for man. He obeyed, and suffered in our stead, and so redeemed us from the curse of the law. The law is by him honoured, its justice, and goodness, and purity, are admitted and maintained, and all its demands satisfied; and now *God is in Christ*, reconciling the world to himself; but *out of Christ* there is no promise of reconciliation. And the language of Heaven seems to be, "O sinner, give up thy vain pretensions to righteousness and to merit. See the lightnings, and hear the thunders of Sinai, the awful penalty of the violated law hovers over thy head; flee for refuge to the hope set before thee in the Gospel; slumber not! linger not! Cavil no longer, but to-day, instantly, ere death cut thee down, "Believe in the Lord Jesus Christ, and thou shalt be saved!"

Now, is it this doctrine that makes void the law? Certainly by no means. It maintains and exalts the dignity of the law.

It is the human fiction, that repentance is enough, without any atonement, to satisfy the law and save us; which degrades the divine law to a level with the impracticable, sleeping, unrepealed laws of human codes. This notion in fact nullifies the law of God, for it supposes that the law is neither obeyed, nor its penalty inflicted; and if so, then what is the use of it! Ah, no! this notion is too gross, too much calculated to bring the divine law, and its Author, the Divine Being, (I almost tremble, when I but express the just consequence,) into utter contempt, ever to be believed, if closely investigated in the light of divine revelation.

And the justness of our reasoning is fully confirmed by an appeal to facts. The doctrine of justification, by faith in the Saviour, *is* much more efficacious in producing good works, than the doctrine that repentance, and such good works as ours, are a sufficient ground of acceptance with God.

And the mode of operation on the mind seems to be, that the doctrine which teaches the necessity of atonement, is calculated to fill the soul with deep humility, seriousness, and anxiety to be saved from the wrath to come; and it leads the sinner to Jesus for help, and none ask him for help in vain. He gives the Holy Spirit to them that ask him, and the spirit helpeth our infirmities.

The other doctrine engenders a spirit of pride, and of self-sufficiency, and little or no seriousness; no anxiety to avoid that evil, which the man thinks it is in his own power at any time to remove. He does not feel his need of help, he does not ask it, and he does not get it; for it is written, "God resisteth the proud, but giveth grace to the humble."

It may be objected, that we "have sublimed and spiritualized the standard of the law, to such a degree, as to cut off all hope of fulfilling it, and of consequence would render all attempts or endeavours to keep it of no use; and indeed, that it is of no use, since we are said to be saved by the righteousness of another; and thus man is set against the law, or made careless about it, and *Antinomianism*, that pernicious heresy, is defended." I answer, that I am not aware of having over-strained the declarations of the Bible; but that truth may be perverted and abused, that the grace of God may be turned into licentiousness; that man may have a true theory in his head, and yet not believe it, and so may lead a wicked life, and "hold the truth in unrighteousness:" This is admitted; still the inference, from what we have said, that endeavours to keep the law are useless, or not required, is denied.

For we maintain not only the sublime spirituality of the divine law, but also that it is eternally in force; that there is in it an eternal fitness, and that it will be the never-abrogated rule of right between the Creator and the creature, and between creatures circumstanced as we are; that there is an *inseparable* connexion between obedience to it and human happiness; and, therefore, it is absurd to suppose it will ever cease to be requisite, or to be useful. The Saviour came not to destroy the law, but to confirm and fulfil the law; not only to save us from the penalty of the broken law, but also to restore our desire and ability to keep it.

And here comes in the necessity of the Scripture doctrine of regeneration. To obey the spiritual law, "Ye must be born again;" if any man be in Christ, he is a new creature. Old things are passed away, behold all things are become new. The man has a new belief and perception of eternal realities, new motives hence arise, new hopes, new dependencies, new antipathies, new pleasures. He is translated out of the kingdom of Satan into the kingdom of God's dear Son; turned from darkness to light; from the power of Satan to God. To as many as believe the Gospel, Jesus gives the *power* to become the sons of God; he gives them the spirit of adoption, they look up to Jehovah and call him Father.

Now then, there is no condemnation to them that are thus in Christ Jesus. But, be it observed, they must walk, not after the flesh, but after the spirit; must cleanse themselves from all filthiness of the flesh, and also of the spirit, perfecting holiness in the fear of God; and must be on earth a peculiar people, zealous of good works.

Thus fighting the good fight of faith, and laying hold on eternal life, they shall eventually finish their course with joy, and have an *abundant entrance*—that is, as under full sail, enter the haven of eternal purity, peace, and felicity.

There the spiritual law *of love* shall still be their rule, and then their *obedience to it will be perfect*, and, partly from that very cause, their bliss will be complete.

These, my brethren, are I believe, the solemn and delightful truths of God's Holy Book; and say now, Do we make void the law? or, does our doctrine establish the law? Is it not evident that *that* which magnifies the law is the Gospel? And this Gospel, the Gospel of God our Saviour, is utterly unlike any other system of religion or morals in the world? The Gospel never abandons the position, that the law is spiritual, and eternally *binding, as a rule.* And, it is only an ignorance of this truth, or a forgetfulness of it, or some false opinions concerning it, that allows the careless, carnal security, and lamentable indifference of so many persons, who are every hour, every moment, still liable to the awful penalty of heaven's violated law, because they will not come to Christ, that they may be saved.

The preacher had closed here, and were he to meet you weekly he would now have done. But, recollecting that most of us will never meet again, under similar circumstances, he is anxious that the discourse of this day, should not be considered as a piece of matter-of-course declamation; he solemnly and seriously requests that those not convinced, will "search the Scriptures, and see whether these things be so" or not; for, if true, their importance is greater than words can express, or mind conceive. Oh, how tremendously awful the penalty of the law! Oh, how great a salvation to be redeemed from its curse, and restored to obedience to it, which is life and peace. This is happiness! this is heaven! Oh, that this may be the portion of us all. Look to Jesus! None but Christ, none but Christ! Let him be all our salvation, and all our desire. If we *abide in him*, we shall bring forth plenteously the fruits of righteousness and holy living, which are to the praise and glory of God.

DISCOURSE III.

DELIVERED TO TWO FAMILIES IN DR. LIVINGSTONE'S HOUSE, AT MACAO, MARCH 3, 1822.

INTRODUCTION.

[Macao, in China, is a small island-like peninsula of a larger islet, in the bay which forms the entrance to Canton. The Chinese Government receives a ground-rent from the Portuguese residents, who are allowed a Government for the management of their own people, and forts for their own protection, but subject and open at all times to the Chinese authorities. Here the European Merchants, during the absence of their ships, retire from Canton, by the permission and the authority of the Chinese Government. The Portuguese have, in Macao, several Parish churches, and about fifty Ecclesiastics.

Here, during the summers of 1818 and 1819, in consequence of there being no Protestant Chaplain in the settlement, Dr. Morrison felt constrained to deduct a few hours from his Chinese pursuits, and prepared Lectures for the Sabbath mornings, which were subsequently printed for distribution in the east.

In 1819 a Chaplain for the Honourable East India Company's Factory arrived in China, and Dr. Morrison discontinued his morning lecture. The following brief discourse was composed on a visit to Macao, during what is called the Canton season, when there was no public service at Macao.]

---

1 COR. XV. 50—58.

" O death, where is thy sting? O grave, where is thy victory?"

THE death of a human being presents to the eye of an observer a shocking spectacle, and most shocking, when the deceased has been an acquaintance, a dear friend, or a beloved relative. The first cessation of life darkens the brightest eye, that it can no longer see, and deafens the quickest ear, that it can no longer hear; and no bodily organ will any more convey our wishes to the spirit, which but a moment ago animated the now lifeless corpse. And but a few hours or days more, and the fairest form, although recently possessing all the health and vivacity of youth, becomes a mass of offensive putrefaction, which makes the most affectionate friend desire, as did Abraham, to have the remains of a late beloved object interred out of sight.

There is nothing that our senses can discover, but what would lead to the supposition that death is the annihilation of our being. When we stand around the re-opened grave, and seeing the dead remains cast up; ask, Can these dry bones live? and of that which formerly constituted the life of our friend, (the soul or the spirit,) our senses can discover nothing. If we invoke the dead, we get no response. If we mentally express our love and affection to the deceased, we cannot perceive that any ear listens; death *seems*, to the eye of sense, to be the destruction of our existence. The unaided reason of man has sometimes acquiesced in the evidence of the senses, and has compared death to the extinguishing of a flame, which ceases for ever; sometimes, however, reason has suggested the probability of a continued existence of the spirit, in a separate state, after the body has returned to dust; but the revelation of our blessed Saviour alone has "brought life and immortality to light." His Gospel removes all doubts on the subject; and not only does it assure us that the separate spirit lives, but that the dead body too shall revive. They "that sleep in the dust of the earth shall awake, some to everlasting life, and some to everlasting shame and contempt." Our theme this day does not, however, lead us to speak of the awful eternity of the wicked, but of the hope of the righteous.

For these there is prepared an eternally happy region, and happy society, in Sacred Scripture called "The kingdom of God." There the Deity manifests the light of his countenance, and the glory of his perfections, so as to diffuse amongst the inhabitants of heaven, a felicity which is, to mortal man whilst on earth, utterly inconceivable; there, too, angelic beings, and the glorified spirits of just men made perfect, form a society, in comparison with which, not to say the unsubstantial pleasures of the gayest society on earth, but the society of the wisest and purest of human beings, is joyless.

But "This I say, brethren, flesh and blood cannot inherit *the kingdom of God;* neither doth corruption inherit incorruption." Heaven is a state of existence and of happiness, of which the human body, as it is now constituted, is incapable. A CHANGE, therefore, of the present mode of existence must take place; "We shall not all sleep, but we shall all be *changed.*" Death is the commencement of that change; the resurrection is the consummation of it. "This corruptible must put on incorruption." That death is the commencement of that change, is true of all those who shall 'quit this world before the last day—ere the morning of the day of judgment dawn; for the Christians that shall be found alive on that morning shall not die, but shall be *changed*, in a moment, in the twinkling of an eye; when the last trumpet shall sound, and the dead shall be raised incorruptible, and we shall be changed. Of the nature of this change, I presume not to speak, nor do I now deem it needful to answer objections to the possibility of a resurrection. That God's power can effect a resurrection of human beings, few will deny; and God's word declares he will raise the dead. St. Paul compares the dead body interred in the earth, to seed sown in the ground; and in allusion to this idea, he says of the body, when dead—"It is sown in dishonour," but, in reference to the resurrection, "It is raised in glory; it is sown a natural body, it is raised a spiritual body." The identity of the human being is preserved whilst the qualities of the body are changed. Dishonour is changed to honour; and the natural or material body to a spiritual body; and again the Scripture saith, this *vile body* shall be fashioned like unto Christ's *glorious* body, according to the working whereby he is able to subdue all things unto himself. Not only will the body

D

be purified and undecaying in its qualities, but it will also be rendered incapable of pain or suffering; in heaven there shall be no more sickness, neither sighing, nor tears.

But is not death the punishment of sin? St. Paul, in his letter to the Romans, saith, "By *one man* (meaning Adam, the first parent of mankind) sin entered into the world, and death by sin; and so death passed upon all men; for that all have sinned."

Had man never sinned who can tell but he would have undergone some *change*, similar to death, whereby he would have been transferred to a superior state of existence. Death in that case would have been simply a dissolution of the existing body, unaccompanied by pain, or agony, or fear; a calmly going to sleep. But now there is in the impenitent sinner's death a dreadful *sting*. Sin, or a violation of God's holy law, a guilty conscience, makes death a most terrific enemy; more terrible than any other foe, and hence called the "King of Terrors."

And this enemy mere human power could never have conquered, this sting human strength never could have extracted. But God the Father, seeing there was no deliverer, with his own arm brought salvation. God so loved (or compassionated) the world, that he gave his only begotten Son, that whosoever believeth in him should not perish, but have everlasting life. Jesus Christ, by his obedience and sufferings, fulfilled the law in our stead, and made atonement for us; the law of God being satisfied, sin is removed from the believer in Christ; and with the removal of sin, the sting of death is taken away. Death is only the beginning of that change which is necessary to translate the Christian, from a world of suffering, to the kingdom of God in heaven; and the resurrection of the body shall complete that change. "Then shall be brought to pass the saying that is written, "Death is swallowed up in victory. O death, where is thy sting! O grave, where is thy victory! Thanks be to God which giveth us the victory, through our Lord Jesus Christ."

Since, then, death is not an eternal sleep, but a resurrection and subsequent never-dying state of existence are certain; and our Saviour, when he comes to judge the world, will award to every one according to the deeds done in the body; and no person's labour shall be in vain in the Lord. Let us be steadfast and immoveable, always abounding in the work of the Lord. *Steadfast* in the belief of the truths taught by our Saviour, and not to be *moved* away from the hope of the Gospel; which looks to a complete deliverance from divine wrath, and from all evil, and an eternity of inconceivable happiness, all accruing to us through the finished righteousness and perfect work of our exalted and adorable Redeemer.

And the person who has this hope in him, should *abound* in all Christian tempers, and in all virtuous practice, according to the duties of his station, holding forth the word of life, whether by a declaration of divine truth, or by an example which shall edify others.

Now, as to labouring in the Lord, it is self-evident that a person must first belong to Christ; and it is not merely having received the rite of baptism in infancy, that constitutes us Christians in the high and beneficial sense which will be finally availing. By baptism we are made members of the visible church; but ere we can be united to Christ, we must be born again. If any man be in Christ, or be a genuine disciple, he is "a new creature;" he is converted, or turned, or changed; he is made a new man. From the universal prevalence of death, may be argued the universal existence of sin and guilt; but Sacred Scripture is explicit in declaring that all mankind have sinned, and come short of the glory of God; that in consequence of sin, and alienation of mind from God, human beings are universally deserving of his displeasure.

Indeed, till persons by repentance and faith return to the Lord, and become united to Christ, the Divine Being is very little in their thoughts, his displeasure is not feared, his favour is not valued, the wonders of mercy and condescension, displayed in the work of human redemption, excite little or no regard; this state of mind, although accompanied with the decencies and common moralities of life, is characteristic of those who do not yet belong to Christ, or who have backslidden from the good ways of the Lord. If, indeed, we violate the moralities which are universally approved for the general good of society, we certainly have no claim to the Christian character; but it is possible to observe these moralities, and still our hearts not be right with God. In a Christian mind, God is the supreme good, his revealed will is the standard of conduct, his declarations of human guilt are confessed to be true, his revelation of mercy, through Christ, is received with deep gratitude, sometimes with grateful exultation, the ordinances of religion, whether personal, domestic, or in the public assembly, give pleasure, because they are the means of what the Scriptures call "Communion with God;" the taste is elevated, it becomes more intellectual, rational, and spiritual, and acquires a disrelish for many of the frivolous and time-killing amusements which are so keenly followed by a large portion of society. The mind, in this state, possesses calm and silent joys which the world knows not of, and which the world can neither give, nor yet take away. The Lord of the universe permits the Christian to call him *Father*—his reconciled God; and, in adversity, so strong is the Christian's affiance in his Almighty Saviour, he can say with Job, "Though he slay me, yet will I trust in him;" and when dying, death has no sting.

March, 2, 1822.

Those whose lot it is to visit distant countries, look naturally with longing affection to the land of their childhood, and to the place of their fathers' sepulchres; but it may never be their happiness to return thither, for death spares neither age nor sex. Death waits not till man attains his wishes. He arrests his victims in foreign lands, as well as at home. He sometimes hurries man from earth within sight of the desired land; there can therefore be no excuse for deferring a preparation for death. Heaven has not promised to ward off death till man chooses to be ready; the compassionate Saviour does not hold out any such hopes. The stroke of death cannot be delayed; but, habitual preparation for it, and a heart set on heaven, makes death's stroke harmless. If we reach our heavenly Father's HOME, and attain to a happy resurrection, it matters not whether our mortal remains be interred in Britain or in China.

As an apology for this brief Exhortation, or Discourse, on such a subject, it may be right to state, that the Congregation consisted only of *four* grown persons; and it is here inserted as a simple "Memorial."

DISCOURSE IV.

PREACHED IN THE HOUSE OF THE RESIDENT, LIEUT. COL. FARQUHAR, SINGAPORE, APRIL 5, 1823.

INTRODUCTION.

[After the death of the late indefatigable Missionary, the Rev. Dr. Milne, in June 1822, Dr. Morrison, having completed his Chinese Dictionary, resolved on a visit to the Anglo-Chinese College at Malacca, and repaired thither in the Spring of 1823.

Having revised and put to press the then unprinted portions of the Chinese Version of the Sacred Scriptures, he visited Singapore, the newly occupied settlement, at the eastern end of the Straits of Malacca, and was most hospitably received by the Resident Authorities, Sir Thomas Stamford Raffles and Lieut. Col. Farquhar. At this flourishing settlement there now reside, under the British Government, about 4,000 Chinese, 5,000 Malays, and 4,000 Bugis, Arabs, Hindoos, &c.

On the top of Government Hill, which overlooks the roads, Sir Stamford lived, in a temporary bungalow, at one end of which he kindly accommodated Dr. Morrison with a room, whilst arranging the projected union of the Anglo-Chinese College with a Malayan College, to be founded by Sir Stamford. In that deal-board and mat-covered apartment, on Saturday, the 4th of April, 1823, the following Discourse was composed; and next day, after reading prayers, was delivered to the Europeans of the settlement, in Col. Farquhar the Resident's house, on the sea beach, amidst a heavy shower of rain, which beat so heavily and loudly on the Malayan covered tent, as to nearly drown the sound of the speaker's voice.

Since that period, we are happy to hear that a pious clergyman, son of the late General Burn, has been appointed Chaplain to Government at Singapore.]

A SPIRIT OF LOVE ESSENTIAL TO HUMAN DUTY.

MARK XII. 30, 31.

"*Thou shalt love the Lord thy God with all thy heart, and with all thy soul, and with all thy mind, and with all thy strength: this is the first commandment. And the second is like, Thou shalt love thy neighbour as thyself. There is none other commandment greater than these.*"

"Do you not therefore err, because ye know not the Scriptures, nor the power of God?" was the answer which our Saviour gave to some Jewish sceptics, who denied that there was any resurrection, in which denial the sect also included a denial of the existence of separate spirits. The reasoning from Scripture, which accompanied this remark, put to silence the cavilling opponent; and at the same time it seemed to confirm the belief of a bye-stander, who was listening to the conversation. He was a scribe; *i. e.* a man skilled in the doctrines and the precepts of the Mosaic law. Perceiving that Jesus had answered the sceptical Sadducee well, he too put a question, not with a good design, but, as St. Matthew says, "to tempt," or to try him; thereby discovering a spirit not unfrequently found amongst pretended enquirers, who ask questions, artfully framed, in order to puzzle, and darken, and confound distinctions between truth and error; not with any design of eliciting what is favourable to piety and virtue.

The question put by the Pharisee, otherwise called a scribe and a lawyer, was this—"Which is the first commandment of all?" or, as St. Matthew expresses it, "Which is the great commandment in the law?" Had this question been put to ancient or to modern philosophers, or were it now put to us, as individuals, it is not likely that any would have given, or that any would now give, the same answer that Jesus gave. I venture to form this conjecture, because I do not perceive that a breach of the first and great commandment, viz. a want of love to God, has been often viewed as any serious offence. Were man to originate a decalogue, I think his first and great commandment would be the injunction of some relative duty between fellow-creatures, instead of that duty which man owes to his Creator. Happily we have the answer given by Him, who came down from heaven, and which we are assured is sanctioned there. Jesus answered the Pharisee by a quotation from Moses: "Hear O Israel, the Lord our God is one Lord," and "Thou shalt love the Lord thy God with all thy heart, and with all thy soul, and with all thy might." (Deut. iv. 4, 5.) And Jesus added, "This is the *first* commandment; and the second is like, namely this, Thou shalt love thy neighbour as thyself." Here the first and great commandment is founded on the simple truth, that there is *one Sovereign Lord of the universe;* and the inference is, that all rational creatures should love him. And the second commandment, "Thou shalt love thy neighbour as thyself," is founded on the same principle. Since there is *one Sovereign Lord,* creatures cannot in truth affirm that they are in duty bound to serve different lords, allegiance to whom requires them to oppose each other. The reasoning is conclusive when put thus—Seeing there is one God and *Father* of all men, therefore all men should love each other, for all are *Brethren.*

In considering this first and great commandment, we must review the perfections and character of God the Father, Son, and Holy Spirit, as displayed in the works of creation, providence, and redemption, and as described in the Book of Divine Revelation. The natural perfections of the Deity, his incomprehensible power and wisdom, his omniscience and other attributes, challenge the esteem, admiration, and adoration of all his creatures. How wonderful, and utterly beyond the comprehension of the human mind, is that power which created the universe; which formed and arranged all the parts even of inanimate matter;

which created the sun, the moon, and the stars; which established the order and harmony that exists in all their motions, and which filled our world, the sea, and the dry land with such multifarious forms of animated being, and placed as lord over all here on earth, endued with a rational soul, his creature man. But the Divine Being does not stand only in the seemingly distant relation of Creator, he comes nearer to us as our Moral Governor, our King, and our God; and we owe the loyal affection of dutiful subjects, to HIM under whose benign government and in whose kingdom we live.

And our God must also be contemplated in the character of our Saviour or Deliverer. When mankind fell under the curse, and became subject to the awful penalty of the violated law, "He (as the Prophet expresses it) saw that there was no man, and wondered that there was no intercessor; and his own arm brought salvation. Other creatures in the Great God's vast empire sinned, and were justly subjected to everlasting punishment; then the Divine Deliverer did not take on him the nature of angels, but the nature of man in the posterity of Abraham."—Behold the mystery! "God manifest in human nature," to deliver guilty man!—"Herein is love," saith St. John, "not that we loved God, but that he loved us, and gave his Son to be the propitiation for our sins."

And now, to all the penitent and obedient of the human family, the Deity is revealed as their Father and their Friend: they are his children, for whom he has prepared an everlasting inheritance, to which he will guide them in safety, and that at no distant period, by his Holy Spirit.

This God (the incomprehensibly great, and infinitely just, merciful, and condescending God) is he whom the first and greatest commandment requires us to love.

The word love, in this connexion, means all those dutiful affections of the mind, which the various relations in which the Deity stands to us require; as, for example, esteem and admiration, reverence, obedience, submission, humility, acknowledgment of our dependence, resignation, gratitude, good-will, ardent attachment or devotedness. The whole of these sentiments and affections are summed up in the scriptural phrase, "Love to God," or in more modern phrase, "True piety;" or as an eloquent preacher expresses it, "The spirit of godliness." And those who possess these sentiments and affections are, with striking propriety, denominated "The people of God."

Esteem, admiration, and reverence express themselves in worship;—secret worship, or that which the Christian daily performs as an individual; social worship, or that performed by families; and public worship, or that performed in the assemblies of God's people.

Obedience, submission, humility, resignation, shew themselves in observing the rules of strict morality, in listening heedfully to the doctrines and admonitions of sacred writ, in bearing the afflictions and inscrutable dispensations of Providence without murmuring or repining, confiding entirely in the wisdom, justice, and goodness of God.

And gratitude, good will, attachment, and devotedness, shew themselves in zealously employing every means to effectuate the declared purposes of the Deity; as, for example, the universal diffusion of the glorious Gospel of the blessed God, in being, in this world, the steward of God's providence to relieve the distressed, to compassionate the aged, to defend the widow and the fatherless, and to diminish the natural and moral evils of this guilty and afflicted world.

Love to God is farther manifested by an unsuspecting affiance or trust in him, and a constant reliance on the eventual fulfilment of his gracious promises, that he will be a father and a friend to his people, that he will never leave them, and never, never forsake them; and hence the Christian, even when appearances are most inauspicious, is still found confiding in him. Though he slay me, (said Job,) yet will I trust in him.

The first and great commandment requires all these sentiments and affections in an intense degree—"Thou shalt love the Lord thy God with all thy heart, and with all thy soul, and with all thy mind, and with all thy strength." How strong this language, how vehemently intense are these expressions!

But can true piety be too ardent? Is a heartless, cold assent to the truth of religion, and a frigid attendance on its forms, a keeping of the great commandment?—Ah, No! We must all plead guilty, I fear, of habitually coming short, very far short, of what is required in this first commandment, in all respects, and in every instance. It would be impossible to exemplify every case in which even the most pious are deficient; but take for example the *indifference* with which they often view *idolatry* and *irreligion*, which the sacred Scriptures consider so offensive to the one living and true God. I mean not that the pietist or truly religious should feel anger or dislike to his fellow men and fellow servants, but that he should feel compassion, and benignity, and zeal to turn men from their dumb idols, their false prophets, and their false gods; and from the service of Satan, the god of this world, the arch-rebel against the Supreme Authority, who is the rightful Sovereign of the universe, who is the Lord our God.

The obligations of the second commandment flow necessarily from the doctrines and duties of the first. "Thou shalt love thy neighbour as thyself." And who is my neighbour? Thy fellow man, wherever he is found—every human being. He is not only thy neighbour, but thy brother. Dost thou say with Cain, "Am I my brother's keeper?" Yes! Our Father in heaven has commanded thee to love him, and to love him as thyself. This is truly a "*hard saying*," who can hear it! However hard it may appear, it is a reasonable saying, built on the doctrine of one God, the Creator, Preserver, and Saviour of men, and might fairly be inferred, even if it were not commanded. Polytheism, which admits of gods many and lords many, also admits of hatred and strife, and wars and conflicts amongst the gods; and if amongst the gods there be strife and hatred, why not also amongst their adherents on earth? But *we* all acknowledge only *one* God, who is our *Father*, and *therefore* we should love each other.

The lowest possible sense of this commandment must be, that we should not dislike, despise, hate, or injure each other. And if even in this negative meaning of the precept mankind obeyed it, how changed for the better would be the face of our world! what an improvement in every society!

But it is not credible that the merely abstaining from disliking, despising, hating, and injuring our neighbour is all that is meant by God's command to love each other: it must denote positive, active good will, and good deeds exercised and performed, towards and for our neighbour; it must include benevolence and beneficence, and these in an intense degree. "Thou shalt love thy neighbour as thyself." The idea which is sometimes brought forward in the form of an objection to this, assumes for granted, that, if we love others as ourselves, we must have all things in common with them; but this by no means follows. A father would not shew his affection for his family by sharing amongst them the whole of his substance, that they might use it as they pleased. He shews his love by husbanding the property, and by supplying their wants as they occur. And does not a good father love his children as himself? he studies and labours for their welfare just as much as for his own; he loves them as sincerely as he does himself. The same sort of feeling or affection ought to be cherished for all our neighbours, for all mankind, making only that distinction which justice requires; a distinction between those more nearly and more distantly related to us. For to a right understanding of a part of a subject, it is always necessary to view that part in connexion with the whole; any particular precept must be viewed in connexion with all the precepts of revealed religion and all the fairly deduced principles of natural religion: justice has claims as well as benevolence.

But even according to the most guarded and most moderate exposition of this second commandment, how elevated and how benevolent is the morality of our blessed Saviour! how distant (yea, infinitely removed) from the spirit of selfishness, from the hard-hearted *individualism* which makes one's apparent or seeming immediate self-interest the master principle. According to the doctrine of Jesus, much that is praised and lauded in the world as great generosity and meritorious benevolence, sinks down to the level of *simple duty;* and if we examine ourselves by the precept of Christ's second commandment, we shall, I fear, find ourselves as much deficient as we before did in reference to the first and great commandment. Yes! who can say that he has loved his God with all his heart, and soul, and strength; and his neighbour as himself? I believe that no merely human being could in truth say so, since the day that Adam sinned. But let us not therefore think that the first and second commandments, which we have this day considered, are not the rule of our duty. The non-attainment of the highest degrees of piety and virtue does not furnish an excuse for us, but must be considered as our sin, and should lead us to the Saviour. Would we but ourselves begin to love God and love our neighbour, as Heaven has directed; and did all who approve of the principle use rational means to diffuse it, what a comparative paradise might this earth of ours still be.

According to the principles taught by our Saviour Jesus Christ, those persons greatly err who place religion, or true piety, in the back ground. To love God is the first, the great, the greatest commandment: to love our neighbour is, indeed, like it; but it must rank second. True morality is necessarily founded on true religion; but to sink religion, and consider morality disconnected with it, is to put down what Jesus taught, and to elevate to a higher place our own notions of the due importance and right order of things.

Our first great duty, as individuals, is to get and to cherish scriptural ideas of the Divine Being; for he has, in the sacred Scriptures, revealed himself to men. And having attained right views of the divine character, we must reverence, obey, and submit to him. Good morals will follow. Make the tree good, and the fruit will be good. A pure spring will send forth pure streams. Pious and virtuous principles will ensure pious and virtuous conduct. This procedure is what enlightened self-love dictates; and if we must love our neighbour as ourselves, it becomes our duty to employ every innocent and virtuous means within our power to diffuse the same knowledge, principles, and conduct amongst our neighbours.

I think they greatly err, who suppose that active, zealous benevolence, and beneficence, are all very well and very praise-worthy; but still, as long as one is harmless, the omission of active, zealous benevolence is not to be censured, and will not be blamed nor punished by heaven at the last, the final judgment. Ah! remember how the Saviour represents that awful day:—"Depart from me, ye cursed."—And why? I was an hungered, and ye gave me no meat; I was thirsty, and ye gave me no drink; I was sick and in prison, and ye visited me not. They reply, with confidence and arrogance, "Lord, we never saw thee." Well, true!—but, inasmuch as ye did it not to one of the least of these (my people, your neighbours), ye did it not to me. I never knew ye. "Depart from me." And these shall go away into everlasting punishment; but the righteous, who are described not only as the *just*, but rather as the *benevolent*, shall go into life eternal.

I mean not now to insinuate that a man may not innocently withhold his aid from some plans and pursuits which other people think benevolent; every man must judge for himself as to the channel of his benevolence. These remarks will only apply to those who are generally indifferent to the welfare of their fellow-creatures.

Whilst I plead the cause of the natives here, I do not forget *our* native land, and our immediate relatives, and our poor kindred; and, some of us can say—our own children. No! let all these have their share of our regard, but let us not limit our regards by the circle of our kindred.

I must confess I think it a fault in European Christians, to speak with but little feeling of kindness and consideration for those we denominate "the Natives." Things, however, are improving, and there are many exceptions to this censure; but still I doubt if we have come up to the soberly interpreted meaning of the divine command, to love them as ourselves. There is a way of putting down all such grave ideas, by a little levity and ridicule: but the subject is too serious for that mode of dismissing it; it involves *eternal* consequences.

In comparison of the impious and the selfish man, who recognises not, nor submits to any heavenly Father; and who, from the selfishness of his heart, feels not at any time as a friend or brother—in comparison, I say, of this man, how happy is he who loves God, and who loves his neighbour, or who is pious and benevolent. When he looks up to heaven, he is permitted to address the supreme Sovereign of the universe, the ever-merciful and the ever-blessed God, the Almighty, as his Father; and when he looks around him in the world, he sees no human being for whom he has not cherished the kindest feelings, and whose good he has not only desired, but promoted to the utmost of his power.

But till man be renewed in the spirit of his mind—whilst the mind is what the Scriptures denominate carnal—it is "*enmity against God*;" and St. Paul describes unregenerated men as "haters of God." "I know you," said Jesus, to some of those around him, "that ye have not the love of God in you." This state of the heart is shewn by a distaste of serious subjects, which have a reference to God, and to the Saviour, and redemption. This distaste is often shewn by those who yet preserve attention to the proprieties of life, and who are prudent in their worldly affairs, as well as those who allow themselves to be profane and profligate. But how can we live quietly in a state of mind that is *inimical* to the great and good God, and the ever-merciful Saviour. The love of God and of Christ should constrain us to cherish love and dutiful affection in return; and, I say it with reverence, should induce us to be "workers together with God," in his plans of mercy to our guilty race. Alas! how many in the world still seem to be "given over to a reprobate mind, to do those things which are not convenient; being filled (as the apostle says) with all unrighteousness, fornication, wickedness, covetousness, maliciousness; full of envy, murder, debate, deceit, malignity, whisperers, backbiters, haters of God, despiteful, proud, boasters, inventors of evil things, disobedient to parents, without understanding, covenant breakers, without natural affection, implacable, unmerciful, who knowing the judgment of God, that they that commit such things are worthy of death, not only do the same, but have pleasure in them that do them." Now seeing the holy law is as our Saviour stated it, and the fact is as the apostle has described, can we wonder at the afflicted condition of the world? And how difficult is it to exercise either individual benevolence to, or a benevolent government over wicked men. Duty is seldom easy, and than these no duty is more difficult. But although difficult, duty must not be relinquished. A heaven-derived principle of love to God, and love to our neighbour, will sustain the mind under very strenuous and long-continued efforts to be and to do good. And may such a principle be implanted in every breast here present; *and in forming this new settlement, may no consideration induce the adoption of regulations in the remotest degree unfavourable to virtue, or that can be construed into giving a license or countenance to vice.* May Christians, by example and by persuasion, endeavour to lead others to know and love God, and to love each other; still allowing perfect liberty of conscience, and of conscientious religious usage and worship, (even to Mohammedans and Pagans;) but *gross and open immorality has no rights,** should not be recognized, nor meet with any support, nor furnished with any pretexts, lest ye be "partakers of other men's sins."

* Said in reference to vices licensed for the sake of the revenue. Pagan China will not license gaming, nor opium-houses. When reasoned with, in the European manner, that to make vice expensive, is the way to diminish it, they reply—No father can license vice in his house to his children, but must *prohibit* it altogether.

DISCOURSE V.

DELIVERED ON BOARD THE WATERLOO, IN THE CHINA SEA, ON SUNDAY, DECEMBER 14, 1823.

INTRODUCTION.

[Dr. Morrison having served the Hon. East India Company in China, in the capacity of Chinese Secretary and Translator to the Select Committee, about fifteen years, received, in consideration of his services, their permission to visit England for two seasons, to recruit his health and see his friends, took a passage on board the Waterloo, Captain Alsager.

On the 9th of December, 1823, the Waterloo quitted the shores of China; and, after touching at the Cape, and St. Helena, reached soundings on the British coast exactly on the hundredth day of being at sea. A thunder storm of considerable severity off the Cape, and a "fiery south-easter" on entering Table Bay, were the only cases of imminent danger that occurred. For passengers, the China ships, with a cargo of tea, are universally allowed to be the most pleasant and comfortable vessels that sail the ocean. Although extremely liable to the usual complaint occasioned by the giddy motion of boats and ships, Dr. Morrison was generally able to read and write; and composed, whilst on board ship, a "Domestic Memoir," for the perusal of his kindred; a School-book, concerning China, consisting of "Ten Conversations between a Father and his Children;"* and also a few discourses, of which the following is one.

When the weather permits, in the Company's ships, "a church is built," as the sailors term it, by arranging handspikes for seats on the quarter deck; a flag is laid on the capstan, for a desk, and the Captain, or some person in his stead, reads prayers on Sundays.

Captain Alsager requested Dr. Morrison to officiate as chaplain, and allowed him to add a short sermon, addressed to the officers and men. The following discourse was the first, and was preached after being five days out, in the China Sea.]

* Since published in London, under the title of "CHINA, a Dialogue, &c. By an Anglo-Chinese."

E

RECONCILIATION.

2 CORINTHIANS, V. 19.

"*God was in Christ reconciling the world unto himself, not imputing their trespasses unto them.*"

To speak of *reconciling* two parties, two men, two nations, or a servant to his master, supposes that some enmity exists between them. But the Almighty God, who created the heavens, the earth, and the ocean, is not the enemy of man. Of all the creatures in the world, man is the first and the noblest. He alone possesses a soul or spirit, that can think and reason, and comprehend, in some degree, the works of the great Creator. And who made man what he originally was—a holy and a happy being? It was the Most High God. He spread abroad the heavens, and placed there the sun, and moon, and stars. He laid the foundations of the earth, and filled the air, the ocean, and the land with living creatures; and to man, whom God created in his own image, he gave dominion over all, requiring only man's obedience to himself, the supreme Lord of the universe. The Divine Being himself pronounced the whole creation "very good," and whilst man was obedient to his Maker, he was the *child*, the *friend* of God: he was not an enemy then; at that time there was no occasion to speak of reconciliation.

But man was created a rational creature, to be governed by reason and religion. He was not like things made of mere matter, the sun, and moon, and stars, which have never gone wrong, and cannot do wrong. Man was made free to obey, and free to disobey; but he was forewarned of the consequence of disobedience. God gave him a law, and told him what would be the consequence of his breaking that law. And to this arrangement who can object?

What could be more reasonable than that the Great Creator should give a law to his creature, man, and require him to obey it; and so doing, be for ever the happy child and friend of God.

Man, however, tempted by a disobedient and malicious Spirit, presumed to think that God's commands might be disobeyed, and no harm follow. He thought that pleasure instead of pain would be the result of his disobedience, and he trusted his own foolish thoughts, and believed the tempter, instead of believing and obeying his Maker and Divine Benefactor. It was disobedience to God's commandments that made man the enemy of God. And a heart disobedient to God's commands, is what is otherwise called sin and wickedness, and carnal or fleshly mindedness. And St. Paul says, "The carnal mind *is enmity* against God, for it is not subject, or obedient, to the law of God. All mankind have become "*enemies to God* by wicked works."

And could not the Almighty justly and easily destroy all his enemies? The angels that sinned he cast out of the abodes of bliss, and has consigned them to everlasting punishment. In our world he has inflicted many and awful calamities, on nations, and on families, and on individuals.

How manifold are the diseases which afflict humanity; some loathsome, some painful and excruciating; the forms of death how numerous! and some of them how awful! He can destroy, by the lightning's flash instantaneously, or by long protracted disease; by the storm on land, or by the tempest at sea; by the deluge of waters that overflows the earth, or by the rending earthquake that swallows up crowded cities. The plague, and the pestilence, and the famine, can at God's command destroy myriads in a day, or an hour. These are punishments which we read of; and some of which we have seen or have felt, which righteous Heaven sends upon the world, because it is in a state of enmity to God by wicked works. And since we see and know assuredly that God sends heavy bodily and temporal calamities, is there not every reason to believe that the

E 2

spiritual and eternal punishments which are threatened will be inflicted after death on all those who live and die with their hearts in a state of enmity against God? Oh, yes! to be so credulous as to believe our own notions, and the devil's temptations, instead of believing the Bible, which contains the revealed will of God, is the same sort of foolish and wicked proceeding that at first brought death into the world, and all our wo.

And what does God require of his creatures? In answer to this it must be declared from the Holy Scriptures, that God is good and merciful, as well as holy and just. His law did not require that which man, whom he made, was not able to perform. The law of God consists of two parts—our duty to our Maker, and our duty to our fellow-creatures. It is thus expressed by divine authority, "Thou shalt love the Lord thy God with all thy heart, and love thy neighbour as thyself." To love God means to reverence him and fear him, as a good child does a kind parent; to desire to know his will and to obey it; to be grateful to him for all his goodness and mercy, and to avoid whatever he forbids; or, in one word, to be religious. To love our neighbour means not only that we should not injure any man, woman, or child, either in their property or person; or minds, by teaching them what is wicked, or seducing them to vice; but also means that we should try to do them good, in all these respects, which may be called being moral. So that, according to the divine law, religion and morality must always go together. To seem to be very religious and to make long prayers, whilst we are immoral, is to deceive ourselves; and whilst we hate religion, and never pray, to pretend that we are honest and good-hearted, is also to deceive ourselves.

The truth is, that no unconverted man loves God and religion; nor does he love his neighbour, and seek his neighbour's good. Heaven knows it: he dislikes or hates God and religion, and he loves inordinately himself, and seeks excessively his own interest; and if he does not do positive injury to his neighbour he is careless about him.

True piety to God and true benevolence to man go together, as heaven's law has joined them. If one be wanting you may be sure the other does not exist.

But are all irreligious and immoral men God's enemies? Yes; that is the point to which we have come, and which is fully proved, both by the declarations of Holy Scripture, and by the history of divine Providence, and by every man's own experience, if he would look into his own heart. How else can you account for a man's neglecting prayer and thanksgiving, for neglecting the Bible and religious books, for never thinking reverently and affectionately of God and religion; but instead thereof, sometimes cursing and swearing, and blaspheming God's holy name, and ridiculing religion, and shunning and despising religious people; and making a jest of vice, and taking pleasure in the company of wicked and immoral people; not only disobeying the Almighty, and being wicked himself, but taking pleasure in those that run into the same excesses, and indulge the same vices as himself. Do not all these things shew that the heart is disaffected to our Maker; has a dislike to, and is at enmity with God?

Now to remain at enmity with God, on whom we depend every moment for life itself, and without whose favour happiness is utterly unattainable;—who can, moreover, justly and easily inflict everlasting punishment upon us, evinces desperate wickedness and consummate fool-hardiness. Oh, man! canst thou rush upon the thick studs of the Almighty's buckler! Can feeble man, whose life is in the breath of his nostrils, dare and defy the eternal God! It is absurd! What then can man do? How shall he be reconciled? Our text furnishes the true answer—"God is in Christ reconciling the world to himself, not imputing their trespasses to them."

But how can this be? Rebellion against the divine law must be punished; a spirit of enmity against the Supreme Being, the Sovereign of the universe, cannot be allowed to pass with impunity. The "*discipline*" of the world does not permit it; and man's trespasses, if imputed to him, will occasion his everlasting ruin. Here is the difficulty. Must

Heaven's threatenings all go for nothing. No! It pleased God the Father to appoint Christ Jesus, the Son of God, to be man's Surety, man's Saviour. He was early promised; his coming was often foretold by ancient prophets; all good men hoped and believed that he would come; and when the time that Heaven thought right did arrive, Christ our Lord and Saviour actually came down from heaven, lived in our world as a poor man, obeyed the law in our stead, taught men more perfectly the will of God the Father, set an example of perfect virtue, died as a sacrifice to atone for man's sins, rose again from the dead, and ascended to heaven to make intercession for all his followers on earth, to confer the Holy Spirit, to sanctify and guide them, and to prepare habitations of bliss for them when they die. To be told that God has done all these things for man's reconciliation, is the Gospel, *the good news*, the happy tidings. *That* Jesus, whom the Jews crucified, was God manifested in a human body; and he burst the bonds of death, rose from the dead, and was exalted a Prince and a Saviour, to give repentance and remission of sins. He is the way, the truth, and the life; none can be reconciled to the Father but by him, and by him all that will, may be reconciled. The *least* sinful, and those who have shewn least enmity, must yet submit to come by the appointed way of reconciliation; and the *most* sinful, he who has shewn the bitterest enmity to God, who has been most irreligious and most immoral, may be reconciled and brought to obedience through Christ. For God is in Christ reconciling the world to himself; all ranks and conditions of men are included; the Gospel is the news of a general pardon for all who desire to submit to the rightful government of the Almighty, and to be at peace with him. And heaven is so high, and earth so low; God is so great, and man so little, that all human distinctions are lost in this divine proclamation of mercy. There is only one way of being reconciled to God for the king and for the beggar, for the rich and for the poor, for the learned and for the unlearned. St. Paul says, "The unrighteous shall not inherit the kingdom of God—neither fornicators, nor idolaters, nor adulterers, nor effeminate, nor abusers of themselves with mankind, nor thieves, nor covetous, nor drunkards, nor revilers, nor extortioners—that is, whilst they continue such; but that even such wicked persons may be reconciled to God, appears from what he immediately adds, (1 Cor. vi. 9—11.) "Such were some of you, but ye are washed; but ye are sanctified; but ye are justified in the name of the Lord Jesus, and by the Spirit of our God."

Some people may think that there was no occasion for Christ Jesus the Mediator to make an atonement, to bring about a reconciliation between God and man; but Heaven knows best what was necessary to reconcile man to God, and Heaven has the best right to decide on that subject. It ill becomes sinful man to tell his offended Maker what is necessary or right. The proud spirit must be brought to submit to Divine Wisdom; every lofty and self-exalting imagination must be humbled; if not, man is still persisting in his opposition and enmity to the divine will. The tempter said at the beginning to our first parents, "If you do disobey Heaven, it is by no means sure that you will die;" and so he says still, to deceive men, "If you do not submit to the Saviour, and only try to be good yourselves without him, you are not likely to be condemned." But in the first instance, man knows by sad experience that what Satan suggested was a lie; and what reason is there to suppose that the suggestions of Satan and of our own foolish hearts shall prove true, in opposition to the inspired declarations of God's Holy Spirit in the Bible!

Now *submission* to Christ, that man may be reconciled to God, is what is required of all; and this submission implies repentance, and faith, and obedience; a sincere desire and endeavour from henceforward to perform all our duties to God and to man, so far as we know them; and constant prayer in our hearts to God to enable us to know our duty better, and always to perform it. And all this is quite practicable, without scholarship, or learning, or riches; so that no man need make an excuse. All must try to perform their duty according to their stations; kings and subjects, and magistrates and people, and parents and children, and masters and servants, and teachers and scholars, and poor and rich, and old and young. For all are God's creatures; and if we fear God, and love and serve him, we shall never desire to ill use or harm any of his creatures. When men are reconciled to God, they become reconciled to each other. The love of God shed abroad in the heart does away with national hatred, family feuds, and personal animosities.

Finally, The man who would make his peace with God must submit to the Saviour Jesus Christ, for *out* of Christ Heaven has not appointed any way of reconciliation; but *in* Christ God is reconciling the world to himself. And oh, how condescending and how kind is the language of Heaven! The Apostle Paul says, for himself and the other Apostles, "Now then we are ambassadors for Christ, as though *God did beseech* you by us, *we pray you* in Christ's stead, be ye reconciled to God." Oh, wonderful! God beseeching, and Christ entreating man to be reconciled. On Heaven's part, then, there is nothing to hinder reconcilliation and friendship—"Wherefore," O men, "let my counsel be acceptable to you. Break off your sins by righteousness," and be at "peace with God, through our Lord Jesus Christ." Only say not to yourselves, "Peace! peace! when there is no peace;" for "there is no peace, saith the Lord, to the wicked;" that is, to him who still *goeth on in his trespasses*; but he that *confesseth and forsaketh them* shall find mercy.

DISCOURSE VI.

DELIVERED ON BOARD THE WATERLOO, NEAR CHRISTMAS ISLAND, DECEMBER 25, 1823.

INTRODUCTION.

[Bethlehem, a small town, about six miles south of Jerusalem, was called the "City of David" in consequence, probably, of David, king of Israel, having been born there: an event which occurred about a thousand years before the coming of Jesus, the Messiah. Bethlehem, or the "City of David," is a place well known, and much frequented by Christians of different countries, Latins, and Greeks, and Armenians; and it is supposed, that the very field is known where the shepherds were watching their flocks, when the angel announced the birth of our Saviour.

Mary, the mother of Jesus, lived at Nazareth, which was about seventy miles north of Jerusalem; and the occasion of her coming to Bethlehem, about eighty miles distance, was, an order issued by the Roman Emperor, Cæsar Augustus, that all persons in Judea should repair to their native place, to have a list of their names taken. Whilst Mary was at Bethlehem, Jesus was born; and on that occasion, an angel from heaven appeared during the night to some shepherds, and speaking audibly, called upon them not to be afraid, for he brought them good tidings, which concerned all people in the world, these tidings were, that *a Saviour was born—Christ, the Lord.*

To commemorate this event, the 25th of December has been fixed on; it is not, however, certain that Christmas-day, as it is called, was the precise time of our Saviour's birth; nor is the keeping of this holiday commanded in the Sacred Scriptures; but if it be observed with decorum, and be not profaned by any excess, the observance of it may be rather useful than otherwise.

The commemoration of any event ought to correspond to the nature of that event; and what we have to-day to commemorate, is not some domestic or national occurrence, but the birth of the Saviour of the world; it seems, therefore, incumbent on us to consider the nature of his salvation, and how it concerns us.]

CHRIST EXALTED.

ACTS, V. 30, 31.

"Jesus, hath God exalted to be a Prince and a SAVIOUR."

A SAVIOUR is a deliverer; one who rescues from some evil. A man who delivers his country from foreign enemies, is sometimes called the saviour of his country; and people speak of saving a man from drowning, or from any similar calamity. Whenever men speak of a Saviour, it is understood that some evil is hanging over, or has actually come upon those who are to be saved. The same as when men speak of a physician, it is understood that there are sick persons to be healed.

Now the evils to which men are subject, are some of them bodily evils, otherwise called natural evils; such as sickness, poverty, and so on: others are mental evils; such as concern the mind, or the thinking part of man—the soul; and these are sometimes called moral, or spiritual evils. Such bodily evils terminate when the body dies—there is no sickness or poverty in the grave; but as the soul, or spirit, never dies, the death of the body does not deliver from those evils which are of a spiritual nature, nor from the punishment which awaits the bodies of the wicked after the resurrection: hence calamities, or evils, are some *temporal,* or enduring only for a few years; and some of them *eternal,* or never-ending. But all human calamities, whether bodily or spiritual, temporal or eternal, are, without exception, the consequence of sinning against God. We are taught, that man was originally made a holy, obedient, and a happy being. Then there was no sickness, no death, no affliction. But man sinned. He disobeyed God, and became wicked and miserable. At the beginning, the Bible assures us, man was made in the image of God;

he resembled the Divine Being in these three things;—in *knowledge*, in *innocence*, in *holiness;* but by transgression he fell into a state just quite the reverse, a state of *ignorance*, and of *guilt*, and of *wickedness*. Now to deliver man from these three evils, the Saviour is appointed, and sustains a threefold character; he is a *Prophet*, a *Priest*, and a *King*. A Prophet, or Teacher, to teach ignorant man; a Priest, or one who offers sacrifice, to atone for man's guilt; and a King, or Prince, to bring man into a state of willing obedience to the divine law.

Since the time when man fell from his original state, he has become ignorant of the Divine Being. He knows not the living and the true God. In many parts of the world, both in ancient and in modern times, as in China for example, people have imagined that there were many gods, and that they were such beings as sinful man himself is; hence they made images of their gods, and worshipped the works of their own hands—a bit of carved wood, or a rude stone. In other parts of the world, where idols or images are not used, as in our own country, there is still great ignorance of God prevailing; and many false opinions, some of which set the divine perfections at variance with each other. There are people who, contrary to Scripture, think that God is so merciful he will not punish sin; and, by this notion, his holiness and his justice are set aside altogether; and these persons live and die without repentance, and never apply by faith to the Saviour.

There is much ignorance also amongst men, concerning the holy and spiritual law of God. Man is very ignorant of his duty to God, and often has no desire to know the truth; and hence it is, that many are so careless and jovial whilst living in disregard of their religious duty; and, consequently, still under the wrath of God. Most of men think, that simply avoiding great crimes, is fulfilling their duty; whereas, the Bible declares every one accursed, who continues not in all things written in the book of the law, to do them.

Further, fallen man is ignorant concerning a future state; the state after death. Some people, who think themselves very wise, have denied that there is any future state, and others have said many foolish things about it; but Jesus Christ, the Saviour, is a divine teacher, who came down from heaven, to instruct man concerning God, and his glorious perfections, and his holy law, and man's duty, and a future state; and therefore he is called, in the Bible, "the light of the world; the sun of righteousness," because when the sun shines, and there is broad day-light, people can see and know what is going on; but ignorance is like the night, and darkness, when people know not whither they go, nor at what they stumble. Christ, our Lord and Saviour, brought life and immortality to light; he has declared plainly that there are two states after death, one of happiness, and one of misery; one of rewards, and one of punishment. A heaven, where there shall be no sorrow, no pain, no death; but life, and peace, and joy for ever and ever; and that there is a hell, a place of remorse and despair, where there is nothing but weeping and wailing and gnashing of teeth.

If men would but listen to the Saviour, they might know their real circumstances; but alas! most men love darkness and ignorance, rather than light and knowledge. Just like some men who are ill, and daily getting worse, but will not listen to the advice of a physician, till they get so bad that no medicine will do them good; they put off from day to day, and, though sorry for it afterwards, it is then too late. Now, the great thing to be effected, in this case, is, first to let these people know their real danger, that they may be induced to use proper means for their recovery. So divine teaching begins by letting men see God's greatness and goodness, holiness and justice; and their own sinfulness, and wickedness, and guilt, and misery; and the awful condition of living in defiance of the Almighty; and the dreadful consequences of dying whilst under the wrath of God, that they may use the means which Heaven has appointed to deliver them from impending ruin, and cause them to look by faith to Christ the Lord, who is a Prince and a Saviour.

II. But one may inquire, if a man be found guilty of

breaking the law, how can he be delivered from that guilt? If a man be guilty of wilful murder, must he not be condemned to die? Who can save him? The answer to this is, that although those who break human laws often cannot be saved from the penalty, God has provided a way to save sinners.

The way which heaven has been pleased to appoint for the delivery of guilty man, is the substitution of a Surety; that is, of a person to bear the punishment due to man in his stead; this person, otherwise called a *Redeemer*, and a *Mediator* between God and man, is Christ the Lord; who, as on this day, was born at Bethlehem, in the land of Judea. *Christ* is a word in the *Greek* language, which means the same as *Messiah* does in the *Hebrew* language, and they both mean a person anointed with oil, or one who has had oil poured on the head; which was an old custom, when prophets, priests, and kings were *appointed*. Therefore the names *Christ*, and *Messiah*, denote that the Saviour, Jesus, was *appointed* to deliver man; and whatever Jesus taught, and whatever he did, is sanctioned in heaven. Christ, the Saviour, was not a *mere* man; that is, although he was truly man, he was not a man only, but he existed before man was made. He was from everlasting, and came down from heaven; he was God and man in one person; and he is therefore sometimes called the Lord; the Lord of heaven and earth; and the Son of man. The Bible says, "He being in the form of God, thought it not robbery to be equal with God, yet took upon him the form of a servant, and was made in the likeness of sinful man." Though he was rich in heaven, yet for our sakes he became poor on earth. In the prophecies of Isaiah, these words refer to him (chap. ix. 6.) "For unto us a child is born, unto us a Son is given; and the government shall be upon his shoulder; and his name shall be called Wonderful, Counsellor, the Mighty God, the Everlasting Father, the Prince of Peace."—"Christ the Lord, was God manifest in the flesh." Thus we learn that the Saviour is almighty, and infinitely *able* to deliver man from guilt and misery.

This is a wonderful subject—no man could reason it out—we are told it by divine authority. The ancient Prophets, Jesus himself, and the Apostles, all bear witness to it. It is not revealed that man may cavil at it; but that he may believe God's testimony and be saved. "Herein is love, not that we loved God, but that he loved us, and gave his Son to be the propitiation for our sins; and not for ours only, but also for the sins of the whole world." "The Saviour was wounded for our transgressions, he was bruised for our iniquities; the chastisement of our peace was upon him, and by his stripes we are healed."

To take away man's guilt, Christ died; but he rose again from the dead, and having shewn himself alive to his disciples, he *ascended* to heaven in their presence; and thus, as the text says, he is *exalted* a *Prince*, and a Saviour, to give repentance and remission of sin.—He is a *Prince*—He is a *King*, to rule over his people, and to defend them. He brings them at first into subjection, and makes them obedient to the divine law; and is to them a Saviour from sin. He gives his Holy Spirit to convince them of their sins, to help their infirmities, to teach them to pray, to be their comforter, and to be their guide; till finally they have endured, or performed, what Divine Wisdom sees meet in this world, and then they are eventually received into the kingdom of heaven. The King of Zion, having rescued his people, will at last crush all his enemies under his feet. And who are his enemies? All those who "will not have him to reign over them;" that is, all those who will not be taught by him, but are self-conceited, and prefer their own notions and speculations, to his heaven-sent instructions; all those who will not have him to be their surety and mediator; but are self-righteous, and think their own goodness sufficient without the Saviour; and all those who profess to call him Lord, and say, "our Saviour, our Saviour," but who will not do those good works, that he commands, nor leave off the sins which he forbids. Though men may say they were *baptized* in his name, and were natives of a Christian country, and never renounced the Christian name; nay, even *fought*, as they think, for the Christian religion, or *preached* the Christian religion; still, if they obey not Christ Jesus, as a king—if they will not submit to his laws, nor keep his commandments—he will, at the day of judgment, say, "Depart from me, for I never knew you, all ye that work iniquity."

To an ignorant, guilty, and sinful world, the birth of the "Saviour, Christ the Lord," is truly matter of unspeakable joy; but the joy of those who are saved by him, will be a spiritual and holy joy; expressed, indeed, it may be, by innocent festivity, but not in revelling and excess; for if in keeping Christmas we run to excess, that goes to prove that the Saviour is not yet *our* Saviour. Oh, that he may subdue us all to himself, make us listen with humility to his instructions; remove from us the guilt of all our past sins, and reign in our hearts for ever!

DISCOURSE VII.

DELIVERED ON BOARD THE WATERLOO, JANUARY, 1824.

JOY IN HEAVEN OVER ONE REPENTING SINNER.

LUKE, XV. 7.

"Joy shall be in heaven over one sinner that repenteth, more than over ninety and nine just persons, which need no repentance."

To repent is to re-think; to think differently from what one did before; to change one's mind, or to come to one's senses again; to come to one's self, as one that has been foolish or mad before: and when a man changes his opinions, and his likings, he changes his conduct. To repent, always denotes a man's changing his thoughts and his actions for the better; and is generally accompanied with sorrow and with shame for the past. There are various forms and degrees of repentance, to distinguish which is of great importance to every man. For example,

If a man associate with gamblers, and lose his property, and be reduced to want, he forms a very different opinion of gambling from that which he did while he was prosperous and winning; and he is vexed with himself, and sorry for his folly, and ashamed of the want to which he is reduced. He seems to repent, but it is only for the *consequences* that he is sorry; if he had continued to win, it is not likely that he would have repented of his gambling;

and if he leave off gambling, it is not because he is convinced that it is a pursuit which wastes that precious time, which Heaven has given us for rational or useful purposes; or because it cherishes a spirit of covetousness, and an unjust desire to obtain our neighbour's property, without giving him an equivalent. If the man's mind were changed, so as to view gambling in this light, he would then repent and leave it off, whether he lost or won.

The same reasoning is applicable to any vice, which injures, either gradually or suddenly, our property, or our health, or our good name in the world; such as the excessive use of intoxicating liquors, or the irregular, extravagant, or unnatural indulgence of the sensual appetite. When a man has squandered away his money, or brought upon himself some loathsome disease, or made himself shunned and despised for his intemperance and debauchery, he may then change his opinion of these vices, because of their bad consequences, and only for that reason; and if he leave them off, it is not because he desires to obey the will of God; and therefore, in this case, he still loves these vices, and almost hates Divine Providence, for having made the consequence of vice to be misery. In such a state of mind as this, a man who is even sick and dying by the consequence of his own vice, however sorry, and fretted, and ashamed he may be, has not undergone that change of opinion and liking which constitutes true repentance. This man's anger, and vexation, and grief, is what the Apostle calls the sorrow of the world, which worketh death; a sort of atheistical sorrow, which still allows a man's heart to remain far off from God. This is the lowest form and degree of that which appears like repentance, for it has regard only to the natural evils which are the consequence of vicious conduct, and does not at all regard vice as a sin against God. Perhaps such a state of mind should not be called repentance, but *remorse*.

But suppose a man's mind so far changed, as to consider all violations of, or deviations from, the divine law, as subjecting him to the punishment that is to be inflicted after death; and, at the same time, this man's mind not

F

so far changed and enlightened, as to perceive the excellence, and goodness, and amiableness of the divine character; and the justice, and reasonableness, and happy tendency, of what Heaven's law requires; although that man may be afraid of the consequences likely to follow his wicked life, or his impious thoughts, still his heart does not hate evil, but only dreads the consequences, and feels aversion to God who has threatened these consequences. And when such a man is sorry, and seems to repent, his repentance has not yet assumed the form and degree that constitutes true and saving repentance. I am afraid you will say that I am refining too much, and as long as a man is sorry for his sins, it is no matter what the exact reason of it may be. However, if you consider that the first and great commandment is to love God, it will appear plain to you, that the mind which thinks the Divine Being has given too strict laws, and annexed too severe punishments, must rather feel aversion or hatred to God, than love to him. And, therefore, a greater change of mind is requisite to bring a man near to God, which is the effect of true repentance.

The Divine Being is a holy and righteous Sovereign. He made the universe, and he made man; therefore his controul over man is most just. The Almighty is infinitely wise and good, therefore the laws which he prescribes, whether they regard our own persons, our behaviour to our fellow creatures, or the affections we ought to cherish towards our Maker, must be infinitely good, and conducive to our happiness; but since God's laws are just and good, our obedience should be cheerful and willing; not with feelings such as a slave must have towards a tyrannical master, but such as a dutiful child should cherish towards a virtuous and kind parent. Not to be obedient to the divine law, is the most wicked rebellion against just authority, and a most presumptuous pretence that we know better what is good for us, than He who made us.

Now, when a man's mind is so changed, that he does not consider the laws of religion and virtue as restraints upon his pleasure or his profit, nor hindrances of his happiness, but, contrarywise, he thinks "God's service perfect freedom;" he then thinks his past disobedience the result of inexcusable ignorance, presumption, wilfulness, and ingratitude. Further, when such a man thinks, not only of the Divine Perfections—God's infinite excellence, wisdom, and goodness, but also of the wonders of redeeming mercy, manifested in our Saviour; he feels still more ashamed, and humble, and sorry for his past folly and wickedness, and for his daily sins and transgressions. There is such a change passed on his mind, that he does not *wish* to sin any more. It is not only the consequences of vice and irreligion that he dreads—he hates every false and every wicked way. He desires to confess, with "shame and confusion of face," his manifold presumptuous sins, and to use means henceforward to yield obedience, from a sense of duty and gratitude; to return as a rebel pardoned by his king; as a prodigal son received by a kind father.—And look at the case of the prodigal, as stated by our Saviour.

The prodigal began his career in a spirit of ungrateful pride and self-sufficiency; abandoned his father's house, and sought for happiness in jovial and riotous living, far off from his real friends and his home; in the same manner as guilty, foolish, proud man does, who labours, as in the very fire, to attain happiness, sometimes from the accumulation of money, or from sensual pleasures, or the distinctions and honours of this life, and ever disappointed, still pursues the fleeting shadow.

The prodigal's wants and misery happily humbled his proud heart, and brought him to himself, to a right understanding of his father's kindness, and the happiness of home; then he repented; his mind was changed; and he came to this happy resolution—"I will arise and go to my Father, and will say unto him, Father! I have sinned against heaven, and before thee, and am no more worthy to be called thy son; make me as one of thy hired servants."

Here there was no design to *excuse*, much less to *justify* himself. No apology on account of his youth, no pretence about having a good heart, notwithstanding his former pride, and ingratitude, and wilfulness. No! this example of a sincere penitent represents him as resting his plea entirely on the goodness and mercy of his Father. He still retains the language of the filial relation, although he acknowledges that he has no claim to it. "*Father* (said he) I am unworthy to be called thy son; but, O give me in my Father's house, a servant's place." Here is a spirit of the deepest humility and self-abasement, and an acknowledgement of his Father's goodness. Here sorrow, shame, affection, hope, all work together in this man's breast, and bring him back again to his duty. He did not stay in a distant country, and send apologies to his Father. No, he arose and came himself. And how was he received? With a frown? No! was he upbraided for the past, and put in a course of trial to see how he would behave for the future? No! When he was yet a great way off, his Father saw him, and had compassion, and ran, and fell on his neck and kissed him, and brought him to the home he had deserted, and took away his filthy ragged garments, and gave him good clothes, and shoes, and a ring; and having found alive a lost son, whom he lamented as dead, he made a feast, and filled his whole house with joy.

And does this at all represent a lost sinner's case? Yes! Our blessed Saviour says, "Joy shall be in heaven over one sinner that repenteth."

How different are the sentiments entertained in heaven and on earth. Alas! who is there amongst men who much cares whether a fellow sinner repents or not; and how many are there ever ready to despise and mock the man who seems at all concerned about his sins. This world, and wicked men and women, are like the people of the far country, where the prodigal wasted his substance with riotous living; and when he began to be in want, none cared for him; the brute beasts were more regarded than he was. He fain would have filled his belly with the husks which the swine did eat, and no man gave unto him. But heaven is like the prodigal's *home;* in that place there is still a kind concern about him. Oh, what compassion! The Spirit of God strives with sinning man; the Spirit is grieved by man's wickedness; the Son of God died for man; and all heaven rejoices, (there is joy in the presence of the angels of God,) when sinful man repents, *i. e.* when man, at first, *out of his mind*, and wandering far off from his heavenly Father's home; feeding on ashes, or trying to ll his stomach with husks; trying to find happiness in drunkenness, in debauchery, or in riches, or in worldly distinctions, and such like low and grovelling, or vain and unsatisfying pursuits:—When he comes to himself, *is restored to his right mind*, and right judgment, and arises, and goes to his heavenly Father, and confesses his follies and his sins, and forsakes them; then there is joy in heaven on his account.

There are some self-righteous, self-conceited people, such as the Pharisees were, in our Saviour's days, who, like the returning prodigal's elder brother, think there is far too much ado made about a sinner's repenting; they do not care whether he repents or not; and they censure those who are a little anxious to induce him to repent; and they are angry because there is such a fuss made about a worthless wretch, (perhaps some poor drunken sailor,) who does actually repent, and come to his heavenly Father, penitent, sober, and in his right mind.

That such self-righteous, cold-hearted people, are very wrong is very evident, unless it be pretended that they are wiser, and better, and more rational, than the all-wise God and his holy angels; but this is too shocking and blasphemous even to be imagined.

And, further, it is a very plain inference from this subject, that a man's repenting, or not repenting, is a matter of great, of vast importance; for in heaven trifling or small matters cannot cause joy or grief. And observe, it is not the repentance of a whole family, or of a whole nation, that is said to give joy, but even the repentance of *one* sinner causes this joy. Oh, yes! it must be true, that real repentance is connected with the saving of a soul, an immortal spirit, from eternal misery, and the preparing it for eternal happiness. And is not this enough to make angels glad? is not this sufficient to cause joy in heaven? for heaven is the land of benevolence and compassion.

It should ever be remembered that repentance, in some cases, is unavailing; and repentance, even in cases where it is admissible, may be deferred till it is too late. When man violates the laws of his fellow-creatures, it often happens that his repentance will not prevent his punishment. There is no proof that when the angels sinned, they were allowed to repent. And when a man has, by vicious excesses, ruined his health, repentance, and even reformation, will not always restore him to health.

But, in reference to man's salvation, the mediatorial work of our Saviour, his death and sufferings in our stead, have made repentance admissible. He came to call sinners to repentance; his servants, the ministers of religion, are directed to go into all the world, and proclaim the good tidings, that the work of redemption is finished; and now God "commands all men, every where, to repent." The good angels are interested about man's repentance; and when but *one* repents, there is joy in their presence. Thus, all that are divine and good, in heaven and on earth, are moved about one man's salvation or condemnation. Their united admonition and entreaty, is, "Repent and believe the Gospel, and thou shalt be saved." To the returning penitent, then, there is no hindrance—none such need despair. No returning prodigal will ever be rejected: quite the contrary, he will be received with demonstrations of joy.

I have only one caution to suggest; let no one defer repentance; for death may surprise thee, and there is no repentance in the grave. The axe is laid ready at the root of the tree; if it bring not forth good fruit, it will ere long be cut down and cast into the fire. To delay repentance is not the suggestion of a friend, but of an enemy. It is a suggestion that comes from the destroyer of men's souls—the father of lies. Take the resolution at once, and, looking to God's Holy Spirit for help, say, "I will arise and go to my Father;" for you have the Saviour's word for it, that you will be welcomed with joy: the act of faith and repentance will make Heaven glad;—and then, O man! do thou go and bring forth fruits meet for repentance.

Exhortation delivered in England.

And one of the meet and becoming fruits of repentance is an anxious desire to bring others to repentance. A sort of missionary spirit is the general result of true repentance. A gracious state in this world is sometimes said to be glory begun, or an incipient degree of the same sort of sentiments, affections, and joys as will be experienced in heaven. Now if sinless angels rejoice in the return of one human creature to obedience and duty through the blessed Redeemer, is it credible that a gracious soul in this life can be indifferent to the repentance of sinners? and if not indifferent to the effect, neither can such a person be indifferent to the means. To bring sinners to repentance is to co-operate with God, who wills not the death of a sinner, but rather that he should repent, return, and live. To use means to bring sinners to repentance is to co-operate with the Divine Redeemer and with the Holy Spirit; it is to glorify God, and to cause joy in heaven.

By a missionary spirit, I mean a desire to win souls to Christ, to bring men to repentance; to find a sacred delight, to feel (as our text suggests) a seraphic, an angelic joy in the good tidings of sinners being brought to repentance.

Those Christians who take no sort of interest in the news of a sinner repenting, who will not aid in any means to bring sinners to repentance, who will neither give their personal services to call men to repent, nor join with God's people to pray that a spirit of repentance may be poured out upon the nations, nor contribute of their property to send forth the heralds of salvation—are wanting in some of the best evidences of the reality of their Christianity. Here is a work that makes heaven glad; but they are frigid and careless about it—it affords them no joy. What proof then do they give of a fitness for heaven?

Repentance and remission of sins are to be proclaimed in God's name amongst all nations; and Heaven wills that one man should be the medium of conveying this proclamation to others; and yet there are professed disciples of the

Saviour who will not at all aid this divine cause. In such cases, is there not a manifest lack of real Christianity?

On the other hand, how great is the encouragement to the missionary spirit amidst apparently small results. Whole districts, tribes, and nations may not be converted; but the repentance of *one* sinner causes joy in heaven. And although multitudes may not throng the road of true repentance, a solitary traveller attracts the attention of angels, and fills their hearts with joy.

And since angels derive joy from the repentance of sinners, they must look with complacency on the use of scriptural means to enlighten the human mind, to convince the conscience of the evil of sin, and to bring men to repentance. And therefore the zealous evangelist at home, in his own town or neighbourhood, as well as the friends of Christian Missions to foreign lands, need not much regard, nor need be much discouraged by human censure, or by man's neglect.

Since human affairs are known to the angels—who indeed are ministering spirits, sent forth to minister to the heirs of salvation—and this knowledge cannot be by any powers approaching omniscience, it follows that spiritual beings must traverse the universe, and communicate knowledge to each other. And if angels communicate the affairs of our world to each other, why may not they communicate such knowledge to the spirits of just men, that have attained the perfection of a heavenly state?

I see no reason to answer this question in the negative; at the same time, I do not presume to make any positive affirmation concerning what is not expressly revealed. But the probability of this knowledge and intercourse, may be useful in leading our meditations more frequently, and more impressively, to the invisible state; and may prevent our being so much absorbed, as men too frequently are, with sublunary things. O, my fellow-sinners—my Christian brethren, all heaven is concerned for our eternal welfare:—forbid it, O blessed God! that we should be stupid and unconcerned.

DISCOURSE VIII.

WRITTEN IN THE INDIAN OCEAN, JAN. 2, 1824.

INTRODUCTION.

[It is the annual custom for two of the ships from China to carry, on their way home, stores to the Cape of Good Hope. The Waterloo, in the season 1823 and 24, was one of those. Anticipating a short stay at the Cape, (which indeed proved to be only four days,) Dr. Morrison prepared the following discourse for the African Missionaries connected with the London Missionary Society.

The Rev. Dr. Philip, Resident Agent at the Cape for the Missions, was then in the interior, awaiting at the different stations, his Majesty's Commissioners, who were making a tour of the Colony. However, several Missionaries, the Rev. Mr. Moffat and others, were then at the Cape, residing in Dr. Philip's house, adjoining a Chapel which he had built. Mrs. Philip, a pious and amiable lady, exerted herself to the utmost, and beyond her strength, to render the families, then "quartered" upon her, as comfortable as possible.

On the Thursday evening, Jan. 29th, 1824, an accustomed service took place in the Chapel, and the stranger from China was expected and pressed to address the Congregation. He readily assented, but the intense heat of Cape Town, and the fatigue of walking about its streets, and paying the usual respects to the local authorities, induced a severe head-ache, to which, from childhood, he has been in all climates constantly subject; and it was totally impossible that he could even read the discourse which he had prepared.

Under these circumstances, Mr. Moffat, instead of preaching a Sermon of his own, read to the people the following Discourse. And the Rev. Mr. *Faure*, Dutch Clergyman at the Cape, who was present, took a copy for the purpose of translating it into the Dutch language.

Cape Town, to an Asiatic, appears quite European; or if not *quite* European, so nearly allied to Europe, as to *seem* European to an old Indian. The closeness of the houses, occasioned by the inhabitants shutting every door and window to keep out the clouds of dust and sand, was, to people from the high seas, perfectly intolerable. Capt. Alsager and the writer of this were, on one occasion, shewn into a room to await the appearance of the master of the house, where they could scarcely breathe, and consequently retreated to the door-way and there took their stand till some external air was admitted into the chamber.]

MISSION OF BARNABAS AND SAUL.

ACTS, XIII. 1, 2, 3.

"Now there were in the church that was at Antioch, certain prophets and teachers; as Barnabas, and Simeon that was called Niger, and Lucius of Cyrene, and Manaen, which had been brought up with Herod the tetrarch, and Saul. As they ministered to the Lord, and fasted, the Holy Ghost said, Separate me Barnabas and Saul for the work whereunto I have called them. And when they had fasted and prayed, and laid their hands on them, they sent them away."

WHEN it is remembered, that the prophets declared the Messiah should be for *a light to the Gentiles*, and for salvation to *the ends of the earth,* Is. xlix. 6; that the angels at the Saviour's birth declared the Saviour's advent was good tidings *to all people,* Luke ii. 10; and that Jesus, when ascending to Heaven, commanded his Gospel to be taught to *all nations*—it is surprising how slow of apprehending this essential truth the first Jewish Christians were. *Eight* years elapsed before any of the Africans attended to this command to preach to the Gentiles—and then Peter required an express revelation from heaven to induce him to go to a Roman military officer, Cornelius—and when he did do so, the Apostles and brethren at Jerusalem censured him for it; and still no Church was formed amongst the Gentiles until persecution, which arose about Stephen, scattered the disciples; and even then some of them, who came as far as Antioch, preached the word to *none* but unto the Jews *only*, (xi. 19.) However, eventually some men of Cyrene, (Africans,) for Cyrene was a place in Africa, "spake unto the Grecians preaching the Lord Jesus;"—and the "hand of the Lord was with them, and a great number believed"—and then a Gentile Church was formed at Antioch, and with this first Gentile Church, raised by African preachers, originated the name *Christian*, as a designation applied to Christ's disciples—and from this same Church the first Mission was sent out. We shall notice,

I. The persons employed on this Mission.
II. Their dedication to the work.
III. The field of their labour.
IV. Their manner of executing the work.

I. *The persons employed* on this Mission were Paul and Barnabas. Of Barnabas little is recorded, Paul's history is well known. From the circumstance of the people of Lystra having supposed Barnabas to be their god Jupiter, and Paul to be the god Mercurius, the patron of eloquence, it is likely that Barnabas was a man of gravity and dignity in his manner, less prompt in his elocution than Paul. However, these two missionaries in addition to their natural qualifications, possessed supernatural endowments of a spiritual nature, and also the power of working miracles for the confirmation of the truth. Still they appear to have been subject, occasionally, to the same bad tempers and passions as other men; for when about to go on a second Mission, they differed in opinion concerning an assistant, and contested the point so sharply, as to cause a separation. Barnabas insisted on taking his relative Mark with them, and Paul obstinately refused to allow it, because Mark had abandoned them on a former occasion.

If men so eminently qualified, so richly gifted, so expressly appointed or called by Heaven, manifested such unconciliating tempers, we should not expect an entire absence of human frailty in modern Missionaries, nor be discouraged when strifes occasionally arise, and separations take place. However, the example of the Apostles in this matter is not for imitation, but should induce watchfulness and caution; for by a sinful indulgence of temper, these two divinely selected servants of God were prevented from walking together in love, and from labouring together for the faith of the Gospel.

Paul, at the time of his wonderful conversion, when he saw a heavenly vision, was told by Jesus, that he would be sent to the Gentiles to open their eyes, and turn them from darkness to light, and from the power of Satan to God; and on the present occasion, when at Antioch with other teachers, the Holy Ghost said, "Separate me Barnabas and Saul, for the work whereto I have called them." The divine operation on the human spirit, or communications from the Spirit of God to the soul of man, is a doctrine every where taught in the Bible from beginning to end; sometimes this influence operates in a manner known to the persons so operated on or influenced, and sometimes not; but of the Holy Spirit's work in striving with men, in regenerating and changing the hearts of men, in suggesting truth to the mind, and in comforting the souls of men, divine Revelation does not admit a doubt. In every age, holy men of God have spoken and acted, in many cases, as they were moved by the Holy Ghost. Not that the Holy Spirit's influences are in all places and all times alike, for in divers manners God spake in times past, by the inspired Prophets, before the coming of his Son; and subsequently, seeing Jesus promised to send the Comforter, and encouraged the children of God to pray for the Holy Spirit, it is manifest the Spirit's operations continue under the reign of the Messiah, that dispensation or method of divine rule under which we live. However, there is one great difference in the ministration of the Spirit in ordinary cases, and during the apostolic age; his suggestions or influences are not in later ages so certainly ascertainable; for our circumstances are different, the written word has long been complete, and it must be our guide. It is the rule according to, and it is the instrument by which the Holy Spirit works. And therefore the Holy Ghost does not now suggest to the churches the names of those who are to be employed in ministering the word of life, whether that be in Christendom or in unchristianized lands, but gives the qualifications requisite, and the willing mind to which intimations the churches should attend with prayerful watchfulness, whilst to the individual concerned, the most abiding and most satisfactory evidence of being called will be a consciousness of unfeigned scriptural motives, and singleness of intention, with a deep sense of gratitude to God, and ardent benevolence to men; a readiness to spend and be spent for the elect's sake, that they may obtain the salvation which is in Christ Jesus, with eternal glory.

II. At Antioch Barnabas and Saul were, as it is said in our text, "recommended to the grace of God." Notwithstanding the express call of the Holy Spirit, received whilst the prophets and teachers were ministering to the Lord and fasting, it was still deemed right again to observe a season of fasting and prayer, at which "they" (the prophets and teachers) laid their hands on the two Missionaries before sending them away. It does not appear in the Sacred Scriptures, that the Jewish Priests were ordained by any peculiar rite; but the Levites were dedicated by the laying on of the hands of the congregation, Num. viii. 10. Moses, at the appointment of Joshua to be his successor, received this command from the Almighty, "Take thee Joshua, the son of Nun, a man in whom is the spirit, and *lay thy hand upon him,* and give him a charge, and put of thine honour upon him, that the congregation may be obedient." (Num. xxvii. 20.) In the New Testament, the Bishops and Presbyters were appointed by the laying on of hands; but "Barnabas and Paul," (the *Apostles* as they are called in chap. xiv. 14.) were not on this occasion first commissioned to teach and to preach Jesus Christ, and therefore the circumstance of now laying hands on them is the more remarkable.

However, what is of the greatest importance here to observe is, the evident anxiety, the earnest desire to obtain, by solemn intercession, the co-operation of the Almighty arm. It implies a strong conviction of the difficulty of the work to be accomplished, and a consciousness of merely human efforts being inadequate. This, indeed, has been the sentiment, and this the feeling of all God's eminent servants, from Moses to Paul, and from his time to the present day. Moses exclaimed, "Who am I, that I should go to Pharaoh, and that I should bring forth the children of Israel out of Egypt! How shall Pharaoh hear me, who am of uncircumcised lips!"—The Prophet Jeremiah wished to decline his arduous office, and expostulated, saying, "Ah, Lord God, I cannot speak, for I am a child!" and Paul, referring to the ministry of "Christ's Gospel," exclaims, "Who is sufficient for these things." Such sentiments and feelings, when arising solely from humility and a desire to obtain divine aid, are exactly what they should be; but when mixed with timidity, the fear of man, distrust, the love of ease, and such unhallowed motives, they are so far wrong, and not to be indulged. When they are sincere and accompanied by love to God, they will not lead a man to decline his Lord's service, but will lead him to fasting and prayer for God's help. And then he may say with humility, "If thy presence go not with me, send me not up hence." And so, as in the cases above referred to, the answers from heaven will be as they were then, gracious and encouraging. The Lord replied to Moses thus, "Certainly I will *be with thee*—say not I am not eloquent, for who hath made man's mouth—have not I the Lord?—Now, therefore, go, and I will be with thy mouth, and teach thee what thou shalt say." Jeremiah received for answer, "Say not I am a child; thou shalt go, and whatever I command thee speak. Be not afraid of their faces, for *I am with thee.*" And when Paul besought the Lord for help, the answer given him was this, "My grace is sufficient for thee."

All these examples should operate as a check both to presumption and to despondency, when men are engaged in the arduous work of the ministry. In the employment of humble, sincere, and zealous efforts, as directed by scripture precepts and examples, let the Lord's co-operation be sought by abstinence and prayer, and then there is every reason to hope, that God will recognize such servants, as "workers together with him." Not that they must therefore be as successful as they wish, but their labour in the Lord, shall be graciously acknowledged and accepted.

III. *The field of labour*, occupied by Barnabas and Saul, on this first mission, was confined to Asia Minor: they did not pass into Europe, but returned to Antioch and Jerusalem: and after Paul went forth a second time, he and Silas did not think of leaving Asia, till the vision appeared to them of a Macedonian Greek, calling and beseeching them to pass over to Europe, and afford help. Judea was a province of the Roman empire, and beyond the limits of that empire they never went. Paul was a Roman citizen, and he never quitted the Roman empire; and there was, as yet, no general law of the empire against the Christian Missionaries: the opposition they met with, was only from the prejudices and enmity of their fellow-subjects; to whom, occasionally, the local magistrates listened, and lent their aid. Being permitted to travel every where, afforded them facilities, such as indeed all Missionaries who labour in the British empire enjoy, but which is not the case with those in some Pagan countries.

It is observable that these two Missionaries, although so eminently furnished by heaven with qualifications for their work, and under no necessity to learn a foreign language, did not go without an assistant; or, as he is called, a "minister," one to serve and assist them. Moses had Joshua for his minister during his life-time, and for his successor after his death. Elijah had Elisha to minister to him, and serve him, and to succeed him; and when the kings of Judah, Israel, and Edom, enquired for a Prophet of the Lord, Elisha was pointed out, as he who had poured water on the hands of Elijah;* *i. e.* performed for him the

* In Java, and other countries of the East, it is still the usage for an attendant to "pour water on the hands" of a person when washing; under the same idea of cleanliness, as is suggested by bathing in a *running stream;* instead of bathing in stagnant water.

duties of a domestic servant. In ancient scriptural times, and in modern Asia still, the relations of Preceptor and Scholar, of elder and younger, always carried with them the idea of principal and helper; of one who is served, and of one who ministers to the other; in the whole of which is preserved a spirit of reciprocal affection and kind efforts, united to promote the good of both, in the pursuit of some common end. It is not the relation of lord and slave, or of a tyrannical master and an oppressed servant; but still of one who directs, and of another who is directed.

The spirit of modern Missionaries have so generally spurned at this sort of relation, although so perfectly scriptural, and so evidently rational, and honourable to both parties; they have robbed themselves of the comfort, and advantage to the cause, which its adoption would have ensured; and strifes, and divisions, have been the consequence of its rejection; and, thereby, consecutive labours being intermitted, the good cause has been injured.

IV. The manner in which Barnabas and Saul, with Mark for their minister, executed the mission, or fulfilled the work to which they were appointed, is stated at considerable length, and affords example and instruction, to all persons who have similar duties to perform, and to all churches who send forth Missionaries.

With such qualifications, and such powers as they possessed, and with such an express warrant from heaven to undertake the mission, many, now-a-days, would anticipate that he who sent them would smooth down every rugged difficulty, and incline all hearts to give them a ready reception. But this was not the case. At Paphos, on the island of Cyprus, a fellow-countryman of their's, a false prophet, opposed them, and used all his influence with the Roman Pro-consul against them. At Perga, their assistant, John Mark, abandoned them. At Antioch, in Pisidia, their countrymen, the Jews, stirred up the religious ladies, (the devout and honourable women,) and the rulers of the city, and raised a persecution against Paul and Barnabas, and expelled them out of their coasts. At Iconium, the Gentiles and the Jews also, with their rulers, made an assault upon them, to use them despitefully and to stone them. Not content with this degree of enmity, these Jews followed Paul and Barnabas as far as the region about Lystra and Derbe, probably a hundred miles from Iconium, and persuaded the people to attempt the murder of the Apostles; and they actually stoned Paul, and dragged his body out of the city, supposing he had been dead. Paul, indeed, from the time that he became a Christian, was not only in labours abundant; but was also, at different times, in stripes above measure, scourged severely; was frequently imprisoned, and often exposed to death; in perils from robbers, from his own countrymen, from heathens, from false Christians; and he met difficulties in all places, by land and by sea, in the city and in the wilderness. He suffered not only from men, but also from the elements—thrice shipwrecked; exposed to hunger and thirst, to cold and nakedness. One inference from these things is, that opposition, and manifold sufferings endured by any servant of God, do not indicate that it is the will of Providence that he should desist from preaching the Gospel.

However, although Paul persevered in his work, he did not always remain in the same place, nor did he always address the same people. When the Jews contradicted and blasphemed, he and Barnabas gave them a solemn warning; and thenceforth, at that place, turned their attention to the Gentiles. And from Iconium, when he found out the design of the Gentiles and Jews, to unite together and murder him, he fled, and went elsewhere. Although a perfect stranger to the fear of man, he did not think it right to throw away his life; but obeyed the precept, "When they persecute you in one city, flee to another," and continue still to publish the Gospel.

We see that Paul could not be intimidated by ill usage; nor could he be flattered by the admiration and adulation of the populace and pagan priests. When the Apostles, Barnabas and Paul, heard of the intention to honour them as the gods Jupiter and Mercury, they were more earnest than ever in testifying against the vanity of idols. Christhan Ministers and Missionaries have not in every age imitated these eminent servants of God; but have sometimes been silenced by the attentions, flatteries, and favours of immoral men possessing wealth or power; they have entered into a sort of compromise with the world: The church shall receive contributions, and external respect, and reverence, and dignity; but on condition that the patrons of the church must not be offended by uncourteous censures for their vices, their vanities, and their idols. The world is very willing to have a religion, if it may have its vicious indulgences passed over in silence. It will idolize for a while even Christ's Ministers, whether Bishops, or Presbyters, or Apostles, on these terms.

But neither fear, nor flattery, nor ridicule, could silence Paul. The scoffing philosophists of Athens might call him "a babbler,"* and "mock" him and his doctrine; he bore his testimony *against* them, and *for* the truth faithfully; and then left them that he might go and address others on the same grand and awful subjects. May all Ministers and Missionaries be enabled to follow his example when assailed in these several ways.

On this Mission Barnabas and Paul addressed all classes of people, and used a variety of means, exhortations, and arguments. They went first to the lost sheep of the house of Israel who were scattered abroad. In the Jewish Synagogue at Antioch, Paul *reasoned* out of the Scriptures, proving that Jesus of Nazareth was the Messiah, who had in his death and resurrection perfected the work of redemption, and had sent the word of salvation to them; and he declared that through Christ they now had preached to them the forgiveness of sins, but they who despised the work of God should perish.

At Lystra he *reasoned* against hero-worship and idolatry, from the principles of natural religion, and exhorted the people to turn from these vanities unto the living God, who made heaven and earth, the sea, all things that are therein.

* Σπερμολογος. "Vulgar prater."

At Thessalonica Paul's manner was to go every Sabbath day into a Synagogue of the Jews, and *reason* with them out of the Scriptures, opening and alleging that Christ must needs have suffered and risen again from the dead, and he declared that this Jesus whom he preached was the Christ.

At Athens he *disputed* in the Synagogue with the Jews, and with the devout or religious people; and he *disputed* in the market-place daily with those that met him, which roused the attention of the Epicurean and Stoic philosophers, who led him to Areopagus, where, in the midst of Mars' hill, he declared to them the God that made the world, who was to them unknown. He insisted on the doctrines of Providence, man's accountableness, repentance, and a future judgment, to be executed by Christ Jesus, whom God raised from the dead.

At Corinth, during the week-days, Paul worked at a mechanical trade in Aquila's house*, and *reasoned* in the Synagogue every Sabbath, and persuaded the Jews and the Greeks—and subsequently in a private house he remained a year and six months *teaching* the word of God.

At Ephesus, he spake boldly in the Synagogue for the space of three months, *disputing* and *persuading* the things concerning the kingdom of God. And here also he *disputed* daily in the school of one Tyrannus.

These labours were not always efficacious, for many opposed and blasphemed, and divers were hardened and believed not; but his efforts were not wholly in vain, for in almost every place there were some who believed and turned to the Lord.

From the example here exhibited to us, it may be fairly inferred that the Scriptures warrant a variety of means to be employed in propagating the Gospel. One means should

* The duties of a Minister or Missionary are generally more than enough for any man's qualifications and strength; but if Paul worked at a trade, he might with equal propriety have traded for his support; and if such secular employments were lawful in him, I know not why a Missionary may not attend to secular affairs for his own support; nor can I see the principle on which the Jesuits' trading for the support of their missions is censured, provided they *traded honestly*.

not be exclusively employed, nor only one manner of exhibiting divine truth be used. Some Christians say that preaching is the great instrument of spreading the Gospel, and despise other means. Some have noticed the silent efficacy of the Sacred Scriptures, and do not allow weight enough to oral instruction. Some declaim against arguing and disputing, and insist that a simple declaration of, or testimony to the truth is best. Now it appears to me a mistake, to exalt one means above another, for they all have their use in different times, places, and circumstances; and christian wisdom consists in rightly timeing the means, not relinquishing any for an exclusive adherence to one favourite method. Knowledge, and prudence, and piety, and the hand of the Lord, going together, will effect the work. Worldly wisdom consists in the employment of insincere specious means, or crafty arts, and implies the exclusion of divine aid. But knowledge and prudence, learning and talents, of every sort, exerted to the utmost, being accompanied with a simple-hearted sincerity, and unintermitted reliance on the Almighty arm, should not be called "worldly wisdom." The wisdom of this world, which the Bible condemns, consists in a self-sufficient employment of human means and crafty devices, accompanied by a neglect or contempt of the Holy Spirit. To employ ignorance, rashness, and a froward furious zeal, under an idea of avoiding "worldly wisdom," is a great error; and, therefore, we conclude no means, whether consisting of oral instruction, preaching, teaching, reasoning, and disputing; or of written or printed communications, the Sacred Scriptures, essays, circular letters, and so forth, should be neglected. The modern method of teaching children, although perfectly justified on principle and by precept, is the only means that I know of which is not sanctioned by express example; for academies or colleges, where a select number of persons are constantly with preceptors, are justified by the example of our Saviour himself; and also by the Apostolic Missionaries, who took young men under their care to assist, and to be instructed and fitted for the work. That these had no fixed abode, or stationary building in which they taught, appears to me a mere circumstance, which does not affect the principle. Modern Missionaries have foreign languages to study, which the Apostles had not; and it is absolutely necessary for them to be stationary whilst learning, and whilst teaching heathen youths.

Translations of the Scriptures are sanctioned by the constant use made of the sacred writings, by our Lord and the Apostolic Missionaries; and their references are generally made to a translation of the Old Testament into the Greek tongue. For it is the meaning, the sense of the Scriptures, that is to be regarded as sacred, not the Hebrew or Greek words. It is the superstition of the Romish Church in China and other countries, to consider the Latin words, "Pater, Filius, Spiritus Sanctus," &c. as sacred, and not to be translated. The Budh Priests, in China, do the same with many of the Sanscrit words of their superstition, and do not translate them. Perhaps Bishop Lowth's idea, (which is adopted in the practice of some Missionaries,) that the word Jehovah is not to be translated, partakes of the same superstition. In the New Testament, the word Jehovah is never used, but is translated as our translators in the English Bible have generally done, by a word corresponding to Lord.

The employment of the pen, in narratives, memoirs, letters, &c. for the diffusion of divine truth in the earth, is fully justified by the sacred writings themselves; and these writings authorize the use of the pen and the press, as a very eminent means of preserving and diffusing the Gospel. If any comparison were to be drawn, (a proceeding which I do not advise,) I know not but writing would appear the *most* efficient means. How great has been the effect upon the human mind produced by the Gospels, or memoirs of our Saviour, written by the Evangelists, and the epistles or letters written by Paul and the other writers of the New Testament!

But although this be admitted, *preaching*, that is, testifying to men by the living voice, the gospel of the grace of God; opening and expounding the Scriptures, teaching the things concerning the kingdom of God, reasoning from principles of natural religion; persuading, and if necessary, disputing with the opponents of the truth, is never to be disused. And as we have apostolic example for preaching *viva voce*, so we have apostolic example for publishing and defending divine truth by means of *written essays* or *letters*. If we take into account the permanent utility of Paul's letters for eighteen centuries past, it would probably appear, that he converted and edified more persons by means of his letters, than he did by all his preaching, and his miracles, and his sufferings put together. If it be objected that the writings of Ministers and Missionaries, and private Christians can never be compared to the inspired Gospels and Epistles, it is granted. No more can the preaching of uninspired ministers be compared to the divine sermons of Jesus, and the inspired preaching of the Apostles; and, therefore, when we argue about the comparative use of means, the argument still holds good: inspired letters being compared with inspired sermons; and uninspired translations and essays, compared with uninspired preaching. An induction of particular facts, as given in church history, from the days of the Apostles to the present time, would, I doubt not, confirm what has been now advanced in favour of a variety of means, viz. colleges or schools of the prophets, translations of the Bible and religious writings, preaching and oral teaching. The admirable Luther used all the three means: he was professor of divinity at the Wittemberg University, a preacher in the same city, and an assiduous writer of religious essays and expositions of sacred writ, by all of which means he converted many individuals, and reformed the religion of nations. But there are not many persons competent to employ all these means; if a man excel in one, the churches should be satisfied. The object to be attained is the communication of truth to the human soul, that it may be enlightened, purified, and saved; and whether this be done to children or adults, by means of a school, or hearing the word preached, or reading the Scriptures, or religious books, containing the sense and meaning of the Holy Spirit in the Scriptures—let God be praised for giving efficacy to the means, and let them be employed zealously and assiduously; for, since all these means are, less or more, rendered effectual, it is manifest that the Lord does not confine himself to any one, to the exclusion of the rest; and therefore it is incumbent on Christians to employ all, or such of them, as circumstances may render most practicable. In one's native country, where instruction can be conveyed to thousands in one's mother tongue, preaching should be extensively employed. Amongst unlettered tribes of men, no use can be made of books, and therefore that means is by the necessity of the case excluded; but a seminary to introduce the knowledge of letters, and to raise up native preachers, would be an important means. In some places, as China for example, it is extremely difficult to become qualified to preach; and it is impossible, under present circumstances, to gather a congregation to preach to. Teaching a few individuals, or writing books in one's own hired house in China, or teaching in a college out of China, and the distribution of Bibles and Tracts amongst Chinese colonists, are the means that can be mostly used. Happily, the Sacred Scriptures are all translated into the Chinese language, and there are a few religious essays, but much more—very much, is still required to be done in qualifying preachers and writers to expound the Scriptures, to testify the Gospel, and to reason with the heathen, to enforce even the principles of natural religion, and declare to them the God that made the heavens, who is to them generally unknown. Heaven, indeed, they speak of, but concerning Him who is higher than the heavens, they are almost totally ignorant. Oh, what a wide field! what an abundant harvest! is there in the regions beyond India, accessible through the medium of the Chinese language! how few the labourers, and how difficult the work.

But, blessed be God, a beginning has been made. Providence has blessed the efforts of his servants, so that the acquisition of the language is now much facilitated. In the Anglo-Chinese College, native books, teachers, and students are provided. By the Chinese Bible, divine truth is made accessible to the educated; and there is one Chinese Protestant set apart to the ministry amongst his countrymen, with the Bible in his own language, for his sole guide and his instructor, under the desired influences of the Holy Spirit.

I thus briefly rehearse to you what God has done by his servants, for it was his co-operation which gave efficacy to the very limited means at first employed; and now that the means are thus far increased, it must ever be remembered, that all that men can do, when they have done their utmost, is but the use of means which cannot be effectual unless the hand of God work with them; the energy of his Holy Spirit must be prayed for and relied on, and then the labour will not be in vain. Men, and the efforts which they make, or the measures they employ, preaching, teaching, writing, must all be considered as instruments in the hand of God, the Father, Son, and Spirit. In the temporal deliverances and national conquests of God's ancient people, his might, and the operation of his hand were always acknowledged. In the spiritual deliverances from Satan's usurpation of the human heart, and the spiritual conquests of primitive disci ples and apostles, "The hand of the Lord" was recognized in those that believed the Gospel and turned to him, and to him they gave the glory.

The churches should esteem and encourage those men who spend or hazard their lives in distant lands for the sake of the Lord Jesus, but they should be careful not to rob God of the honour that is due to his name, for this is the very principle of pagan idolatry, and of all impiety. Men sacrifice to their net and to their drag, and pay a sort of worship to the mere human instrument of good, forgetting the divine hand which wielded it.

These Notes were added when the same discourse was read in England.

Although we have not assembled to-day expressly for missionary purposes—yet, in as much as I believe it capable of demonstration, that one part of the design of Christians forming societies or churches, is the diffusion of Gospel light throughout the world—you will not deem the discourse of this day irrelevant to the object of our meeting. I fear Christian churches still view the propagation of the Gospel, rather as an act of voluntary benevolence than as a duty binding in all Christians, and all churches to the full extent of their means. Christians are too selfish in supposing that their own edification is the sole object of associating together in church fellowship, and they do not, perhaps, consider sufficiently that indifference to the great object of extending the Redeemer's kingdom, is rather presumptive evidence against their being subjects of his kingdom. Alas! where is the loyalty of many to Zion's king? I speak of what comparatively ought to exist. Whilst I rejoice that in this highly privileged land, there are so many of every rank in society who are faithful servants and subjects of the most High God—may they daily increase, and may hundreds and thousands be raised up to spend their fortunes, and sacrifice their lives, in his spiritual and just wars against Satan's usurped dominion over the children of men.

Leaf Square, May 2, 1824.

And I by no means wish you to *begin* in distant regions, but to *begin* in your own neighbourhood, by teaching the rising generation those things that promote their usefulness in this life, and their happiness in the next.

DISCOURSE IX.

DELIVERED ON BOARD THE WATERLOO, FEBRUARY 29, 1824.

INTRODUCTION.

[During the night of February 22, 1824, whilst sailing fast homeward, with a fine fair breeze, something gave way at the fore-top-mast stunsail; a man was ordered up by the second officer, then on duty, to replace it. The evening was fine, and there was some moon-light; but the man, having over-reached himself to pass a rope, fell; and, from the moment of his fall into the sea, was never more heard or seen. The ship was put about; a boat lowered down; and the officer on duty went out himself, and rowed about in every direction, hoping to find the man clinging to the life-buoy, which was instantly cut from the quarter. But every effort was unavailing. The men returned; the boat was hoisted in; and the ship steered her course. Poor Benjamin Hill, the unfortunate sailor who fell, thus suddenly ended his mortal career, and sunk in a watery grave. Almost every voyage such casualties occur. They produce a momentary impression of seriousness on the minds of the ship's company, but generally leave no evidence of a lasting beneficial result, for no new truths are communicated to the mind. Since the Writer left China, in the short space of two years, three persons whom he knew there, have in Europe committed suicide; one in Paris, who returned home rich; one in Edinburgh said to be prosperous, but disappointed in further schemes of ambition; and the officer on duty, in this melancholy case, who shot himself when embarking for another voyage.

The Sabbath after the loss of Hill, the following exhortation was delivered to the men.]

PREPARATION TO MEET GOD.

AMOS, IV. 12.

"Prepare to meet thy God."

HUMAN beings, whether nations or individuals, are in this world subject to the government of the Almighty. The world is his, and men are all his creatures, accountable to him for their conduct. This principle is applicable to all nations, and to all individuals :—to Jews and to Heathens; to Greeks and to Barbarians; to Mohammedans and to Hindoos; to the rich and poor; to the learned and ignorant. His kingdom extendeth over all, and his sceptre is a sceptre of righteousness. Justice is the habitation of his throne, and his judgment is according to truth. But nations and individuals too often cast off the fear of God, and obedience to him, and live and act as if they were accountable to no superior authority; during which time the Almighty, who delights in mercy, graciously employs means to bring men to repentance. For this purpose the prophet Amos was employed and sent to Judah and Israel, to remonstrate with them, and forewarn them of the calamities that would befal them, unless they repented and reformed. Heaven had already sent many calamities to chastise them, and bestowed many mercies to awaken their gratitude; but they still continued their impiety and wickedness, and therefore greater calamities were denounced, when God himself should enter into judgment with them; in the prospect of which, the words of the text were addressed to them by the Prophet, as from the Almighty himself—"Prepare to meet thy God, O Israel."

To every man it is appointed once to die, and after death the judgment; for the Scriptures testify that God hath appointed a day, in which he will judge the world in righteousness, by that person whom he hath ordained for this purpose — Jesus Christ. St. Paul declares we must all appear before the judgment-seat of Christ; and, therefore, to every man it may with truth and propriety be said—" Prepare to meet thy God"—prepare either to justify thyself, or to contend with him—or *prepare for a gracious reception, by previous and immediate submission to mercy*. If man would think seriously, and believe the truth sent down from heaven, instead of believing the lies suggested by Satan and a wicked heart, he would soon be convinced that self-justification is as impracticable as to overcome Omnipotence. No sophistry can conceal man's guilt from Him who searcheth the heart, and " declareth unto man what is his thought;" and no power can resist His who "formeth the mountains, and createth the wind;" whose word makes the earth tremble, and sends forth the desolating tempest; whose providence can turn the morning of impious hope into darkness and bitter disappointment; and who can tread the powerful wicked, on the high places of the earth, under his feet. Resistance to the Almighty is so palpable a fallacy, it is not usually suggested to the human mind by the deceiver of mankind: it is his mode of destroying, rather to employ misrepresentation than to urge direct opposition; to suggest that sin is not so great an evil as some people would represent it; and that the Almighty will not require a strict account of man's thoughts, words, and actions: or he persuades men to put far away the evil day, and suggests that it is yet *too soon to prepare to meet one's God;* by which delusion, persisted in day after day and year after year, many suddenly pass to the bar of God, (it is to be feared,) wholly *unprepared*. The misinterpreting the *mercy* of God is another destructive fallacy by which many are deceived. That God is merciful, is as true as that God is just. But to whom is he merciful? to the man who mocks at sin, and still goes on in his trespasses? No such thing! The Bible declares that God is angry with the wicked every day;—against such the wrath of God is revealed from heaven;—to such sinners God is a consuming fire. But, to him that confesseth and forsaketh his sins, the Lord sheweth mercy, and multiplies pardons. God is merciful, but he will not be mocked; and the hypocrite cannot deceive him. He is most merciful to the man who is sincerely sorry for his sin, and who obediently submits to the Saviour as Heaven has directed: but to the man who makes light of sin, and who despises or neglects the Saviour, the Gospel does not promise mercy. Now, concerning what is sin, and what is duty, man must derive his opinions from reason and from revelation. The *will of God*, as far as it can be ascertained, must decide what is right and what is wrong; not man's own notions, in opposition to, or differing from the Divine Will.

By looking over this book of Amos, from which the text is taken, we may see some of the *sins* on account of which divine judgments were threatened. The period spoken of is nearly 2,500 years ago; about 800 years before the Romans conquered England. The first sin mentioned is *cruelty*. The Edomites pursued their brothers of the kingdom of Judah with the sword, and *cast off all pity*. The anger of Edom did *tear perpetually*, and he "*kept his wrath for ever*." The inhabitants of Damascus cruelly treated those of Gilead, and threshed them, as with threshing instruments of iron. And the Ammonites, for the purpose of enlarging their borders, or extending their territories, stormed the cities of Gilead, and ripped up their women with child. The divine law requires of the different nations of mankind charity and good will to each other, an endeavour to promote each other's welfare; and of individuals is required a spirit of benevolence, which not only forbids hurting or injuring either man or woman, whether in their persons, their character, or their property, but also requires that they should be assisted to the utmost of any man's power. A feeling of *indifference* about other people begins a violation of the divine law; and cruelty to them closes it, or carries the offence to the greatest degree. How many cruelties are still practised by the nations of Europe in their wars undertaken for trivial causes, such as a desire to enlarge their border, or to extend their territory! When the Almighty shall make inquisition for the blood of hundreds and thousands of those who have been unmercifully treated, or cruelly murdered, how will those men, who have instigated or perpetrated these cruelties, be prepared to meet their God?

Gaza is threatened because they carried away captive the whole captivity, and cruelly delivered them up to Edom as slaves, (ch. i. 6.); and how much displeasure must Heaven have felt against the professed Christians of Europe, who have cruelly carried away, and still carry away, from their homes, thousands of defenceless persons, and sell them as slaves. When our Saviour said, "Blessed are the merciful, for they shall obtain mercy," the declaration implied, that the unmerciful, or cruel, were accursed.

Another sin with which the people of that day were charged by the Prophet, and which the Almighty declares his determination to punish, is contempt for and disregard of the divine law, with the dissemination of false opinions in religion and morals. "They despised the law of the Lord, and have not kept his commandments, and their lies caused them to err." In many places, in the Sacred Scriptures, the children of men are charged with this contempt for the divine precepts; and this wickedness is cherished by *believing lies*, or *false opinions*. Some scornful men pique themselves on not being *believers;* they would have others think that they are too knowing to *believe;* whereas in fact no one is more *credulous* than a *wicked* man. He too believes; but he will *believe a lie* that promises impunity to the sinner, rather than *believe the truth* which threatens his punishment. As in the case of our first parents, he will believe Satan when he says, "You may sin and yet not die," rather than believe the Almighty when he declares, "In the day thou sinnest thou shalt assuredly die." The prophet Isaiah, too, describes the rulers of Jerusalem scorners and despisers of the divine law, and of his threatenings: they said, with contempt and defiance, 'When the overflowing scourge shall pass through, it shall not come near unto us; for we have made a covenant with death, and with hell are we at agreement: we have made lies our refuge, and under falsehood have we hid ourselves.' False opinions make sinners feel careless and secure; and a sort of *faith in the devil*, a belief in lying excuses for sin, embolden them still to go on, and to err more and more from the right way. Men know very well that the third commandment forbids making use of the name of the Almighty on trivial occasions; and yet how frequently is the commandment despised and violated, without the least feeling of remorse, because people believe that it is a sufficient excuse that they mean no harm! But meaning harm, or not meaning harm, is not at all noticed in the commandment. Mean harm to whom? How could men harm the Almighty, in their sense of harm? If it be intended that they mean no harm to their neighbour, the excuse is equally fallacious. This commandment speaks of man's duty to his Maker, not of his duty to his fellow-creatures. It commands us to reverence, in our speech, the divine name; and we violate that precept whenever we use it with irreverence. The precept is very express—"Thou shalt not take the name of the Lord thy God in vain, for the Lord will not hold him guiltless that taketh his name in vain." Now, the lie, or false opinion, which people commonly *believe*, is, that they will be held "*guiltless*," because they swear, or invoke the divine name, out of merriment, or from surprise, or from habit, without direct malice; none of which excuses can be reasonably inferred from the precept as at all availing.

This is but one example of many other false opinions that cause men to err, and persist in sin with an easy conscience. Men believe, or half believe, with now and then slight misgivings, such excuses for sin, and a neglect of duty towards God, as would not impose on a mere fool, if they referred to duties owing himself.

Men who have a right to command, properly enough insist on strict, prompt, and implicit odedience, and admit of no silly excuses; and shall the high commands of righteous Heaven be despised and disregarded, and the divine authority insulted by silly excuses, and man yet be "*guiltless*," in direct contradiction to the divine declaration! Were it not the fact that man appears to believe such lying absurdities, it might be supposed impossible that he could so far deceive himself, or be such a dupe to the deceiver of mankind.

Another false opinion very prevalent is, that young men may be vicious with impunity—that youth is an excuse for vice; but it is an opinion not at all countenanced in the Bible, any more than that it is excusable for persons, in certain situations, to disregard the divine laws: as for example, that strict morality does not apply to *sailors* or *soldiers*, or to *politicians*, or to great *generals* and *conquerors*. In some of these cases the parties would not plead for an *entire* exemption, but that various forms of wickedness are *excusable* in them, from their peculiar circumstances; and a little sophistry may be employed to support the pretext: but when examined by the holy law revealed in the Bible, all such pretexts will prove to be a part of those lies which cause men to err. (Isa. xliv. 20.) "A deceived heart turns man aside, that he cannot deliver his soul, nor say—is there not a lie in my right hand?"

Even the ministers of religion are not free from being the dupes of false opinions, and the defenders of them, by which they confirm others in their wicked ways, and destroy instead of saving men. Thus saith the Lord, "I have seen folly in the prophets of Samaria, who have caused my people Israel to err; for both *prophet* and *priest* are profane; the land is full of adulterers, and because of swearing the land mourneth. I have seen also in the prophets of Jerusalem an horrible thing; they commit adultery, and walk in lies; they strengthen also the hands of evil doers, that none doth return from his wickedness." (Jer. xxiii. 10—14.) And how do they strengthen the hands of evil doers?—by bad example, and by "walking in lies," or defending false opinions.

You see how impartial the Bible is. Some people have represented it as made up kingcraft and priestcraft; but it is as severe against wicked kings and magistrates, and wicked prophets and priests, as against wicked poor men; and therefore the accusation is not true. The Bible evidently contains the righteous will of the most high and heart-searching God, before whom all craft, and hypocrisy, and false excuses, are naked and open to view; and by whom they are abhorred, and will be punished, unless men, by repentance and application to the Saviour, prepare to meet their God.

In farther confirmation of what I have now said, concerning the impartiality of the Bible, the sin next pointed out, in the 2d chapter and 1st verse of Amos, is *bribery* and *oppression*. The magistrates sold the righteous for silver, and the poor man for a pair of shoes. Then, the smallest bribe, even the value of a pair of shoes, would induce the magistrates to give up a poor man to the will of his merciless oppressor. Of this sin, I believe British magistrates are remarkably free. The laws will not permit it; and the poor man's cause is heard as well as the rich, and even-handed justice dispenses the same law to both. In private life wicked masters will be tyrannical; and bad servants will neglect their duty, in minute cases, which the law of man cannot well reach: but these sins are known in heaven.

Lewdness, the source of so many calamities, even in this life, is next threatened with God's displeasure; and drunkenness, that brutalizing sin, which renders man beastly, or foolish, or mad; which unfits him for duty, destroys health, and wastes property; which makes children rob their parents, and husbands starve their families; which makes a man a prey to vagabonds and villains, reduces him to beggary, brings him to highway robbery, or to murder, and to the gallows.

Further, the Prophet charges Judah and Israel with *hard-hearted impenitence*, in the midst of many calamities sent from heaven to chastise and to warn them. The Almighty sent famine, or a want of bread—"Yet have ye not returned unto me, saith the Lord."—"I have withholden the rain, so that two or three cities wandered unto one city to drink water, but they were not satisfied; yet have ye not returned unto me, saith the Lord. I have overthrown some of you, and others were as a firebrand plucked out of the burning;

H

yet have you not returned unto me, saith the Lord." This hard-hearted impenitence, notwithstanding both judgments and mercies, is a very common sin. Every deliverance from sickness or from death, or from any imminent danger, should lead us to serious reflection, to repentance and to prayer, to reformation, and to the Saviour. But a hard impenitent heart denies the goodness of divine Providence, and attributes mercies and blessings to good-luck, and afflictions to chance; and, under this unhappy state of mind, man will not return to the Lord, nor submit to the hand that chastises him.

In the midst of this hard-hearted ungrateful impenitence, the prophet says, "The people of that time put far away the evil day," and indulged in luxury and carelessness; they stretched themselves upon their magnificent couches, selected the best of the lambs and calves for intemperate feasts; chanted to the sound of the viol, invented to themselves instruments of music, drank wine in bowls, and perfumed themselves with the chief perfumes; but they were not grieved nor concerned for the affliction of their poor and oppressed brethren, who suffered from famine, pestilence, and war.

And to sum up these *sins*, they hated the days appointed for prayer and religious instruction, and wished them gone, that they might make more money to consume upon their lusts; to sell corn, and set forth wheat with their unjust measures, and false balances to deceive and to defraud. And after all this, they hated him that rebuked them, and abhorred him that spoke uprightly.

Yet in the midst of all this wickedness, they kept up some form of religion for a fair pretext; they had certain holidays, and offered sacrifices, and sung anthems.

The wickedness, and folly, and hypocrisy of Judah and Israel, too much resemble what is the case in our own day; and the use we should make of the prophet's censures, is, for every man to examine his own heart, to judge himself, and prepare to meet his God.

The way to prepare, is not to try to cover over or hide our transgressions, for that is impossible. Nor must we think, that because we have wholly, or almost forgotten many of our evil-doings, and our ways that have not been good, therefore, Heaven has forgotten them; nor should we set up the idle pretext, that we have not been "great sinners," that we have had "a good heart," or that we were "young," or any such-like excuses; for there is no proof that Heaven will admit such pretexts, but abundant proof may be produced from the Sacred Scriptures, and from reason, to the contrary.

If you ask me—"Then how shall we *prepare?*" I answer, "Confess, and forsake your sins." Arrangements are made by the divine goodness to allow of pardon to those who do so. To explain what I humbly believe the Scriptures teach on this solemn subject, I will make a comparison, not as being exactly the same as the reality, but as something like it.

Suppose a man who cannot swim, in the midst of the ocean, struggling to keep himself up, and to save himself from drowning; unless some one help him, it is evident he cannot struggle long, and must eventually perish. But if a life-buoy be thrown out to him, and he sees it, and gets on it till a boat comes and picks him up, he will be saved. But if, through pride or perverse folly, he will not avail himself either of the buoy or the boat, he will, by struggling, soon be exhausted, and must sink.

The drowning man resembles a poor sinner; the life-buoy resembles our Saviour. The man who feels that he is perishing, who sees Jesus, and casts himself upon his Almighty arm, will be saved, and finally taken to heaven. The man who proudly or perversely thinks he can save himself, and will not receive the Saviour's assistance, must perish.

The man who gets on the buoy, resembles the Christian who believes in Christ Jesus; and the man who will not get on the buoy, resembles him who believes he can save himself, and so neglects or rejects Jesus Christ the Saviour. The one believes the truth and is saved, the other believes a falsehood and perishes. It is difficult to suppose any

H 2

DISCOURSE X.

DELIVERED IN THE SCOTCH SECEDER'S CHAPEL, MILES'S LANE, LONDON, APRIL 11, 1824.

INTRODUCTION.

[The personal and relative duties of Christians are from Sabbath to Sabbath, the theme of animating discourses from the pulpit; and the mercies of God our Saviour are daily exhibited to guilty men that they may be saved. I would this morning take a wider range, and digress a little to those duties which Christian churches owe to those still large portions of the great human family, which heretofore have remained unacquainted with revealed religion; and endeavour to ascertain our duty from a review of the past. The subject cannot be so interesting to each individual, as that which concerns his or her personal salvation; but yet, as it concerns the salvation of others, it should not be uninteresting to any Christian.]

THE MISSIONARY'S REHEARSAL.

ACTS, XIV. 26, 27.

"*And thence sailed to Antioch, from whence they had been recommended to the grace of God for the work which they fulfilled. And when they were come, and had gathered the church together, they rehearsed all that God had done with them, and how he had opened the door of faith unto the Gentiles.*"

BARNABAS and Paul, from Attalia sailed to Antioch, from whence they had been recommended to the grace of God, for the work which they fulfilled; and when they were come (to Antioch) and had gathered all the church together, they *rehearsed* all that God had done with them, and how he had opened the door of faith unto the Gentiles.

He was an inhabitant of Africa, Simon, of Cyrene, who bore the cross of Christ our Saviour, when led forth to crucifixion, and certain men of Cyrene, in Africa, first preached, or *told* the good news*, concerning the Lord Jesus, to the Grecians at Antioch.

Antioch was a large town, the capital of Syria, about 200 miles north of Jerusalem, (Acts, xi. 20.) Here these African preachers founded a Helenistic,† or Greek proselyte church. Here the disciples were first called Christians, and from this church the first formal Christian Mission was sent forth. This church continued famous for several ages, and produced, 300 years afterwards, the celebrated preacher Chrysostom, the bishop and patriarch.

Barnabas and Saul being separated for the missionary work, to which the Holy Spirit called them, were sent forth, after fasting, prayer, and the laying on of hands. They made a missionary tour of about 1,500 miles, in that part of the then Roman empire now called Asia Minor. They themselves were subjects of the Roman empire, and beyond its limits they did not go. They did not even pass at this time into the European part of the empire. They were absent about two years, speaking, as opportunities offered, both to Jews and Gentiles, concerning the Lord Jesus, and testifying the Gospel of the grace of God. They met with much opposition, and had some success, the Lord working with them, and several Christian societies or churches were formed in different places.

These things occurred about twelve or thirteen years after our Saviour's ascension, whilst Claudius I., the then Emperor of Rome, and his generals, were in Britain, waging

* Ευαγγελιζομενοι. † Ελληνιστας.

war against the chief, Caractacus, and effecting the conquest of our uncivilized pagan ancestors.

An interesting and edifying narrative of the transactions and discourses of these two divinely appointed Missionaries, is contained in the 13th and 14th chapters of the Acts of the Apostles.

When they returned to Antioch, they gathered the church together, as our text says, and *rehearsed* all that God had done with them, and now he had opened the door of faith unto the *Gentiles*.*

The words in which Barnabas and Saul, (or Paul as he was now called, for he seems to have changed his name during his absence,†) *rehearsed* their transactions, are not given us; but by looking over the narrative, we can ascertain the substance of their *rehearsal*. At Cyprus, they had, apparently, but one convert; and at this early part of their tour, John, their assistant deserted them, and went from Perga to Jerusalem. At Antioch, in Pisidia, the Jews, their own countrymen, persecuted them, but some of the Gentiles heard the word gladly, and glorified the word of the Lord.

At Iconium, both Jews and Gentiles attempted to stone them to death; at Lystra, the Pagan priests idolized them, and called them gods; at Derbe they preached the Gospel and taught many; and on their return, passing through Lystra, Iconium, and Antioch, (at each of which places some few appear to have become disciples,) they confirmed their minds, and exhorted them to continue in the faith, and bear patiently afflictions, for these must be passed through in the Christian's way to the kingdom of God. And having (χειροτονησαντες) elected or appointed senior disciples, or elders to preside in the new formed societies or churches, they commended them to the Lord, with fasting and prayer. During this Mission the Lord not only accompanied their discourses, reasonings, and instructions, with the energies

* Εθνεσι.

† Supposed to have been changed in compliment to Sergius *Paulus*, the convert at Cyprus.

of his Holy Spirit on the minds of some of the hearers, but also enabled the Apostles to perform several miracles. Elymas, the sorcerer, was punished with temporary blindness, and the man at Lystra, who had been lame from his infancy, was restored to the perfect use of his limbs.

It does not appear in what language these two Missionaries usually spoke; whether in Greek, or in the dialects peculiar to the several provinces of the empire through which they passed, but there is every reason to believe that they could make themselves understood in any of the languages or dialects wherever they came.

After rehearsing the proceedings of this first Mission, to the assembled church at Antioch, Barnabas and Paul abode a long time, it is supposed about two years, in Syria, defending the proceedings of the late Mission against bigoted Jewish brethren, who taught that the Mosaic rites were essential to salvation. With these people the Missionaries had "no small dissention and disputation." At Phenice and Samaria, however, as they went south to Jerusalem, and declared the conversion of the Gentiles, they "caused great joy to all the brethren."

At Jerusalem the church received them, and heard their report; but still opinions were divided: some Pharisees who believed, insisted that the law of Moses must be observed by the Gentile converts, and there was "much disputing" at their meeting. Finally, the argument suggested by Peter, that since the Almighty put no difference between the Jew and the Gentile, but "purified the hearts" of both by the faith of the Gospel, it was not for them to impose the yoke of a ritual on the necks of the new disciples, which Heaven had not imposed. Barnabas and Paul supported this argument, by declaring the wonders which God had already wrought among the Gentiles, without any Mosaic rites; and James concurred in, and confirmed the same sentiment, by a reference to prophesies concerning the Gentiles. He gave it as his "sentence," or fixed opinion, that the Gentiles who had turned to God, should not be "troubled" with any Mosaic rites, but only be required to abstain from idolatry and vice. This motion was carried by the Apostles and Elders, with the whole church. A letter was written, couched in the terms employed by James, and sent back to Antioch by Judas and Silas, together with Barnabas and Paul. When the multitude of believers at Antioch heard the epistle from Jerusalem read to them, they rejoiced for the consolation afforded to their minds by it. The deputies from Jerusalem, Judas and Silas, delivered exhortations calculated to confirm the faith of the disciples, and so closed the proceedings which arose out of the Mission undertaken and accomplished by Barnabas and Paul.

From the Sacred Scriptures we may derive *general principles*, which will apply to all cases; but not particular precepts for every possible case. Nor, unless we be in exactly the same circumstances as the examples recorded in Scripture, would our exact imitation of them be always right. That human means, such as preaching and teaching, should be employed for the diffusion of our holy Religion, is what I would call a general principle, fairly derived from the Bible: but since modern Missionaries have not such an express call by the Holy Spirit as Barnabas and Saul had, since they have not the gift of tongues, and since they have not the power of working miracles, they cannot be exact imitators of those two divinely appointed Missionaries. Although at the present day we hope ministers and missionaries are moved by the Holy Ghost to undertake the work, we cannot attain to certainty on that subject, with respect to any individual. When, indeed, we see the fruits of the Spirit, the work of the Lord, prospering in the hands of his servants, and men converted and purified by the Gospel, then we know that God is working with them, and may fairly infer, that these servants were called to the work, when the churches recommended them to the grace of God and sent them forth.

Barnabas and Paul *rehearsed* to the church all *that God had done with them*. In this great work the Lord himself is the prime mover, the principal agent; he is the Head, the

Captain, the King; men are the servants, or instruments by which he works: but still they are moral instruments; they should zealously co-operate, they should be active workers together with God, and him they must always acknowledge. And those servants that honour him, he will honour. A zealous use of suitable means, and a humble reliance on divine aid must always go together. To sit still, and do nothing, but wait till Heaven shall miraculously convert the nations, which some persons recommend, is a course as unscriptural and irrational, as to be all bustle and activity, in the use of means, without any regard to the Supreme Agent. As if man—unaided man, could overcome the God of this world, and conquer Satan's kingdom. How futile such an attempt! and how impious to presume to take Heaven's work out of Heaven's hand! Man, unaided, can effect no good, but the Almighty, without means, can accomplish his purposes; still he is pleased in carrying on the renovation of the world, to employ human means; and he is infinitely wise, and this arrangement must be infinitely good; it is, therefore, ours to be unwearied and abounding in the work of the Lord, employing, as experience may suggest, the most appropriate means.

The Spiritual Church I consider a theocracy, adumbrated by the theocracy of the Jewish nation. Jehovah is king. The kingdom is spiritual; the omniscient God, the Father of Spirits, is the sovereign Ruler. He requires no vicegerent on earth; and there is none. The churches on earth, like the tribes of Israel, or the provinces of an empire, are equal amongst themselves, and amenable only to their Divine Head.

But whilst maintaining this fundamental principle, these several tribes, or provinces, or churches, may have laws and regulations for the preservation of peace and order amongst themselves, without at all infringing upon, or casting off the supreme rule of their Divine Sovereign. Of the power and supremacy of God our Saviour we would never lose sight.

Since the time when Barnabas and Paul rehearsed to the

church at Antioch the result of their two year's mission in Asia Minor, how manifold have been the labours, the afflictions, the persecutions, the schisms, the heresies, the corruptions, the declensions, and the revivals of the churches; and how varied the circumstances, and the characters of those whom God has employed to extend the spiritual kingdom of the Redeemer. "To the Messiah are given dominion, and glory, and a kingdom; that all people, and nations, and languages, should serve him." This the prophet declared in these very words more than five centuries before the Saviour's advent; and now, in our days (eighteen centuries subsequent), do we see the prophesy partly fulfilled, which is a pledge of its complete accomplishment at some future day.

Acting on the principles which have just now been recognized, and in the faith of the divine promises, the London Missionary Society, seventeen years ago, recommended the person who now addresses you,* by prayer and the laying on of hands, to the grace of God, and sent him forth to the work to be fulfilled; and through God's mercy he stands here this day to "*rehearse*" to this assembled church all that God has done with him. The Divine Providence has led him by a way that he knew not, and in paths which could not be by us foreseen. After so explicit a recognition of the divine rule and government of the world and the church as has just now been made, it will not be necessary to refer to it in every step of our *rehearsal;* for we desire to acknowledge God in all our ways, and magnify his gracious Providence, although we may not in words always refer to it.

Barnabas and Saul were separated to the work by an *express* injunction from Heaven; Acts, xiii. 2. "The Holy Ghost said, separate me Barnabas and Saul for the work

* Jan. 8th, 1807, ordained in Dr. Nichols's Chapel.

whereunto I have called them;" but the Missionary of whom we now speak had no *such* call. Gratitude to the Saviour, to whom the written word led his mind, and a desire to promulgate the salvation which is in Jesus, induced him to offer his services to the church. Some letters of Vanderkemp, recorded in the Evangelical Magazine nearly twenty years ago, decided him to say, in reply to enquiries for Missionaries, "here am I, send me." He would readily have gone to Africa with the unfortunate traveller, Mungo Park, and Anderson, his brother-in-law, as a Missionary, in the settlement the formation of which Park contemplated. Park and Anderson soon finished their mortal career. Finally, China was suggested to him as the sphere of his labours, and he acquiesced.

In the first apostolic Mission, Barnabas and Saul were united, and they had Mark for their minister, or helper, or servant, in whatever they might require. But the first Protestant Chinese Missionary went quite alone. Barnabas and Saul did not leave their own empire, they travelled not more than two thousand miles, and were absent but two years.

China is seventeen thousand miles from England, through some stormy seas and under scorching suns; it is a land in which foreigners, and above all, European foreigners, are interdicted; but Providence conducted him thither in safety, and provided for him a residence and temporal support.

The prophet Ezekiel, who lived about the time of the Chinese Confucius, received his commission from Heaven in these words, "Son of man, go, get thee unto the house of Israel, and speak with my words unto them, for thou art not sent to a people *of a strange speech and of a hard language*, but to the house of Israel." And such is now, (after innumerable difficulties have been overcome by former labourers,) the situation of ministers in England; to them the churches say, "go with the Bible, and thousands of good books to assist you; and speak in your mother tongue, and to your own people, a people prepared by many admitted Christian truths, the words of divine revelation. But the Chinese Missionary was sent to "a people of a strange speech, and of a hard language." An ancient and copious language, entirely unlike any other language under heaven. Even with the best assistance to acquire it, the Chinese language may be justly called "a hard language," and the then difficulty of obtaining assistance, rendered the acquisition of it more so. Natives in China are not allowed to teach it to foreigners, which makes it difficult to procure their aid, and when obtained, they know only their mother tongue, and for want of a medium of communicating their ideas to foreigners, they are ill qualified to teach. I would here remark, that a competent knowledge of some Asiatic languages is a more difficult task, and a more rare attainment, even amongst Missionaries, both Roman Catholic and Protestant, than is generally supposed. And Missionary Societies do not, perhaps, lay stress enough on *furnishing the means* for a speedy and extensive acquisition of foreign languages by their Missionaries. However,

By persevering labour and undivided attention, considerable progress was made in the Chinese language; and by many years' application and great expense,* books have been written and printed, which will render this "strange speech" more easy of acquisition to those who may hereafter be sent forth to teach the nations beyond the Ganges.

Out of China also, from under the influence of malicious informers, and a persecuting government, books and teachers are now provided at the Anglo-Chinese College, an institution originated for the furtherance of the Gospel, and to promote the temporal and spiritual well-being of the Chinese. By the aid of the lamented Milne, this institution was reared and tuition commenced; and by his help, as is well known, the whole of the canonical Scriptures were translated, and have been printed and sent forth to the

* The Hon. the East India Company expended £15,000 on printing Morrison's English and Chinese Dictionary.

world. Oral instruction has been given to many, and some Christian Tracts have been written in Chinese, and extensively circulated. Several individuals have their minds much influenced by the truth, and *one*, to whom Milne was the means of conversion, is now left amongst his countrymen in China, as a teacher of Christianity, having, in his own tongue, *the Bible alone*, and we hope the Holy Spirit of God as his guide. This is a brief rehearsal of what God hath done by his servants in this case. Milne has been removed, we hope, to his eternal rest, but there are yet four or five labourers, who, since the Chinese Mission commenced, have entered and yet remain on the field.

It is now no longer a question, as it once was in England, whether the Chinese language be acquirable or not for religious purposes. We have now, in our own tongue, copious Chinese philological books, a Chinese Bible, a Chinese Christian College, and a converted native Chinese teacher; and should we not be thankful and be encouraged.

Pioneers, who *make ways and approaches*, are thought to hold a humble place in the army, in the republic of letters, and in the churches. The conqueror, the author of genius, and the dignified prelate or popular preacher, who enter into other men's labours, are those who appear to effect great things; the pioneer is forgotten. Missionaries who *first* enter pagan lands, are only pioneers. They may clear a little ground, make roads, plough and sow, (very necessary labours to be sure,) but the field is as yet unsightly. When the blade shoots up above ground, it is encouraging; but the husbandman must still exercise long patience, till the ear be formed, filled, and ripened—and the yellow waving harvest be gathered in. And ere this be effected, it may be that a part of the promised crop is blasted and lost. I fear the patience of British Christians will be tried, if not exhausted, before the fruits of the Chinese Mission exhibit any striking appearance. Some of the means which we employ, (particularly the Anglo-Chinese College,*) are, I fear, not popular. And we are told we ought to *preach* more; that *preaching* is the great instrument of conversion; the divine command is, we are told, go and *preach* the Gospel to every creature.

To obviate this objection, and that the truth may appear, permit me to examine briefly this subject.

The modern sense of the word "preach," is to proclaim or publish in religious orations, or to address with earnestness and vehemence, and inculcate religious truths on a congregation, or an assembly of many persons. Now in our English Bible, when the word preach is used, it does not always mean what the modern use of the word implies. There are *six*† *different* Greek words in the Acts of the Apostles that our English translators have rendered by the one word "*preach*," and if they had used six different English words, the word preach would not have stood so prominent. The

1st word, Κηρυσσω, means, "to *proclaim* as a public herald, or crier."—"What ye hear in the ear, *preach* ye upon the house tops." (Matt. x. 27.) In St. Luke it is, "*proclaim*" ye upon the house tops. When this term is used, the very words of the proclamation are generally given. As (Matt. iii. 1.) John came *preaching*, or *proclaiming* in the wilderness of Judea—"Repent ye, for the kingdom of Heaven is at hand." Another example is in Matt xxiv. 14. "This Gospel of the kingdom shall be *preached*, or proclaimed, in all the world, for a witness unto all nations, and then shall the end come."

Had this been the only term employed, the objection would have seemed to be conclusive, though not quite so, for a proclamation may be made in writing, as well as by

* "A fixed residence had been formed at *Siam* for the French Missionaries, together with a *Seminary* for instructing the youth in the languages of the circumjacent nations, who had all settlements, or *Camps*, as they were called, at the capital." About A.D. 1663, (vide Mosheim, Vol. V. p. 16.)

I should like to know the subsequent fate of this seminary.

† See Campbell on the Gospels, Vol. I.

the voice. Thus (Ezra i. 1.) Cyrus, king of Persia, made *a proclamation* throughout all his kingdom, and *put it in writing*. And (in Acts xv. 21.) it is said, Moses of old time hath in every city them that *preach* him—but how? by "being *read* in the synagogue every Sabbath-day." Thus you see *reading* the Scriptures is called *preaching*.

2d. The next word that our translators render *preach* is Ευαγγελιζω, "*To tell glad tidings* or joyful news." (Acts v. 42.) "And daily in the temple and in every house, they ceased not to teach and to *preach* Jesus Christ." They *taught* the people many general truths of religion, and *told them the good news* concerning Jesus Christ. But this *preaching* was sometimes only conversation in a house, perhaps only with a single family, or only with some of the members of a family. When Philip was sitting in the Ethiopian's chariot, and conversing with him, (Acts xiii. 35.) it is said, Philip "*preached* unto him Jesus;" but one man speaking to another in a carriage, cannot, in the modern sense, be called "*preaching*." It should be read, Philip *told him the good news* concerning Jesus.

A 3d word, Καταγγελλω, means, "To declare plainly, or openly, an explicit statement of a truth; but this may be not a sermon, but a single sentence. In Romans i. 8. the word is translated "spoken of," instead of preached. "Thus I thank God your faith is *spoken of*, or *talked about*, throughout the whole world," not your faith is *preached*.

A 4th word, λαλεω, means, "To speak, to tell, to announce, to report, to spread a report." It is sometimes rendered, "*preaching*" the word, and sometimes "*speaking*" the word. The disciples, who were scattered on the persecution which arose about Stephen, went to Antioch, "*preaching* the word." A commentator,* who seems to think that ordinary disciples should not preach, remarks, that the original word here means only, *speaking* or *talking* about. And on the other hand, I have heard it rather objected to some Missionaries, that their discourses to the heathen were more like *talking* to them than *preaching*.

* Scott, in loco.

I

But both these remarks arise from too much stress on the *modern use* of the word *preach.* To preach the Gospel, is to *tell about the Saviour,* whether to an individual or to many, in a private house or in the temple—*to spread the report,* to talk about the good news sent from heaven to all people.

There are two more words translated preaching, viz.

The 5th word, διαλεγομαι, which means, "To reason, to argue, to dispute." Acts xx. 7. "Paul preached unto them, or reasoned with them."—xxiv. 25, "Paul preached or reasoned of righteousness, temperance, and judgment to come."—xviii. 19. "Paul entered into the synagogue, and *preached,* i. e. *reasoned,* or disputed with the Jews.

Lastly, the 6th word, παρρησιαζομαι, which means, "To speak freely, plainly, boldly." Barnabas told the other Apostles how Saul had *preached boldly, spoken freely and openly,* at Damascus, in the name of the Lord Jesus.

These examples will, I hope, convince you that *speaking* to individuals, or families, or *to students in a school or college, concerning the Lord Jesus,* and *telling the good news of salvation by him,* as well as proclaiming to a multitude, either by the living voice or by written documents, the command of God, to repent and believe the Gospel; are all, in the scriptural sense of that phrase, so many ways of *preaching* the Gospel.

Beside, the Saviour's last commission is thus expressed by St. Matthew, xxviii. 19, "Go ye, and *disciple* all nations, *teaching* them to observe all things whatsoever I have commanded you." This *teaching* of *disciples,* is in the manner of a *master teaching his pupils.* An *instructor* who is attended by *scholars* from day to day, in the manner of the antient ambulatory schools which existed in almost every part of the world; in China, in Greece, and in Judea. If stress were to be laid on the phraseology, it would justify schools and colleges, where masters and pupils, teachers and scholars meet daily, rather than the desultory sermons, or earnest harangues of an itinerant missionary, probably addressed but once to the same people.

But I have no intention of setting up one means of

spreading the Gospel in opposition to another, but to justify the use of that means to which we are, in China, almost exclusively "*shut up*:" and I wish to evince that every means of spreading abroad in the world, the report concerning Jesus the Saviour, and making known to the children of men the salvation which is to be found in him, is in reality preaching, or proclaiming the Gospel.

An institution, where teacher and scholar, master and disciple, remain together for some years, is particularly desirable in a mission to a people wholly unacquainted with the history and doctrines of the Bible. It is extremely difficult to reach the understanding and conscience of a very ignorant person in Christendom, as some ministers have testified;* but how much more difficult is it where the first principle of religion, viz. that a Supreme Being exists, is not recognized or known; then, as Brainerd said, "There is no foundation to build upon." How much the Missionary has to teach them before he can tell them any truths, that appear "good tidings" to them! Just as our Saviour, (Luke xx. 1.) is said to have *taught* the people in the temple, and *preached the Gospel*. These were two topics; teaching man the existence and the perfections of the great Creator; and man's duty, that "God is,"—and that he rewards and punishes the children of men, is not *preaching the Gospel;* this is not *telling the good tidings of salvation* through Christ, of mercy and forgiveness to the repenting sinner. Nor will this blessed intimation be esteemed Gospel or *good news*, by him who knows not God, nor feels that he is a sinner. The disciples of Confucius deny that there is any future existence of separate spirits. Death, they say, is like the extinction of a flame; it is annihilation of the living principle, and if heaven would punish man, there exists nothing after death capable of receiving punishment. Their language affords no term for *God Almighty*, a Being *distinct from*, and *superior to* the heavens and the earth. Their gods are all inferior to the powers of nature, and were formed or brought into existence by *Heaven*.

* Foster on Popular Ignorance.

But then, if so, it may be said, *heaven* is equivalent to *God*. No, the word sometimes appears to approach to the idea of a supreme Being; but when examined into, it denotes only the purer and more subtle parts of the chaotic mass which ascended to the upper regions, leaving below the grosser parts, which form the earth and water. And yet in a confused manner, heaven and earth are described as two great powers, and man is the third, but over these, there is found no supreme God. "*God that made the world*," is to them unknown; their language affords no established term that can apply to *Him*. Now, it must appear plain, even from this slight view of the subject, how little impression a passing discourse, addressed by a despised foreigner, to an ignorant and sometimes a proud and contemptuous audience must make; and still more so, when it is remembered that the language of the foreigner is probably not very perspicuous, and his knowledge of many of the people's opinions and prejudices not very accurate. I once overheard a man, who had heard me frequently speak concerning Jesus, tell his friend, that Christianity was the same as Buddhism, and he said it with a sneer. He now, I hope, understands the subject better, after hearing me talk about the Gospel for several years. On my quitting China I left him, at his own request, a complete copy of the Sacred Scriptures, that he might read it and lay to heart the parts which he found easy.

What I infer from these remarks is, the desirableness of having the same persons around a Christian Teacher for a considerable period of time, that they may attain a full understanding of the Christian Religion; and that they may spread the report amongst their countrymen; and in such cases as indicate true conversion, they may be employed entirely in disseminating the seed of the word; and thus oral instruction be united with the written word distributed amongst the people.

It appears to me that our Saviour *commenced* his Mission in this way. He selected twelve disciples or scholars, beside the seventy, and had them always about him to be fully instructed; and their subsequent preachings and writings were the means of radicating the Gospel in the western world. Our dislike to the religious language of Rome, may lead some to turn away with disgust from the term, "The College of Apostles;" but this is being offended with mere words, and that without reason. The manner in which our Saviour appeared was very similar to that of the moral philosophers of antiquity; it was similar to that of the Chinese moralist, Confucius,* who also had seventy disciples more closely attached to him: these were ambulatory schools or colleges. The pupils remained with the master till they understood his doctrines, and then they spread them by discourses, or conversations, or books. I am pointing out only a general resemblance, and not affirming that the manner was the same in every particular.

It may be affirmed, that lectures given in a chapel or place of meeting, would produce the same effect as I am contending for, in a school or college. To which I answer, if the heathen would assemble regularly and constantly, as Christian societies do, a considerable part of the same effect would be produced; but by no means the whole of it. However, the heathen, who despise the foreigner and his new religion, which would turn them from the religion of their fathers, and call their attention a short time from their business or amusement, will not often attend any place of meeting; and when a few of them can be assembled, the impression is not at all equal to that made on those who are instructed all the day. We have tried both means at Malacca, a ndthere is no comparison as to the degree of Christian knowledge obtained by the students, and by the labouring men who come occasionally to hear the evening lecture in the town.

Further, such an institution as that which I am now advocating, is much required for continuing a succession of well-instructed European Christian Teachers to labour in that immense field opened by the nations which use the Chinese language. I have already noticed, that a competent knowledge of some Asiatic languages, is not an easy

* It is remarkable that Confucius also had seventy or seventy-two disciples, more eminent than the rest, whose images are now worshipped with his.

or common attainment; I knew four Roman Catholic Missionaries who had been fourteen years in Peking, and could not read a word of Chinese; and I knew an Italian priest, who lived thirty years on the Chinese frontier, as agent for the Missions, who was still more ignorant of the language, for he could neither read nor speak it. Now, to be told by Christians at home, to go and teach, and preach, and convert the heathen, without even adverting to the *laborious schooling* which a man must undergo before he can either teach or preach, is often disheartening; because there appears a want of consideration and feeling for a poor Missionary's peculiar and difficult circumstances. He has, at first, no Christian society nor Christian ordinances; and if he reads much in religious European books, to make up for these defective circumstances, his attention is withdrawn from the studies preparatory to Christian usefulness amongst the heathen; and if he does not labour hard at his pagan studies, years will elapse before he can either teach or preach; and death may occur before he is of any use at all to the heathen, as a Christian teacher. If, on the other hand, he does fag at the Pagan language, their history and opinions, in order to reason with them, and persuade them concerning the Gospel, he is in danger of becoming barren of religious and Christian affections. Further, he has often an extensive correspondence to keep up with Christian people at home, to write journals and official letters to societies; to keep accounts, and attend to pecuniary details; matters in which he has, probably, never been instructed. And all these things put together, viz. defective means of acquiring the language, opinions, and manners of the people he has to teach; the importunity of those who desire him to shew immediate fruits of his labour; his own anxiety to be useful; the various calls of missionary and domestic management—these all keep his mind so much on the stretch, as to affect his health and spirits, and it may be, in some of the many deaths we have had, hastened that event. The mental labours and anxieties of Milne were extreme.

To obviate these difficulties, as well as for other purposes, the Anglo-Chinese College is instituted. There, Missionaries may have every facility for acquiring the language, history, and philosophy of China, without any extraneous cares, till they be competent to teach and to preach Jesus Christ; and by these facilities, their health and lives be preserved, as well as their direct usefulness be greatly accelerated.

We have already remarked, that primitive Societies (or Churches) of Christians were formed on the principle of uniting teachers and disciples, not only to worship together, as some have lately affirmed, but also to be instructed in Christian knowledge; and not only, I believe, for these two ends, but also to raise up and send forth Missionaries. In May, 1823, during your Christian Festival in the metropolis, one of the speakers, (Mr. Fletcher,) whose speech I read in the Atlantic Ocean, made this remark; "every Christian Church, in proportion as the end of its formation is accomplished, is a *Missionary Society;* a society established not only for its own edification, but for the enlargement of the Redeemer's kingdom." This is a sentiment which in China I have long entertained, and therefore, have been grieved, sometimes, to see the work of Missions considered by most of the churches, as a work in which they might or might not interest themselves, just as they pleased.

The church at Antioch, to which we have to-day made frequent reference, had several prophets and teachers; as Barnabas, and Simeon, that was called Niger, "or the black man," and Lucius of Cyrene, and Manaen, who had been brought up with Herod the tetrarch, and Saul. These taught the disciples and ministered to the Lord; and some of them, as we have seen, went on a missionary tour. It has long been my wish to form, at the Anglo-Chinese Mission House, and at the college, a central *Home* beyond the Ganges, for teachers and preachers; from whence some of the number may go forth occasionally on missionary tours, two and two, perhaps an European and a native disciple together; and when they have finished their tour, let them return to refresh their minds and re-establish their health, and attend to studies to fit them for new stations, as they may be discovered or present themselves. Even now, qualified teachers are much wanted to *write books* for the idolatrous heathen, for the catechumens, for converts, and for native preachers.

In the first century of the Christian era, not only did Providence employ the preaching of the Apostles and disciples, but also their writings; the memoirs of Jesus, and the letters of the Apostles, for the instruction of believers and the spread of the Gospel. And history informs us, that the Christians had not only *schools* for children, but also "*academies*" erected in several large cities, in which persons of riper years, especially such as aspired to be public teachers, were instructed in different branches, both of human learning and of sacred erudition. St. John erected, it is said, a school of this kind at *Ephesus;* and one of the same nature was founded by Polycarp at *Smyrna;* and the Catechetical School formed at Alexandria, is supposed to have been erected by St. Mark. There were also at Rome, Antioch, Cæsarea, Edessa, and in several other places, schools of the same nature, though not all of equal reputation.*

The writings of well-educated and studious men have, in every age, been a very principal means employed by Providence to preserve and extend the true religion.

During the first and second centuries, it is beyond all doubt that the pious diligence and zeal with which many learned and pious men recommended the Sacred Writings, and spread them abroad in translations, contributed much to the success and propagation of the Christian doctrine. And when Christians were calumniated and misrepresented by Pagan writers, "Those who, by their *apologetic* writings in favour of the Christians, destroyed the poisonous influence of detraction, rendered no doubt, signal service to the doctrine of Christ. Nor were the writings of such as combated with success the ancient heretics without their use, especially in the early periods of the church." †

Many of those whom Providence has made most eminently useful, were persons who, like Paul, received the

* Mosheim, Vol. I. p. 119. † Ibid. Vol. I. p. 151.

benefit of early instruction under some good teacher. A long list of names might be selected from history, were it necessary, and these would prove that colleges, and books, and preachers, have not hindered each other; but have all co-operated, under the divine blessing, for the furtherance of the Gospel.

Jerom of Prague travelled into England for the sake of his studies, and he carried hence the books of Wickliffe, and promoted, with the labours of Huss, the reformation in Bohemia; some youths of Bohemia, who studied at Oxford, also carried home religious truth. Luther's judgment was, that the *written* word of God, laid open and rightly explained to the people (either orally or by printed expositions) is the most powerful engine for the destruction of the kingdom of Satan. The divine blessing attended his labours, and the circulation of judicious expositions of various parts of the Scriptures. Aleander burnt Luther's books, but that increased men's curiosity to read them, and Luther re-published them with additional arguments, and in more correct composition. Luther recommended to the churches in Saxony the study of the *Latin tongue*, that there might be *men capable of instructing foreign nations*,* by which he seems to have meant the other nations of Europe.

The London Missionary Society, at the suggestion of the late Dr. Milne, in January, 1823, resolved to employ means to obtain correct versions of the Sacred Scriptures into the languages of Cochinchina, Japan, and Siam. The two first of these are closely allied to the Chinese language, which is, indeed, read by educated Cochinchinese and Japanese; I therefore beg to recommend the study of the Chinese language, and desire the countenance of Christians to the Anglo-Chinese College, that there may be *men capable of conveying Christian instruction to these foreign nations.* The Society's Missionaries, by the very liberal aid of the Bible Society, have already made and printed a translation of the whole Bible into the Chinese language; but one of the

* Milner, Vol. IV. p. 608—227. Vol. V. p. 460.

translators died, and the revision which he and his colleague unitedly desired to make, has not been effected. Other labourers should be prepared and qualified to revise, correct, and superintend future editions of the Chinese Bible; and those who desire the end, should encourage the means.

The perfection to which printing has been brought, and the ease of Chinese printing, afford wonderful facilities for the preservation and diffusion of Christian knowledge. How often in China, where the voice of no Christian could reach me, have I been instructed, reproved, and consoled, by the writings of good men who lived centuries ago, and by books which had been printed hundreds of years before their pages were opened to my perusal. How wonderfully, and with what a beneficial effect, are the pious sentiments of Christians of all communions, and of every nation, collected, and sent forth to every region, by the Bible Society's sheets of correspondence, by the Missionary Journals and Registers, by religious Tracts, and similar productions of the press. These instruct and gladden the hearts of thousands, and hundreds of thousands, to whom it would be impossible to convey the same good by the living voice.

Concerning the College, I will make only one more remark. In it the Chinese students are taught the English language, in order to open to them the stores of knowledge which so richly abound in English authors and English translations. By this means, pious writers of former ages, and of the present day, will be made useful to an extent they themselves never could have contemplated; their works will be read in China and Japan, and will contribute, we hope, to the salvation of sinners, the joy of angels, and the glory of God.

Feb. 6th, 1825, at Mr. Stratten's.

However, it is God alone who can open the door of faith unto the Gentiles; we would use the means but not rest in them—our hope is in God, and in him only.

I have this morning endeavoured to point out to you the means which are, in my humble opinion, the most appropriate for diffusing Christian knowledge in the farther East, and I hope you will see it to be right to assist in so good a cause. The strongest motive I can suggest to you is, the love of Christ. Let that constrain you, and then your motives and your practice will assuredly be exactly what they ought. In the degree that we value Christian knowledge for ourselves, in the same degree shall we be anxious to communicate it to others. If we count all things but loss for the excellency of the knowledge of Christ, we shall consider the communication of that knowledge the greatest good that we can possibly bestow on a fellow creature; and it is not only so, but it is likewise the most acceptable service that we can perform in the sight of God.

On another Occasion.

I do not this evening plead for pecuniary aid in behalf of the Anglo-Chinese College, but only assert its right to a small portion of assistance from every church, that ever utters the prayer dictated by the Divine Saviour, "Thy kingdom come." You have had this day to assist yourselves. This is a duty. But you must also labour that you may have to give to him that needeth, as well as provide for your own wants. It is sometimes said, both in reference to gifted labourers and pecuniary resources, and even by principals of Scotch Universities, that "there is much still to be done at home; and whilst wants exist at home, it is Quixotic to send help abroad." This tale is specious, and suits our selfishness; but it assumes as a correct principle, that till all our wants and wishes are satisfied, we should not alienate any thing belonging to us, or that *seems* to belong to us; for in fact there is no good that we possess that is strictly ours. Man is but a steward; all things belong to God. However, apart from this consideration, I deny that we must wait until all our own wants be supplied, ere we supply others. I have not food enough for one hearty meal, but my brother has none. England abounds in Bibles, and preachers, and pious books; but there are pagan lands that have comparatively none.

Now, what does the Christian principle say—Shall I eat the whole of my scanty meal, and give my brother none? or shall I share it with him? I say, share it with him. Help yourselves this evening, and at a future day, help the Anglo-Chinese College. I promise you not thanks; I insist upon it as a duty. Let it not be said of us—all seek their own, not the things which are Jesus Christ's;—all seek their own edification only, not the enlargement of the Saviour's kingdom.

DISCOURSE XI.

WRITTEN ON BOARD THE WATERLOO, MARCH 3 AND 4, 1824.

WISDOM'S WAYS.

PROVERBS, III. 17.

"Her (Wisdom's) ways are ways of pleasantness, and all her paths are peace."

THE Divine Being,—the Father, Son, and Holy Spirit, the only living and true God,—is the *Supreme Wisdom*. His knowledge of what is best, and of the means of effecting it, is infinite: hence, in the New Testament, he is styled "The only wise God." The creation of the universe is ascribed to his wisdom. "The Lord, by wisdom, hath founded the earth; by understanding hath he established the heavens. By his knowledge the depths are broken up, and the clouds drop down the dew." And, in the work of human redemption, the angels are said to perceive the "manifold wisdom of God."

The Almighty is the source of all created wisdom. The wonderful instincts of animals are from him; the skill of ingenious men is his gift; and the powers, or faculties, of the human soul, fitting it for the attainment of wisdom, both natural and spiritual, are from God.

Wisdom's ways, spoken of in our text, denote the *paths of human duty, in which Heaven directs man to walk, and which lead to happiness.*

There is a large party of men in the world, (some of them ingenious and learned men, but proud opposers of the true wisdom,) who set up notions of their own, instead of, or in opposition to, that wisdom which cometh down from Heaven: their system the Bible calls the *wisdom of this world*, which shall come to nought, and end in disappointment and misery.

There is no age nor condition in life in which a man can be placed, that can prevent his finding the ways of true wisdom. He may know them, and walk in them, if he will, although ever so poor, and although he may not know a letter of a book. Therefore no man should be discouraged, but think and act for himself, in this matter, as becomes a man. Nor should any man deceive himself so far as to imagine, that because he has no scholarship, it is therefore excusable in him to disregard the ways of wisdom, and wander in the downward paths of folly. Nor may those who have some scholarship think that they are superior men, and above attending to those instructions of wisdom, which are suited to poor people and servants. The ways of heavenly wisdom are for all ranks and conditions of men.

I. Let us, therefore, try to ascertain from the Bible what those *ways* are. And, in the first place, it is written, (Ps. iii. 10.) "The *fear of the Lord* is the *beginning of wisdom*." The Lord is that great and awful Being who made the world, and who rules over it as the King of kings and Judge of all mankind. He is that gracious and merciful Being who hears the groaning of the prisoners, and of those appointed to death; who hears the prayers of the distressed, and sends help from his holy temple. He is the Giver of life and health to the poor, and of power and wealth to the great amongst men. He is the Creator and Benefactor, the Father of all intelligent creatures; and therefore all good angels and good men fear him. They fear him, not as a cruel master, not as an enemy; but as a Superior, as a Father, as the greatest and best of Beings. Some people cavil at the word *fear*, as if it denoted a degrading feeling;—like a child being afraid in the dark, or a coward being afraid of another man, or of some danger that threatened him: but this is not fair; it seems to suppose that the Almighty is an imaginary being, or that he is our equal, or that he is a bad being, all of which are very shocking suppositions. For a child to fear, as well as to love, a good parent, is a very proper feeling: for a man to be afraid of an earthquake, which makes the mountains tremble, is not cowardice. Since a good parent will not be angry with, nor chastise or punish a child, without just cause, a child should always be afraid of incurring such a parent's displeasure; for this is the same as being afraid to do wrong; and to be afraid of incurring the divine displeasure is the beginning of wisdom. The fear of the Lord implies a knowledge of the Almighty's greatness, and goodness, and justice, and a desire never to do any thing undutiful, or bad, or unjust; and he who does not desire to possess this fear is a bad man by his own confession; and he who curses and swears, and pretends not to be afraid of the divine punishments, is as great a fool as the man who defies the lightning or the earthquake. Boys sometimes think that swearing and bad language makes them look manly, but it only shews that they are fools. Our Saviour said, "Fear not them that kill the body, and after that have no more that they can do; but I will forewarn you whom ye shall fear. Fear Him, who, when he hath killed, hath power to cast both soul and body into hell. Yea, I say unto you, *fear Him*." Any of you who have a reverence for God, and a dread of wicked language and conduct, be not afraid when your comrades swear at you, and treat you with contempt and ridicule, and call you Methodists; these sneers are all trifles, compared with the cruel mockings, and tortures, and deaths, which many confessors and martyrs have endured, without fear, and without impatience. Never be ashamed to own that you fear God, and then you need fear none else. It was a proper answer given by a soldier-officer,* who refused a challenge, "I am not afraid to

* Colonel Gardiner.

fight, but I am afraid to sin." Man may mock me, and call me a coward; but as I think duelling sinful, I fear God and not man. The *fear of the Lord* is the beginning of wisdom; it lies at the foundation of all true religion and morality. It checks and puts a stop to all profane thoughts, and language, and conduct. Hence the Bible describes the wicked man as one who has *cast off the fear of God*, and as one who has no fear of God before his eyes.* He who truly *fears God* is a religious and holy man, or, in other words, a pious and moral man.

Now, since this reverence for the Divine Being is the beginning of wisdom's ways, it follows, that some modern notions about leaving religion out of the education of children is a foolish method. A regard to the Almighty in the human heart, is the main-spring of all that is good: without it, all the machinery of education will not work, nor produce a good man. Every body knows that reading and writing, known by a man of bad principles, only makes him more mischievous than he could well be without them. And the same is true of the higher branches of education; although they polish the surface of society, they may exist together with the utmost depravity, cruelty, and injustice, and therefore the utmost folly. Yes! religion *is* the beginning of wisdom! If you ask me, "What religion?" I answer, "*The fear of the Lord.*" That is true religion; and if a man is not afraid of sinning against God Almighty—if you hear him make a jest of what is sinful—he is evidently not possessed of the *true religion*. He must still be numbered with the fools, as the Bible calls those who make a mock at sin, and who in vain pretend to belong to any church: but he who is *afraid of offending Heaven* has certainly begun to be wise, and has commenced the true religion; has entered the porch of the true church, and will advance as he increases in knowledge.

Having now ascertained the right way of setting out in the pursuit of wisdom, let us, in the

* Deut. xxviii. 5. 8. "If thou wilt not—fear this glorious and fearful (or awful) name," the Lord thy God, "the Lord will make thy plagues wonderful."

II. Next place, enquire concerning her *paths*, said to be pleasant and peaceful. And,

(1.) *A humble, teachable disposition*, and a desire and strenuous endeavour to learn, is declared to be one of the paths of wisdom; in confirmation of which, I shall quote some of the paragraphs in the Book of Proverbs.

(Prov. i. 8.) "My son, hear the instruction of thy father, and forsake not the law of thy mother." The advice and admonitions of good parents, next to the instructions derived from Heaven, should be carefully listened to and remembered by those who mean to do well; for parents have most right to direct, and they feel a deeper interest in their children than any other persons. Orphans should attend to the good advice given by teachers and the ministers of religion, or by older people and superiors, who themselves set a good example. The churches and chapels at home afford the means of instruction to all who, instead of wandering about the streets and fields, choose to attend them. And there are many small cheap books and tracts, containing excellent instruction, which those that can read may easily avail themselves of.

(Prov. xiii. 1.) "A wise son heareth his father's instructions, but a scorner heareth not rebuke." And there is a promise annexed to a diligent study of what is good. (Chap. ii. ver. 2.) "If thou incline thine ear unto wisdom, and apply thy heart to understanding; if thou seekest her as silver, and searchest for her as for hid treasures; then shalt thou understand the fear of the Lord, and find the knowledge of God; for the Lord giveth wisdom, out of his mouth cometh knowledge and understanding."

The Divine Wisdom condescends to entreat and persuade thoughtless man, and says, (Prov. i. 22.) "How long, ye simple ones, will ye love simplicity? and the scorners delight in their scorning, and fools hate knowledge? Turn ye at my reproof: behold, I will pour out my spirit unto you; I will make known my words unto you."

And, finally, against those who will not listen to the divine instruction a threatening is denounced. Heaven says to proud and untractable, unteachable men, "Because

I have called, and ye refused; I have stretched out my hand, and no man regarded; but ye have set at nought all my counsel, and would none of my reproof: I also will laugh at your calamity; I will mock when your fear cometh; when your fear cometh as desolation, and your destruction cometh as a whirlwind; when distress and anguish cometh upon you:—for that they hated knowledge, and did not choose the fear of the Lord."

In these passages of Sacred Scripture, the good and the evil, the blessing and the curse, are set before us; the path of wisdom, and the path of folly; the different conduct and fate of the humble learner, and of the proud scorner. "A man's pride shall bring him low; but honour shall uphold the humble in spirit." (Prov. xxix. 23.) Therefore, (chap. iii. ver. 5.) "Trust in the Lord with all thy heart, and lean not to thine own understanding.—Be not wise in thine own eyes; but in all thy ways acknowledge the Almighty, and he will direct thy paths."

(2.) But the humble and teachable disposition so strongly inculcated, does not imply an easy acquiescence with whatever any body may suggest; quite the reverse! It is accompanied by a *firm resistance* to the enticements of evil men and bad women. (Prov. i. 10.) "My son, if sinners entice thee consent thou not." If they say, 'Cast in thy lot among us—let us all have one purse,' and so entice you to steal or to rob, "Walk not thou in the way with them: refrain thy foot from their path, for their feet run to evil, and make haste to shed blood."

(Prov. ii. 10.) "When wisdom entereth into thy heart and knowledge is pleasant to thy soul; discretion shall preserve thee, understanding shall keep thee, and deliver thee from the way of the evil man, from the man that speaketh froward things"—who rejoices to do evil, and delights in the frowardness of the wicked; and will deliver thee from the strange woman, from the abandoned woman, who flattereth with her words, who forsaketh the guide of her youth (her father or her husband,) and forgetteth the covenant of her God;—for her house inclineth unto death, and her paths unto the dead. None that go unto her return again,

neither take they hold of the paths of life. (Prov. v. 2.) "Her feet go down to death, and her steps take hold on hell;" therefore, O man, remove thy way far from her, and come not nigh the door of her house, "Lest thou give thine honour unto others, and thy years unto the cruel—lest strangers be filled with thy wealth, and thy labours be in the house of a stranger," and thou mourn at the last, when thy flesh and thy body are consumed (by loathsome disease), and remorse extort from thee the exclamation—"How have I hated instruction, and my heart despised reproof—I have not obeyed the voice of my teachers, nor inclined mine ear to them that instructed me!"

He who does not firmly resist the fair speeches of impudent and abandoned women, (Prov. vii. 21.) "goes after her as an ox to the slaughter, or a fool to the correction of the stocks; for her house is the way to hell, going down to the chambers of death." (Prov. ix. 17.) "The simple fool who turneth into her house, knoweth not that the dead are there, and that her guests are in the depths of hell." This strong language is dictated by divine wisdom, to confirm the resolution of those who have any regard for their own honour or welfare in this world, or any concern for the salvation of their souls.

(3.) And the same divine wisdom which so strongly dehorts men from a licentious life, recommends *honourable marriage and conjugal fidelity;* for man's ways are before the eyes of the Lord, and he pondereth all his goings.

(4.) Another path of wisdom pointed out in this Sacred Book, is *prudence and diligence* in temporal and secular concerns. An improvident thoughtlessness, carelessness about the future, is condemned by an allusion to that feeble insect the ant, Prov. vi. 6. "Go to the ant, thou sluggard, consider her ways and be wise, which having no guide, overseer, or ruler, provideth her meat in the summer, and gathereth her food in the harvest." If the feeble insect, without guide, overseer, or ruler, provides for itself, how inexcusable is it in a man to live in a careless, improvident manner, and squander in riot and dissipation, what should afford him support when he is sick or unemployed.

The happy effects of diligence and prudence are strongly expressed in these words, "Seest thou a man diligent in his business, he shall stand before kings, he shall not stand before mean men." The proof of this is every day seen, in the respectability to which well-principled, industrious men attain; whereas, to the sluggard or dissipated man, *poverty and want* come upon him as one that travelleth apace, and terribly as the approach of an armed enemy whom he cannot resist.

(5.) A peaceable disposition, and living in harmony with other people, is pointed out as another path of wisdom. He is called a wicked man who soweth discord—but a soft answer turneth away wrath. The beginning of strife is as when one letteth out water; you cannot always stop it when you wish; "therefore leave off contention before it be meddled with."

(6.) And to this end useful conversation is enjoined, and the avoiding of tale-bearing, and excessive talking. (Prov. x. 19.) "In the multitude of words there wanteth not sin, but he that refraineth his lips is wise. The tongue of the just is as choice silver; the heart of the wicked is little worth; the lips of the righteous feed many; but fools die for want of wisdom. The tongue of the righteous useth knowledge aright, but the mouth of fools poureth out foolishness. A wholesome tongue is a tree of life, but perverseness therein is a breach of the spirit. The lips of the wise disperse knowledge, but the heart of the foolish doth not so."

A fool's lips enter into contention, and his mouth calleth for strokes. A fool's mouth is his destruction, and his lips are the snare of his soul. The words of a tale-bearer are as wounds, and they go down into the innermost parts of the belly.

"Answer not a fool according to his folly"—*i.e. not* in the same foolish manner; but answer him according to his folly, *i.e.* give him such an answer as his foolish speech requires to shew its folly, lest he be wise in his own conceit. Men, who by vicious bad language corrupt each other, and teach vice to young boys, have a great deal

to answer for beside their own sins: if a man cannot say much that is useful, he may at least forbear saying what is vicious and corrupting; there is no occasion to be eternally muttering and talking. And connected with good conversation—

(7.) *Truth* may be noticed. "Lying lips are an abomination to the Lord; but they that deal truly are his delight. The lip of truth shall be established for ever; but a lying tongue is but for a moment. A righteous man hateth lying, but a wicked liar is loathsome, and cometh to shame. The getting of treasures by a lying tongue, is a vanity tossed to and fro of them that seek death. A false witness shall not be unpunished, and he that speaketh lies shall perish." And with truth must be joined *sincerity:* "Faithful are the rebukes or censures of a friend, but the kisses or flatteries of an enemy are deceitful." "He that rebuketh or findeth fault with a man, shall find more favour than he that flattereth with the tongue." To *truth* and *sincerity*, will *honesty* be added, for "divers weights are an abomination to the Lord, and a false balance is not good."

(8.) Another of wisdom's paths, is the *keeping good company.* "He that walketh with wise and good men, shall be wise, but a companion of fools shall be destroyed. Go from the presence of a foolish man when thou perceivest not in him the words of knowledge. Make no friendship with an angry man, and with a furious man thou shalt not go."

(9.) *Contentment* is also a path of wisdom, for "better is a little with righteousness than great revenues without right; therefore be not envious against evil men (who are prosperous,) neither desire to be with them, for he that maketh haste to be rich shall not be innocent."

(10.) Finally, the path of wisdom requires *sobriety*, or the moderate use of inebriating liquors; for "wine is a mocker, strong drink is raging, and whosoever is deceived thereby, is not wise. Contentions, babbling, wounds without cause, redness of eyes, sorrow and wo," are the consequences of intoxication, and the drunkard and glutton shall come to poverty, and be the slaves of lewdness and perverse conduct.

Thus I have noticed *ten* of those paths which wisdom

pronounces *pleasant;* docility, firmness, honourable marriage, prudence, diligence, peaceable disposition, truth, useful conversation, good company, contentment, and sobriety. These, added to the fear of God, will render a man's life tolerably pleasant, under any circumstances, much more so than all the pleasures of sin can do under the most prosperous circumstances. The paths of folly, in which so many tread, are the opposite of these, and those who tread in them, are proud, unteachable mockers and scorners, silly dupes of designing men and women, or who themselves seduce and corrupt the innocent, having no real affection for any woman, and beloved by none; and imprudent, idle, and extravagant; and quarrelsome; liars, and deceitful, whose mouths are filled with impious and indecent language; companions of profligate people, discontented and murmuring against Providence, and seeking to drown their mental miseries in habits of intoxication; and who, in the midst of all these hateful and unhappy modes of living, have every reason to fear that misery awaits them after death. Now,

Although an entire deliverance from afflictions, of one kind or another, is not to be expected in this guilty world; it is easy to see, that in comparison of the paths of wicked folly, wisdom's ways are, indeed, ways of pleasantness, and all her paths are comparatively peace. Endeavour, then, O men, to remember the instructions of Divine Wisdom, and pray God, for Christ's sake to grant you the aid of his Holy Spirit, to avoid the broad road that leads to destruction, and to enter in at the strait gate that leads to eternal life. If you would remember these things, whether at sea or on shore, you would find them contribute to your daily comfort, and ensure your lasting happiness.

DISCOURSE XII.

Composed at Sea.

DELIVERED AT KINGSBRIDGE, DEVONSHIRE, MARCH 21, 1824; AND AT THE REV. DR. WAUGH'S, WELLS STREET, LONDON, MARCH 28.

INTRODUCTION.

[In a land far off, the most populous nation in the world, on the eastern limits of Asia, from whence your preacher has returned for a short season, the name of Jesus is hated by the rulers, and by most of the people. A native of that land is, through dread of the oppressor, afraid to have about his person, or in his house, either book or any written paper which contains the name of Jesus, that blessed name, which is your only hope.

Compared with such a state of things, how truly may the people of this country say, "to us the lines have fallen in pleasant places, and we have a goodly heritage." In Great Britain, princes, and nobles, and legislators, join with the ministers of the Gospel, and beseech men to receive the Bible. *(How cheering to me, after many years exile and solitude, is such an assembly as this!)* Who can estimate the value of the Sabbath, and the Bible, and the ordinances of God's house!—And is it possible that those nations which now hate the name of Jesus, and are slavishly attached to their idols, and their ancient sages, and their superstitions, and their vices, can ever be converted? Is it not a hopeless task to endeavour to reclaim them? We say, no! and the reason we assign is this—"The most High God ruleth in the kingdom of men." For the encouragement of my own mind, and for your encouragement my fellow Christians, I have chosen the following words as my text.]

GOD THE SUPREME RULER.

DANIEL, IV. 32.

"The most High ruleth in the kingdom of men."

HUMAN governments, whether the supreme authority be vested in a senate, a king, or an emperor, have, indeed, immense power over their fellow creatures; and the will of these governments, which thousands, or hundreds of thousands of armed men can enforce, seems, at times, quite irresistible. The absolute despots of Asia, and of other parts of the world, have often done whatever their caprice dictated with the persons and the property of their numerous subjects. And whilst millions have continually trembled at the oppressor's frown, the monarchs themselves have been puffed up with pride, and deemed themselves omnipotent as gods, and have forgotten their dependance on the Almighty; or have practically acted, as if they were amenable to no higher authority. The sovereign of Babylon,* that mighty monarch, whilst walking on an elevated terrace, and surveying the great city which he had embellished, said, either mentally or audibly, with vain self-complacency, Dan. iv. 30. "Is not this great Babylon that I have built, for the house of the kingdom, by the might of my power, and for the honour of my majesty." But whilst the word was in the king's mouth, there fell a voice from Heaven, denouncing a punishment of his pride and self-sufficiency, which punishment would last till he should learn to know and acknowledge, that "The most High ruleth in the

* Nebuchadnezzar is called Nabuchodnosor II. by Rollin, reigned over Chaldea, Assyria, Arabia, Syria, and Palestine, forty-three years. Ante J. C. 603.

kingdom of men;" and He giveth earthly thrones to "whomsoever he will;" and sometimes setteth up over nations "the basest of men." The doctrine taught is, that the most High God is the supreme ruler over the nations and the kingdoms of the earth; and as his wisdom and justice may direct, he roots out and pulls down, or builds up and plants; no power on earth can obstruct his designs. The illustration of this much-neglected truth, I shall draw from a slight survey of the Book of Daniel, in which our text lies, and make such inferences in passing, as may tend to instruct, reprove, or admonish.

I. Daniel himself, the writer of this book, strikingly exemplifies how the *Divine Ruler can and does employ some of all ranks and conditions of men as his special and beloved servants on earth.* Kings and courtiers, shepherds and fishermen, philosophers and unlettered men, have, according to Sacred Writ and the history of the church, all been especially employed by divine Providence. The kings, David and Solomon, were writers of parts of divine Revelation; Daniel and Joseph, were courtiers or statesmen, under heathen monarchs; and this Daniel was twice declared, by a divine message, to be "a man greatly beloved" in the heavenly world;—a clear proof that no secular duties, nor any station in society, is incompatible with the service of God. Daniel was, when a young lad, carried away (as a prisoner by a victorious army that had ravaged his native country,) to a foreign land, and there appointed to the menial duties of the royal harem. And from the age of eighteen till ninety, he served the pagan princes of successive dynasties with fidelity, and at the same time preserved a conduct that was pleasing to Heaven. The Jews, of late years, being grieved that Daniel's prophesies point so clearly to Jesus of Nazareth, as the true Messiah, will not allow him the title of *prophet*, alleging as a reason, that he lived as a courtier, instead of living secluded from mankind, as did the prophets Elijah and others. But Heaven did not, because he was a courtier, withhold from him the gift of prophesy; and therefore how futile is it in man to with-

hold the name. Beside, our Saviour has designated him "Daniel *the prophet*," Matt. xxiv. 15. There are those in our day who despise the poor and unlettered, as if Heaven never employed them, as he did formerly the prophet Amos, who was a herdsman, and the fishermen of Galilee, who were the first Missionaries of the Saviour; and there are those in the lower walks of life, who seem to think that kings and statesmen cannot be faithful servants of the most High. But a review of sacred history, and human records, will shew, that there is no reason for such a supposition; nor is it often necessary to quit one's station in society, in order to serve the Lord; but it is practicable to serve him wherever we are, whilst we faithfully purpose, as did Daniel, not to defile ourselves, nor to be unfaithful in the things that concern our God. Daniel was a man of prayer, and neither flattery nor frowns could turn him aside. He would not desist from prayer to save his life; although it would have been no very artful subterfuge to substitute for his *usual* devotions, mental prayer, unknown to man; or to have retired to his closet, and shut to the door. But no, when his enemies at court, who envied the influence of the captive Jew, obtained the foolish and impious decree, that no person in the empire should for thirty days ask a petition of God or man, but only from the king; Daniel, *knowing the decree* was signed, went into his house, kneeled upon his knees three times a day, *with his chamber windows open* towards Jerusalem, and prayed and gave thanks before his God, *as he did aforetime.* For he thought it not right to conceal his prayers on this occasion, nor to *act* a lie, or do what implied an untruth, as a discontinuance of his usage would have been. Whilst praying, he was discovered, and suffered the penalty of his disobedience to the king's commands, for he obeyed a higher authority. He was cast in amongst lions, but the lions in the den could not hurt him: For the most High hath power, either to employ the ordinary course of nature in his government, or to stop it, or to change it, as he sees fit. He bids the ravenous lions not devour, and the fiery furnace not burn, and it is done. Daniel came forth unhurt from the den;

and his friends, Shadrach, Meshach, and Abednego, who would not worship the king's golden image, walked in the midst of the burning fiery furnace and felt no harm. They trusted that God would see meet to deliver them; but if not, they were prepared to suffer. Their courage and firm resistance to the royal mandate did not arise from a foreknowledge that they should be delivered; but from faith in the divine power, and submission to the divine wisdom. "Our God, said they, is able to deliver us from the burning fiery furnace," and out of thy hand, O king; "but if not"—if he should not see fit to do so, be it known unto thee, O king, that we will not serve thy gods, nor worship the golden image which thou hast set up. They trusted in God and were delivered. These examples shew that the divine government, or providence, extends to individuals, and if to some individuals, why not to all individuals? Individuals constitute nations, and great affairs arise from small beginnings. A general providence implies a particular providence, as effects imply a cause; or as the motion of a great machine implies attention to the minute wheels.

The character of Daniel, president of the empire; of Shadrach, and his two friends, who also held offices under government; of Nehemiah, cup-bearer to Artaxerxes, king of Persia; and the extraordinary circumstances which occurred to them, gave them, in all probability, such influence in the empire, as must have contributed to ameliorate the condition of the Jews in captivity, and, eventually, was the means of obtaining decrees for their restoration. Nor may we omit here the name of Esther, the captive Jewish orphan girl, who was raised by Providence to be queen of Persia, and the saviour of her nation. And be it observed, that the enemies of these just persons, of Daniel, of Shadrach, of Mordecai, and Esther, fell into the pit which they dug for the innocent. Daniel's malicious and intended murderers were themselves devoured by wild beasts; those who heated the furnace were themselves burnt; and wicked Haman was hanged on his own gallows; for God knoweth (however complicated the case) how to deliver the righ-

I have called, and ye refused; I have stretched out my hand, and no man regarded; but ye have set at nought all my counsel, and would none of my reproof: I also will laugh at your calamity; I will mock when your fear cometh; when your fear cometh as desolation, and your destruction cometh as a whirlwind; when distress and anguish cometh upon you:—for that they hated knowledge, and did not choose the fear of the Lord."

In these passages of Sacred Scripture, the good and the evil, the blessing and the curse, are set before us; the path of wisdom, and the path of folly; the different conduct and fate of the humble learner, and of the proud scorner. "A man's pride shall bring him low; but honour shall uphold the humble in spirit." (Prov. xxix. 23.) Therefore, (chap. iii. ver. 5.) "Trust in the Lord with all thy heart, and lean not to thine own understanding.—Be not wise in thine own eyes; but in all thy ways acknowledge the Almighty, and he will direct thy paths."

(2.) But the humble and teachable disposition so strongly inculcated, does not imply an easy acquiescence with whatever any body may suggest; quite the reverse! It is accompanied by a *firm resistance* to the enticements of evil men and bad women. (Prov. i. 10.) "My son, if sinners entice thee consent thou not." If they say, 'Cast in thy lot among us—let us all have one purse,' and so entice you to steal or to rob, "Walk not thou in the way with them: refrain thy foot from their path, for their feet run to evil, and make haste to shed blood."

(Prov. ii. 10.) "When wisdom entereth into thy heart and knowledge is pleasant to thy soul; discretion shall preserve thee, understanding shall keep thee, and deliver thee from the way of the evil man, from the man that speaketh froward things"—who rejoices to do evil, and delights in the frowardness of the wicked; and will deliver thee from the strange woman, from the abandoned woman, who flattereth with her words, who forsaketh the guide of her youth (her father or her husband,) and forgetteth the covenant of her God;—for her house inclineth unto death, and her paths unto the dead. None that go unto her return again,

neither take they hold of the paths of life. (Prov. v. 2.) "Her feet go down to death, and her steps take hold on hell;" therefore, O man, remove thy way far from her, and come not nigh the door of her house, "Lest thou give thine honour unto others, and thy years unto the cruel—lest strangers be filled with thy wealth, and thy labours be in the house of a stranger," and thou mourn at the last, when thy flesh and thy body are consumed (by loathsome disease), and remorse extort from thee the exclamation—"How have I hated instruction, and my heart despised reproof—I have not obeyed the voice of my teachers, nor inclined mine ear to them that instructed me!"

He who does not firmly resist the fair speeches of impudent and abandoned women, (Prov. vii. 21.) "goes after her as an ox to the slaughter, or a fool to the correction of the stocks; for her house is the way to hell, going down to the chambers of death." (Prov. ix. 17.) "The simple fool who turneth into her house, knoweth not that the dead are there, and that her guests are in the depths of hell." This strong language is dictated by divine wisdom, to confirm the resolution of those who have any regard for their own honour or welfare in this world, or any concern for the salvation of their souls.

(3.) And the same divine wisdom which so strongly dehorts men from a licentious life, recommends *honourable marriage and conjugal fidelity;* for man's ways are before the eyes of the Lord, and he pondereth all his goings.

(4.) Another path of wisdom pointed out in this Sacred Book, is *prudence and diligence* in temporal and secular concerns. An improvident thoughtlessness, carelessness about the future, is condemned by an allusion to that feeble insect the ant, Prov. vi. 6. "Go to the ant, thou sluggard, consider her ways and be wise, which having no guide, overseer, or ruler, provideth her meat in the summer, and gathereth her food in the harvest." If the feeble insect, without guide, overseer, or ruler, provides for itself, how inexcusable is it in a man to live in a careless, improvident manner, and squander in riot and dissipation, what should afford him support when he is sick or unemployed.

The happy effects of diligence and prudence are strongly expressed in these words, "Seest thou a man diligent in his business, he shall stand before kings, he shall not stand before mean men." The proof of this is every day seen, in the respectability to which well-principled, industrious men attain; whereas, to the sluggard or dissipated man, *poverty and want* come upon him as one that travelleth space, and terribly as the approach of an armed enemy whom he cannot resist.

(5.) A peaceable disposition, and living in harmony with other people, is pointed out as another path of wisdom. He is called a wicked man who soweth discord—but a soft answer turneth away wrath. The beginning of strife is as when one letteth out water; you cannot always stop it when you wish; "therefore leave off contention before it be meddled with."

(6.) And to this end useful conversation is enjoined, and the avoiding of tale-bearing, and excessive talking. (Prov. x. 19.) "In the multitude of words there wanteth not sin, but he that refraineth his lips is wise. The tongue of the just is as choice silver; the heart of the wicked is little worth; the lips of the righteous feed many; but fools die for want of wisdom. The tongue of the righteous useth knowledge aright, but the mouth of fools poureth out foolishness. A wholesome tongue is a tree of life, but perverseness therein is a breach of the spirit. The lips of the wise disperse knowledge, but the heart of the foolish doth not so."

A fool's lips enter into contention, and his mouth calleth for strokes. A fool's mouth is his destruction, and his lips are the snare of his soul. The words of a tale-bearer are as wounds, and they go down into the innermost parts of the belly.

"Answer not a fool according to his folly"—*i.e.* not in the same foolish manner; but answer him according to his folly, *i.e.* give him such an answer as his foolish speech requires to shew its folly, lest he be wise in his own conceit. Men, who by vicious bad language corrupt each other, and teach vice to young boys, have a great deal

to answer for beside their own sins: if a man cannot say much that is useful, he may at least forbear saying what is vicious and corrupting; there is no occasion to be eternally muttering and talking. And connected with good conversation—

(7.) *Truth* may be noticed. "Lying lips are an abomination to the Lord; but they that deal truly are his delight. The lip of truth shall be established for ever; but a lying tongue is but for a moment. A righteous man hateth lying, but a wicked liar is loathsome, and cometh to shame. The getting of treasures by a lying tongue, is a vanity tossed to and fro of them that seek death. A false witness shall not be unpunished, and he that speaketh lies shall perish." And with truth must be joined *sincerity:* "Faithful are the rebukes or censures of a friend, but the kisses or flatteries of an enemy are deceitful." "He that rebuketh or findeth fault with a man, shall find more favour than he that flattereth with the tongue." To *truth* and *sincerity*, will *honesty* be added, for "divers weights are an abomination to the Lord, and a false balance is not good."

(8.) Another of wisdom's paths, is the *keeping good company.* "He that walketh with wise and good men, shall be wise, but a companion of fools shall be destroyed. Go from the presence of a foolish man when thou perceivest not in him the words of knowledge. Make no friendship with an angry man, and with a furious man thou shalt not go."

(9.) *Contentment* is also a path of wisdom, for "better is a little with righteousness than great revenues without right; therefore be not envious against evil men (who are prosperous,) neither desire to be with them, for he that maketh haste to be rich shall not be innocent."

(10.) Finally, the path of wisdom requires *sobriety*, or the moderate use of inebriating liquors; for "wine is a mocker, strong drink is raging, and whosoever is deceived thereby, is not wise. Contentions, babbling, wounds without cause, redness of eyes, sorrow and wo," are the consequences of intoxication, and the drunkard and glutton shall come to poverty, and be the slaves of lewdness and perverse conduct.

Thus I have noticed *ten* of those paths which wisdom

pronounces *pleasant;* docility, firmness, honourable marriage, prudence, diligence, peaceable disposition, truth, useful conversation, good company, contentment, and sobriety. These, added to the fear of God, will render a man's life tolerably pleasant, under any circumstances, much more so than all the pleasures of sin can do under the most prosperous circumstances. The paths of folly, in which so many tread, are the opposite of these, and those who tread in them, are proud, unteachable mockers and scorners, silly dupes of designing men and women, or who themselves seduce and corrupt the innocent, having no real affection for any woman, and beloved by none; and imprudent, idle, and extravagant; and quarrelsome; liars, and deceitful, whose mouths are filled with impious and indecent language; companions of profligate people, discontented and murmuring against Providence, and seeking to drown their mental miseries in habits of intoxication; and who, in the midst of all these hateful and unhappy modes of living, have every reason to fear that misery awaits them after death. Now,

Although an entire deliverance from afflictions, of one kind or another, is not to be expected in this guilty world; it is easy to see, that in comparison of the paths of wicked folly, wisdom's ways are, indeed, ways of pleasantness, and all her paths are comparatively peace. Endeavour, then, O men, to remember the instructions of Divine Wisdom, and pray God, for Christ's sake to grant you the aid of his Holy Spirit, to avoid the broad road that leads to destruction, and to enter in at the strait gate that leads to eternal life. If you would remember these things, whether at sea or on shore, you would find them contribute to your daily comfort, and ensure your lasting happiness.

DISCOURSE XII.

Composed at Sea.

DELIVERED AT KINGSBRIDGE, DEVONSHIRE, MARCH 21, 1824; AND AT THE REV. DR. WAUGH'S, WELLS STREET, LONDON, MARCH 28.

INTRODUCTION.

[In a land far off, the most populous nation in the world, on the eastern limits of Asia, from whence your preacher has returned for a short season, the name of Jesus is hated by the rulers, and by most of the people. A native of that land is, through dread of the oppressor, afraid to have about his person, or in his house, either book or any written paper which contains the name of Jesus, that blessed name, which is your only hope.

Compared with such a state of things, how truly may the people of this country say, "to us the lines have fallen in pleasant places, and we have a goodly heritage." In Great Britain, princes, and nobles, and legislators, join with the ministers of the Gospel, and beseech men to receive the Bible. *(How cheering to me, after many years exile and solitude, is such an assembly as this!)* Who can estimate the value of the Sabbath, and the Bible, and the ordinances of God's house!—And is it possible that those nations which now hate the name of Jesus, and are slavishly attached to their idols, and their ancient sages, and their superstitions, and their vices, can ever be converted? Is it not a hopeless task to endeavour to reclaim them? We say, no! and the reason we assign is this—"The most High God ruleth in the kingdom of men." For the encouragement of my own mind, and for your encouragement my fellow Christians, I have chosen the following words as my text.]

GOD THE SUPREME RULER.

DANIEL, IV. 32.

"The most High ruleth in the kingdom of men."

HUMAN governments, whether the supreme authority be vested in a senate, a king, or an emperor, have, indeed, immense power over their fellow creatures; and the will of these governments, which thousands, or hundreds of thousands of armed men can enforce, seems, at times, quite irresistible. The absolute despots of Asia, and of other parts of the world, have often done whatever their caprice dictated with the persons and the property of their numerous subjects. And whilst millions have continually trembled at the oppressor's frown, the monarchs themselves have been puffed up with pride, and deemed themselves omnipotent as gods, and have forgotten their dependance on the Almighty; or have practically acted, as if they were amenable to no higher authority. The sovereign of Babylon,* that mighty monarch, whilst walking on an elevated terrace, and surveying the great city which he had embellished, said, either mentally or audibly, with vain self-complacency, Dan. iv. 30. "Is not this great Babylon that I have built, for the house of the kingdom, by the might of my power, and for the honour of my majesty." But whilst the word was in the king's mouth, there fell a voice from Heaven, denouncing a punishment of his pride and self-sufficiency, which punishment would last till he should learn to know and acknowledge, that "The most High ruleth in the

* Nebuchadnezzar is called Nabuchodnosor II. by Rollin, reigned over Chaldea, Assyria, Arabia, Syria, and Palestine, forty-three years. Ante J. C. 603.

kingdom of men;" and He giveth earthly thrones to "whomsoever he will;" and sometimes setteth up over nations "the basest of men." The doctrine taught is, that the most High God is the supreme ruler over the nations and the kingdoms of the earth; and as his wisdom and justice may direct, he roots out and pulls down, or builds up and plants; no power on earth can obstruct his designs. The illustration of this much-neglected truth, I shall draw from a slight survey of the Book of Daniel, in which our text lies, and make such inferences in passing, as may tend to instruct, reprove, or admonish.

I. Daniel himself, the writer of this book, strikingly exemplifies how the *Divine Ruler can and does employ some of all ranks and conditions of men as his special and beloved servants on earth.* Kings and courtiers, shepherds and fishermen, philosophers and unlettered men, have, according to Sacred Writ and the history of the church, all been especially employed by divine Providence. The kings, David and Solomon, were writers of parts of divine Revelation; Daniel and Joseph, were courtiers or statesmen, under heathen monarchs; and this Daniel was twice declared, by a divine message, to be "a man greatly beloved" in the heavenly world;—a clear proof that no secular duties, nor any station in society, is incompatible with the service of God. Daniel was, when a young lad, carried away (as a prisoner by a victorious army that had ravaged his native country,) to a foreign land, and there appointed to the menial duties of the royal harem. And from the age of eighteen till ninety, he served the pagan princes of successive dynasties with fidelity, and at the same time preserved a conduct that was pleasing to Heaven. The Jews, of late years, being grieved that Daniel's prophesies point so clearly to Jesus of Nazareth, as the true Messiah, will not allow him the title of *prophet*, alleging as a reason, that he lived as a courtier, instead of living secluded from mankind, as did the prophets Elijah and others. But Heaven did not, because he was a courtier, withhold from him the gift of prophesy; and therefore how futile is it in man to with-

hold the name. Beside, our Saviour has designated him "Daniel *the prophet*," Matt. xxiv. 15. There are those in our day who despise the poor and unlettered, as if Heaven never employed them, as he did formerly the prophet Amos, who was a herdsman, and the fishermen of Galilee, who were the first Missionaries of the Saviour; and there are those in the lower walks of life, who seem to think that kings and statesmen cannot be faithful servants of the most High. But a review of sacred history, and human records, will shew, that there is no reason for such a supposition; nor is it often necessary to quit one's station in society, in order to serve the Lord; but it is practicable to serve him wherever we are, whilst we faithfully purpose, as did Daniel, not to defile ourselves, nor to be unfaithful in the things that concern our God. Daniel was a man of prayer, and neither flattery nor frowns could turn him aside. He would not desist from prayer to save his life; although it would have been no very artful subterfuge to substitute for his *usual* devotions, mental prayer, unknown to man; or to have retired to his closet, and shut to the door. But no, when his enemies at court, who envied the influence of the captive Jew, obtained the foolish and impious decree, that no person in the empire should for thirty days ask a petition of God or man, but only from the king; Daniel, *knowing the decree* was signed, went into his house, kneeled upon his knees three times a day, *with his chamber windows open* towards Jerusalem, and prayed and gave thanks before his God, *as he did aforetime*. For he thought it not right to conceal his prayers on this occasion, nor to *act* a lie, or do what implied an untruth, as a discontinuance of his usage would have been. Whilst praying, he was discovered, and suffered the penalty of his disobedience to the king's commands, for he obeyed a higher authority. He was cast in amongst lions, but the lions in the den could not hurt him: For the most High hath power, either to employ the ordinary course of nature in his government, or to stop it, or to change it, as he sees fit. He bids the ravenous lions not devour, and the fiery furnace not burn, and it is done. Daniel came forth unhurt from the den;

and his friends, Shadrach, Meshach, and Abednego, who would not worship the king's golden image, walked in the midst of the burning fiery furnace and felt no harm. They trusted that God would see meet to deliver them; but if not, they were prepared to suffer. Their courage and firm resistance to the royal mandate did not arise from a foreknowledge that they should be delivered; but from faith in the divine power, and submission to the divine wisdom. "Our God, said they, is able to deliver us from the burning fiery furnace," and out of thy hand, O king; "but if not"—if he should not see fit to do so, be it known unto thee, O king, that we will not serve thy gods, nor worship the golden image which thou hast set up. They trusted in God and were delivered. These examples shew that the divine government, or providence, extends to individuals, and if to some individuals, why not to all individuals? Individuals constitute nations, and great affairs arise from small beginnings. A general providence implies a particular providence, as effects imply a cause; or as the motion of a great machine implies attention to the minute wheels.

The character of Daniel, president of the empire; of Shadrach, and his two friends, who also held offices under government; of Nehemiah, cup-bearer to Artaxerxes, king of Persia; and the extraordinary circumstances which occurred to them, gave them, in all probability, such influence in the empire, as must have contributed to ameliorate the condition of the Jews in captivity, and, eventually, was the means of obtaining decrees for their restoration. Nor may we omit here the name of Esther, the captive Jewish orphan girl, who was raised by Providence to be queen of Persia, and the saviour of her nation. And be it observed, that the enemies of these just persons, of Daniel, of Shadrach, of Mordecai, and Esther, fell into the pit which they dug for the innocent. Daniel's malicious and intended murderers were themselves devoured by wild beasts; those who heated the furnace were themselves burnt; and wicked Haman was hanged on his own gallows; for God knoweth (however complicated the case) how to deliver the righ-

I have called, and ye refused; I have stretched out my hand, and no man regarded; but ye have set at nought all my counsel, and would none of my reproof: I also will laugh at your calamity; I will mock when your fear cometh; when your fear cometh as desolation, and your destruction cometh as a whirlwind; when distress and anguish cometh upon you:—for that they hated knowledge, and did not choose the fear of the Lord."

In these passages of Sacred Scripture, the good and the evil, the blessing and the curse, are set before us; the path of wisdom, and the path of folly; the different conduct and fate of the humble learner, and of the proud scorner. "A man's pride shall bring him low; but honour shall uphold the humble in spirit." (Prov. xxix. 23.) Therefore, (chap. iii. ver. 5.) "Trust in the Lord with all thy heart, and lean not to thine own understanding.—Be not wise in thine own eyes; but in all thy ways acknowledge the Almighty, and he will direct thy paths."

(2.) But the humble and teachable disposition so strongly inculcated, does not imply an easy acquiescence with whatever any body may suggest; quite the reverse! It is accompanied by a *firm resistance* to the enticements of evil men and bad women. (Prov. i. 10.) "My son, if sinners entice thee consent thou not." If they say, 'Cast in thy lot among us—let us all have one purse,' and so entice you to steal or to rob, "Walk not thou in the way with them: refrain thy foot from their path, for their feet run to evil, and make haste to shed blood."

(Prov. ii. 10.) "When wisdom entereth into thy heart and knowledge is pleasant to thy soul; discretion shall preserve thee, understanding shall keep thee, and deliver thee from the way of the evil man, from the man that speaketh froward things"—who rejoices to do evil, and delights in the frowardness of the wicked; and will deliver thee from the strange woman, from the abandoned woman, who flattereth with her words, who forsaketh the guide of her youth (her father or her husband,) and forgetteth the covenant of her God;—for her house inclineth unto death, and her paths unto the dead. None that go unto her return again,

neither take they hold of the paths of life. (Prov. v. 2.) "Her feet go down to death, and her steps take hold on hell;" therefore, O man, remove thy way far from her, and come not nigh the door of her house, "Lest thou give thine honour unto others, and thy years unto the cruel—lest strangers be filled with thy wealth, and thy labours be in the house of a stranger," and thou mourn at the last, when thy flesh and thy body are consumed (by loathsome disease), and remorse extort from thee the exclamation—"How have I hated instruction, and my heart despised reproof—I have not obeyed the voice of my teachers, nor inclined mine ear to them that instructed me!"

He who does not firmly resist the fair speeches of impudent and abandoned women, (Prov. vii. 21.) "goes after her as an ox to the slaughter, or a fool to the correction of the stocks; for her house is the way to hell, going down to the chambers of death." (Prov. ix. 17.) "The simple fool who turneth into her house, knoweth not that the dead are there, and that her guests are in the depths of hell." This strong language is dictated by divine wisdom, to confirm the resolution of those who have any regard for their own honour or welfare in this world, or any concern for the salvation of their souls.

(3.) And the same divine wisdom which so strongly dehorts men from a licentious life, recommends *honourable marriage and conjugal fidelity;* for man's ways are before the eyes of the Lord, and he pondereth all his goings.

(4.) Another path of wisdom pointed out in this Sacred Book, is *prudence and diligence* in temporal and secular concerns. An improvident thoughtlessness, carelessness about the future, is condemned by an allusion to that feeble insect the ant, Prov. vi. 6. "Go to the ant, thou sluggard, consider her ways and be wise, which having no guide, overseer, or ruler, provideth her meat in the summer, and gathereth her food in the harvest." If the feeble insect, without guide, overseer, or ruler, provides for itself, how inexcusable is it in a man to live in a careless, improvident manner, and squander in riot and dissipation, what should afford him support when he is sick or unemployed.

The happy effects of diligence and prudence are strongly expressed in these words, "Seest thou a man diligent in his business, he shall stand before kings, he shall not stand before mean men." The proof of this is every day seen, in the respectability to which well-principled, industrious men attain; whereas, to the sluggard or dissipated man, *poverty and want* come upon him as one that travelleth apace, and terribly as the approach of an armed enemy whom he cannot resist.

(5.) A peaceable disposition, and living in harmony with other people, is pointed out as another path of wisdom. He is called a wicked man who soweth discord—but a soft answer turneth away wrath. The beginning of strife is as when one letteth out water; you cannot always stop it when you wish; "therefore leave off contention before it be meddled with."

(6.) And to this end useful conversation is enjoined, and the avoiding of tale-bearing, and excessive talking. (Prov. x. 19.) "In the multitude of words there wanteth not sin, but he that refraineth his lips is wise. The tongue of the just is as choice silver; the heart of the wicked is little worth; the lips of the righteous feed many; but fools die for want of wisdom. The tongue of the righteous useth knowledge aright, but the mouth of fools poureth out foolishness. A wholesome tongue is a tree of life, but perverseness therein is a breach of the spirit. The lips of the wise disperse knowledge, but the heart of the foolish doth not so."

A fool's lips enter into contention, and his mouth calleth for strokes. A fool's mouth is his destruction, and his lips are the snare of his soul. The words of a tale-bearer are as wounds, and they go down into the innermost parts of the belly.

"Answer not a fool according to his folly"—*i. e. not* in the same foolish manner; but answer him according to his folly, *i.e.* give him such an answer as his foolish speech requires to shew its folly, lest he be wise in his own conceit. Men, who by vicious bad language corrupt each other, and teach vice to young boys, have a great deal

to answer for beside their own sins: if a man cannot say much that is useful, he may at least forbear saying what is vicious and corrupting; there is no occasion to be eternally muttering and talking. And connected with good conversation—

(7.) *Truth* may be noticed. "Lying lips are an abomination to the Lord; but they that deal truly are his delight. The lip of truth shall be established for ever; but a lying tongue is but for a moment. A righteous man hateth lying, but a wicked liar is loathsome, and cometh to shame. The getting of treasures by a lying tongue, is a vanity tossed to and fro of them that seek death. A false witness shall not be unpunished, and he that speaketh lies shall perish." And with truth must be joined *sincerity:* "Faithful are the rebukes or censures of a friend, but the kisses or flatteries of an enemy are deceitful." "He that rebuketh or findeth fault with a man, shall find more favour than he that flattereth with the tongue." To *truth* and *sincerity*, will *honesty* be added, for "divers weights are an abomination to the Lord, and a false balance is not good."

(8.) Another of wisdom's paths, is the *keeping good company*. "He that walketh with wise and good men, shall be wise, but a companion of fools shall be destroyed. Go from the presence of a foolish man when thou perceivest not in him the words of knowledge. Make no friendship with an angry man, and with a furious man thou shalt not go."

(9.) *Contentment* is also a path of wisdom, for "better is a little with righteousness than great revenues without right; therefore be not envious against evil men (who are prosperous,) neither desire to be with them, for he that maketh haste to be rich shall not be innocent."

(10.) Finally, the path of wisdom requires *sobriety*, or the moderate use of inebriating liquors; for "wine is a mocker, strong drink is raging, and whosoever is deceived thereby, is not wise. Contentions, babbling, wounds without cause, redness of eyes, sorrow and wo," are the consequences of intoxication, and the drunkard and glutton shall come to poverty, and be the slaves of lewdness and perverse conduct.

Thus I have noticed *ten* of those paths which wisdom

pronounces *pleasant;* docility, firmness, honourable marriage, prudence, diligence, peaceable disposition, truth, useful conversation, good company, contentment, and sobriety. These, added to the fear of God, will render a man's life tolerably pleasant, under any circumstances, much more so than all the pleasures of sin can do under the most prosperous circumstances. The paths of folly, in which so many tread, are the opposite of these, and those who tread in them, are proud, unteachable mockers and scorners, silly dupes of designing men and women, or who themselves seduce and corrupt the innocent, having no real affection for any woman, and beloved by none; and imprudent, idle, and extravagant; and quarrelsome; liars, and deceitful, whose mouths are filled with impious and indecent language; companions of profligate people, discontented and murmuring against Providence, and seeking to drown their mental miseries in habits of intoxication; and who, in the midst of all these hateful and unhappy modes of living, have every reason to fear that misery awaits them after death. Now,

Although an entire deliverance from afflictions, of one kind or another, is not to be expected in this guilty world; it is easy to see, that in comparison of the paths of wicked folly, wisdom's ways are, indeed, ways of pleasantness, and all her paths are comparatively peace. Endeavour, then, O men, to remember the instructions of Divine Wisdom, and pray God, for Christ's sake to grant you the aid of his Holy Spirit, to avoid the broad road that leads to destruction, and to enter in at the strait gate that leads to eternal life. If you would remember these things, whether at sea or on shore, you would find them contribute to your daily comfort, and ensure your lasting happiness.

DISCOURSE XII.

Composed at Sea.

DELIVERED AT KINGSBRIDGE, DEVONSHIRE, MARCH 21, 1824; AND AT THE REV. DR. WAUGH'S, WELLS STREET, LONDON, MARCH 28.

INTRODUCTION.

[In a land far off, the most populous nation in the world, on the eastern limits of Asia, from whence your preacher has returned for a short season, the name of Jesus is hated by the rulers, and by most of the people. A native of that land is, through dread of the oppressor, afraid to have about his person, or in his house, either book or any written paper which contains the name of Jesus, that blessed name, which is your only hope.

Compared with such a state of things, how truly may the people of this country say, "to us the lines have fallen in pleasant places, and we have a goodly heritage." In Great Britain, princes, and nobles, and legislators, join with the ministers of the Gospel, and beseech men to receive the Bible. *(How cheering to me, after many years exile and solitude, is such an assembly as this!)* Who can estimate the value of the Sabbath, and the Bible, and the ordinances of God's house!—And is it possible that those nations which now hate the name of Jesus, and are slavishly attached to their idols, and their ancient sages, and their superstitions, and their vices, can ever be converted? Is it not a hopeless task to endeavour to reclaim them? We say, no! and the reason we assign is this—"The most High God ruleth in the kingdom of men." For the encouragement of my own mind, and for your encouragement my fellow Christians, I have chosen the following words as my text.]

GOD THE SUPREME RULER.

DANIEL, IV. 32.

"*The most High ruleth in the kingdom of men.*"

HUMAN governments, whether the supreme authority be vested in a senate, a king, or an emperor, have, indeed, immense power over their fellow creatures; and the will of these governments, which thousands, or hundreds of thousands of armed men can enforce, seems, at times, quite irresistible. The absolute despots of Asia, and of other parts of the world, have often done whatever their caprice dictated with the persons and the property of their numerous subjects. And whilst millions have continually trembled at the oppressor's frown, the monarchs themselves have been puffed up with pride, and deemed themselves omnipotent as gods, and have forgotten their dependance on the Almighty; or have practically acted, as if they were amenable to no higher authority. The sovereign of Babylon,* that mighty monarch, whilst walking on an elevated terrace, and surveying the great city which he had embellished, said, either mentally or audibly, with vain self-complacency, Dan. iv. 30. "Is not this great Babylon that I have built, for the house of the kingdom, by the might of my power, and for the honour of my majesty." But whilst the word was in the king's mouth, there fell a voice from Heaven, denouncing a punishment of his pride and self-sufficiency, which punishment would last till he should learn to know and acknowledge, that "The most High ruleth in the

* Nebuchadnezzar is called Nabuchodnosor II. by Rollin, reigned over Chaldea, Assyria, Arabia, Syria, and Palestine, forty-three years. Ante J. C. 603.

kingdom of men;" and He giveth earthly thrones to "whomsoever he will;" and sometimes setteth up over nations "the basest of men." The doctrine taught is, that the most High God is the supreme ruler over the nations and the kingdoms of the earth; and as his wisdom and justice may direct, he roots out and pulls down, or builds up and plants; no power on earth can obstruct his designs. The illustration of this much-neglected truth, I shall draw from a slight survey of the Book of Daniel, in which our text lies, and make such inferences in passing, as may tend to instruct, reprove, or admonish.

I. Daniel himself, the writer of this book, strikingly exemplifies how the *Divine Ruler can and does employ some of all ranks and conditions of men as his special and beloved servants on earth.* Kings and courtiers, shepherds and fishermen, philosophers and unlettered men, have, according to Sacred Writ and the history of the church, all been especially employed by divine Providence. The kings, David and Solomon, were writers of parts of divine Revelation; Daniel and Joseph, were courtiers or statesmen, under heathen monarchs; and this Daniel was twice declared, by a divine message, to be "a man greatly beloved" in the heavenly world;—a clear proof that no secular duties, nor any station in society, is incompatible with the service of God. Daniel was, when a young lad, carried away (as a prisoner by a victorious army that had ravaged his native country,) to a foreign land, and there appointed to the menial duties of the royal harem. And from the age of eighteen till ninety, he served the pagan princes of successive dynasties with fidelity, and at the same time preserved a conduct that was pleasing to Heaven. The Jews, of late years, being grieved that Daniel's prophesies point so clearly to Jesus of Nazareth, as the true Messiah, will not allow him the title of *prophet*, alleging as a reason, that he lived as a courtier, instead of living secluded from mankind, as did the prophets Elijah and others. But Heaven did not, because he was a courtier, withhold from him the gift of prophesy; and therefore how futile is it in man to with-

hold the name. Beside, our Saviour has designated him "Daniel *the prophet*," Matt. xxiv. 15. There are those in our day who despise the poor and unlettered, as if Heaven never employed them, as he did formerly the prophet Amos, who was a herdsman, and the fishermen of Galilee, who were the first Missionaries of the Saviour; and there are those in the lower walks of life, who seem to think that kings and statesmen cannot be faithful servants of the most High. But a review of sacred history, and human records, will shew, that there is no reason for such a supposition; nor is it often necessary to quit one's station in society, in order to serve the Lord; but it is practicable to serve him where-ever we are, whilst we faithfully purpose, as did Daniel, not to defile ourselves, nor to be unfaithful in the things that concern our God. Daniel was a man of prayer, and neither flattery nor frowns could turn him aside. He would not desist from prayer to save his life; although it would have been no very artful subterfuge to substitute for his *usual* devotions, mental prayer, unknown to man; or to have retired to his closet, and shut to the door. But no, when his enemies at court, who envied the influence of the captive Jew, obtained the foolish and impious decree, that no person in the empire should for thirty days ask a petition of God or man, but only from the king; Daniel, *knowing the decree* was signed, went into his house, kneeled upon his knees three times a day, *with his chamber windows open* towards Jerusalem, and prayed and gave thanks before his God, *as he did aforetime*. For he thought it not right to conceal his prayers on this occasion, nor to *act* a lie, or do what implied an untruth, as a discontinuance of his usage would have been. Whilst praying, he was discovered, and suffered the penalty of his disobedience to the king's commands, for he obeyed a higher authority. He was cast in amongst lions, but the lions in the den could not hurt him: For the most High hath power, either to employ the ordinary course of nature in his government, or to stop it, or to change it, as he sees fit. He bids the ravenous lions not devour, and the fiery furnace not burn, and it is done. Daniel came forth unhurt from the den;

and his friends, Shadrach, Meshach, and Abednego, who would not worship the king's golden image, walked in the midst of the burning fiery furnace and felt no harm. They trusted that God would see meet to deliver them; but if not, they were prepared to suffer. Their courage and firm resistance to the royal mandate did not arise from a foreknowledge that they should be delivered; but from faith in the divine power, and submission to the divine wisdom. "Our God, said they, is able to deliver us from the burning fiery furnace," and out of thy hand, O king; "but if not"—if he should not see fit to do so, be it known unto thee, O king, that we will not serve thy gods, nor worship the golden image which thou hast set up. They trusted in God and were delivered. These examples shew that the divine government, or providence, extends to individuals, and if to some individuals, why not to all individuals? Individuals constitute nations, and great affairs arise from small beginnings. A general providence implies a particular providence, as effects imply a cause; or as the motion of a great machine implies attention to the minute wheels.

The character of Daniel, president of the empire; of Shadrach, and his two friends, who also held offices under government; of Nehemiah, cup-bearer to Artaxerxes, king of Persia; and the extraordinary circumstances which occurred to them, gave them, in all probability, such influence in the empire, as must have contributed to ameliorate the condition of the Jews in captivity, and, eventually, was the means of obtaining decrees for their restoration. Nor may we omit here the name of Esther, the captive Jewish orphan girl, who was raised by Providence to be queen of Persia, and the saviour of her nation. And be it observed, that the enemies of these just persons, of Daniel, of Shadrach, of Mordecai, and Esther, fell into the pit which they dug for the innocent. Daniel's malicious and intended murderers were themselves devoured by wild beasts; those who heated the furnace were themselves burnt; and wicked Haman was hanged on his own gallows; for God knoweth (however complicated the case) how to deliver the righ-

I have called, and ye refused; I have stretched out my hand, and no man regarded; but ye have set at nought all my counsel, and would none of my reproof: I also will laugh at your calamity; I will mock when your fear cometh; when your fear cometh as desolation, and your destruction cometh as a whirlwind; when distress and anguish cometh upon you:—for that they hated knowledge, and did not choose the fear of the Lord."

In these passages of Sacred Scripture, the good and the evil, the blessing and the curse, are set before us; the path of wisdom, and the path of folly; the different conduct and fate of the humble learner, and of the proud scorner. "A man's pride shall bring him low; but honour shall uphold the humble in spirit." (Prov. xxix. 23.) Therefore, (chap. iii. ver. 5.) "Trust in the Lord with all thy heart, and lean not to thine own understanding.—Be not wise in thine own eyes; but in all thy ways acknowledge the Almighty, and he will direct thy paths."

(2.) But the humble and teachable disposition so strongly inculcated, does not imply an easy acquiescence with whatever any body may suggest; quite the reverse! It is accompanied by a *firm resistance* to the enticements of evil men and bad women. (Prov. i. 10.) "My son, if sinners entice thee consent thou not." If they say, 'Cast in thy lot among us—let us all have one purse,' and so entice you to steal or to rob, "Walk not thou in the way with them: refrain thy foot from their path, for their feet run to evil, and make haste to shed blood."

(Prov. ii. 10.) "When wisdom entereth into thy heart and knowledge is pleasant to thy soul; discretion shall preserve thee, understanding shall keep thee, and deliver thee from the way of the evil man, from the man that speaketh froward things"—who rejoices to do evil, and delights in the frowardness of the wicked; and will deliver thee from the strange woman, from the abandoned woman, who flattereth with her words, who forsaketh the guide of her youth (her father or her husband,) and forgetteth the covenant of her God;—for her house inclineth unto death, and her paths unto the dead. None that go unto her return again,

neither take they hold of the paths of life. (Prov. v. 2.) "Her feet go down to death, and her steps take hold on hell;" therefore, O man, remove thy way far from her, and come not nigh the door of her house, "Lest thou give thine honour unto others, and thy years unto the cruel—lest strangers be filled with thy wealth, and thy labours be in the house of a stranger," and thou mourn at the last, when thy flesh and thy body are consumed (by loathsome disease), and remorse extort from thee the exclamation—"How have I hated instruction, and my heart despised reproof—I have not obeyed the voice of my teachers, nor inclined mine ear to them that instructed me!"

He who does not firmly resist the fair speeches of impudent and abandoned women, (Prov. vii. 21.) "goes after her as an ox to the slaughter, or a fool to the correction of the stocks; for her house is the way to hell, going down to the chambers of death." (Prov. ix. 17.) "The simple fool who turneth into her house, knoweth not that the dead are there, and that her guests are in the depths of hell." This strong language is dictated by divine wisdom, to confirm the resolution of those who have any regard for their own honour or welfare in this world, or any concern for the salvation of their souls.

(3.) And the same divine wisdom which so strongly dehorts men from a licentious life, recommends *honourable marriage and conjugal fidelity;* for man's ways are before the eyes of the Lord, and he pondereth all his goings.

(4.) Another path of wisdom pointed out in this Sacred Book, is *prudence and diligence* in temporal and secular concerns. An improvident thoughtlessness, carelessness about the future, is condemned by an allusion to that feeble insect the ant, Prov. vi. 6. "Go to the ant, thou sluggard, consider her ways and be wise, which having no guide, overseer, or ruler, provideth her meat in the summer, and gathereth her food in the harvest." If the feeble insect, without guide, overseer, or ruler, provides for itself, how inexcusable is it in a man to live in a careless, improvident manner, and squander in riot and dissipation, what should afford him support when he is sick or unemployed.

The happy effects of diligence and prudence are strongly expressed in these words, "Seest thou a man diligent in his business, he shall stand before kings, he shall not stand before mean men." The proof of this is every day seen, in the respectability to which well-principled, industrious men attain; whereas, to the sluggard or dissipated man, *poverty and want* come upon him as one that travelleth space, and terribly as the approach of an armed enemy whom he cannot resist.

(5.) A peaceable disposition, and living in harmony with other people, is pointed out as another path of wisdom. He is called a wicked man who soweth discord—but a soft answer turneth away wrath. The beginning of strife is as when one letteth out water; you cannot always stop it when you wish; "therefore leave off contention before it be meddled with."

(6.) And to this end useful conversation is enjoined, and the avoiding of tale-bearing, and excessive talking. (Prov. x. 19.) "In the multitude of words there wanteth not sin, but he that refraineth his lips is wise. The tongue of the just is as choice silver; the heart of the wicked is little worth; the lips of the righteous feed many; but fools die for want of wisdom. The tongue of the righteous useth knowledge aright, but the mouth of fools poureth out foolishness. A wholesome tongue is a tree of life, but perverseness therein is a breach of the spirit. The lips of the wise disperse knowledge, but the heart of the foolish doth not so."

A fool's lips enter into contention, and his mouth calleth for strokes. A fool's mouth is his destruction, and his lips are the snare of his soul. The words of a tale-bearer are as wounds, and they go down into the innermost parts of the belly.

"Answer not a fool according to his folly"—*i.e. not* in the same foolish manner; but answer him according to his folly, *i.e.* give him such an answer as his foolish speech requires to shew its folly, lest he be wise in his own conceit. Men, who by vicious bad language corrupt each other, and teach vice to young boys, have a great deal

to answer for beside their own sins: if a man cannot say much that is useful, he may at least forbear saying what is vicious and corrupting; there is no occasion to be eternally muttering and talking. And connected with good conversation—

(7.) *Truth* may be noticed. "Lying lips are an abomination to the Lord; but they that deal truly are his delight. The lip of truth shall be established for ever; but a lying tongue is but for a moment. A righteous man hateth lying, but a wicked liar is loathsome, and cometh to shame. The getting of treasures by a lying tongue, is a vanity tossed to and fro of them that seek death. A false witness shall not be unpunished, and he that speaketh lies shall perish." And with truth must be joined *sincerity:* "Faithful are the rebukes or censures of a friend, but the kisses or flatteries of an enemy are deceitful." "He that rebuketh or findeth fault with a man, shall find more favour than he that flattereth with the tongue." To *truth* and *sincerity*, will *honesty* be added, for "divers weights are an abomination to the Lord, and a false balance is not good."

(8.) Another of wisdom's paths, is the *keeping good company*. "He that walketh with wise and good men, shall be wise, but a companion of fools shall be destroyed. Go from the presence of a foolish man when thou perceivest not in him the words of knowledge. Make no friendship with an angry man, and with a furious man thou shalt not go."

(9.) *Contentment* is also a path of wisdom, for "better is a little with righteousness than great revenues without right; therefore be not envious against evil men (who are prosperous,) neither desire to be with them, for he that maketh haste to be rich shall not be innocent."

(10.) Finally, the path of wisdom requires *sobriety*, or the moderate use of inebriating liquors; for "wine is a mocker, strong drink is raging, and whosoever is deceived thereby, is not wise. Contentions, babbling, wounds without cause, redness of eyes, sorrow and wo," are the consequences of intoxication, and the drunkard and glutton shall come to poverty, and be the slaves of lewdness and perverse conduct.

Thus I have noticed *ten* of those paths which wisdom

pronounces *pleasant;* docility, firmness, honourable marriage, prudence, diligence, peaceable disposition, truth, useful conversation, good company, contentment, and sobriety. These, added to the fear of God, will render a man's life tolerably pleasant, under any circumstances, much more so than all the pleasures of sin can do under the most prosperous circumstances. The paths of folly, in which so many tread, are the opposite of these, and those who tread in them, are proud, unteachable mockers and scorners, silly dupes of designing men and women, or who themselves seduce and corrupt the innocent, having no real affection for any woman, and beloved by none; and imprudent, idle, and extravagant; and quarrelsome; liars, and deceitful, whose mouths are filled with impious and indecent language; companions of profligate people, discontented and murmuring against Providence, and seeking to drown their mental miseries in habits of intoxication; and who, in the midst of all these hateful and unhappy modes of living, have every reason to fear that misery awaits them after death. Now,

Although an entire deliverance from afflictions, of one kind or another, is not to be expected in this guilty world; it is easy to see, that in comparison of the paths of wicked folly, wisdom's ways are, indeed, ways of pleasantness, and all her paths are comparatively peace. Endeavour, then, O men, to remember the instructions of Divine Wisdom, and pray God, for Christ's sake to grant you the aid of his Holy Spirit, to avoid the broad road that leads to destruction, and to enter in at the strait gate that leads to eternal life. If you would remember these things, whether at sea or on shore, you would find them contribute to your daily comfort, and ensure your lasting happiness.

pretended science and philosophism, which set themselves in opposition to the religion of Jesus; but where in the tents of infidel philosophy, or in the temples of paganism, or in the mosques of mahomedanism, are to be found such sublime truths concerning God, such accurate statements concerning what man is; such gracious revelations of divine mercy; and such glorious hopes to them that walk uprightly, as are exhibited in thy lovely tabernacles, O Jehovah, God of Hosts!

But it is not privilege alone that is to be learned in Christian churches; the Lord said to Moses concerning the first tabernacle, "There will I meet with thee, and commune with thee of all things which I have *given thee in commandment* to the children of Israel." Christians, who should not forsake the assembling of themselves together, are to come together not only for prayer and praise, but also to hear what God the Lord will speak from his word in matters of duty, as well as in matters of privilege, and to exhort one another to love and to good works. Our attachment to the Saviour must be manifested by obedience to all his commandments. The Christian life, like that of our blessed Lord, should be a life of active benevolence, going about doing good. Not a life of monastic, selfish, and unsocial seclusion, which the folly of the human mind has every where suggested, as well in Pagan as in Christian lands. Oh no!—Apostolic, (which is the true primitive) Christianity, knows nothing of inactive, antisocial, selfish contemplation. Of the Holy Bible, nine tenths are made up of precepts and exhortations concerning man's duty to God, and to his fellow creatures. I trust, that on this occasion, whatever is right and expedient will be done: and to goad a willing mind, is not the practice that a generous nature approves.*

Remarks on another occasion.

And there is one duty of which it becomes me to put you in mind, viz. that of assisting, as God shall give ability, to

* A collection for the chapel was to be made.

The happy effects of diligence and prudence are strongly expressed in these words, "Seest thou a man diligent in his business, he shall stand before kings, he shall not stand before mean men." The proof of this is every day seen, in the respectability to which well-principled, industrious men attain; whereas, to the sluggard or dissipated man, *poverty and want* come upon him as one that travelleth apace, and terribly as the approach of an armed enemy whom he cannot resist.

(5.) A peaceable disposition, and living in harmony with other people, is pointed out as another path of wisdom. He is called a wicked man who soweth discord—but a soft answer turneth away wrath. The beginning of strife is as when one letteth out water; you cannot always stop it when you wish; "therefore leave off contention before it be meddled with."

(6.) And to this end useful conversation is enjoined, and the avoiding of tale-bearing, and excessive talking. (Prov. x. 19.) "In the multitude of words there wanteth not sin, but he that refraineth his lips is wise. The tongue of the just is as choice silver; the heart of the wicked is little worth; the lips of the righteous feed many; but fools die for want of wisdom. The tongue of the righteous useth knowledge aright, but the mouth of fools poureth out foolishness. A wholesome tongue is a tree of life, but perverseness therein is a breach of the spirit. The lips of the wise disperse knowledge, but the heart of the foolish doth not so."

A fool's lips enter into contention, and his mouth calleth for strokes. A fool's mouth is his destruction, and his lips are the snare of his soul. The words of a tale-bearer are as wounds, and they go down into the innermost parts of the belly.

"Answer not a fool according to his folly"—*i.e. not* in the same foolish manner; but answer him according to his folly, *i.e.* give him such an answer as his foolish speech requires to shew its folly, lest he be wise in his own conceit. Men, who by vicious bad language corrupt each other, and teach vice to young boys, have a great deal

to answer for beside their own sins: if a man cannot say much that is useful, he may at least forbear saying what is vicious and corrupting; there is no occasion to be eternally muttering and talking. And connected with good conversation—

(7.) *Truth* may be noticed. "Lying lips are an abomination to the Lord; but they that deal truly are his delight. The lip of truth shall be established for ever; but a lying tongue is but for a moment. A righteous man hateth lying, but a wicked liar is loathsome, and cometh to shame. The getting of treasures by a lying tongue, is a vanity tossed to and fro of them that seek death. A false witness shall not be unpunished, and he that speaketh lies shall perish." And with truth must be joined *sincerity*: "Faithful are the rebukes or censures of a friend, but the kisses or flatteries of an enemy are deceitful." "He that rebuketh or findeth fault with a man, shall find more favour than he that flattereth with the tongue." To *truth* and *sincerity*, will *honesty* be added, for "divers weights are an abomination to the Lord, and a false balance is not good."

(8.) Another of wisdom's paths, is the *keeping good company*. "He that walketh with wise and good men, shall be wise, but a companion of fools shall be destroyed. Go from the presence of a foolish man when thou perceivest not in him the words of knowledge. Make no friendship with an angry man, and with a furious man thou shalt not go."

(9.) *Contentment* is also a path of wisdom, for "better is a little with righteousness than great revenues without right; therefore be not envious against evil men (who are prosperous,) neither desire to be with them, for he that maketh haste to be rich shall not be innocent."

(10.) Finally, the path of wisdom requires *sobriety*, or the moderate use of inebriating liquors; for "wine is a mocker, strong drink is raging, and whosoever is deceived thereby, is not wise. Contentions, babbling, wounds without cause, redness of eyes, sorrow and wo," are the consequences of intoxication, and the drunkard and glutton shall come to poverty, and be the slaves of lewdness and perverse conduct.

Thus I have noticed *ten* of those paths which wisdom

pronounces *pleasant*; docility, firmness, honourable marriage, prudence, diligence, peaceable disposition, truth, useful conversation, good company, contentment, and sobriety. These, added to the fear of God, will render a man's life tolerably pleasant, under any circumstances, much more so than all the pleasures of sin can do under the most prosperous circumstances. The paths of folly, in which so many tread, are the opposite of these, and those who tread in them, are proud, unteachable mockers and scorners, silly dupes of designing men and women, or who themselves seduce and corrupt the innocent, having no real affection for any woman, and beloved by none; and imprudent, idle, and extravagant; and quarrelsome; liars, and deceitful, whose mouths are filled with impious and indecent language; companions of profligate people, discontented and murmuring against Providence, and seeking to drown their mental miseries in habits of intoxication; and who, in the midst of all these hateful and unhappy modes of living, have every reason to fear that misery awaits them after death. Now,

Although an entire deliverance from afflictions, of one kind or another, is not to be expected in this guilty world; it is easy to see, that in comparison of the paths of wicked folly, wisdom's ways are, indeed, ways of pleasantness, and all her paths are comparatively peace. Endeavour, then, O men, to remember the instructions of Divine Wisdom, and pray God, for Christ's sake to grant you the aid of his Holy Spirit, to avoid the broad road that leads to destruction, and to enter in at the strait gate that leads to eternal life. If you would remember these things, whether at sea or on shore, you would find them contribute to your daily comfort, and ensure your lasting happiness.

and his friends, Shadrach, Meshach, and Abednego, who would not worship the king's golden image, walked in the midst of the burning fiery furnace and felt no harm. They trusted that God would see meet to deliver them; but if not, they were prepared to suffer. Their courage and firm resistance to the royal mandate did not arise from a foreknowledge that they should be delivered; but from faith in the divine power, and submission to the divine wisdom. "Our God, said they, is able to deliver us from the burning fiery furnace," and out of thy hand, O king; "but if not"—if he should not see fit to do so, be it known unto thee, O king, that we will not serve thy gods, nor worship the golden image which thou hast set up. They trusted in God and were delivered. These examples shew that the divine government, or providence, extends to individuals, and if to some individuals, why not to all individuals? Individuals constitute nations, and great affairs arise from small beginnings. A general providence implies a particular providence, as effects imply a cause; or as the motion of a great machine implies attention to the minute wheels.

The character of Daniel, president of the empire; of Shadrach, and his two friends, who also held offices under government; of Nehemiah, cup-bearer to Artaxerxes, king of Persia; and the extraordinary circumstances which occurred to them, gave them, in all probability, such influence in the empire, as must have contributed to ameliorate the condition of the Jews in captivity, and, eventually, was the means of obtaining decrees for their restoration. Nor may we omit here the name of Esther, the captive Jewish orphan girl, who was raised by Providence to be queen of Persia, and the saviour of her nation. And be it observed, that the enemies of these just persons, of Daniel, of Shadrach, of Mordecai, and Esther, fell into the pit which they dug for the innocent. Daniel's malicious and intended murderers were themselves devoured by wild beasts; those who heated the furnace were themselves burnt; and wicked Haman was hanged on his own gallows; for God knoweth (however complicated the case) how to deliver the righ-

I have called, and ye refused; I have stretched out my hand, and no man regarded; but ye have set at nought all my counsel, and would none of my reproof: I also will laugh at your calamity; I will mock when your fear cometh; when your fear cometh as desolation, and your destruction cometh as a whirlwind; when distress and anguish cometh upon you:—for that they hated knowledge, and did not choose the fear of the Lord."

In these passages of Sacred Scripture, the good and the evil, the blessing and the curse, are set before us; the path of wisdom, and the path of folly; the different conduct and fate of the humble learner, and of the proud scorner. "A man's pride shall bring him low; but honour shall uphold the humble in spirit." (Prov. xxix. 23.) Therefore, (chap. iii. ver. 5.) "Trust in the Lord with all thy heart, and lean not to thine own understanding.—Be not wise in thine own eyes; but in all thy ways acknowledge the Almighty, and he will direct thy paths."

(2.) But the humble and teachable disposition so strongly inculcated, does not imply an easy acquiescence with whatever any body may suggest; quite the reverse! It is accompanied by a *firm resistance* to the enticements of evil men and bad women. (Prov. i. 10.) "My son, if sinners entice thee consent thou not." If they say, 'Cast in thy lot among us—let us all have one purse,' and so entice you to steal or to rob, "Walk not thou in the way with them: refrain thy foot from their path, for their feet run to evil, and make haste to shed blood."

(Prov. ii. 10.) "When wisdom entereth into thy heart and knowledge is pleasant to thy soul; discretion shall preserve thee, understanding shall keep thee, and deliver thee from the way of the evil man, from the man that speaketh froward things"—who rejoices to do evil, and delights in the frowardness of the wicked; and will deliver thee from the strange woman, from the abandoned woman, who flattereth with her words, who forsaketh the guide of her youth (her father or her husband,) and forgetteth the covenant of her God;—for her house inclineth unto death, and her paths unto the dead. None that go unto her return again,

neither take they hold of the paths of life. (Prov. v. 2.) "Her feet go down to death, and her steps take hold on hell;" therefore, O man, remove thy way far from her, and come not nigh the door of her house, "Lest thou give thine honour unto others, and thy years unto the cruel—lest strangers be filled with thy wealth, and thy labours be in the house of a stranger," and thou mourn at the last, when thy flesh and thy body are consumed (by loathsome disease), and remorse extort from thee the exclamation—"How have I hated instruction, and my heart despised reproof—I have not obeyed the voice of my teachers, nor inclined mine ear to them that instructed me!"

He who does not firmly resist the fair speeches of impudent and abandoned women, (Prov. vii. 21.) "goes after her as an ox to the slaughter, or a fool to the correction of the stocks; for her house is the way to hell, going down to the chambers of death." (Prov. ix. 17.) "The simple fool who turneth into her house, knoweth not that the dead are there, and that her guests are in the depths of hell." This strong language is dictated by divine wisdom, to confirm the resolution of those who have any regard for their own honour or welfare in this world, or any concern for the salvation of their souls.

(3.) And the same divine wisdom which so strongly dehorts men from a licentious life, recommends *honourable marriage and conjugal fidelity;* for man's ways are before the eyes of the Lord, and he pondereth all his goings.

(4.) Another path of wisdom pointed out in this Sacred Book, is *prudence and diligence* in temporal and secular concerns. An improvident thoughtlessness, carelessness about the future, is condemned by an allusion to that feeble insect the ant, Prov. vi. 6. "Go to the ant, thou sluggard, consider her ways and be wise, which having no guide, overseer, or ruler, provideth her meat in the summer, and gathereth her food in the harvest." If the feeble insect, without guide, overseer, or ruler, provides for itself, how inexcusable is it in a man to live in a careless, improvident manner, and squander in riot and dissipation, what should afford him support when he is sick or unemployed.

The happy effects of diligence and prudence are strongly expressed in these words, "Seest thou a man diligent in his business, he shall stand before kings, he shall not stand before mean men." The proof of this is every day seen, in the respectability to which well-principled, industrious men attain; whereas, to the sluggard or dissipated man, *poverty and want* come upon him as one that travelleth apace, and terribly as the approach of an armed enemy whom he cannot resist.

(5.) A peaceable disposition, and living in harmony with other people, is pointed out as another path of wisdom. He is called a wicked man who soweth discord—but a soft answer turneth away wrath. The beginning of strife is as when one letteth out water; you cannot always stop it when you wish; "therefore leave off contention before it be meddled with."

(6.) And to this end useful conversation is enjoined, and the avoiding of tale-bearing, and excessive talking. (Prov. x. 19.) "In the multitude of words there wanteth not sin, but he that refraineth his lips is wise. The tongue of the just is as choice silver; the heart of the wicked is little worth; the lips of the righteous feed many; but fools die for want of wisdom. The tongue of the righteous useth knowledge aright, but the mouth of fools poureth out foolishness. A wholesome tongue is a tree of life, but perverseness therein is a breach of the spirit. The lips of the wise disperse knowledge, but the heart of the foolish doth not so."

A fool's lips enter into contention, and his mouth calleth for strokes. A fool's mouth is his destruction, and his lips are the snare of his soul. The words of a tale-bearer are as wounds, and they go down into the innermost parts of the belly.

"Answer not a fool according to his folly"—*i.e. not* in the same foolish manner; but answer him according to his folly, *i.e.* give him such an answer as his foolish speech requires to shew its folly, lest he be wise in his own conceit. Men, who by vicious bad language corrupt each other, and teach vice to young boys, have a great deal

to answer for beside their own sins: if a man cannot say much that is useful, he may at least forbear saying what is vicious and corrupting; there is no occasion to be eternally muttering and talking. And connected with good conversation—

(7.) *Truth* may be noticed. "Lying lips are an abomination to the Lord; but they that deal truly are his delight. The lip of truth shall be established for ever; but a lying tongue is but for a moment. A righteous man hateth lying, but a wicked liar is loathsome, and cometh to shame. The getting of treasures by a lying tongue, is a vanity tossed to and fro of them that seek death. A false witness shall not be unpunished, and he that speaketh lies shall perish." And with truth must be joined *sincerity:* "Faithful are the rebukes or censures of a friend, but the kisses or flatteries of an enemy are deceitful." "He that rebuketh or findeth fault with a man, shall find more favour than he that flattereth with the tongue." To *truth* and *sincerity*, will *honesty* be added, for "divers weights are an abomination to the Lord, and a false balance is not good."

(8.) Another of wisdom's paths, is the *keeping good company*. "He that walketh with wise and good men, shall be wise, but a companion of fools shall be destroyed. Go from the presence of a foolish man when thou perceivest not in him the words of knowledge. Make no friendship with an angry man, and with a furious man thou shalt not go."

(9.) *Contentment* is also a path of wisdom, for "better is a little with righteousness than great revenues without right; therefore be not envious against evil men (who are prosperous,) neither desire to be with them, for he that maketh haste to be rich shall not be innocent."

(10.) Finally, the path of wisdom requires *sobriety*, or the moderate use of inebriating liquors; for "wine is a mocker, strong drink is raging, and whosoever is deceived thereby, is not wise. Contentions, babbling, wounds without cause, redness of eyes, sorrow and wo," are the consequences of intoxication, and the drunkard and glutton shall come to poverty, and be the slaves of lewdness and perverse conduct.

Thus I have noticed *ten* of those paths which wisdom

pronounces *pleasant;* docility, firmness, honourable marriage, prudence, diligence, peaceable disposition, truth, useful conversation, good company, contentment, and sobriety. These, added to the fear of God, will render a man's life tolerably pleasant, under any circumstances, much more so than all the pleasures of sin can do under the most prosperous circumstances. The paths of folly, in which so many tread, are the opposite of these, and those who tread in them, are proud, unteachable mockers and scorners, silly dupes of designing men and women, or who themselves seduce and corrupt the innocent, having no real affection for any woman, and beloved by none; and imprudent, idle, and extravagant; and quarrelsome; liars, and deceitful, whose mouths are filled with impious and indecent language; companions of profligate people, discontented and murmuring against Providence, and seeking to drown their mental miseries in habits of intoxication; and who, in the midst of all these hateful and unhappy modes of living, have every reason to fear that misery awaits them after death. Now,

Although an entire deliverance from afflictions, of one kind or another, is not to be expected in this guilty world; it is easy to see, that in comparison of the paths of wicked folly, wisdom's ways are, indeed, ways of pleasantness, and all her paths are comparatively peace. Endeavour, then, O men, to remember the instructions of Divine Wisdom, and pray God, for Christ's sake to grant you the aid of his Holy Spirit, to avoid the broad road that leads to destruction, and to enter in at the strait gate that leads to eternal life. If you would remember these things, whether at sea or on shore, you would find them contribute to your daily comfort, and ensure your lasting happiness.

pretended science and philosophism, which set themselves in opposition to the religion of Jesus; but where in the tents of infidel philosophy, or in the temples of paganism, or in the mosques of mahomedanism, are to be found such sublime truths concerning God, such accurate statements concerning what man is; such gracious revelations of divine mercy; and such glorious hopes to them that walk uprightly, as are exhibited in thy lovely tabernacles, O Jehovah, God of Hosts!

But it is not privilege alone that is to be learned in Christian churches; the Lord said to Moses concerning the first tabernacle, "There will I meet with thee, and commune with thee of all things which I have *given thee in commandment* to the children of Israel." Christians, who should not forsake the assembling of themselves together, are to come together not only for prayer and praise, but also to hear what God the Lord will speak from his word in matters of duty, as well as in matters of privilege, and to exhort one another to love and to good works. Our attachment to the Saviour must be manifested by obedience to all his commandments. The Christian life, like that of our blessed Lord, should be a life of active benevolence, going about doing good. Not a life of monastic, selfish, and unsocial seclusion, which the folly of the human mind has every where suggested, as well in Pagan as in Christian lands. Oh no!—Apostolic, (which is the true primitive) Christianity, knows nothing of inactive, antisocial, selfish contemplation. Of the Holy Bible, nine tenths are made up of precepts and exhortations concerning man's duty to God, and to his fellow creatures. I trust, that on this occasion, whatever is right and expedient will be done: and to goad a willing mind, is not the practice that a generous nature approves.*

Remarks on another occasion.

And there is one duty of which it becomes me to put you in mind, viz. that of assisting, as God shall give ability, to

* A collection for the chapel was to be made.

GOD THE SUPREME RULER.

DANIEL, IV. 32.

"*The most High ruleth in the kingdom of men.*"

HUMAN governments, whether the supreme authority be vested in a senate, a king, or an emperor, have, indeed, immense power over their fellow creatures; and the will of these governments, which thousands, or hundreds of thousands of armed men can enforce, seems, at times, quite irresistible. The absolute despots of Asia, and of other parts of the world, have often done whatever their caprice dictated with the persons and the property of their numerous subjects. And whilst millions have continually trembled at the oppressor's frown, the monarchs themselves have been puffed up with pride, and deemed themselves omnipotent as gods, and have forgotten their dependance on the Almighty; or have practically acted, as if they were amenable to no higher authority. The sovereign of Babylon,* that mighty monarch, whilst walking on an elevated terrace, and surveying the great city which he had embellished, said, either mentally or audibly, with vain self-complacency, Dan. iv. 30. "Is not this great Babylon that I have built, for the house of the kingdom, by the might of my power, and for the honour of my majesty." But whilst the word was in the king's mouth, there fell a voice from Heaven, denouncing a punishment of his pride and self-sufficiency, which punishment would last till he should learn to know and acknowledge, that "The most High ruleth in the

* Nebuchadnezzar is called Nabuchodnosor II. by Rollin, reigned over Chaldea, Assyria, Arabia, Syria, and Palestine, forty-three years. Ante J. C. 603.

kingdom of men;" and He giveth earthly thrones to "whomsoever he will;" and sometimes setteth up over nations "the basest of men." The doctrine taught is, that the most High God is the supreme ruler over the nations and the kingdoms of the earth; and as his wisdom and justice may direct, he roots out and pulls down, or builds up and plants; no power on earth can obstruct his designs. The illustration of this much-neglected truth, I shall draw from a slight survey of the Book of Daniel, in which our text lies, and make such inferences in passing, as may tend to instruct, reprove, or admonish.

I. Daniel himself, the writer of this book, strikingly exemplifies how the *Divine Ruler can and does employ some of all ranks and conditions of men as his special and beloved servants on earth.* Kings and courtiers, shepherds and fishermen, philosophers and unlettered men, have, according to Sacred Writ and the history of the church, all been especially employed by divine Providence. The kings, David and Solomon, were writers of parts of divine Revelation; Daniel and Joseph, were courtiers or statesmen, under heathen monarchs; and this Daniel was twice declared, by a divine message, to be "a man greatly beloved" in the heavenly world;—a clear proof that no secular duties, nor any station in society, is incompatible with the service of God. Daniel was, when a young lad, carried away (as a prisoner by a victorious army that had ravaged his native country,) to a foreign land, and there appointed to the menial duties of the royal harem. And from the age of eighteen till ninety, he served the pagan princes of successive dynasties with fidelity, and at the same time preserved a conduct that was pleasing to Heaven. The Jews, of late years, being grieved that Daniel's prophesies point so clearly to Jesus of Nazareth, as the true Messiah, will not allow him the title of *prophet*, alleging as a reason, that he lived as a courtier, instead of living secluded from mankind, as did the prophets Elijah and others. But Heaven did not, because he was a courtier, withhold from him the gift of prophesy; and therefore how futile is it in man to with-

hold the name. Beside, our Saviour has designated him "Daniel *the prophet*," Matt. xxiv. 15. There are those in our day who despise the poor and unlettered, as if Heaven never employed them, as he did formerly the prophet Amos, who was a herdsman, and the fishermen of Galilee, who were the first Missionaries of the Saviour; and there are those in the lower walks of life, who seem to think that kings and statesmen cannot be faithful servants of the most High. But a review of sacred history, and human records, will shew, that there is no reason for such a supposition; nor is it often necessary to quit one's station in society, in order to serve the Lord; but it is practicable to serve him wherever we are, whilst we faithfully purpose, as did Daniel, not to defile ourselves, nor to be unfaithful in the things that concern our God. Daniel was a man of prayer, and neither flattery nor frowns could turn him aside. He would not desist from prayer to save his life; although it would have been no very artful subterfuge to substitute for his *usual* devotions, mental prayer, unknown to man; or to have retired to his closet, and shut to the door. But no, when his enemies at court, who envied the influence of the captive Jew, obtained the foolish and impious decree, that no person in the empire should for thirty days ask a petition of God or man, but only from the king; Daniel, *knowing the decree* was signed, went into his house, kneeled upon his knees three times a day, *with his chamber windows open* towards Jerusalem, and prayed and gave thanks before his God, *as he did aforetime*. For he thought it not right to conceal his prayers on this occasion, nor to *act* a lie, or do what implied an untruth, as a discontinuance of his usage would have been. Whilst praying, he was discovered, and suffered the penalty of his disobedience to the king's commands, for he obeyed a higher authority. He was cast in amongst lions, but the lions in the den could not hurt him: For the most High hath power, either to employ the ordinary course of nature in his government, or to stop it, or to change it, as he sees fit. He bids the ravenous lions not devour, and the fiery furnace not burn, and it is done. Daniel came forth unhurt from the den;

and his friends, Shadrach, Meshach, and Abednego, who would not worship the king's golden image, walked in the midst of the burning fiery furnace and felt no harm. They trusted that God would see meet to deliver them; but if not, they were prepared to suffer. Their courage and firm resistance to the royal mandate did not arise from a foreknowledge that they should be delivered; but from faith in the divine power, and submission to the divine wisdom. "Our God, said they, is able to deliver us from the burning fiery furnace," and out of thy hand, O king; "but if not"—if he should not see fit to do so, be it known unto thee, O king, that we will not serve thy gods, nor worship the golden image which thou hast set up. They trusted in God and were delivered. These examples shew that the divine government, or providence, extends to individuals, and if to some individuals, why not to all individuals? Individuals constitute nations, and great affairs arise from small beginnings. A general providence implies a particular providence, as effects imply a cause; or as the motion of a great machine implies attention to the minute wheels.

The character of Daniel, president of the empire; of Shadrach, and his two friends, who also held offices under government; of Nehemiah, cup-bearer to Artaxerxes, king of Persia; and the extraordinary circumstances which occurred to them, gave them, in all probability, such influence in the empire, as must have contributed to ameliorate the condition of the Jews in captivity, and, eventually, was the means of obtaining decrees for their restoration. Nor may we omit here the name of Esther, the captive Jewish orphan girl, who was raised by Providence to be queen of Persia, and the saviour of her nation. And be it observed, that the enemies of these just persons, of Daniel, of Shadrach, of Mordecai, and Esther, fell into the pit which they dug for the innocent. Daniel's malicious and intended murderers were themselves devoured by wild beasts; those who heated the furnace were themselves burnt; and wicked Haman was hanged on his own gallows; for God knoweth (however complicated the case) how to deliver the righ-

teous, and reserve the unjust to their deserved punishment. I observe in the

Second place, that the past fulfilment of many prophecies, should lead us confidently to expect the accomplishment of those yet future. The Book of Daniel begins by stating, that "*the Lord gave*" Jehoiakim, king of Judah, (for the Lord reigneth and *gives* empires to whom he will,) into the hand of Nebuchadnezzar, king of Babylon. And Daniel prefaced his interpretation of that king's dream, by saying to him, "The God of Heaven *hath* GIVEN thee a kingdom, power, and strength, and glory."—And to a descendant of his, king Belshazzar, he said, "The most High God GAVE Nebuchadnezzar, thy father, a kingdom, and majesty, and glory, and honour; and for the majesty that God gave him, all people, nations, and languages, trembled and feared before him—whom he would he slew, and whom he would he kept alive, and whom he would he set up, and whom he would he put down." How striking is this description of the great warriors and despots of the earth. But (says the faithful statesman) when the king's heart was lifted up, and his mind hardened in pride, he was *deposed* by Providence from his kingly throne; and they took his glory from him, and he was driven from the sons of men; and his heart was made like the beasts; his reason departed from him, and his dwelling was with the wild asses; they fed him with grass like oxen, and his body was wet with the dew of heaven—till he knew that the *most High God ruleth* in the kingdom of men, and that *He appointeth over* it whomsoever he will." And then, adds the aged courtier, Daniel, (speaking from himself,) "And thou, O Belshazzar, hast not humbled thy heart, though thou knewest all this, but hast lifted up thyself against the Lord of Heaven."—Thou hast profaned the sacred vessels of his house, hast praised the gods of silver, gold, brass, iron, wood, and stone, but the God in whose hand thy breath is, and whose are all thy ways, who has entire controul over thee, thou hast not glorified. God hath numbered thy kingdom and finished it; thou art weighed in the balances and found wanting; thy kingdom is divided, and *given* to the Medes and Persians. In that very night was Belshazzar, king of the Chaldeans, slain, and Darius, the Mede, took the kingdom. In this was the doctrine of our text verified, and thus Daniel lived to see the end of that first monarchy, concerning which he received divine revelations. He lived, too, to the time of the return of the captivity of which Jeremiah had spoken so decidedly, whose prophesies Daniel studied, and for the fulfilment of which he prayed.

The present generation can, by the light of history, see the fulfilment of other parts of the prophesy in the dissolution of the ancient Persian, the Macedonian, and the Roman empires; and we now see that *kingdom set up*, which is described as an everlasting kingdom—the Spiritual kingdom of the Messiah, to whom " is given dominion and glory;" that " *all peoples, and nations, and languages, should serve him.*" (Dan. vii. 14.) All dominions shall eventually serve and obey him, (chap. vii. ver. 27.) The stone cut out without hands, which smote the emblematic image, became a great mountain, and *filled the whole earth.* This stone denoted Christ's kingdom, which the God of heaven set up " during the prevalence of the Roman authority," (*Scott,*) " and which shall never be destroyed, nor left to other people; but shall break in pieces, and consume all (Pagan and Anti-christian) kingdoms, and it shall stand for ever." The fulfilment, in such an extraordinary manner, of the predictions contained in Daniel's book, proves that he spake by inspiration of the Almighty; and since the Most High hath, in successive ages, accomplished the things foretold, the present generation has the strongest possible evidence, that the things not yet done, shall in due time be likewise accomplished. " For the Most High God ruleth in the kingdom of man."

It has appeared to me a strange question, which some professing Christians have put to me, viz. whether it was likely that certain Asiatic countries would *eventually* be evangelized? The prophecies now quoted and referred to, seem so clearly and decidedly to intimate, that the God of Heaven designs that the *kingdom* which he hath set up shall be *universal,* that any doubts of the *eventual universality* of Messiah's reign, appear to imply a doubt whether Omnipotence can effect the design which Heaven has formed. It appears to imply the existence of the same sort of *credulity* which is so frequently combated in this book, viz. *a belief* that the *earth* rules, and not that "the Heavens do rule;"—it implies a belief that the Most High does *not* rule over the nations, and that he *cannot* give them to whom he will; that the human heart cannot be stirred up to will and to do what he ultimately designs, or that he cannot crush all his determined enemies under his feet. Unless people harbour the secret belief of the weakness of Omnipotence, why array a host of objections about the prejudices of natives, their everlasting attachment to ancient usages, the difficulty of their languages, the hostility of pagan governments? &c. In the lapse of ages since Daniel wrote, have no inveterate prejudices against Christ's Gospel been removed? Have no ancient usages been deserted? Have no hard languages been learned? Have no hostile empires been overthrown? Where are the empires represented by the great image—the head of gold, the arms of silver, the body of brass, and the legs of iron? The gold, silver, brass, and iron, *i. e.* the the Babylonian, Persian, Grecian, and Roman empires, *have* all been broken in pieces, by "the stone cut out without hands;" this has been effected, and who shall hinder that stone, which has broken to pieces so many hostile powers from becoming a great mountain and *filling the whole earth!* The Lord God omnipotent reigneth; hath he said, and will he not do it! What Christian dares contradict and blaspheme, by surmising there *are some* peoples and nations, and languages, who will not, and can never be made to serve him? Here the question may be set at rest—has Heaven declared that "*all* peoples, and nations, and languages, shall serve" the Son of Man—the King of Zion. The sure word of prophesy answers in the affirmative; speak then no more of difficulties, nor ever doubt that the thing spoken shall eventually be accomplished, for we repeat the reason, the Most High ruleth in the kingdom of men, and none can stay his hand, nor check him by the impious question—What doest thou?

But then it may be asked, do you anticipate an universal Christian monarchy? No. The Messiah himself hath declared that his *kingdom is not of this world:* Jesus reigns in the hearts of his subjects, and their obedience to him is spiritual. The Jews who expected the Messiah to appear as a temporal prince, were disappointed. The Millenarians of the fourth century, who looked for a temporal reign of the Saviour in Judea, and the delights of a terrestrial paradise, looked in vain; the crusades of Christian princes to recover, by force of arms, the Holy Land, were not made successful; the aim at universal sovereignty by the Roman Pontiffs has been nugatory. But still the Saviour's kingdom has wonderfully increased. If the Messiah were a temporal prince, then might his servants fight. But bodily subjection in his kingdom does not make a man a subject, and physical force cannot conquer the mind. The weapons used in his wars are not carnal, they are spiritual—truth and knowledge. The king's command to his servants is—"Go into all nations and proclaim the Gospel." This, and this only, is the weapon to be employed for bringing the nations into subjection to the Prince of Peace. We now pass on to another remark—It is right to pray for the accomplishment of promises.

III. The prophet, to whom was revealed so clearly the certainty of things then future, says, (Dan. ix. 1.) "In the first year of Darius, who was king over the realm of the Chaldeans, I, Daniel, understood by books the number of the years whereof the word of the Lord came to Jeremiah the prophet, that he would accomplish seventy years in the desolations of Jerusalem; and I set my face unto the Lord God, to seek by prayer and supplications, with fasting, and sackcloth and ashes." But says an objector, Why pray for what was promised? would it not be done whether he prayed or not? This is the undutiful language of a hard impenitent heart, of a proud and disobedient spirit, which always severs what God in wisdom has joined together; human duty and the divine operation, the means and the end. Daniel was a patriot and a pious man; in his prayer he, by a confession of the sins of his countrymen of all ranks, acknowledged the justice of God, and magnified the divine faithfulness, by a reference to the law of Moses, where all the evil that had actually befallen Judah and Jerusalem, was, in case of disobedience, clearly foretold. He adored the just and holy God, and being encouraged by promises of restoration, he, as a man who loved his country, dutifully prayed, that the promised restoration might speedily be effected; O Lord, said he, *defer* not. That man cares little for any anticipated good who will not ask for it. Is there no moral fitness visible in the creature imploring blessings from the Creator? in the sinner supplicating forgiveness? And if Daniel felt a deep interest in, and prayed for his country, that the mercy promised should be conferred; shall Christians *as men*, feel nothing for *human kind;* nor ever pray that the mercy promised to all nations may be soon conferred. If our hearts feel no interest in the prosperity and enlargement of the Messiah's kingdom, it is sufficient to excite a doubt whether we be, indeed, subjects of that kingdom. But, further—

Heaven is pleased to work by the instrumentality of men; and the revealed will of God should induce all his people to use means to effect that which is revealed as Heaven's final design. It is a strange perversion to interpret the declarations of the king's intentions, as a sort of interdict on all his subjects, forbidding them to use any means to forward the accomplishment of those declared designs. Heaven, no doubt, can effect the conversion of the nations without our aid; but have those persons, who (in the spirit of inhumanity and disaffection) will not come to the help of the Lord, and of their fellow sinners, any reason to expect his approbation? When God's servants declare, according to the Scriptures, that it is the Lord's purpose that all nations shall serve Christ, and that the Lord alone can convert the soul; there are those who immediately infer, that all human means are to be neglected, and expect that heaven will, without means, miraculously change the hearts of men. But the Bible does not sanction this inference, nor the notion thus entertained.

When the time came that the Almighty would deliver Israel out of Egypt, he employed Moses and Aaron; and when he would restore the captives from Babylon, although we are assured that he stirred up the spirit of Cyrus, king of Persia, to rebuild the temple, there is every reason to believe that Daniel's name and influence were the means of leading to that event; and the Apostles were "workers together with God." Indeed, this doctrine of human agency being employed by Heaven, is so fully taught in Sacred Scripture, that those pagan princes who have punished his people, and other nations, as well as those who have served them, are called his servants. In Ezek. xxix. 18. it is thus written—"Son of man, Nebuchadnezzar, king of Babylon, caused his army to serve a great service against Tyrus—yet had he no wages, nor his army, for the service that he had served. I have, therefore, given the land of Egypt to them, because they served for me, saith the Lord God." And Cyrus is, by the mouth of Isaiah, called the Lord's anointed, and his shepherd, who would perform the Lord's pleasure concerning Jerusalem. Having the promises, let us, therefore, pray and work, for eventually, our labour shall not be in vain in the Lord. False theories always lead to extremes. Those err egregiously who trust solely to human efforts, and (as some do) deride appeals to heaven for the out-pouring of the Holy Spirit; and those who affirm, that conversion being Heaven's work, the use of means is unnecessary, and may be neglected, do not less err from the truth.

In matters that concern our individual salvation, as well as in what concerns the kingdom of our Saviour, let no theory or system prevent our praying and working; but let us be encouraged by the promise, that he will give the Holy Spirit to them that ask him; and since it is God that worketh in us, let us work out our own salvation with fear and trembling. Finally, we observe,

IV. The Lord has not deserted any nation. It is remarkable that Heaven vouchsafed such a revelation of future events to a pagan monarch, as was contained

L

in Nebuchadnezzar's dream; and from this we may learn, that although the Almighty set apart Abraham's posterity as a peculiar people, and for important purposes, he at no period forsook the rest of the nations, but ruled over them in justice and mercy, giving them rain from heaven, and fruitful seasons, filling their hearts with food and gladness. They have been the Lord's servants for judgment or for mercy; and some of them, as Cyrus, have been expressly called by name, and girded for their work, although they have not known him. And though it must be allowed, that ignorance, and iniquity, and cruelty, abound amongst the nations, there is yet amongst many of the heathen, a spirit of faith that the "Heavens do rule," and that man is accountable to superior powers; and their consciences either accuse or exonerate them. They have, many of them, an accurate sense of natural justice between man and man; and they teach often, as we do, (whatever their practice may be,) truth, benevolence, chastity, and charity. I speak generally of what I have seen and read in modern pagan books—to this praise there are particular exceptions, similar to what is the case in the nations of Christendom: the heathen of that part of the world where I have been, may be divided into three classes, viz. those who believe in Providence, and endeavour, in some degree, to do what they *think* right; next, those who acknowledge the doctrine in theory, but disregard it in practice, as profligate professors of Christianity do; and thirdly, those who deny the doctrine of Providence, and profess atheism, and annihilation at death. The Chinese divide their sects into *three*: two of them, called the Budh and the Taou sects, are religionists, who believe in gods, separate spirits, and a future state of rewards and punishments; and the third sect, the followers of Kung-foo-tsze, or, as he is called in Europe, *Confucius*, who doubt the existence of gods, deny a future state, and consequently any other rewards or punishments than the natural consequences of vice in this life. The *Téen*, or heaven, of which they speak, is not God, but nature. They teach the practice of truth, justice, and benevolence, to promote personal, domestic, and national happiness; and for the dignity which it confers on man; whom it elevates, they say, to a sort of equality with that great power in nature, the Heavens. Heaven, earth, and sage men are, according to them, three *equals*, and co-workers, essential to each other. We have, to-day, allowed that Heaven condescends to employ men; but they blasphemously teach that Heaven cannot dispense with the sage's services.

The heathen have the means of inferring the being and perfections of God from his works; but in this matter their foolish heart is darkened, and they commonly change his glory into a corruptible image. They have knowledge enough to convince them of sin, but of the means of obtaining the remission of sin, they have no correct information; therefore, apart from all other considerations, a benevolent heart will ever delight in using means to convey to them revealed religion, and thereby communicate the knowledge of God, and of his Christ. The character of pagan countries, like the character of Christendom, is black enough, it need not be exaggerated; nor should the little knowledge and morality they have amongst them be *over-rated*, as has been done by some persons, who would discourage, and if they had power, would absolutely prohibit all efforts to evangelize them. It is a fact, that there are many of the heathen more correct men than many people called Christians; and this is frequently the case with the nominal Christians in small colonies in pagan countries, where the check of public opinion rests on the natives, but is removed from the foreigners. And what crime can be named that does not exist, and even abound, in Christendom! All this is granted, but the comparison should not be between profligate nominal Christians, and a few of the best of the heathen; but between them and the Christians who adopt the principles, imbibe the spirit, and practice the precepts of their religion. And, indeed, the man who has not done this, however well educated, or however high his station in society, is not a competent judge of the merits of this question. I really do not argue, that his nominal Christianity makes him a whit better or happier than the paganism of India or China does the natives of those regions. If the principles of Christianity do not regulate his conduct, purify his heart, bring him near to God, moderate him in prosperity, and soothe him in affliction—in what respect is he a Christian? The merely looking at food upon the table, will not nourish, and strengthen, and make healthy and comfortable, the man who does not choose to eat of it. To him the best and the worst food are alike; but, all must allow, that such a man is not a fit judge of the matter. However, I will not pursue this subject. We should all do well to remember that, as St. Paul said, he is not a Jew who is one merely outwardly. So, the merely being born in Christendom, does not necessarily make us Christians, or real subjects of Messiah's kingdom; still it should also be remembered, that we thereby enjoy great advantages, for which we must be accountable; and if neglected or despised, it may be more tolerable in the day of judgment, for the men of heathen lands than for us.

The king Nebuchadnezzar, after he was recovered from his deplorable state of madness, published a decree, to inform his empire of the signs and wonders that the High God wrought towards him; in this decree he states, that when his understanding returned to him, he "Blessed the Most High, and praised and honoured him that liveth for ever and ever; the king of heaven, whose works are truth, and his ways judgment, and those that walk in pride he is able to abase:—before him all the inhabitants of the earth are reputed as nothing, and he doeth according to his will in the army of heaven, and among the inhabitants of the earth." This is now the language of the same man, who had before set up the lofty image of gold, and commanded all his subjects to worship it, on pain of being burnt to death; and who impiously demanded—who that god was, that could deliver out of his hand. How altered the language! How changed the man! The penitentiary decree which he published, is thought an evidence of his conversion to God—but of that subject man cannot speak with certainty. However, we may infer from what is related, that no change is too hard for the Lord to effect; and therefore, since he ruleth over all, none need despair, however great the difficulties in the eventual accomplishment of his promises. Let individual Christians, and let all the churches in all lands, and in all ages, praise and honour him, for he liveth for ever and ever; his dominion is an everlasting dominion, and his kingdom is from generation to generation.

My fellow Christians, before I close, let me recommend the application of the doctrine of our text to your personal and domestic concerns. The *Most High ruleth: the Lord reigneth:* our affairs are not left to blind chance: it is not an enemy who governs the world. Satan is a powerful and cunning adversary; but he is not supreme. The Lord's arm is omnipotent; he can defend, and support, and carry us safely through all dangers and difficulties. Live near to God and then you are safe.

Are there any here who live at a distance from God? How insecure!—Are there any who set God at defiance? Oh, what madness!—Oh, my brother! my sister! acknowledge the Divine Power, and submit to his just dominion, and to his gracious and paternal rule, and then no human nor infernal enemy can do you lasting harm. Impenitent sinner! tremble for thy fate, for neither riches, nor influence, nor health, nor youth, can secure thee against God. Nor rocks, nor hills, falling on thee, can hide thee from the awful effects of his justice. There is no darkness, nor shadow of death, where the workers of iniquity may hide themselves. But in Jesus, the Redeemer, is to be found for the penitent a hiding place. Let his love melt thine impenitent heart; flee by faith to him and thou too wilt be safe.

Remarks at Dr. Waugh's Chapel, March 28, 1824.

Your venerable pastor, this afternoon, in reference to the pecuniary aid of British Christians towards the enlargement of the Redeemer's kingdom, used the word "generosity." Now, at the risk of being called a caviller, I do object to the use of this word, because but little has been done by us, and that little is done for Jesus Christ. Is the propagation of the Gospel not his cause! Is not the support of Gospel ordinances in this land his cause! Now, try how it will sound for us to talk of *generosity* to Jesus Christ; who, (as many of you heard well illustrated this afternoon,) "*gave* HIMSELF *a sacrifice for us,*" and is set forth a propitiation for our sins. Churches, or Christian Societies are not only designed for their own edification, but also to promote the furtherance of the Gospel. And if we give a fiftieth or a hundredth part of our income, and a hundredth part of our time to this cause, shall we call such doings—*generosity!* Alas, for the low feeling of the churches and of the ministers in this matter. How few of the ministers devote themselves to the enlargement of the Saviour's kingdom, beyond the comforts of home and their own country; and how few Christians make their persons, and their labours, and their property, whether much or little, *subservient* to the cause of Christ. Is not St. Paul's complaint still true in a very great degree, notwithstanding all the stir and activity of British Churches—" All seek their own, not the things which are Jesus Christ's?" That a reasonable portion of what God hath given us, be employed by us, in supporting and diffusing the blessed Gospel, is a solemn duty, which no Christian man or woman may innocently leave undone. It should not be called *charity* or *generosity*. Shall we have the ordinances of religion, even to satiety and loathing, and not help our starving brethren in pagan lands? Alas, for the selfishness of Christians. By such meagre doings, how can we have the heart to pray, Thy kingdom come? But it will come—we may be selfish, but help will arise from some other quarter; for the Most High ruleth in the kingdom of men, and his resources are inexhaustible.

Address at Newcastle-on-Tyne—High Bridge, Church of Scotland Chapel.

More than thirty years have elapsed, since, in this house of prayer, he who this night addresses you, attended as a child, the ministry of the Gospel; and then, by God's blessing, had his mind gradually imbued with the principles of our holy religion. In addition to the instruction given from the pulpit, he was required to commit to memory portions of Holy Writ, hymns of praise and adoration, and the form of sound words sanctioned by the Scottish Church: to these were added domestic instruction, and the many prayers of a father, to whom prayer was a delight. The child of that period has been, in the course of Divine Providence, conducted to distant regions, to a people of a hard language and a strange speech; there to use means of conveying to the people the treasures of divine truth and mercy, which have been entrusted to the churches by Almighty God, for the salvation of a lost world;—he has assisted materially in rendering Moses and the Prophets, Christ and the Apostles, legible, in the mother-tongue of hundreds of millions of our fellow creatures, our brethren and our sisters of the great human family. And he who was then instructed here, and, a bashful boy, stood in that spot, to be publicly catechised, now stands before you to bear witness to the grace, and mercy, and faithfulness of God our Saviour:—he stands before you as an instance of divine goodness; as an example of the benefit of early religious instruction; as an encouragement to the fathers and mothers of families in this congregation, to spare no pains in the religious education of their children; and he stands before the youths of this congregation as a stimulus to those, here present, to listen to the voice of heaven-derived truth, conveyed by their parents, their spiritual pastors, and by the Bible itself; for all these co-operate, being accompanied by the energies of the Holy Spirit, in convincing of sin, in awakening the conscience, in imparting spiritual life, and quickening those who are dead in trespasses and sins.

Your preacher has long been deprived of the benefit of Christian ordinances in a pagan land, and he has learned to value them more than he ever before did; and he would that all here present were more and more convinced, and were at all times more sensible of their inestimable worth, that they might more cheerfully support them at home, and lend their assistance to send them abroad. This land of churches, of Sabbaths, and of Bibles, is, in comparison of many regions, a truly happy land. And how awful the condemnation of those of us will be, who despise, or neglect, or abuse such inestimable privileges! May it be yours, my friends, rightly to appreciate them, and to improve them! Especially do I rejoice, that there are so many in this congregation who care for the religious education of the children, and that the children delight in learning wisdom's ways. In the distant regions beyond the Ganges, and in the land of the "rising sun,"* children do not enjoy those spiritual advantages which children in this country enjoy, not because Heaven has withheld the means, as many impiously suppose; but because of the selfishness of Christians, which has prevented them from using the means in their power, to communicate those privileges to others. I hope brighter days are near at hand, when the churches will all exert themselves more in the great duty of disseminating the Gospel, than they have ever yet done. When Cain's sullen selfish speech—"Am I my brother's keeper?" shall be reversed, and Christians shall all acknowledge the sacred solemn duty of caring for their brethren of mankind, irrespective of geographical limits; for God has made of "ONE *blood*," all nations of men—and all men are brethren; even the Pagan Chinese maintain the principle, (whatever their practice may be,) that *(Tëen hëa wei yih këa)* "The whole world is but one family."

* *Jih-pun*, or Japan, denotes, in Chinese, "The source of day."

DISCOURSE XIII.

DELIVERED AT WINDSOR CHAPEL, NEAR MANCHESTER, OCT. 31, 1824.

THE CHURCH AMIABLE.

PSALM LXXXIV. 1.

"*How amiable are thy tabernacles, O Lord of Hosts!*"

When the posterity of Abraham were, by the hand of Moses, delivered from that state of slavery to which the Egyptians had reduced them, and were crossing the deserts of Arabia, proceeding to the land of promise, a *spacious tent* was, by divine command, erected in the wilderness, to be at once a palace for the Divine Presence as Israel's king, and a place of the most solemn public worship; this tent, set up in the wilderness, was the first Tabernacle. "Let them make me a sanctuary," said the Almighty, "that I may dwell among them."—"And there," said Jehovah to his servant Moses, "will I meet with thee, and I will commune with thee, from above the mercy seat, from between the two cherubim, (which are upon the Ark of the Testimony,) of all things which I give thee in command, unto the children of Israel." This Tabernacle was carried by the Israelites into Canaan, and during about five hundred years, continued the place of public worship, to which the several tribes resorted, till it was succeeded by the magnificent temple reared by king Solomon.

The Psalm which I have taken as the subject of discourse on this occasion, was written by king David, when expelled from Jerusalem, by his abandoned and rebellious son Absalom. In it the pious and afflicted monarch, agreeably to his usually devout manner, expresses his ardent attachment to the House of God. A pious commentator* has thus rendered the whole Psalm—

"How lovely are thy tabernacles,
O Jehovah, God of Hosts!
My soul longeth, yea, languisheth,
For the courts of Jehovah!
My heart and my flesh cry out for the living God!
Yea, as the sparrow findeth a house
And the swallow a nest for herself,
Where she may lay her young;
So I seek thine altars, Jehovah God of Hosts,
My King and my God.

Happy they who dwell in thy house,
They will be for ever praising thee.
Happy the men whose strength thou art,
Confidence reigns in their hearts.
Though they pass through a desolate valley,
Yet shall they drink from a fountain:
Yea, the rain shall cover it with blessings;
They shall go from strength to strength,
Till each appeareth before God in Zion.

O Jehovah, God of hosts, hear my prayer;
O God our shield, behold and regard
The person of thine anointed.
For better is a day in thy courts,
Than a thousand *spent elsewhere!*
I had rather be a door-keeper
In the house of my God,
Than dwell in the tents of the wicked.
For a sun and a shield is God, Jehovah.
Jehovah will give grace and glory;
No good thing will he withhold
From those who walk uprightly.

O Jehovah, God of Hosts,
Happy is the man who trusteth in thee!

* Boothroyd.

Now, this beautiful ode, expressive of the delight which the inspired penman took in the place where God was pleased graciously to reveal himself, and descriptive of the benefits and the bliss derived from an attendance there, is applicable to Christian churches, consisting of redeemed and regenerated persons; and also to the edifices where they assemble to worship God and to learn his will. And both the ancient Jewish Tabernacle, and the Christian Church, are emblematic of heaven, which is called by St. Paul, the greater and more perfect tabernacle, not made with hands, into which Christ, the great High Priest, not by blood of goats and calves, but by his own blood, has entered, having obtained eternal redemption for us.

An assembly of real believers constitutes a church, a spiritual temple composed of living stones—of which temple, the Divine Redeemer is the chief corner-stone. In such a church God dwells and communes with his people. The priests of this temple are the ministers of Jesus Christ;—"Wise-hearted men, in whom the Lord puts wisdom and understanding, to know how to work for the service of the sanctuary, according to all that the Lord hath commanded." (Exod. xxx. 1.) By the instrumentality of these men, "opening and alleging," from the Sacred Scriptures, the infinitely important, and inexpressibly gracious truths of divine revelation, the glorious perfections and the merciful designs of the Almighty, are exhibited or manifested to the children of men. And by the devotional parts of the Christian service, men unite in humble confessions, petitions, and thanksgivings to the Supreme Judge, the Divine Father, and bountiful benefactor of mankind. If you, my fellow Christians, who delight in God's house, had been exiled from it, and had seen nothing but pagan temples rising in its stead, you would have been able to enter more fully into the feelings of the Psalmist, when he exclaimed—"How amiable are thy tabernacles, O Lord of Hosts!" Then, instead of the spiritual presence of the living and true God, which you here enjoy, you would there have, perhaps, a carved image of something merely human, or brutal, or ludicrous, or obscene, set up as the object of worship and of prayer.

Instead of the soul-cheering development of the heaven-derived plans of mercy, founded on the sacrifice and atonement of God our Saviour; yonder, there are only the human and heart-chilling fictions that require man, ever-sinning man, to atone for his own sin; a never-to-be-effected work, which is productive only of disappointment, and remorse, and sorrow; or else of false hopes, which will eventually leave the sinner in unutterable despair. Instead of that sweet fellowship which true Christians enjoy when they go to the House of God in company; other lands have only the selfishness of solitary superstition, on the one hand, or licentious crowds at frantic festivals, carrying in procession, or hurrying towards, their idol gods. How lovely are thy tabernacles, O Lord of Hosts, in comparison of these! Alas, how much undervalued by those who enjoy the privilege of attending them! and by how many in this land neglected and despised. There is reason to apprehend, that even pious people do not usually value, as they deserve, the blessings derived to themselves and their children, from God's house of prayer, and Christian ordinances there dispensed; and this undervaluing of them arises, as is the case in other matters, from the abundance of the blessing.

Instead of having to travel from other districts and remote provinces, to assemble with God's people in the tabernacle dedicated to Jehovah; a house of prayer is to be found in almost every street. How inexcusable are those who will not frequent public worship, who will not enter where God dwells, and where the mercy of our Saviour is proclaimed to sinners! How few of the most pious can sincerely join with the royal Psalmist, and say in truth, "My soul longeth, yea, even fainteth for the courts of the Lord; my heart and my flesh crieth out for the living God?" And in the case of others who do attend the house of prayer, it is more matter of usage, and mere formality, than of desire, or a sense of duty. People go to hear some popular speaker, or to see some stranger; but few of us, it is to be feared, come hither to meet with God, who dwells in his church; and to commune with the Father of Spirits. But, since there is, in this christianized land, a large portion of persons baptized as professed disciples of Christ, who will not enter within the gates of God's house; we always rejoice in those who do: for these put themselves in the way of receiving instruction from the divine word, and of learning the way of salvation. How much to be pitied are those who prefer almost any assembly, before the assembly of those who meet to worship God; who will spend on places of public amusement, or of riotous festivity, their time, and their property, and their health; but who will not come to hear the revelation of divine mercy in that place where Jehovah dwells; or if they do occasionally enter the courts of the temple, it is not as devout worshippers, and docile learners, but to gratify curiosity, or to exercise their critical acumen on the language or manner of the preacher. I fear, that amongst many of us who seem to delight in God's house, and who regularly attend it, those faults just alluded to are also to be found. Ah, my Christian brethren, we should know and feel better, than to be drawn to the Christian temple by the mere wisdom of words, or music of eloquence, or to see a person from India or from Africa. I say not, that all regard to these and such like circumstances is sinful; but they should hold a very subordinate place to more sacred and spiritual motives. Although all the churches and chapels of the land are not sufficient to contain half the population, how thinly are some of them attended! But the people alone are not always to blame when churches and chapels are deserted. If systems of religion, originating in merely human ratiocination, supersede in public preaching, the divine truths of Christ's blessed Gospel, then is the glory departed. Such an edifice may be a temple of reason, a school of ethics, or a lecture-room for the moral philosophy of the day—but it no longer deserves the name of *a Bethel, a House of God;* nor, since God's truth, as revealed in the Sacred Page, is not there exhibited, nor spiritual sacrifices offered through the blood of atonement, can God be said to dwell there. God dwells with the humble and the contrite in heart, but the proud mind, or the proud assembly, which would rather dictate to Heaven what divine revelation should contain, than receive with reverence and gratitude what it actually *does* contain, cannot hope for the divine presence. The ancient temple, our heavenly Father's house, was once perverted and turned into a house of merchandise, a den of avaricious, covetous persons; and it is possible that Christian churches may be perverted, and turned into temples of superstition, or pagan-like mummery, or stalls for priestly sloth and lazy indifference; or a stage for the display of man's wisdom, or merely human eloquence; and in such cases, it is not the people alone who are to be blamed for the mixed motives with which such places are attended, or perhaps not attended at all.

Under the Christian dispensation, no building can be called a House of God, irrespective of the nature of the instruction which is given in it, and the offerings of prayer and praise there presented. The instruction given must be scriptural, and the Gospel preached must be Christ's Gospel, not another Gospel, which, indeed, can be no Gospel; for there is no other name given under heaven by which we can be saved, but his; he alone is able to save to the uttermost all that come unto God by him; and he alone can present our prayers and our praises with acceptance before his Father. It is incumbent, then, on the ministers of religion, not to desecrate places set apart for the ministry of the Gospel, by robbing them of their true glory, which consists in the scriptural and full exhibition of the whole revealed will of God; and especially the message of free, complete, and wholly unmerited mercy, through the mediation of Christ Jesus. Whilst the glorious perfections of God, as displayed in all his works, but especially in redemption, are exhibited to sinful men, the places of public worship will be intrinsically amiable, and be so esteemed by some, whatever they may be thought of by others. Where God, in Christ, reconciling the world to himself, is set forth as the Father, the Friend, the almighty Protector, the Guide, the Saviour, and the everlasting portion of his people, there God dwells. And the Christian who seeks and finds his satisfaction in the enjoyment of Christian ordinances in such a place, may be said to dwell in God's house. "*Happy*, or blessed," said the Psalmist, "are they that dwell in thy house, they shall be still praising thee."

Happiness is the pursuit of all men. The Chinese place the word happiness, in large characters, continually before their eyes, on walls and doors, and even at the back of the stage which is erected for comedy and broad-farce; happiness is their constant aim, still ever unattained; but not only do they fail to find it who seek it in mere amusement, honours, or pleasures, or riches—to whom it is ever a fleeting shadow pursued in vain: but absolute or perfect happiness, is to all unattainable in this life, because sin has poisoned all the springs of bliss; yet, after this admission is made, it is still, we know, true that there is a large portion of happiness to be enjoyed from waiting on God in the courts of his house, as well from what Christian ordinances now confer, as from what they lead the mind to anticipate in the heavenly world; for, as has been well said, "grace is glory begun." Those exercises of mind which constitute the happiness of a humble and devout worshipper in God's house of prayer, are similar in kind to those that will be experienced in the general assembly of ransomed sinners round the throne in glory. Are they not then happy who dwell in God's house, and are ever praising him, for the past blessings of Providence and grace, and in hope of those that are yet to come? God is their strength, confidence in God reigns in their hearts, and though they now pass through a desolate valley, they by the way drink from a living fountain, and draw water out of the wells of salvation; yea, the showers of spiritual influence from on high, fill the pools here and there with blessings. And the Christian traveller is refreshed and strengthened, till he finishes his course, and appears before God in the heavenly Zion.

A day spent in God's house in preparation for eternity, is better than a thousand spent elsewhere. The sabbatical rest, and the ordinances of religion, which may be enjoyed by the inhabitants of this country, constitute an invaluable blessing. Compared with those who are compelled, in the pursuit of their lawful concern, to take long voyages, where, on the mighty deep, the Sabbath comes, but no rest, no retirement, no house of prayer. Or those who live in Pagan lands, in places where no Sabbath is observed, no Christian congregations meet, where the animating influence of Christian society is entirely withdrawn; there, at the recollection of past days of delight and happiness, found in God's house, the soul cries out—"How amiable are thy tabernacles, O Lord of Hosts; my soul longeth, yea, even fainteth for the courts of the Lord. My heart and my flesh crieth out for the living God!" The exile and the wanderer then envies the very birds of the air; the sparrow and the swallow find nests for themselves, where they may rest; it may be near the altars of Jehovah, from which the pious mourner is secluded. It is the great abundance of Christian ordinances in this land, that makes it so desirable a home to the Christian; and I know that some who are obliged to dwell in foreign lands, away from the assemblies of God's people, regret their absence from home on this account, more than on any other. I know it by experience, and I mention it to you this day, with a desire that all here present may think more highly of the privileges they enjoy, and avail themselves of them more *assiduously*; or, in cases where that is not required, more *gratefully*; and that those who may have heretofore frequented the tents of the wicked, places of dissipation or riot, may see the evil of such a preference, and adopt the spirit of the Psalmist's resolution, rather to be a door-keeper, to sustain the lowest office in God's house, although he was possessed of royal dignity, than take up his abode with those who did not fear God. To this thought, the young in this congregation would do well to take heed, for they that go with wise and good men, will learn wisdom and goodness; but the companion of fools will be destroyed. Man is weak and wicked, and himself prone to ill; if he associate only with others, weak and wicked as himself, they all descend lower and lower in the depths of ungodliness or profligacy, onward and onward in that guilty path which leads to the regions of despair and endless woe. Whereas, those that join themselves to the sincere worshippers of Jehovah, and obedient disciples of Messiah, the anointed Saviour of men, are in the way to receive grace and glory. For God is a *Sun* and a *Shield*, he will give grace and glory, and no good thing will he withhold from those that walk uprightly, and who present their prayers to the Lord God of Hosts, with a reference to the person of God's anointed. The world is in moral and spiritual darkness; the surmises of Pagan philosophers, and the theories of antichristianism, cannot clear away the dark gloom that hangs over the head of a guilty creature. But God our Saviour, as he is revealed in the assemblies of his people, is *a sun*, and dispels, with the bright and glorious rays of his blessed Gospel, the darkness, and the gloom, and the dread which hover round the head of guilty man; and in the face of God's anointed, the light of this sun shines with beams of free, unmerited, unbought mercy, to the soul of the penitent; and life and immortality are brought to light, with a lustre and a soul-reviving glow, of which the natural sun, glorious and delightful as it is, when beaming forth on a world of night, and dispelling the darkness and the gloom, is but a faint resemblance. My brethren, have ye been translated out of darkness into God's marvellous light? or are ye still sitting in the darkness of unbelief, and in the region and gloomy shadow of spiritual death? If ye have seen the light of Jehovah's countenance, as he reveals himself in the sanctuary—the holy place of Christian assemblies and ordinances; ye require no arguments to induce you to love, and to support, and to frequent the services of his house. But if this light has not yet shone into your hearts, it is because ye have closed your eyes against the light. For the sun of the glorious Gospel of the ever blessed God shines upon you, and around you, in his house of prayer, if ye would but lift up your eyes and see:—Oh Lord, open thou the eyes of all such here present, that they may see marvellous things out of thy law; lift thou up the light of thy countenance upon them, that in thy light they may see light;—thou that didst at first cause the light to shine out of darkness, shine into their hearts, to give the light of the knowledge of the glory of thyself in the face of Jesus Christ!

And ye Christians, who remember with melancholy

M

regret the days which are past, when the light of the Lord shone upon you, but which are now exchanged for days of darkness and gloom, that divine sun is eternally the same;—your sins of presumption, or of carelessness, or of speculative security, have gathered the clouds which intervene, and cause the darkness of which you complain. The sanctuary, the house of prayer, is not to you an object of desire as it once was; peradventure ye have become wise in your own conceits, and undervalue the truths which have to you become common-place, and which have lost the charm of novelty. Or it may be a fulness of bread, a luxurious, and elegant, and over-abundant exhibition of spiritual delicacies, has made you loathe simple food; or feuds of a secular and personal nature, although connected with religion, have imbittered your spirit; and the agitation of bad passions, or other causes have dimmed the spiritual eye, and caused the Lord to hide his face from you. Sure we may be, that the cause of our obscurity is not in yonder sun, but the cause of obscurity, and gloom, and eclipses, and the darkness of night, is, the changes which take place on our earth, or something that interposes between his beams and us.

This sun has shone and illumined the saints of the Most High in every age, since the beginning of the world; it lighted up the road that led them to Messiah, the Lamb slain from the foundation of the world; it shines upon the souls of the faithful in afflictions and distresses, in sickness and in death; and in yonder brighter world, this sun shall no more go down, but shall beam forth an unspotted, unobscured orb of light and love for ever and ever.

The Lord God is a sun and a *shield*. Not only does he supply his people with the light of life; but he is also exhibited in the sanctuary as a *defence*. No weapon that is formed against his church's peace shall prosper. How manifold have been the machinations, and how varied and desperate the forms of assault intended to overthrow and annihilate the Church of God upon earth. Learning, and talent, philosophy, and science, falsely so called, enlisted with zeal on the side of the enemy; and persecution, and fire, and sword, wielded by the rulers of the earth, leagued together to oppose Messiah's reign, and to crush his rising kingdom, have all proved inefficient to the end proposed. For he *must* reign till he hath put all his enemies under his feet. And they that trust in the Lord shall be as Mount Zion, which cannot be moved. As the mountains are round about Jerusalem, so the Lord is round about his people, from henceforth, even for ever. He is a defence against all enemies. Our help, my Christian friends, is in the name of the Lord, who made heaven and earth. Oh what a shield is God to his people; it is a shield wielded by an Almighty arm, and guided by infinite wisdom and skill. Divine foreknowledge secures the church against any sudden or unexpected assault, and the omnipotent power of Jehovah renders that shield, which he throws around his church, impregnable to every foe, either from earth or from hell. Happy the people who resign themselves to his care, who flee to him for refuge, and who renounce all,—the least trust in any inferior power.

Oh, what a consolation are these sublime truths to the humble Christian, however poor, or afflicted, or distressed, or neglected, by man. Oh blessed Gospel, blessed Bible, which givest to the disconsolate such cheering revelations of divine benignity! Truly, O Jehovah, thou givest grace, and thou givest glory. Thou hast laid the foundation in the atoning sacrifice of Emmanuel, and thou hast led us to hope that the Spiritual Temple shall be finished with shouts of grace, grace unto it. The Lord will *give* grace and glory. All must be resolved into the free *gift* of God. The *gift* of God is eternal life. He spared not his own Son, but *gave* him up to the death for us all, and how shall he not with him also freely *give* us all things. These are the words of an Apostle, and how striking the similarity of language used by him and by Israel's King—"No good thing," said the pious monarch, "will he withhold from those that walk uprightly. O Jehovah, God of Hosts, happy is the man who trusteth in thee! Here, Christians, every thing is promised that Heaven considers good for upright persons; it is not what we consider good, but what

Infinite Wisdom considers good, and that is not always prosperity. Inspired and Holy Writ has recorded, that sometimes, (perhaps oftener than we imagine,) it is good to be afflicted. Chastisement indicates parental care and an ardent affection, and therefore we should not consider afflictions as positive and unmixed evil—if heavenly glory be at the end of all these graciously afflictive dispensations, how happy the result! Oh, what an exhilirating view of the matter did Paul take, when oppressed and afflicted, persecuted, and scorned, imprisoned and scourged, and hungry and thirsty; and in cold and nakedness, ill-fed and ill-clothed—in the midst of all these, he said, "Our light afflictions, which are but for a moment, work out for us a far more and exceeding and eternal weight of glory;" these afflictions are not worthy to be compared with the glory which shall be revealed in us. Truly so! A moment and eternity! earthly suffering and heavenly bliss! Man's wrath and God's love!—Who would ever think of drawing a comparison? Oh thou afflicted, discomforted, poor, and friendless; or aged and destitute Christian, lift up thy head and rejoice in God thy Saviour. And thou, man of God, who art rich and increased in goods, but whose mind is elevated above these things, in themselves perishable and fleeting, bless God who has taught thee not to trust in uncertain riches, but in himself; and who has led thee to adopt the ejaculation of the royal Psalmist, in the closing lines of that ode, which has been the subject of our discourse—

> "O Jehovah, God of Hosts,
> Happy is the man who trusteth in thee."

He is indeed *happy*, and happiness is no where else to be found.

Now, my hearers, these views of life and of death, of time and of eternity, and of the gracious character of God, our Creator, Preserver, and Redeemer, are those that are exhibited in the courts of God's house; and do they not justify the exclamation of king David—"How amiable are thy tabernacles, O Lord of Hosts?" There are some young persons in this country, exposed to the attacks of a

pretended science and philosophism, which set themselves in opposition to the religion of Jesus; but where in the tents of infidel philosophy, or in the temples of paganism, or in the mosques of mahomedanism, are to be found such sublime truths concerning God, such accurate statements concerning what man is; such gracious revelations of divine mercy; and such glorious hopes to them that walk uprightly, as are exhibited in thy lovely tabernacles, O Jehovah, God of Hosts!

But it is not privilege alone that is to be learned in Christian churches; the Lord said to Moses concerning the first tabernacle, "There will I meet with thee, and commune with thee of all things which I have *given thee in commandment* to the children of Israel." Christians, who should not forsake the assembling of themselves together, are to come together not only for prayer and praise, but also to hear what God the Lord will speak from his word in matters of duty, as well as in matters of privilege, and to exhort one another to love and to good works. Our attachment to the Saviour must be manifested by obedience to all his commandments. The Christian life, like that of our blessed Lord, should be a life of active benevolence, going about doing good. Not a life of monastic, selfish, and unsocial seclusion, which the folly of the human mind has every where suggested, as well in Pagan as in Christian lands. Oh no!—Apostolic, (which is the true primitive) Christianity, knows nothing of inactive, antisocial, selfish contemplation. Of the Holy Bible, nine tenths are made up of precepts and exhortations concerning man's duty to God, and to his fellow creatures. I trust, that on this occasion, whatever is right and expedient will be done: and to goad a willing mind, is not the practice that a generous nature approves.*

Remarks on another occasion.

And there is one duty of which it becomes me to put you in mind, viz. that of assisting, as God shall give ability, to

* A collection for the chapel was to be made.

rear *tabernacles* dedicated to Jehovah, throughout the whole earth. To excite your *gratitude*, I have already alluded to the temples dedicated, by deluded votaries, to dumb idols, or to apostate demons, in various parts of the world; but gratitude to God and to the former benefactors of our race, whom Heaven employed to originate spiritual blessings in our native land, is not to be confined to *mere* feeling. Although, even if it were, I fear we seldom *feel* enough on this subject. However, it is not enough to *feel* grateful or to *express* thankfulness; gratitude should rouse us to *exertion*, for the purpose of establishing tabernacles to Jehovah in all lands; that all nations, and peoples, and languages, may also exult in those *lovely edifices*, where mercy and salvation are revealed to the children of men. There is no possible good work at all comparable to the originating, amongst any tribe of men, a Christian Church. Alas, that there should be so often a spirit of cavil, and censorious criticism, in reference to those who have gone before us in good works of this kind; because, forsooth, it has been discovered that the operators were not perfect, that frailty and imperfection attended them and their efforts! Did a right spirit prevail amongst Christians, it would subdue or annihilate the spirit of censorious cavil, and lead to an emulation and imitation of those who first erected tabernacles to Jehovah in these lands, the beneficial effects of which have so far exceeded all calculation. Oh, what would Christian Missionaries in some parts of the world not do, or suffer, to witness a hundredth part of the Christian temples which adorn this land, rising up in the regions in which they labour. But next to Heaven's aid, they require the constant and energetic co-operation of the churches at home, and it is incumbent on those who rejoice from Sabbath to Sabbath, in the enjoyment of the unspeakable privileges of God's house, and the loveliness of his sanctuary, to co-operate assiduously to convey similar bliss to all mankind. And when Christians arrive at the house not made with hands, eternal in the heavens, that better and infinitely more perfect tabernacle, if they can look back and review the occurrences of earth, what can possibly yield satisfaction equal to that arising from having begun and finished, in new districts or regions of the world, tabernacles appropriated to the worship of Jehovah! For those who have been brought to delight in Jehovah's tabernacles on earth, shall be there gradually fitted for the inheritance of the saints in the realms in light and glory, and unmixed happiness, before the throne of God and of the Lamb. And there all the ransomed millions washed in the Redeemer's blood, shall assemble, and remain for ever in those eternal mansions. Oh, my brethren, to be instrumental in *saving* a soul from death, in *rescuing* an immortal spirit from misery, and in placing it amongst the inhabitants of Heaven—how great the felicity! O Lord of Hosts, happy are they that dwell in thy house on earth, they will be ever praising thee; but infinitely more happy are they who attain to the heavenly inheritance, and who shall there dwell for ever in thy lovely tabernacles; then, indeed, shall the tabernacle of the Lord be with men, and he shall dwell amongst them, communicating pure and ineffable felicity. To those blessed regions the Divine Redeemer has already ascended, and prepares mansions for all his followers. Let us, therefore, look to Jesus, rely on his Almighty aid, imitate his holy example, and gather consolation from the hope of being, after having passed through this desolate valley, for ever with him.

"Lord of the worlds above,
How pleasant and how fair
The dwellings of thy love,
Thy earthly temples are!
To thine abode
My heart aspires,
With warm desires
To see my God.

"The Lord his people loves;
His hand no good withholds
From those his heart approves,
From pure and pious souls:
Thrice happy he,
O God of hosts,
Whose spirit trusts
Alone in thee."

DISCOURSE XIV.

DELIVERED AT DR. RAFFLES' CHAPEL, LIVERPOOL, IN BEHALF OF MORAVIAN MISSIONS, JULY, 1824.

INTRODUCTION.

[The Association in London for the aid of Moravian Missions, requested Dr. Morrison to preach two Sermons at Liverpool, on his way to Ireland, in 1824. The following discourse was composed for that purpose, in the residence of the author's father-in-law, John Morton, Esq. at Liverpool. A Quaker lady, Mrs. Hannah Kilham, who has herself visited the shores of Africa as a teacher of Christianity, thus expressed herself on the subject of the following discourse, in a letter to the author.

TO DR. MORRISON.

Esteemed Friend,—I am quite sorry to have given thee the case of an inquiry respecting the manuscript which thou kindly sent, and for which, indeed, I have felt greatly indebted. It was read with deep interest and pleasure, and not considering it as of private communication, I took the liberty to allow a few friends, who had the gratification of being with thee at the time it was mentioned, to read it also; and it is now in the care of Robert Forster, who is out on a journey for two days. On his return, I intend immediately to have it forwarded to Hackney.

I cannot but greatly desire, that principles so consonant with the grand doctrines of Christianity, as taught by our Holy Redeemer, should be most fully declared to the world, and pressed home upon the consciences of all professing Christians. The appeal which has been made, appears to me so strong, so clear, and undeniable, not only on the *fraternity* of mankind, but on the claims, which an acknowledgment of that fraternity must involve, that I cannot but believe it greatly desirable, that many others should have the privilege of hearing it; and would hope that it may be felt as a debt due to society at large, to have this appeal, by means of the press, brought into a current, through which it may be instrumental in conveying into wide circulation a correspondent feeling.

"What hast thou that thou hast not received?" may be justly inquired of those stewards to whom have been committed the precious gifts, the sense and feeling of the truth, and of the just demands of Christian duty. I earnestly wish nothing may be withheld that would tend to arouse to a consciousness of the just demands of the great Parent of the Universe, and the claims of brotherhood in the family of man; claims, which the supineness of human nature is so often disposed to turn away from, as with the deaf ear, and the cold insensible heart. But the day is brightening. I am, with earnest desire, that infinite goodness may be pleased to bless thy labours, and render them, through his own power, instrumental to the everlasting welfare of many in that land so interesting, to which thy attention has been led, and in which his providential care has been thy shelter; and trusting in the continuance of the same divine support in thy future labours in his cause, I am, with much respect and esteem,

Thy sincere friend,

H. KILHAM.

Robt. Howard's, Bruce Grove, Tottenham,
13th of 9th Month, 1825.]

THE KINDREDSHIP OF THE NATIONS.

ACTS, XVII. 26.

"God hath made of one blood all nations of men."

SOME of the principles contained in divine revelation, are so different from the commonly received opinions of the world in its present state of apostacy from God, that they are generally overlooked and disregarded, either as preposterous, or as inapplicable to men of the existing generation. The pacific spirit of the Gospel, in opposition to wars—the meek and long-suffering virtues of our holy religion, in opposition to resentful duels, are examples of what I refer to; and the doctrine taught in my text, viz. the *kindredship* of all mankind, is amongst the number of disregarded, although heaven-derived truths.

The *pride* of man,—that satanic sin,—has induced in individuals, families and nations, a constant effort to elevate themselves above their neighbours, to claim a superiority, not only in exterior and existing temporal circumstances, but also to claim a superior origin to that of their neighbours; and, as if in the most impious opposition to the declaration of the great Creator, to arrogate to themselves, a being derived from *better blood* than their neighbours. We hear Christian, as well as Pagan princes, and others, boasting of their descent, and of their being derived from the blood of eminent ancestors of a supposed superior race; whereas the divine declaration by the mouth of Heaven's inspired servant is, that God hath made of *one blood* all nations of men; and of course, likewise all the families and individuals of those several nations. The important truth, that all nations are derived from the same first pair of human beings, and are therefore related to each other, and equal amongst themselves, is ridiculed as a useless truism, only fit to be laughed at; and with the principle is swept away at once the whole code of laws, and table of moral duties, which require and inculcate justice, and peace, and benevolence, and fraternal feelings amongst men of different nations. And, in opposition to this truth, the principles of a selfish individualism, a clanship, or self-idolizing patriotism, are introduced and designated prudence and virtue; and then self-aggrandizement, and national hatred, and warfare, become the pursuits of mankind, which are lauded by poets and praised by politicians, and echoed by the multitude; and acquiesced in, and sometimes advocated, even by the disciples of Jesus, and the ministers of his religion.

But since God has made of *one* blood all nations of men; since there is *one* God and Father of all, and he made human beings of the same material, there is a manifest kindredship and equality amongst all mankind. Infidelity may attempt to prove that there are different races of men, and pagan fancy may attribute their existence to different gods, or various powers; but since our discourse is not now addressed to such persons, but to professed Christians, we shall argue from the acknowledged principles of that holy religion; and shall deny the existence of any noble blood that raises some men superior to their fellows; or that disconnects them from the duties binding on our common humanity; or that elevates them to a place amongst the gods of pagan fancy. Too long have false notions of individual superiority, of family greatness, and of the right of some nations to dominate over the rest; and notions of a mistaken patriotism led men to despise and disregard, if not to hate and injure, his fellows, for all of whom we this day claim the rights of *consanguinity* and of *brotherhood.*

The Lord of heaven and earth, who giveth to all mankind life and breath and all things, made the world, and determined the bounds of men's habitation, to dwell on all the face of the earth. Mankind acknowledge one Creator, one divine Father, and their dwelling place is the sole property of one great Lord; they are the subjects of *one* divine King; and I see not why the principles of reciprocal duty, which are binding on brothers of the same family, and on subjects of the same kingdom, should not apply to them.

The time was, when every petty chieftain in this land cherished hate and feud, and practised bloodshed and murder against his neighbouring petty chieftain, who was equally rancorous; but the more extended dominion of one Prince imposed the duties of fellow-subjects on each other, and those duties have been felt and are now fulfilled in a very useful degree; and in the existing British empire, formerly, separate and distinct nations, which once lived in rancorous hostility, and gloried in doing mischief to each other, are now united as fellow subjects, and are bound, not only to forbear to injure one another, but are bound to exert themselves to do each other good; and shall spiritual Christians not carry forward this principle to its fair and conclusive extent—*i.e.* to all the nations over whom God their King and Saviour reigns? There still exists, not only with merely professed Christians, but also with many who seem truly religious, a sort of disesteem for, and disregard about, other portions of their heavenly Father's territory, and other branches of the human family, and which feelings are quite at variance with the sober dictates of reason and revelation. And there is a way of praising one's native country, and of acting for it, which generally throws injurious reflections on other parts of God's world, and of his creatures, which reflections often wear an air of impiety to God, and injustice to men.

The progress of navigation and geography, which enable so many persons to circumnavigate the globe and visit all countries, tends much to the development of the philanthropic spirit, which our text suggests. The hideous and distorted pictures formerly drawn of the rest of the nations, either by ignorance or artifice, as well as the representations of savage innocence, have, in all cases proved untrue, and human nature is found much the same in every land. It is depraved, and vicious, and degraded by superstition; but it is improvable by the diffusion of knowledge, by human kindness, and can be renewed by the grace of God. The objection of a frigid infidelity, that some tribes of men are sunk so low, that they cannot be raised, and that some are so invincibly attached to their idols, and their superstitions, and their vicious usages, that they can never be changed, has no foundation in truth. Esquimaux and Hottentots, New Hollanders and Otaheiteans, Negroes and Sandwich Islanders, Tartars and Hindoos, and Chinese, have all of them yielded to the kindness of men, the grace of the Saviour, and the mercy of God; and have been changed, and civilized, and sanctified, and glorified.

The great point yet to be gained is, to induce the Christian Churches to use somewhat proportionate means to communicate spiritual benefits to the rest of their brethren of mankind.

None will dispute the doctrine which we have laid at the foundation of this discourse, viz. the kindredship of all mankind; but many will argue that Christians should pretty much confine their attention to their own country, *i. e.* to those of their brethren of mankind, who live under the same civil government.

But does Christianity sanction or inculcate this sentiment?

Before the call of Abraham, *i. e.* during the first two thousand years of the world's existence, there was no distinction made in Heaven's dispensations amongst the nations of the earth. And the separation of one small country from the rest of the world, was a temporary arrangement made by divine Providence to preserve truth in the earth till Messiah should come. Around the Jews a partition wall was set up, but Jesus broke it down. Was God the God of the Jews only? or was he not also the God of the Gentiles? Is Jesus the Saviour of the Jews only? or the Saviour of men only, who live under some one civil Government? Is he not declared to be given as the Saviour of the world; and is it not promised that all nations shall serve him? I enter not this day into the disputes of theologians, concerning what they call general and particular redemption; for it is not necessary to my argument, since they all agree that the redemption which is in Jesus, extends to some of all nations, peoples, and languages.

And as the design of this salvation is not confined to any one country, so the command of Zion's king to his people is, not to confine their notification of his redeeming work to any one country, but to go into all the world and proclaim the Gospel to every human creature. I am aware that the pagan notions of patriotism are commonly received in our land, and are warmly advocated by a spirit of selfish aggrandizement; and that infidels have charged the religion of Jesus with not inculcating the virtue of patriotism. I acknowledge the charge to be true; I believe it does not inculcate the commonly received notion of patriotism. And although wise and good men think otherwise, and perhaps sneer at the expression, I do believe, that the religion of Jesus, properly understood, makes men *citizens of the world*. It calls upon them not to confine their attention, or their benevolent efforts, only to persons who live under the same civil government with themselves; but to extend their attention, and their care, and their benevolent concern to all human beings whom their Creator has made of the same blood as themselves; who occupy, as well as themselves, a part of their heavenly Father's wide domain; who, as well as themselves, live under his government, and if living under one and the same government, impose duties on men, shall Christians reject the government of God, and deny the duties owing to their fellow subjects in his empire! Shall Christians limit or extend their concern and their efforts to promulgate Christ's Gospel, just as human governments may be narrowed or extended!

I am persuaded, that few or none will advocate such a cause, or such a sentiment; but they may argue, that as our facilities are generally greater in our own neighbourhood, and in our own country, our efforts to do good must begin, and be proportionably greater there: and to this modification of duty, I see no reason to object; but still argue, that the degree of attention and care given by Christian Churches to the rest of mankind, is very far below what the necessities of our brethren of mankind require; and which our relation to them, as well as the commands of our Saviour, make it the duty of Christians to give.

It is true, that there are now a few voluntary associations of pious individuals throughout the united kingdom, who make, of late years, some small efforts to send Christianity to the pagan world; and there is much said of an old society, for diffusing Christian knowledge in the British colonies. But what, after all, have the national churches of England and Scotland done, to carry into effect the divine precept, Go and proclaim the Gospel to all the world? What has this Christian state, which insists on being united with the church, and in which union the national church glories;—what has it done, from the impulse of Christian benevolence, for the rest of the nations? Where is the fraternal feeling amongst the nations of Christendom, which Christiany requires of them towards each other, and towards the rest of those national families which are made up of God's offspring on the face of the earth? The eternal feuds and wars of these Christian states in Europe, which are its disgrace in the regions of paganism, and which prove they have no just claim to the Christian name, call forth an immense degree of effort, and of zeal, and of devotedness, and of pecuniary sacrifice, and of personal service; in comparison of which, oh how languid, and feeble, and niggardly, and cowardly, are all the efforts to do good to the rest of mankind, which have yet been made by the self-called Christian world. *The* small society of Christians, called *Moravians, seem to have made benevolent efforts for the rest of the nations, pretty much the business of their lives;** but the more spiritual and most devoted Christians of other Protestant Churches, have as yet done scarcely any thing beyond the limits of their respective civil governments.

I am very well aware of the difficulty of doing good to a fellow-creature, whose heart is under the influence of Satan, the great enemy of man; whose heart is itself enmity against God, and who does not love his neighbour, but himself only. I am not ignorant of the difficulties which the selfishness, and the animosities of ambitious Rulers of nations; and the avarice, and lust, and irregularities of foreign visitors, have created and thrown in the way of benevolent efforts for the rest of mankind. And difficulties also arising from things not criminal, as distance of place, insalubrious climates, differences of language, and of all the habitudes of life.

The difficulties are, indeed, many—they are not denied; but it is maintained, that they are not insurmountable; that duty is generally difficult, and not to be neglected because difficult. Difficulties, moreover, give way before sincerity and perseverance in the use of means. Heaven's blessing, and Heaven's help, are sent down on men who attempt honestly and humbly to perform a duty. And it should be observed, that benevolent efforts are so rare in the world, people cannot be all at once convinced that professions of benevolent design are sincere. When the late Dr. Milne, a Missionary to the Chinese, first opened gratuitous schools for Chinese youths, the parents suspected he had some bad design, cloaked over with the pretext of benevolence, and they hesitated to allow their children to attend and receive instruction; but patient perseverance, and the non-appearance of any malevolent tendency, gradually convinced them that the design was good, and that the foreign missionary was really a benevolent man; and they now

* Although the writer considers the brethren amiable and useful, and worthy of sympathy and aid; he yet thinks their discipline not fitted for general adoption.

send their children with confidence, and from the villages come and solicit the establishment of new schools. The human understanding is, indeed, very much blinded, and the human heart is very hard; but still the light of truth can be, though dimly, distinguished and ascertained, and kindness can soften, and grace can melt the heart. The truth is, benevolence has so rarely led men to foreign climes from the nations of Christendom, that the rest of the nations have a right to be suspicious of them; but the real Christians have no good reason to infer, that because avarice, ambition, and other crimes that might be named, are unwelcome visitors in pagan lands, that, therefore, unfeigned benevolence will, when really ascertained, be likewise unwelcome. However, it will require time to enable the nations to see and test the reality of professed benevolence. But,

There is another view of the subject which must be taken, and which makes Christian Missions binding on the churches, whatever the difficulties may be, or whatever the reception given them may be. According to divine revelation, the whole world of human beings is guilty before God, and justly subject to a penalty greater than human language can describe. From the Court of Heaven, a pardon is proclaimed to every one that confesses his guilt and renounces his crimes. Of the way that this pardon has been procured, it is not now necessary to speak. The Divine Redeemer came from heaven and proclaimed this pardon to the nation of the Jews, and left a standing order to all who accepted of it themselves, to proclaim it to others. If I be asked why he did not himself visit every land, and proclaim the good tidings?—I confess my ignorance; I do not know why Heaven chooses to make one man the medium of temporal and spiritual good to another; but I do know that such questions, proceeding from a weak and wicked creature, and disputing the goodness and justice of God, indicate a presumptuous and impious spirit. The commandments of a father are not to be disobeyed and neglected, because an infant child cannot discern their fitness. Much less, may the commandments of the eternal and all-wise God be neglected and disobeyed, till a creature but of yesterday, and who knows nothing, shall be satisfied concerning their fitness.

The societies or churches of those who have themselves accepted Heaven's pardon, are bound, by the Saviour's command, to proclaim it to every human being to whom they can obtain access. It does not remain with them to reason about the probability of other guilty rebels receiving it. For that they are not answerable; but they are answerable for the presumption of repressing it, or for neglecting to promulgate it, because there are difficulties attending the performance of their duty.

And what shall we think of their tender mercies, if it were left to their pleasure, whether to tell of Heaven's pardon to a dying fellow-criminal or not, when it shall be known that they *could* do it and *would* not? However, I appeal not to the compassion of Christians, in reference to the rest of the nations, but ground my appeal on its being an indispensable duty to send forth heralds of salvation throughout the earth, a duty which no church can innocently omit.

As it would be an absurd proposal for every Christian man or woman, or every family, to quit their country and their home, and go forth to distant parts of our own empire, or to foreign nations, to preach Christ's Gospel; the circumstances of the case suggest the necessity of co-operation, and of an organized system for carrying into effect the duty binding on the churches. A few must give their personal services, and if they have fortunes, devote these also, and go forth, making the Gospel without charge, either to the heathen or to the churches. Some have done so, would that there were many more. And others have pursued their lawful secular callings, and thereby have been enabled to do the work of evangelists gratuitously; but there are faithful men and women, who neither have property nor occupation, by which they can maintain themselves whilst engaged in the Missionary work, and to supply the wants of these, the churches at home are bound to contribute, according as the Almighty, in the course of his

N

gracious and righteous Providence, may have enabled them. And each Christian must determine for him or herself in the sight of God, to what extent they shall contribute; I know of no earthly authority that has any right to interfere, or to dictate on this subject. God loveth a cheerful giver to his cause, and I may add, without presumption, that no gift proceeding from vanity, or ostentation, or obtained by importunity or flattery, or that does not proceed from a principle of obedience, and gratitude, and love to God is likely to be acceptable. Who is it that giveth strength to the strong, and wealth to the rich? They that serve God, and they that contribute to his cause in the world, do but give to him of his own, and we dare not praise them and flatter them, if they did give a hundred fold more than they commonly do. And in as much as the sacrifice of those Christians, who remain at home and contribute of their property, is so small, compared with those who give their personal services in foreign parts, the Christians at home ought to lend their aid without solicitation, and rejoice to find opportunities of co-operating with those who actually labour abroad. As the duty is not laid on any individual, by express revelation from Heaven, but falls on the churches in their collective capacity, all ought to feel it; for we are all equally related to our fellow men in remote parts, and are all under equal obligations to our Divine Redeemer. The idea of obligation between Missionaries and Christian contributors, I put entirely out of the case; for they should all serve the Lord Christ, and be anxious to fulfil their duty to their neighbour; but if I were to admit the notion of reciprocal obligation, I would be inclined to say, that there is most on the side of Christian contributors, who are indebted to the men who enable them, by personal services, to aid Christ's cause in the world. However, I will not dwell on such a theme as this.

The nations which have not yet received the religion of Jesus, are very numerous, and their state and circumstances very various; and therefore, the means employed to convey to them divine truth, should be appropriate, and accommodated to their particular circumstances.

The great object of Christian Missions, is to proclaim the mercy of God to guilty creatures—*i. e.* to preach Christ's Gospel, and with it, the whole of revealed religion:—it is to convey divine truth, as revealed in the Sacred Scriptures, to the human mind. Now, the means of doing this are not all equally applicable in all cases; but yet some means may be used in every case.

In the united kingdom, where Christianity has long been introduced, and where the people generally receive the fundamental truths of the existence of one great Supreme God, the creator, preserver, and final judge of men, and where Christian teachers can convey instruction in their mother tongue, public preaching is a very efficient means of conveying divine truth to the human mind.

But, in a newly occupied region, where Christianity is unknown, and where there are no admitted truths on which to build a superstructure of reproof, advice, or consolation; and where the teacher is a foreign Missionary, and speaks but imperfectly the language of the people to be instructed; this practice of public preaching does not apply so well. Schools and conversations are more appropriate means; or some institution of a collegiate nature, where native students may be kept for years together, and receive daily instruction in Christian principles, that they may subsequently go forth and teach their own people, whose opinions and prejudices, and errors, and vices, they are more familiarly acquainted with, and can speak more pointedly to, than most foreign missionaries ever can. And there are some nations in which the governments will not allow the public preaching of foreigners, and where more private means of conveying the Gospel to men's understandings and hearts must be employed.

Further, in countries where letters are known and books abound, and where there exists a taste for reading, the press is a most efficient means of proclaiming the Gospel; but it is one which does not apply to unlettered and ignorant tribes of men. To China, Japan, Corea, Loo-choo, and Cochinchina, in all of which places the Chinese language is read, translations of the Sacred Scriptures, and the multiplication of appropriate Christian books, afford facilities of conveying divine truth to men, which cannot be employed amongst many of the people of Africa and other regions where letters are not known.

Thus it will appear, that male and female schools, catechists, collegiate institutions, preachers, translators, the writers of good books, may all, under different circumstances, be employed and co-operate in evangelizing the world. In this great harvest there are, as yet, but few labourers; and it is incumbent on the churches, to pray the Lord of the harvest to thrust forth labourers into the harvest; and, with their prayers, to join their efforts to qualify fit agents, to afford them the means of going to distant regions, and assist them when there, till in each country the inhabitants themselves shall be able to teach each other, and not require foreign supplies: when the period which prophecy authorizes us to hope for shall have arrived, when it shall be no longer necessary to say to each other, Know the Lord, for all shall know him from the least even to the greatest.

Of those who desire the enlargement of the Redeemer's kingdom, a much larger proportion should devote themselves to those regions of the world which are, as yet, so ill supplied, both amongst the uncivilized and the cultivated nations of men; and this will require proportionably greater effort amongst the Christians who remain at home; not only in contributing of their property, but also in associating for direct encouragement of the several missions, as circumstances may lead their attention to one or another of them. But this will not be done till Christians see it to be a more serious duty than they do at present—a duty, for the performance or omission of which they must be accountable at the great day of judgment. At present, Christians view it more as matter of taste than of duty. If they take a fancy to assist missions, well; if they do not feel so inclined, they think it also well.

But seeing all mankind are related to each other, not only neighbours, but brethren; may the divine precept, to love our neighbour and our brother, be violated and disregarded without guilt? Is it an innocent thing to render void the commandments of God? or attend to them, or neglect them, as may suit our taste and fancy? Let us endeavour to view affairs of duty, with that seriousness of mind that we shall see to be right, when we endeavour to realize our appearance before the judgment seat of Christ. The present life is a period of labour and of service; and if our duties be slurred over now in a spirit of carelessness and indifference, instead of being honestly and faithfully performed to our fellow creatures, how can we expect that the Omniscient Judge will say to us—Well done good and faithful servant? Many persons, who seem very pious people, spend too much on the comforts and elegancies of life, and too little on their Saviour's cause. I am not endeavouring to inculcate any thing extravagant and outrageous; but a plain, palpable, common-sense Christian duty, manifestly deduced from all our Christian principles, and the generally acknowledged truths of our holy religion. I inculcate universal philanthropy, not existing as a merely visionary sentiment, but embodied in real acts of substantial good; and the good to which we now allude, as you Christians know, is above all price, for the redemption of the soul is infinitely precious; and if a soul die in its iniquity, through the neglect of Christian churches, it, indeed, because of its iniquity, suffers death justly; but still, in another respect, its blood is chargeable on them.

These, my brethren, are awful considerations, arising out of the scriptural doctrine of the kindredship, or consanguinity of mankind, and other collateral truths of divine revelation. A flippant spirit of selfishness, or laboured dissertations about the locality of Christian effort, may deride doctrines which impose duties that bear upon all mankind; but with the Bible in our hands, and sound ratiocination founded on the Bible, I see no ground for derision, when the welfare of mankind is the subject of conference, or of expostulation. Some good people like not the generality of our views, and would confine us at home entirely; not only to the British dominions, but almost to the very street in which we happen to dwell. Now, if there were Christhan men resident in every street in the world, we could see a propriety in every one confining his attention to his own street; but this is not the case, and therefore we must remind the Christians, that God has made of one blood all nations of men; and that, therefore, all the duties arising out of kindredship or brotherhood, are binding upon them. Say not then with the sullen frown and rebellious mood of murderous Cain, "Am I my brother's keeper?" for this speech breathes, at the same moment, cruelty and impiety: rather say, I will love him as myself, and strain every nerve to do him good, for his own sake, for our heavenly Father's sake, and for God our Saviour's sake. Amen! Be it so!

"Behold the mountain of the Lord
In latter days shall rise
On mountain tops above the hills,
And draw the wondering eyes.
To this the joyful nations round,
All tribes and tongues shall flow;
Up to the hill of God, they'll say,
And to his house we'll go.

"The beam that shines from Sion hill
Shall lighten every land;
The King who reigns in Salem's tow'rs
Shall all the world command.
Among the nations he shall judge;
His judgments truth shall guide;
His sceptre shall protect the just,
And quell the sinner's pride.

"No strife shall rage, nor hostile feuds
Disturb those peaceful years;
To ploughshares men shall beat their swords,
To pruning-hooks their spears.
No longer hosts encountering hosts
Shall crowds of slain deplore;
They hang the trumpet in the hall,
And study war no more.

"Come then, O house of Jacob! come
To worship at his shrine;
And, walking in the light of God,
With holy beauties shine."

DISCOURSE XV.

DELIVERED AT BRISTOL MISSIONARY ANNIVERSARY, AUGUST 2, 1824.

INTRODUCTION.

[My Christian Friends, your preacher for this evening is not, in ordinary cases, fond of apologies, and should not now make any, did he not think that justice to you and to himself required it. It is generally known, by those who attend meetings like the present, that he has been long in a distant country, occupied chiefly in philological labours, and the exceptions are so few, he may say he never preached. That your edification may not be hindered by disappointment this evening, he states the fact. Beside, on this anniversary, the subject of missions has been thrice advocated, and the claims thereof so powerfully argued; and the difficulties* thereof so well illustrated; and the final success thereof so scripturally exhibited, that nothing remains to be said. All that preachers on this occasion can now do is, but to reiterate truths similar to those which have already been addressed to you.]

THE NATIONS SHALL RENOUNCE LIES AND VANITIES.

JEREMIAH, XVI. 19.

"*O Lord, my strength, and my fortress, and my refuge, in the day of affliction. The Gentiles shall come unto thee from the ends of the earth, and shall say, 'Surely our fathers have inherited lies, vanity, and things wherein there is no profit.'*"

WITHOUT a minute enquiry, on this occasion, into the connection in which this passage of Sacred Writ stands, we deduce from it the three following propositions:—

First. That the idols of the nations, are false, vain, and useless.

Secondly. That the most remote nations shall eventually be convinced that the idols of their fathers are false, and shall abandon them: and

Thirdly. That the worshippers of the true God have, therefore, every encouragement to use diligently, suitable means to turn the nations from their idolatry, looking to God as their strength.

The first of these propositions requires not here any laboured proof. Amongst us it is now universally acknowledged, that our fathers, who in former ages worshipped idols, inherited only lies, vanity, and things wherein there is no profit. But there are hundreds of millions of our fellow creatures, who follow implicitly their idolatrous fathers, and are not convinced of the vanity of idols, in the literal sense of the expression; and of the manifold superstitious, foolish, and sometimes cruel usages, connected with them. The idols of ancient Greece, and Rome, and Britain, have perished from under the heavens, and have been swept from the face of the earth; but in various other parts of the world idols still remain in unnumbered multitudes; not only amongst tribes of men, who may with truth be called uncivilized and savage, but also among hundreds of millions to whom these terms cannot with truth be applied; for it is a misuse of terms to call the inhabitants of India and China uncivilized. Their difference from civilized Europe, consists wholly in their being unchristianized. To civilize people, is, (according to authorities,) to reclaim them from savageness and brutality; from what is coarse and rude, to polish their manners, and so forth. Now the fact is, that in China, for example, there is quite as much mildness and civility in the intercourse of human beings, as in Europe, and sometimes more. And men's actions are as much regulated by law and by etiquette, and so are as much polished, as in any nation they can be, till Christianity regenerates and purifies the heart, and fills it with love to God and man, and diffuses abroad, amongst all ranks, something more humane than human nature ever attains to, without Christianity. Were Greece and Rome civilized before they were christianized? It is the universal opinion that they were. But did their civilization elevate them even to pure deism, as it is called, and drive away their dumb idols! I believe there is no evidence that it did; nor has civilization done so in India or China; nor does past experience authorize the hope that civilization will ever overthrow idolatry, or turn men from Satan and demons, and lying vanities, and foolish superstitions, to the living and true God. It is idle in some advocates of Missions, and others not altogether hostile to them, to cry out, "*First* civilize, and then christianize; for civilization may, and does exist without Christianity;" it has existed, and does at this day exist, with the most gross and vulgar idolatry. It is *revealed religion* alone, whether as in the Jewish dispensation, or under the Christian system, or that partly derived from both, viz. Mahomedanism, that has ever overthrown idolatry. Art, and science, and civilization, never have, by themselves, turned men from superstitious idolatry to the worship of God. Not to refer to the overthrow of idolatry in the ancient European pagan world, which was effected by Christianity; the existing case of the uncivilized, illiterate, South Sea Islands, having cast their idols to the moles and the bats, whilst civilized China, with all its ancient and modern literature, retains them, is very strongly in point to prove our doctrine. In China, there is not a street, nor a shop, nor a palace, nor a hovel, nor a college, nor a poor fisherman's boat, that has not an idol; a carved image of wood, or a porcelain goddess, or a molten divinity of clay, or a literary god of bronze, or a stone idol cut by the mason, or a rude unfashioned piece of rock. The literary disciples of Confucius, who doubt the existence of demons, and who deny a future state in which the human spirit either enjoys or suffers, still kneel down to the image of their master, or worship a scroll with the shadow of a man, and so seem, however paradoxical it may appear, a sort of idolatrous atheists; but to the most High God, who *created the universe*, the Lord of heaven and earth,—so partial is the exception, it may safely be affirmed, no altar is erected in China or in Corea, in Japan or Cochinchina. And together with their false gods, there goes along an immense host of superstitious usages, and vain conceits, and false hopes, and false fears; and to support the one, and to allay the other, an innumerable multitude of things that cannot profit, are invented and practised. The minute detail of these fooleries may amuse curiosity, but cannot be of any material use. It is a condition of human nature to be deeply lamented, and the more that man is restored to the knowledge and the image of God, the more he will lament it. Men who possess the Christian soul of Paul, will feel their spirits stirred in them, when they behold cities and nations wholly given to idolatry; but the mere man of this world, or the well-educated and scientific sceptic, in India or China, sees nothing to lament in it; nor, to remove this idolatry, or elevate the condition of the human soul, does he consider an object worthy of his attention or care.

For it is not the idolaters alone who inherit from their fathers lies, vanity, and opinions which cannot profit; these are often found even after idolatry has been thrown aside. False opinions concerning the Divine Being and his moral government assume, by the influence of the spirit of delusion, an endless variety of forms, which, if left to themselves, become, in every succeeding generation, more rivetted in the human mind, by the veneration which we are taught to have for our fathers. That we should follow our fathers, is a doctrine sometimes inculcated by Christian advocates; but when transported to the Missionary in Pagan lands, where it is also inculcated, it makes directly against his Christianity.

"You conceited young man," said an aged Chinese father, to his now Christian son, "do you think yourself wiser than your father, and wiser than the emperor, and all the mandarins? Begone, thou fool, and adhere to the religion of thy fathers, who were wiser and more ancient, and had more sages sprung up amongst them in this thy native and heaven-favoured land, than all the Europeans from whence this new religion came."

The young man, however, who was situated, in respect of Judea, at the ends of the earth, was convinced that his father, and his father's fathers, had for many centuries inherited lies, vanity, and things wherein there is no profit, and he remained firm to his Christianity, and was kind to his aged father, and contributed to the old man's comfort and ease, mourning only for the hardness of his heart, that would not, whilst advocating the rights of a father on earth, submit to our Almighty Father in heaven. The prophesy of our text was fulfilled, as it had been in millions of instances before, and as it will continue to be till the end of time. For, as we observed in the second place, it is certain, because,

II. God has said it—or as the scripture phrase is, He hath promised it. The nations *shall* abandon their dumb idols, their lies, vanities, and useless superstitions. This prophesy has been gradually fulfilling in every age since Jeremiah lived. Nations the most powerful, and amongst the most ancient, have relinquished their beloved idols, and abandoned their priests and their sorcerers, and the religion of their fathers; and why may not those that yet remain idolatrous be hereafter converted? Has the Gospel lost its power? is the Lord's arm shortened, that he cannot save? Cannot the Holy Spirit of God quicken those that are dead in trespasses and sins? These questions we put to the Christians. To the sceptic, we maintain that the nature of man is substantially the same all over the world; and since revealed religion has produced certain effects, wherever it has been made fully known, it is fair to expect similar effects from it in future. But to the Christian, we adhere to the ground given us in our text; the divine promise.

By the mouth of his holy prophet here, and by various prophets in other parts of the Sacred Pages, we are assured the Gentiles shall come from the ends of the earth, and renounce their idols, which their fathers had worshipped, and the lies and the vanities to which they had devoted themselves. Men may bring forward, in proud array, a thousand difficulties, and scare us with tales of Indian caste, and Asiatic unchangeableness, and magnify a million-fold, the real difficulties. The Christian knows that God is almighty, and possesses infinite resources; and human beings all round the world are his creatures, and his word is faithful and true, and never has, nor ever will fail of being accomplished; and therefore the nations shall come from the ends of the earth, and abandon their idols. The Lord God omnipotent reigneth, and his kingdom ruleth over all. His almighty power can change the hearts of kings and rulers, can level mountains and raise vallies; can make all his mountains a way, and cause his high ways to be exalted. And then willing converts shall come from far; and lo! these from the north and from the west, and those from "the land of *Sinim*," which last name some interpret *of Sina*, or China.

'But if the Almighty has promised the consummation you anticipate, (says an objector,) no doubt he will himself accomplish it; he does not require man's help. We know well that Heaven can, by a miracle, convert the nations, and it will never be done till he does effect it in a miraculous manner.'

To this we answer, that if by a "miraculous manner," be intended a change of sentiment and heart, effected without divine truth being conveyed to the understanding and conscience; we deny that such has heretofore been the proceeding of Divine Providence, and therefore it is not to be expected in time future. And we affirm, that in time past, individuals and nations have been turned from their lying vanities, by the truths of Christ's Gospel, addressed in various ways to the understanding and affections of men; and that there is a standing order given by the Redeemer, to continue such means, till all the kingdoms of this world shall become the kingdoms of our Lord Jesus Christ. We argue, that the intimation of Heaven's final intention, is a reason why Christian churches should use means; for God is pleased, in the general government of the world, both physical and moral, to use means to effect the thing finally intended. If Heaven had not revealed that the nations should abandon, at some period, the lies and vanities of their fathers; the language of adversaries, who affirm, that Heaven is pleased with all the various forms of idol-worship, and that the uncalled for interference of the busy Christian zealots, is a nuisance in the earth, would have had a specious appearance of truth. And certainly there would be little encouragement to use means to effect a change, which, perhaps, Heaven never intended should take place. But as the matter now stands, we know God designs, that eventually the Gentiles from the ends of the earth shall come to him, and shall say—Surely our fathers have inherited lies, vanity, and things wherein there is no profit. Shall *man* make gods? they shall be astonished at the absurdity, and reject the idols with scorn and abhorrence, in spite of prejudice and caste, and the ancient veneration of their sires. Let the Christian churches, therefore, use diligently scriptural means to convey Christ's Gospel to the *Gentiles, even to the ends of the earth.*

III. Now, as the church is the human agent in this great work, and must employ the means we were to speak of in the third place, I will give my sentiments concerning it. The church of our Lord Jesus Christ is *one* to him, and he knows every member of it; but to the human eye, it is made up of many parts. And in this church, this *ecclesia*, or assembly, as visible to the human eye, there are, it is to be feared, many persons not true members of it; and who can be distinguished, certainly, only by the divine eye of our Redeemer, who is the Head, the President, (if I may so speak,) of this assembly or church. Like a field of corn, it contains good grain, and here and there, mixed among the good grain, some noxious or useless weeds, which the discerning eye of the husbandman can easily distinguish. It is not expedient, whilst growing up, to separate them, because, when eradicating the weeds, the good grain would be liable to injury. They must grow together till the harvest, and then they shall be separated for ever. The idea, therefore, of a perfectly pure church on earth does not seem scriptural: and let not members of churches take for granted, that their being so, necessarily implies, that they are true members of Christ's body. There is a danger that those who try to make their churches as pure as possible, should instil the dangerous error, which has just been noticed; viz. that every member of their church is really converted.

There we leave the hint in passing, and remark, that by the phrase, "the Church," in this discourse, is not meant any section of professed Christians throughout the world; or in any country, whether great or small; whether connected or unconnected with any government, in any quarter of the world: for we believe that the church of Christ, of which we speak, is not confined to any nation; but is *placed amongst the nations,* for the good of mankind, irrespective of political or geographical distinctions; and that her *efforts should embrace the whole world,* without the narrowness of feudal bigotry, or pagan-derived notions of patriotism. *God's world is the Christian's country;* and he should feel none of those violent partialities for particular spots of his heavenly Father's territory; nor any of those malevolent antipathies to other regions than those in which he was born, which are so generally felt by men who know not God, and still considered amiable or pardonable in those that do. Now, since the church of Christ is, as we believe, set in the midst of the nations, for the benefit of the whole world, she should *proportion her efforts more equally* than she has heretofore done, according to the wants and necessities (of a moral and religious nature) which exist in different parts of the world. She has, it is to be feared, become too much nationalized and entangled with the politics of the several European governments; and has imbibed the idea, that her exertions, and her cares, are to be narrowed or extended by the political limits of the several nations, where her members reside; and so she has been led to neglect, or perform very carelessly her duty to the rest of the nations; and has not communicated to them Christ's Gospel. I have spoken of the church as one; but if we consider her, as the truth requires, made up of many local churches, or assemblies, or congregations of God's faithful people, and use the term church in the plural, our reasoning will be the same. Even in this day of missions, the churches, whether national or not national, *do not proportion their efforts, in that equitable degree* which the necessities of our Father's world require; and the churches cannot in justice claim the character of good stewards of Christ's mysteries, nor of obedient soldiers of the Captain of salvation, nor of loyal subjects of Zion's King, for they have not promulgated those mysteries, nor obeyed the orders given, nor *sought to enlarge* the kingdom. Your preacher this day appears amongst you as a representative of Eastern Asia; and knowing, as I do, the command of God our Saviour to the churches, to make known the Gospel to every human creature; I am astonished to find Christians so often referring all their missionary efforts to charity, in the ordinary sense of that term. A missionary sermon, is a charity sermon. Now the churches cannot conceal it from us, that Heaven has made it their *solemn duty* to proclaim the Gospel to the ends of the earth; and if they thought rightly, they would feel as Paul did, when he said, "Wo to me, if I preach not the Gospel." Yes! were matters as they ought to be, we should hear from the bench of English Bishops, and from the Scotch General Assembly, as well as from every Pastor of congregational churches, thoughout the land, a sincere confession—"Wo to us, if we assist not to proclaim Christ's Gospel to *the ends of the earth.*"

Charity indeed! Here is a world of guilty rebels; and the world's god has put into the hands of men, pardoned and saved by mercy, a proclamation of mercy and pardon to all who will accept of it; and has given a solemn injunction to go and proclaim it, to the ends of the earth—to every creature—to each rebel; and these pardoned rebels think it, in themselves, a charity to do so: and this proclamation has been in their possession eighteen centuries, and yet one half of mankind has even now scarcely heard distinctly of it; so indolently and carelessly have successive generations done their duty. And there are professing Christians in our land, and ministers of Christ's religion, who think they have nothing at all to do with Christian missions, which are designed to proclaim this divine mercy, to the ends of the earth: and who think that the Lord's servants must all of them stay in their native country; and that when Heaven chooses, Heaven will convert the rest of the nations by a miracle. But alas! how impious and rebellious this language, which is every day heard! how insulting to common sense!

But, perhaps, say some, the Gentiles at the ends of the earth will not thank us for our message. Thank us! their reception, or non-reception of the message, their gratitude or ingratitude, are not chargeable on us, nor are they the rule of our duty. It is ours to obey the King's command; to go and proclaim it. But then, says the spiritual casuist, we shall make their case worse. They had better never hear of mercy than reject it; and therefore we had better not go and proclaim it. Oh! how shocking the presumption and self-conceit of spiritual pride. It is assumed by this objector, that man's tender mercies are greater than God's—how blasphemous! The objector assumes, that he is wiser than God; and disobedience to Heaven is justified by the assumption of being more merciful, as well as wiser than the God of mercy, and than He, who is the infinitely wise God! When driven from this ground, the caviller next comes forward, and asks, if we would have every body become Missionaries, and form a crusade, in the ridiculous sense of that term, and desert our native land? and he asserts, that there is work enough to be done at home. There are plenty of pagans at home. And a Principal of a university will tell us not to give a shilling to foreign missions, till all the work is done at home. Now,

I have endeavoured to prove, that Christ's church on earth is not limited to any political government, the extent of which is what people commonly call home. The *homes* of an Englishman, Scotchman, and Irishman, were once very different; and under that opinion, they were something worse than careless about each other—they often thought it meritorious to hate each other: and they called this malevolent feeling an *ardent patriotism*. But now, in reference to such matters as we speak of, any part of our united kingdom is considered home: and even India, though not called home, is allowed to have a claim, as being filled with fellow-subjects. But has the great Head of the Church, either by the letter, or spirit, or scope of any thing that he or his apostles taught, ever countenanced the idea, that the Church on earth shall thus confine, by political limits, her attention and her care? Did the principles or practice of the apostles countenance this idea? The peculiar attention paid to Judea by our Saviour and his apostles, was not on the ground of that being their native country; but on the ground of the inhabitants of that country having been heretofore God's peculiar people; in which circumstance, they were not to have, and have not, any successors. Jesus threw down the middle wall of partition between Jew and Gentile, and ever since that time, the nations of the earth are all on the same, and on *an equal* footing, as viewed by the Christian revelation. The Church of Christ on earth has no exclusive home, but should *feel at home in any part of her Father's world;* and should *equalize* her care and anxieties for the good of the whole of mankind. She should not care less, nor use less effort for one part, than for another; unless, indeed, she had some special notification from Heaven to do so, which she has not. I think the prevailing idea of the excessively disproportioned claims of *home*, not supported by Scripture nor reason. As to the cavil about English Christians all quitting their native land, it is meant only as a sneer—and sneers are not often easily answered, although they may be easily retorted. The answer I would give to the cavil is this, that it opposes what is not affirmed—no crusade is by me advocated; but, it is affirmed, every Christian ought to do his utmost to promulgate the Gospel.

o

If the church be compared to an army; there, when a general order is given, it is expected that every officer and soldier should do his duty, which is to do his utmost, to carry that order into effect; and his utmost doings will be regulated by his station and his strength. In the general order to promulgate the Gospel, which has been given by the King of Zion to the church, every Christian is bound to consider him or herself as included. And no one can innocently stand by, and say, "this matter does not concern me." No Christian Minister can innocently say, The proclamation of the Gospel to the ends of the earth, is a matter with which I have nothing to do; I am a settled Minister, a stated pastor; I need not feel any interest in it. No! every Christian and every Minister, should rather say, "This too is my concern, and God helping me, I will do something to assist." If not, how shall they, in that particular, give in their account with joy, and not with grief? How can any Christian Minister pique himself on saying, "Yes, I heard of the general order to proclaim the Gospel to every creature, and I paid no attention to it; I did nothing to assist, but I endeavoured to explain it away, as binding only on the apostles; or I tried to prove that it was impracticable, and the scheme visionary; or I endeavoured to shew, that the time of using means was not yet come, or as a French Abbé has lately said, the time has gone by." It is not true, that we want every body to become missionaries; but we want many more than have yet become so. We want the bishops, and presbyters, and pastors, and teachers, to imitate the apostolic church at Antioch, and choose from amongst themselves some of their most experienced, and wisest, and holiest men—men separated by the Holy Ghost from worldly ambition, and schemes of self-aggrandizement, and selfish notions of domestic comfort, to go forth to the nations, to proclaim the Gospel. The churches should send forth their Pauls and their Barnabases, with young men like Mark to minister to them, and assist them; and when they die, to succeed them, as Joshua did Moses; and as Elisha did Elijah, that the work may not cease.

The thing that is most wanted is *personal service.* The missionary work is still, by the churches, deemed, in comparison of the ministry at home, a low service. I know I shall be told, that this is not true, that it is very much esteemed and praised. That it is very much praised is true, and it cannot be the meaning of your preacher, that he is not sufficiently praised; but praises are very easily bestowed: if the service were *really esteemed* by the churches and ministers, a greater number of experienced men would enter into it. If it were really thought to be preferment to become a Missionary; we should have many more candidates from men esteemed in the churches than we have. Those whom the churches look up to, are thought to do great things, if they become members of a deputation, to go abroad, and forthwith come back again; or, as to some, if they will condescend to become Directors, instead of Missionaries. And so the truth comes to be, that there are nearly as many directors as missionaries; as many generals as soldiers in this spiritual warfare. I solemnly avow the highest respect for individuals, who are directors, and for those who have been members of deputations, whilst I speak of the subject generally. The men of eminence in the churches cling to home, and now and then preach a missionary sermon, and the churches laud them for it, and they laud the churches for their liberality; and all parties devolve the actual labour, and the conflict, in foreign lands, on the inexperienced. When chaplains, and ministers, and bishops are wanted for India, with a good income, and a pension, *after a limited* service, you will find men of standing in the churches come forward; and you will find eminently good men, who will undertake deputations, and become superintendants for a time; but none of these will undertake the hard and everlasting duty abroad, which is expected of the Missionary; were it duly esteemed, no discomforts nor difficulties would prevent men from engaging in it; for if fear, or the love of ease, prevent men engaging in a high and honourable calling, then is the charge of coward and sluggard justly applicable. To convince, I must speak what I conceive to be plain truths.

o 2

created the universe, the Lord of heaven and earth,—so partial is the exception, it may safely be affirmed, no altar is erected in China or in Corea, in Japan or Cochinchina. And together with their false gods, there goes along an immense host of superstitious usages, and vain conceits, and false hopes, and false fears; and to support the one, and to allay the other, an innumerable multitude of things that cannot profit, are invented and practised. The minute detail of these fooleries may amuse curiosity, but cannot be of any material use. It is a condition of human nature to be deeply lamented, and the more that man is restored to the knowledge and the image of God, the more he will lament it. Men who possess the Christian soul of Paul, will feel their spirits stirred in them, when they behold cities and nations wholly given to idolatry; but the mere man of this world, or the well-educated and scientific sceptic, in India or China, sees nothing to lament in it; nor, to remove this idolatry, or elevate the condition of the human soul, does he consider an object worthy of his attention or care.

For it is not the idolaters alone who inherit from their fathers lies, vanity, and opinions which cannot profit; these are often found even after idolatry has been thrown aside. False opinions concerning the Divine Being and his moral government assume, by the influence of the spirit of delusion, an endless variety of forms, which, if left to themselves, become, in every succeeding generation, more rivetted in the human mind, by the veneration which we are taught to have for our fathers. That we should follow our fathers, is a doctrine sometimes inculcated by Christian advocates; but when transported to the Missionary in Pagan lands, where it is also inculcated, it makes directly against his Christianity.

"You conceited young man," said an aged Chinese father, to his now Christian son, "do you think yourself wiser than your father, and wiser than the emperor, and all the mandarins? Begone, thou fool, and adhere to the religion of thy fathers, who were wiser and more ancient, and had more sages sprung up amongst them in this thy native and heaven-favoured land, than all the Europeans from whence this new religion came."

The young man, however, who was situated, in respect of Judea, at the ends of the earth, was convinced that his father, and his father's fathers, had for many centuries inherited lies, vanity, and things wherein there is no profit, and he remained firm to his Christianity, and was kind to his aged father, and contributed to the old man's comfort and ease, mourning only for the hardness of his heart, that would not, whilst advocating the rights of a father on earth, submit to our Almighty Father in heaven. The prophesy of our text was fulfilled, as it had been in millions of instances before, and as it will continue to be till the end of time. For, as we observed in the second place, it is certain, because,

II. God has said it—or as the scripture phrase is, He hath promised it. The nations *shall* abandon their dumb idols, their lies, vanities, and useless superstitions. This prophesy has been gradually fulfilling in every age since Jeremiah lived. Nations the most powerful, and amongst the most ancient, have relinquished their beloved idols, and abandoned their priests and their sorcerers, and the religion of their fathers; and why may not those that yet remain idolatrous be hereafter converted? Has the Gospel lost its power? is the Lord's arm shortened, that he cannot save? Cannot the Holy Spirit of God quicken those that are dead in trespasses and sins? These questions we put to the Christians. To the sceptic, we maintain that the nature of man is substantially the same all over the world; and since revealed religion has produced certain effects, wherever it has been made fully known, it is fair to expect similar effects from it in future. But to the Christian, we adhere to the ground given us in our text; the divine promise.

By the mouth of his holy prophet here, and by various prophets in other parts of the Sacred Pages, we are assured the Gentiles shall come from the ends of the earth, and renounce their idols, which their fathers had worshipped, and the lies and the vanities to which they had devoted themselves. Men may bring forward, in proud array, a thousand difficulties, and scare us with tales of Indian caste, and Asiatic unchangeableness, and magnify a million-fold, the real difficulties. The Christian knows that God is almighty, and possesses infinite resources; and human beings all round the world are his creatures, and his word is faithful and true, and never has, nor ever will fail of being accomplished; and therefore the nations shall come from the ends of the earth, and abandon their idols. The Lord God omnipotent reigneth, and his kingdom ruleth over all. His almighty power can change the hearts of kings and rulers, can level mountains and raise vallies; can make all his mountains a way, and cause his high ways to be exalted. And then willing converts shall come from far; and lo! these from the north and from the west, and those from "the land of *Sinim*," which last name some interpret of Sina, or China.

'But if the Almighty has promised the consummation you anticipate, (says an objector,) no doubt he will himself accomplish it; he does not require man's help. We know well that Heaven can, by a miracle, convert the nations, and it will never be done till he does effect it in a miraculous manner.'

To this we answer, that if by a "miraculous manner," be intended a change of sentiment and heart, effected without divine truth being conveyed to the understanding and conscience; we deny that such has heretofore been the proceeding of Divine Providence, and therefore it is not to be expected in time future. And we affirm, that in time past, individuals and nations have been turned from their lying vanities, by the truths of Christ's Gospel, addressed in various ways to the understanding and affections of men; and that there is a standing order given by the Redeemer, to continue such means, till all the kingdoms of this world shall become the kingdoms of our Lord Jesus Christ. We argue, that the intimation of Heaven's final intention, is a reason why Christian churches should use means; for God is pleased, in the general government of the world, both physical and moral, to use means to effect the thing finally intended. If Heaven had not revealed that the nations should abandon, at some period, the lies and vanities of their fathers; the language of adversaries, who affirm, that Heaven is pleased with all the various forms of idol-worship, and that the uncalled for interference of the busy Christian zealots, is a nuisance in the earth, would have had a specious appearance of truth. And certainly there would be little encouragement to use means to effect a change, which, perhaps, Heaven never intended should take place. But as the matter now stands, we know God designs, that eventually the Gentiles from the ends of the earth shall come to him, and shall say—Surely our fathers have inherited lies, vanity, and things wherein there is no profit. Shall *man* make gods? they shall be astonished at the absurdity, and reject the idols with scorn and abhorrence, in spite of prejudice and caste, and the ancient veneration of their sires. Let the Christian churches, therefore, use diligently scriptural means to convey Christ's Gospel to the *Gentiles, even to the ends of the earth.*

III. Now, as the church is the human agent in this great work, and must employ the means we were to speak of in the third place, I will give my sentiments concerning it. The church of our Lord Jesus Christ is *one* to him, and he knows every member of it; but to the human eye, it is made up of many parts. And in this church, this *ecclesia*, or assembly, as visible to the human eye, there are, it is to be feared, many persons not true members of it; and who can be distinguished, certainly, only by the divine eye of our Redeemer, who is the Head, the President, (if I may so speak,) of this assembly or church. Like a field of corn, it contains good grain, and here and there, mixed among the good grain, some noxious or useless weeds, which the discerning eye of the husbandman can easily distinguish. It is not expedient, whilst growing up, to separate them,

God that is to effect the change. To him we look. Those who think our attempts arrogant or presumptuous, mistake the matter, and attribute to us notions of self-sufficiency which we do not possess; on the contrary, we renounce self-dependence, and we adopt the prophet's words in our text, as expressive of our real sentiments—"O Jehovah, our strength, and our fortress, and our refuge, in the day of affliction, our eyes are towards thee, to cause the Gentiles to come from the ends of the earth, and to cast off the lies, and the vanities, and the profitless things, which they inherited from their fathers. And is any thing too hard for God! Hath he spoken, and will he not do it!

Shall the Redeemer, who was wounded for man's transgressions, and bruised for man's iniquities, and died on the accursed tree to redeem man from the curse of the law, not see of the travail of his soul and be satisfied?—O ye Christians, to-day, or whenever ye remember the death of Jesus, remember the millions in various lands to whom his atoning sacrifice has not been preached; and remember his last command—"Go and preach the Gospel to every creature," and then the guilt of indifference to the cause of missions will appear.

DISCOURSE XVI.

DELIVERED AT THE REV. MR. COLLISON'S CHAPEL, WALTHAMSTOW.

THE CONSTRAINING POWER OF THE SAVIOUR'S LOVE.

2 COR. v. 13, 14, 15.

"*For, whether we be beside ourselves it is to God, or whether we be sober it is for your cause; for the love of Christ constraineth us, because we thus judge, that if one died for all, then were all dead; and that he died for all, that they which live should not henceforth live unto themselves, but unto him who died for them and rose again.*"

THE persons speaking in the verses which I have now read were Paul and Timothy, whose names are joined in the commencement of this letter, which begins thus: "Paul an apostle of Jesus Christ, and Timothy our brother, unto the church of God which is at Corinth, with all the saints which are in all Achaia." In the first instance, then, the words *we* and *us* refer to these two servants of God. An account of the first introduction of the Gospel at Corinth is given in the 18th chapter of the Acts of the Apostles, where it appears that Christianity there met with much opposition. St. Paul, as his manner was, first addressed himself to the Jews: he reasoned in the synagogue every Sabbath, and testified that *Jesus* of Nazareth was the Christ, or promised Messiah. The Jews, however, opposed and blasphemed, and probably mocked the pretensions of Jesus, as many of their posterity have done, up to the present day. Paul was therefore compelled to quit them with this solemn declaration: "Your blood,—the blood of your self-murdered souls,—be upon your own heads, I am clean; from henceforth I will go unto the Gentiles." Paul accordingly left the house of Aquila the Jew, and entered a certain man's house named *Justus*, probably a Roman, one that worshipped God. And at this place Paul remained a year and six months, teaching the word of God among the people. Crispus, a chief ruler of the synagogue, one that presided in the Jewish assemblies, who expounded the law, and directed in many things the consciences of the people, believed the truths of the Gospel, and all his house united with him; and many of the pagan Corinthians hearing, believed, and were baptized; and so was formed the first Christian church at Corinth. Corinth, as is well known, was rich, and learned, and profligate; and the disciples who formed the first Christian church there, were in some degree infected with the character of the place; and hence, as appears from both St. Paul's letters to them, there existed strifes, and divisions, and various irregularities, and pretenders to the wisdom of words, and superior rationality, and who gloried in showy appearances, and who calumniated the Apostle, representing him, in the way Festus did, as a madman, one "beside" himself, a deranged person. To such pretensions and allusions there is frequent reference in both the epistles to the Corinthians, and the last allegation is particularly met in the first sentence which we have chosen as the subject of this discourse; "If we be beside ourselves, it is to God; or whether we be sober, it is for your cause;" *i.e.* if when we preach to you the sublime truths concerning our Lord Jesus Christ, and the awful realities of eternity, we be accused of enthusiasm, fanaticism, or madness, like people "beside" themselves, we regard not the accusation; for we walk by faith, not by sight; we obey God rather than men; we believe God and not men; we perform a duty which God has laid upon us: if we be considered beside ourselves, the appearances induced arise entirely from our regard to the will of God. Or, on the other hand, if we appear sober, to be dispassionate, and to descend to subjects that are simple and easy, mere common-place topics, to reason with you as carnal persons, to feed you with milk as babes; we are prompted to this line of conduct by regard to your spiritual welfare;—it is for your cause. And again, when we appear to disregard ourselves, and to neglect the ordinary rules of prudence, as to our own ease and safety, our own wealth and prosperity, we feel fully justified in our own minds: for in addition to the motives which we have expressed, *the love of Christ constraineth us;* it is his love manifested towards us, in dying for our eternal salvation, which induces us to pay that little regard to temporalities that we do; it is his love which raises us above the spirit of selfishness which prevails so much in the world. Christ's love bears us away with itself; it causes us to love after the similitude of that love by which we are influenced. Since God so loved the world as to give his Son for it, and since Christ so loved the world as to pour out his life for it; so we, influenced by the same love, desire to spend and to be spent for the glory of God and the salvation of immortal souls. For we thus judge, that since one died for all, then were all dead; the death of Jesus Christ for all, implies that all were dead in trespasses and sins, legally and spiritually dead, and liable to the second death. Jesus died that they might live; he died to atone for their sins, and to deliver them from going down into the pit of destruction, into the lake of fire which will never be quenched, which is the second death. But, adds the Apostle, Jesus not only died to deliver men from so great a death, he also rose again from the dead, for their justification; and having risen from the grave he ascended to heaven, to confer the quickening influences of the Holy Spirit, to regenerate or give a new life to the children of men, to give a spiritual, holy, heavenly life, to dead, corrupted, sinful souls.

Now then, say St. Paul and his fellow servant, *we* thus judge that if one died for all, then were all dead; and that all those who are made alive in consequence of the death of Christ, should not live to themselves, but to him who died for them. The Christian's not living to himself, is on the supposition that he is no longer his own property, or master, or Lord. What! says St. Paul in his first letter to the Corinthians, Know ye not, that ye are not your own? for ye are bought with a price; therefore, glorify God in your body and in your spirit, which are God's. And when addressing the Romans, he says—None of us liveth to himself, and no man dieth to himself; for, whether we live we live unto the Lord, or whether we die we die unto the Lord; living, therefore, or dying, we are the Lord's.—The doctrine taught is evidently this; the disciple of Jesus Christ, the true Christian, his person, soul and body, his faculties, the powers of his mind, and the members of his body, belong to Christ; his time, his property, all he is, and all he possesses, belong to the Saviour; and all should be employed not to please or to gratify self; but be used as the Saviour has directed. All must be dedicated or devoted to the Saviour's cause. The love of Christ, the love of God our Saviour, in yielding himself to death for human beings, guilty and vile in the sight of pure and divine intelligences is, without controversy, the astonishment of the universe. Man, when he is called to make a sacrifice, dwells on the worthiness of the object in whose behalf he makes it; or takes into account the nearness of the relation. For a good, benevolent, and meritorious person, some would even dare to die. For a friend, a father, a sister, or a wife, there are men who would suffer much and risk their lives; but God commendeth his love towards us, in that whilst we were yet sinners, Christ died for us.

Should an earthly monarch die for the vilest wretch in his dominions, a father yield himself to death for the most abandoned and most worthless son, or a master for the basest slave—it were all nothing, O Christian! in comparison of Christ dying for thee! Christ's love, is love that passeth knowledge! O the height of bliss and glory, from which he descended; and O, the depth of misery, from which he raises the penitent and humble soul! In our present state of imperfect knowledge it is, I imagine, utterly impossible to comprehend the height and the breadth, the depth and the length of the love of Christ. For passing over the consideration of the dignity of his person, and the depth of his humiliation, and the cruel form in which death was inflicted, and the ignominious circumstances attending it; there was, in the Saviour's death, a sting, the venom of which is unknown to us; there was in it, the *curse* of the law, the wrath of justice, the inconceivable and indescribable agony and anguish which the punishment of sin occasioned; for on him were laid the iniquities of us all, and he bore the mighty load! and this was his own free and unconstrained proceeding—the compassion of his own soul prompted him to this. It was love to perishing sinners that brought the Saviour from heaven to earth, and which led him through a series of sufferings, indignities, and insults, to the cross on Calvary. The tongue of angels cannot express, the mind of angels cannot conceive, the Saviour's love. And Oh! how low are man's ordinary conceptions of this amazing subject.

At times, indeed, when the terrors of an awakened conscience flash in a man's face; when death, and hell, and the unknown horror and miseries of the invisible state cross the imagination; the feeling of gratitude for deliverance is a little aroused, and the perception of the Saviour's love somewhat sharpened. When heaven and eternal bliss, and the rivers of pleasure near the throne of God and of the Lamb, are vividly seen by faith, the workings of a grateful heart to the Saviour indicate some sense of his love; and the Christian mourns with shame on account of his past forgetfulness and daily inattention to so grand a theme; but, after all, O how feeble the impression, how indistinct the perception of the love of Christ which usually exists in the hearts and understandings of Christians. But according to the Apostle, the love of the divine Redeemer should originate in the hearts of Christians a corresponding sentiment, which shall be the master principle, the strongest motive that operates in a man's breast; the constant, never-wearied feeling of attachment and devotedness, which shall grow more intense as the believer advances in life, and go with him through the vale of death, into the eternal world. In the life, the labours, and sufferings of the Apostle Paul, a striking example is exhibited of the constraining power of divine love. He forsook all, took up his cross, and followed Christ. Being called to the work of the Lord, neither kindred, nor country, nor ease, nor respectability, could allure; not contempt, nor reproach, nor penury and want, nor bodily sufferings, nor mental anxiety, nor death could intimidate him. In the history of many of the other apostles and disciples, and confessors and martyrs, in every age, there have been bright examples of the *constraining* power of the Saviour's love; it has carried his servants (sometimes the weakest lambs of his flock) onward with an overpowering force, through all that was becoming, and dignified, and faithful, even in the midst of the keenest opposition, and persecution, with fire and sword; and has made them more than conquerors. He that loved them and redeemed them by infusing his own Spirit into their souls, made them equal to the conflict against earth and hell, and gave them the victory. Ask, in the memoirs of faithful men of God in every age, who have endured afflictions, for the cause of the Redeemer, who have borne great persecutions, who have been exiled from kindred, or banished from their country, or resisted to blood striving against sin? ask, what was the principle that actuated them? and invariably will it be found that *the love of Christ* was that which constrained them, was that which supported them and carried them through.

The dedication of our persons and services to God might be inculcated on the ground of what is called natural religion. For we belong to the great Creator of all; His property we are, and Him, it is reasonable we should serve. No man can justly say, my tongue is my own, and I will use it as I will, to oppose the truth, or to revile, or to blaspheme. No mere steward can justly say, the property I have in keeping is my own, and I will use it as I please. Divine authority, and Divine right and justice forbid these pretensions; and hence, I say, we might argue self-dedication to God, on the ground of simple *duty*, as creatures. And even in this view of the case, the heart and the affections, and cheerful obedience and devotedness, are by the law justly required. But notwithstanding that these claims on the part of Heaven can be fairly urged; the blessed Gospel of God our Saviour, as set forth in our text, prefers resting the claim on the powerful influence of the Saviour's love: and it is the recognition of this principle, or spirit of love, as the ruling principle, which is the prominent mark by which all true disciples are distinguished. A spirit of frigid philosophism, and visible disaffection to the Saviour, amounting sometimes to a palpable loathing, and dislike of the very mention of love to Christ, especially mark the formalist, the mere moralist, and the fallacious pretenders to a superior degree of rational Christianity.' But he who has not the love of God in him, is in heart a rebel against the Most High; and he who is not constrained by the love of Christ, who does not make this his glory and his delight, is heretical and antichristian. If any man in the Christian church love not the Lord Jesus Christ, he is *anathema maranatha*: He is accursed, and shall be destroyed, unless he repent of his unnatural resistance of divine love. Love to God is essential to the happiness of an immortal spirit; and to win the human soul, what more could have been done than has already been done? God so loved the world in its ruined condition, as to give his Son Jesus Christ, to suffer and to die for its salvation—that whosoever will, may be restored to the Divine favour; Christ Jesus loved us, so as to die for our guilty race. Herein is love, not that we loved God, but that he loved us. Here is God manifest in the flesh dying for rebel man;—and here is wretched, puny, proud man, standing aloof and unmoved, and his heart unaffected, and callous and hard, and cold as a stone; *but*, for a human heart not melted, not influenced by the Saviour's love, it is not possible, we believe, for all heaven, nor will it be possible to all eternity, to furnish a stronger moral motive. If Christ's love melts not man's heart—if it remove not the heart's enmity to God, nothing can; it must be, (we say it not in anger, but in grief,) in that unhappy case, the soul must be under an anathema; for it has resisted the utmost means that Heaven can employ to subdue its enmity, and remove its curse. As far as the exhibition of the most powerful motives can go, the utmost has been done; and the condemnation of that soul must appear, to the pure and holy intelligences of Heaven, as doubly just—just in the first instance, on account of sin; and just in the second instance, for having neglected, or rejected, so great a salvation.

Oh! the infatuation of sinners, who remain careless, and secure, and unmoved, and destitute of grateful love to the Saviour, after having heard the joyful sound. Alas, who are they that are "beside" themselves! The Christian zealots, as they are called, who knowing the terror of the Lord, endeavour to persuade men to flee from the wrath to come? or, they who seem indifferent and at ease, whilst they yet have reason to fear that the wrath of God abideth upon them? Who are they that are "beside" themselves? those who, knowing that we must all appear before the judgment seat of Christ, are ever exercising themselves to preserve a conscience void of offence towards God and towards man? or, those who live as they list, as if man were not accountable to heaven's great Lord; and who, notwithstanding, yet dream of attaining to the bliss of heaven after death? It were, perhaps, only to irritate the feelings, to retort the charge of mental aberration back from the zealous Christian, on the secure and self-sufficient worldling; but it is not difficult to see the folly and insanity of passing through time, absorbed totally in its pleasures, or its business, and entirely neglecting eternity; or, of maintaining a careless spirit of indifference to the cause of God and of Christ, and of the eternal welfare of millions, and the destinies of our own immortal spirits. The supposition and allegation that Paul's zeal approached to madness, or that the zeal of Christians, in every age, exceeded the requirements of the case, must arise from a disbelief of the alleged facts and principles to which the case refers; there must be a lurking disbelief of the evil of sin; of the danger of everlasting punishment; of the necessity of the Saviour's mediatorial work; there must be a disbelief, that he actually was a divine person clothed with humanity, suffering and dying for the redemption of men; there must be a lurking presumption in the mind, that heaven's future happiness can be attained without Christ's salvation. We thus judge, because we do not think it possible that a right understanding of the case, and a firm belief of the facts and principles adverted to, are compatible with indifference, or an unexcited state of mind. I think it is said of the sceptic Hume, when he heard the zealous Whitfield preach, that if he believed what Whitfield did, he would act as Whitfield acted. The truth is, that both in respect of our personal salvation, and of the salvation of other men, and the evangelization of other lands, the utmost zeal that has ever been manifested in the use of means, such as Paul employed, has not at all equalled what the most sober and dispassionate view of the subject evidently demands. It is the neglect of means, such as teaching and preaching, and the distribution of Bibles, and of pious books, in every accessible part of the world, with a view to instruct, and convince, and convert the children of men, which is chargeable with mental aberration; because it is expecting the end without the means; it is expecting a harvest without sowing the seed; and to act thus, may indeed be denominated fanatical, if that term denotes a totally *unfounded* expectation of some wished-for good. But he who diligently sows the seed of divine truth early and late, who begins in the morning of life, and in the evening withholds not his hand; who is instant in season and out of season in disseminating God's word; who reproves, and rebukes, and exhorts his kindred, and his friends, and his neighbours; or who goes to the savages of the Southern Sea, or to the civilized millions of Eastern Asia, with Christ's Gospel in his heart, and on his tongue, is *not* "beside" himself; but is doing what the soberest mind, that is at all well-affected to God and Christ, and the souls of men, must approve. A practice like that of the Apostle *Paul*;—that is, continually, and at all risks, teaching the things concerning the kingdom of God; proclaiming the glad tidings of salvation through Christ to Jews and to Greeks; going from house to house making known the Saviour; spending and being spent for his sake; making great sacrifices, and enduring great afflictions, devoting the whole soul to the great work of communicating Christian knowledge, is according to the maxims of the most perfect reason; for it is employing the means which God has appointed to promote the temporal and eternal happiness of man. Nor is a comparative disregard of those things which are seen and temporal, with a supreme attention to those which are unseen and eternal, the mark of being "beside" one's-self. Alas! how much do they mistake, who imagine that a plodding and perpetual anxiety about this world, is a mark of wisdom, and of a sane mind; whilst the never dying spirit and its affairs are neglected. If indeed a supreme regard to things temporal and personal were a mark of wisdom and sound mind, then would the great majority of the men of this generation deserve the character of being wise and rational.

But if a high-toned feeling of affection for the Saviour, a feeling of the constraining power of his love, a sacrifice of self, of personal and domestic considerations for Christ's sake, be a mark of wisdom, then is there not much wisdom or sound judgment in the world; for as yet it may be said, as it was said in the apostolic age, when duty is contrasted with the doings of Christians, "All still seek their own, not the things which are Jesus Christ's."

We would not be unjust or querulous; there is *some* regard with many professors to the affairs of the Saviour's kingdom, and there is *much* regard with a few; but oh, when the churches bring their conduct, their feelings, and affections to the standard of apostolic precept, and apostolic example, where shall we find the symptoms of that intense zeal which Paul experienced, and that devotedness which he practised? Earthly Monarchs, great Leaders and Captains, and human Patrons, often receive the offer of life and fortune in their service; almost every country, from the rising to the setting sun, has furnished most striking examples of this sort; and superstition, or false religion, has many devotees, prompted to the greatest sacrifices for the sake of their system. And the Christian cause has, in ages that are past, produced many honoured names, who have not counted their lives dear unto themselves, that they might manifest their gratitude and attachment to the Captain of Salvation; and in the present age (we mean not to deny it) there are many who love our Lord Jesus Christ in sincerity, and are his devoted and zealous servants; yet, after all this admission, we fear that when the rule is applied generally to professed disciples of the Nazarene, Jesus, the Son of God, it will be found that both men and devils are more zealously served than he is—that living kings and captains, and dead deified heroes and canonized saints, in different nations of the world, have more of men's affections, and time, and property, and actual personal service, than our adorable Redeemer.

When we look round on the ten or fifteen thousands of Christian ministers in this highly favoured land, how great a number is there who exhibit no symptoms of feeling the constraining power of the love of Christ? Is there not reason to fear that personal and domestic comfort, and the aggrandisement of their families, generally take the precedence of all other claims?

And of the private Christians, possessed of wealth and of leisure, how small is the proportion who consecrate their time and their property to the Saviour's cause. The principle seems scarcely admitted that God our Saviour has the *first claim* upon us. We give not the first fruits of our increase to him, but are satisfied with leaving the gleanings to Christ's cause, after we have appropriated and hoarded up for our own old age, or our posterity, the rich harvest that heaven entrusted to us; and then mark, in many instances, the consequence; the man who distrusted Providence, and filled his own barns, never arrives at old age, and posterity is corrupted by his wealth, for which they never laboured, and in Satan's service is squandered, what Christ's disciple would not spend in his Master's cause.

Alas! in this prudent, and I fear ostentatious age, how

few who seem carried forwards to personal sacrifices, and disinterested labours, by the constraining power of our Lord's love? How few of the disciples live to him who died for them! There are some, blessed be God! we deny it not. The associated efforts of many individuals and many churches to educate the young, to visit with the Gospel destitute villages, and to carry the glad tidings of salvation to the ends of the earth, indicate the existence of much love to the Saviour in the land, which is a foundation on which to build the hope of still brighter and better days. Yet, alas! among the baptized and professed Christians of this land, how large is the number of those who still continue the devotees of amusement and frivolity; who spend on mere self-gratification their time, and their property, and the exertions of their minds. Day after day, and night after night, do the trifles of fashion and amusement occupy their thoughts and their conversations; and yet are they to be found in churches or in chapels at least once of a Sunday. In such cases, how evident the defect of Christian love and living to the Saviour. How little evidence have they that they are indeed Christians.

And there are, too, men in Christian societies, whose hearts are wholly set on the accumulation of wealth and fortune. How industrious, how laborious are they. Early and late do they fix their attention on schemes of gain, laying up treasures on earth, anxious to leave riches to their children or near relatives, whilst Christ's cause is either neglected, or receives some scanty crumbs from their well-spread table; they live to themselves, and not to him who died for them.

Again, the lettered men of this land, who profess the Christian name, what do they study to promote the diffusion of Christ's gospel throughout the world? Alas! this is but rarely their object. Their own fame, or the agreeable or the fashionable pursuits of literature, are those to which they attend; and the living languages of mankind, amongst nations to which the gospel has not yet reached, are left to here and there a solitary individual; and scholars and divines will spend their lives in perusing, or in translating dead pagan books into English, whilst the translation or composition of Christian books, for the instruction of hundreds of millions of living pagans, is by them totally neglected. These instances will convince every pious mind that much yet remains to be done, to evince the general existence of the love of Christ in the hearts of his professed disciples throughout the Christian churches of this land. But I must close:

This subject should lead us all to self-examination, and to put to ourselves this question:—To what has the love of Christ constrained me? and, first of all, has it constrained me to hate sin? for they were the sins of men which crucified the Lord of Glory. A hatred of sin is the first and the best evidence of the love of Christ being efficacious in producing a corresponding love in our hearts; for a love to the Saviour and a love of sin cannot exist together in the same heart. He that loves sin, hates the Saviour; therefore, the first effect of the love of Christ being shed abroad in any heart, is inducing it to crucify the flesh with its affections and lusts. Take St. Paul's reasoning and advice on the subject: "In that Christ died, he died unto sin once; but in that he liveth, he liveth unto God: likewise reckon ye yourselves to be dead indeed unto sin, but alive unto God, through Jesus Christ our Lord. Let not sin therefore reign in your mortal bodies, that ye should fulfil it in the lusts thereof." And take St. Peter's admonition: "Forasmuch as Christ hath suffered for us in the flesh, arm yourselves likewise with the same mind, for he that hath suffered in the flesh hath ceased from sin, that he should no longer live the rest of his time in the flesh to the lusts of men, but to the will of God." Thus you see that the love of Christ must constrain us, in the first place, to deny ungodliness and worldly lusts, and to live soberly, righteously, and godly in this present world, adorning the doctrine of God our Saviour in all things, and by well doing putting to silence the ignorance of foolish men. This first effect of the Saviour's love terminating in ourselves is essential to the Christian character, and without it the utmost apparent zeal for the enlargement of the visible church, for the increase of education, or for the conversion of the nations to Christianity, will not prove any real attachment to the Saviour. Wilful and habitual sin in professed disciples is like crucifying the Son of God afresh, trampling his blood under foot, and exposing him to open scorn. It will, at the great day of judgment, be in vain to say, "Lord! Lord! have we not prophesied in thy name, and in thy name done many wonderful works," and shewn great zeal for thy cause in the world, if we love and serve sin. He will say, Depart from me, all ye that work iniquity, I never knew you: they that loved me kept my commandments, but ye despised and disobeyed them. True zeal and ardent affection to the cause of our Lord, is not shewn by assailing the sins and ignorances of other men, and indulging our own; but since, humanly speaking, our own sins are most within our own reach, they will be first cast away, whenever our hatred of sin is real. And ministers, and parents, and teachers have need most especially to regard this, when attempting to communicate moral and religious instruction to the young, if they would have God's blessing rest on their labours.

There have been periods of the church, when pious good men seemed to neglect the external diffusion of Christian principles, and to retire within themselves, and let their love to Christ terminate in holy contemplations, and devout admiration of his infinite and ineffable grace. The present is an age of external effort and exertion, and as man, weak and wicked, is ever prone to go to extremes, there is a danger of being hurried onward to activity by the impulse of men's opinions, instead of being actuated by an internal principle of love to Christ. I may, therefore, be permitted to suggest to you, my fellow Christians, the propriety of self-examination on this point, to see whether you are drawn by the cords of divine love, or with the bands of man's opinion. Alas! if man's opinion only, or chiefly, or the importunity of zealous individuals, are the things which carry us forward to support schools, and to advocate the cause of education, and the building of chapels, and the raising up of ministers, and printing Bibles, and sending forth missionaries, and all the while the crucified Redeemer be forgotten, or overlooked by us, in the secret movements of our souls; although man cannot know it, the Saviour knows it, and he cannot possibly accept with approbation our contributions and our doings; for in such case it is not him we serve, but our own vanity, or our own good name. It is the praise of man we are aiming at, and not the praise of God.

These hints will, I hope, induce us all to cherish a spirit of watchfulness, and to be instant in prayer, that our motives may be pure and sincere, that our eye may be single, that it may never be turned away from the cross and crown of our divine Lord; that we may be workers together with him, and labour or suffer with him; that we may now fight the good fight of faith, lay hold on eternal life, be ever cleaving to Jesus, for our life is hid with Christ in God; and that we may be permitted at last to reign with him for ever and ever, joining in the celestial song of Moses and the Lamb, and reciting, throughout eternity, the praises of him who *loved* us, and washed us from our sins in his own blood; to whom be glory and dominion, Amen and Amen!

Topics of an Exhortation founded on the preceding Discourse.

The cause of Christian missions is the cause of Christ.

He has commanded them to be undertaken.

The heathen nations are given to him as his inheritance.

When he sees their conversion, he sees of the travail of his soul, and is satisfied.

He has commanded ordinary means to be used:—*Go and teach all* nations.

The idea of *waiting* for miraculous interference has been acted on, but does not seem warranted. Chinese, supposed to be the most difficult language under heaven, has given way to the use of means.

Christian missions are Christ's cause, and love to him should constrain every Christian to aid in sending forth missionaries, and supporting them, till churches be formed amongst the heathen.

SCHOOLS.

Neglect of children raises up careless men and women, who neglect the next generation, and onwards the world grows worse.

Tuition of children raises up a generation of men and women who teach the next generation of children, and the world is improved.

To assist the poor in educating their children is doing them the greatest service.

And to bring little children to the Saviour must be pleasing to him.

Jesus, the Son of God, who once
For us his life resign'd,
Now lives in heaven, our great High Priest,
And never-dying Friend.
Through life, through death, let us to him
With constancy adhere;
Faith shall supply new strength, and hope
Shall banish every fear.

To human weakness not severe
Is our High Priest above;
His heart o'erflows with tenderness,
His bowels melt with love.
With sympathetic feelings touch'd,
He knows our feeble frame;
He knows what sore temptations are,
For he hath felt the same.

But tho' he felt temptation's pow'r
Unconquer'd he remain'd;
Nor 'midst the frailty of our frame,
By sin was ever stain'd,
As, in the days of feeble flesh,
He pour'd forth cries and tears;
So, though exalted, still he feels
What every Christian bears.

Then let us, with a filial heart,
Come boldly to the throne
Of grace supreme, to tell our griefs,
And all our wants make known:
That mercy we may there obtain
For sins and errors past,
And grace to help in time of need,
While days of trial last.

DISCOURSE XVII.

DELIVERED AT HOXTON ACADEMY CHAPEL, FEBRUARY 6, 1825.

REGARD TO THE AFFAIRS OF OTHERS.

PHILIPPIANS, II. 4.

"*Look not every one on his own things, but every one also on the things of others.*"

THIS sentence of St. Paul's letter to the Christians at Philippi, I consider as a precept addressed to those only, whose hearts are imbued with a principle of love to God and man; for if addressed to an unregenerated heart, or a mind destitute of a principle of piety and benevolence, it would produce nothing but mischief. A *selfish* creature's looking on the things or affairs of others, and intermeddling with them, can effect no good to that other person: but, contrariwise, may do him much harm. The looker-on, if he sees wants, does not relieve them, if he sees imperfections, he exposes them, instead of endeavouring to hide and remove them; if he sees inconsistencies and follies, he ridicules them and pours forth his contempt; if he sees weaknesses, he endeavours to avail himself of them, to benefit and aggrandize himself: therefore it is only he who loves God with all his heart, and his neighbour as himself, that can look on the things of others, and attend to them, in a manner that is beneficial to those other persons. But all sincere Christians profess to love God and their neighbour; therefore I shall feel justified, in addressing Christians on this occasion, to exhort them, individually and collectively, not only to look to their own affairs, but also to the affairs of others. And in the way in which I have guarded the application of this principle, I shall not feel myself justly chargeable with an endeavour to inculcate a spirit of improper interference; the spirit of a meddlesome person; a troublesome busy-body: nor yet shall I feel justly charged with calling upon persons to *neglect* their own affairs, and officiously *interfere* with the affairs of others; or, as the Chinese express it, neglect their own field, and affect to cultivate their neighbour's;—leave their own door choked up with snow, and run to sweep the snow off their neighbour's house-top. There are such persons in the world, but Scripture and reason condemn them; and although selfishness, and a hard-hearted indifference to the cause of God and man, may caricature, and with such allegations calumniate an enlarged benevolence; we maintain that it is not difficult to distinguish a pernicious busy-body, from an ever active and benevolent good man. Religion must not be neglected and set aside, because there are hypocrites; nor must a Christian draw back and retire within himself, because there are ambitious, bustling, noisy, and would-be philanthropists.

Our text says, "Look not every man on his own things," and a caviller may say, it teaches a man to overlook his own affairs and neglect them, in order that he may attend to the affairs of others, which is a proceeding altogether unreasonable. But those acquainted with the idiom of the original language, know that the meaning of the passage is not thus; but that it directs every man to look at, or regard, in all he says and does, not his own welfare *only* or *solely*, but also to have a regard (at the same time that he studies his own welfare) to the temporal and spiritual welfare of others. It is well known that the New Testament teaches Christians to be sober, to be vigilant, to be watchful, to be industrious in all that concerns their own hearts, their personal and domestic interests, and to seek the good of the land they live in; and therefore every candid reader will interpret the expression in our text, in the way which has now been done, and consider it as directed against the demon or idol of *self*, which regards not the discomfort, the ignorance, the want, the misery of others; but which is wholly absorbed about its own things. Self-gratification, which is totally regardless of the misery occasioned to others, is the cruel idol worshipped by the man of pleasure; self-interest is the idol of the covetous, a false god, much worshipped in Christendom, as well as in pagan lands; self-aggrandizement is the idol of the ambitious; and self-ease, self-comfort, and self-edification constitute a sort of household god, secretly worshipped by many a pious Christian.

But "charity seeketh not her own" exclusively; a spirit of heaven-derived benevolence loves her neighbour as herself, regards not only her own gratification, interest, aggradizement, ease, comfort, edification, and happiness; but also desires and labours to promote all these in reference to other persons, families, districts, and nations. The idol of self is thrown down, and God and his creatures are restored to that place in our affections and regards, which is their just right.

Although each person cannot make his or her individual exertions universally beneficial to others, still a spirit of universal benevolence can be cherished, and be productive of the greatest benefit, by disposing the heart to do good to others, whenever or wherever, on every possible occasion, an opportunity is presented. Those who cherish this spirit never say, when it is in the power of their hand to do good, "This is not my concern; that man is not a Jew, but a Samaritan; or he is a Jew, and not a Samaritan, and I will pass by on the other side, and leave him in his distress, and will turn my attention home, for charity begins at home." No; the principle we advocate would prevent this selfish pretext; and I do maintain, (although the sentiment be in opposition perhaps to the opinions of some good men,) that the idea of *universal* benevolence is not a useless visionary notion; but it is a rational, scriptural, christian idea; and my reason is this:—Christians are in scripture taught to imitate the universal benignity of the Deity, whose tender mercies are over all his works, and who causes his sun to rise and shine on all the nations, and on all classes of persons, and sendeth rain on the just and on the unjust. And Christians are further taught in that very Letter of St. Paul, in which our text lies, to imitate not only the extent, but the degree of the Saviour's *benevolence;* if we can apply the word benevolence to the inexpressible and utterly inconceivable charity, which induced him to look upon our lost and ruined world, and interfere to effect our eternal salvation. Let the same mind, says St. Paul to the Christians at Philippi, be in you, which was also in Christ Jesus, who, (although in the form of God—and incomprehensibly glorious and blessed—and equal with God—still, although thus rich in glory and blessedness;) for our sakes emptied himself, and became poor, and made himself of no reputation; and assumed the form of a servant, and the likeness of men; and laid himself low, and submitted to death, even the ignominious and cruel death of the cross. Now it was in pity to all ranks and conditions of men, and for polluted, guilty, wretched, creatures in all nations, and amongst all peoples and languages, that he thus humbled himself and shed his blood;—and never can benevolence so disinterested, or to such a degree, or to such an extent, be equalled, any more than the infinite beneficence of the Deity can be equalled by the puny efforts of feeble man: but still, you perceive the Bible commands Christians to imitate the one as well as the other; to cherish the same mind that was in Christ Jesus, when he looked on the affairs and died for the redemption of the world. Universal benevolence, then, is a scriptural idea; and to cherish such a sentiment, a christian duty.

And how wonderfully comprehensive is the precept that requires this duty—Be ye imitators of God and of the Saviour! The *natural* perfections of the Deity are indeed inimitable; we cannot imitate omnipotence and create a world; nor can we imitate omniscience, and therefore should not affect to judge the world: but we are commanded to imitate the moral perfections of God Almighty, Father, Son, and Spirit ;—to be just as God is just; to be holy as he is holy; pure as he is pure; merciful as he is merciful; and in benignity and charity to resemble him; to forgive as he forgives us; to be patient as he is patient to us; and every one of us to look on the affairs of others, as Christ Jesus looked upon ours;—with similar mercy, and with similar exertions; to bear with others; to labour for others; to suffer deprivations and insults; and, if necessary, death for the sake of others.

Be ye imitators of God, and like-minded with Christ.—Oh, what a rule of Christian ethics is this! and how gloriously *peculiar* is our holy religion in this! Neither ancient nor modern Pagans could say to the people, "Be ye *imitators* of your gods," without saying with the same breath, "Be ye vicious, or impure, or cruel;" nor can the priests of Mahommed tell the Musselmen to *imitate* their prophet, without implying the same absurdity.

Did that principle of benevolent concern for others generally prevail, it would prevent, and in every instance in which it does exist, it does prevent injustice and injuries, and the withholding of rights, and it insures the bestowment of positive good. If the people of Europe called Christians, had looked with a benevolent eye on the affairs of the sons of Africa, how could the abominable Slave-trade ever have been suffered to grow to that horridly cruel and malignant height that it did? If the people of this land called Christians, had looked with a benevolent eye on the poor families around them, how could their children have remained, generation after generation, growing up, and living, and dying in gross ignorance and vice; whilst those who had it in their power to instruct gratuitously, and those whom the funds of the country maintained for the purpose of instructing the people, very generally stood by unconcerned? If at this day the christian churches cherished the principle of benevolent concern for others, to the degree which comes at all near to an imitation of the Saviour, would they view with that apathy which they still do, the situation of hundreds of millions of the human family in the eastern hemisphere, beyond the Ganges, and in other regions; and seem to grudge (as some pious people do) the scanty, miserably disproportioned aid afforded to them? Many more instances of selfish unconcern for others could be brought forwards, every one tending to shew, that still, in our day, of which we think so highly, and which we praise so loudly; still, in comparison of what Christian churches should do, it may in truth be said of them—"All seek their own, not the things which are Jesus Christ's." All look upon their own things; no man cares for the things of others. I speak thus, not because I despise the day of small doings; nor because I am insensible of the willing and devoted aid of many poor Christians, whose mite, given with grateful hearts to the Saviour, constitutes nearly their all; nor do I mean to insinuate that there are no opulent Christians, who contribute largely to benevolent objects of different kinds; but I speak thus, because I take the churches collectively, and I do not confine Christian duty to the bestowment of money, but extend it to the concern which Christians ought to manifest for others, by their *personal services;* I maintain that Christians should allow themselves to be incommoded; and sacrifice their personal and domestic comforts occasionally, or frequently, or perpetually, as circumstances may require; that they should sometimes quit their homes, and their kindred, and their country, from a kind regard to the welfare of other tribes and nations of men. I am now endeavouring to inculcate a general principle applicable to all Christians, both in their individual and associated capacities, which if admitted and adopted, would, with Heaven's blessing, speedily improve the moral and spiritual condition of our comparatively happy land, and of all the rest of the nations; this I am endeavouring to do—but I am not intending to censure this or that individual; nor to point to this man or that woman, and dictate what he or she should do. Of the extent of Christian effort for the sake of others, every individual must answer to God his Saviour, and to his own conscience.

Nor do I require Christians, not even missionaries (whom some people consider a sort of devotees), to reject the comforts which the God of nature, and their reconciled and gracious Father in heaven gives them: I do not require them to starve themselves either with hunger or with cold, nor to destroy their health by excessive exertions; but my doctrine requires Christians to make their personal and domestic comforts and affairs, *subordinate* and *subservient* to the cause of Jesus Christ. It requires Christians to make the prosperity and enlargement of the Redeemer's kingdom their *first* object; and the comfort of themselves and families the *second*. If a man or woman *can*, in the course of Divine Providence, aid in any way, the blessed cause of promoting the salvation and happiness of others, and *will* not, because doing so occasions some discomfort, either actually present, or anticipated; then do I say there is in the case of that man or woman, a gross dereliction of duty, and a heinous offence against Zion's King, although I do not say that Jesus will certainly punish the individuals as rebels, and utterly reject them.

We, of the evangelical school, profess to believe that the Saviour (in a manner we do not pretend to understand, nor presume to describe, yet not less really than if we could do both the one and the other) emptied himself of his divine glories and heavenly riches, and put himself in our place, as our surety, to suffer the just penalty of a violated law in our stead; and by so doing deliver us from inconceivably great and interminably lasting miseries: and yet, after all this profession of obligation, there are very few Christians who will part with a moiety of their wealth for the Saviour's sake; there are very few comparatively, who will take the trouble to teach the ignorant in their own neighbourhood concerning the Saviour, which knowledge, they yet profess to believe, is essential to salvation; how few parents, how few mothers will part with their children, that they may go to preach the gospel in remote lands: or in distant parts of our own empire; and how few of the Christian men or women in comfortable or opulent circumstances, will quit their comforts and their homes for Christ's sake. It is very strange indeed, that such persons can so seldom see it to be *their* duty to make any material effort either at home or abroad. If the rich do not, amongst Protestants, give money to procure an indulgence to commit positive sin, yet most of the well-conditioned and opulent evidently think, that a pecuniary contribution purchases an indulgence for the omission of personal service. I do not desire to over-rate the services of any class of men; nor do I expect that the utmost exertions of all the opulent and well-educated men and women in the land, can or will produce a saving effect, without the co-operation of the Lord's hand working with them; but whilst speaking on this subject, it appears incumbent on me to point out the duties and defects of all such. It is my sincere conviction, that there is, in the United Kingdom, a want of fidelity in the public teachers of religion, on this subject; that the Christians are too much flattered and praised, when they simply perform—and perform many of them but very imperfectly—their duty in caring for the spiritual and eternal welfare of others. And who of us is not disposed to over-rate our feeble heartless services in our Saviour's cause? Alas! where do we find the mind that was in Christ prevailing in the Churches?

He, left his Father's bosom and his heavenly home, humbled himself to death, and descended to hell, for me—to save me from thence—says yonder man or woman; and still neither that man nor that woman will quit the comforts of their terrestrial home, though millions are destitute of the means of knowing the Saviour; and they will, in Christian lands, spend their strength and waste their time, and be filled with an intense zeal, to settle in their own way, metaphysical subtleties; whilst millions require to be taught the being of God; the evil of sin; and the existence of a Saviour. But, to descend to a lower standard than an imitation of Jesus, how few of the spiritual Christians, to accomplish their object, emulate the enterprise of the secular merchant; or the fortitude, courage, and perseverance of the ambitious! How few do as much for the spiritual interests of men, as the celebrated Howard did to alleviate the temporal sufferings of guilty criminals! In yonder eastern regions how many Britons are there, who, for the sake of temporal support, or the acquisition of a fortune, endure an exile of twenty or thirty years, and all the discomforts of a foreign land, and of insalubrious climates; and most of these young persons go from the families of the comparatively opulent in this country. The love of self enables them to do all this: but how disproportioned are those whom the love of Christ their Saviour carries forth and keeps there. No! of the churches, our text reversed is yet true.—Every man looks on his own things, and none, or next to none, regards the things of others.

It may be said to the preacher, and what would you have us do? are not great exertions made by British Christians to instruct their own people at home; and to send Christian instruction to other nations? Are not books and teachers; the Bible and tracts, and missionaries, preachers, and catechists sent forth in every direction, and what more can the Christians do? Are not the national churches of Scotland, England, and Ireland supported at a large expense? and are not the unendowed congregational churches, though unsupported by the state, active and zealous even to excess? How can you say that we care not for the spiritual wants of others? Is there not a British and Foreign Bible Society, and British and Foreign School Society, and Sunday Schools without number?—and the liberality and generosity of the Christian public supports them all.

In answer to this interrogatory remonstrance, I say that, without pretending to exactness, I suppose nine-tenths of all this exertion is for the Christians themselves, and not for others: and when I speak of the Christian churches, I include with the people, the ministers of religion, some of whom are opulent and not industrious; and must bear the censure which applies also to laymen, who seek only great things for themselves, and care not for the wants of others. Our text justifies all the activity, and zeal, and anxiety to do good, of the most intensely zealous, at the same time that it condemns the indifferent and selfishly careless professor of Christianity. And although the efforts of British Christians, when all stated together

Q

in the same paragraph, may appear considerable, and to some persons prodigiously great, and even excessive; they are—when measured by the obligation arising from the divine command; and from the example of our crucified Redeemer; and by the crying necessities of others; and the capability of many Christians to do a hundred times more than they do—these efforts must still be denominated feeble and deficient. There are some pious persons think they do well to check the zeal of this nation to relieve the spiritual wants of other nations; and there are some ministers who seem to say to the churches—"Look every man to his own things, and don't look at, nor trouble yourselves with the affairs of others:" and after giving such advice, they go and pray that the Saviour's kingdom may come! nor do they seem to perceive, nor will they admit, that such advice and such prayers are inconsistent. There is a grossly antichristian idea still has place in the breasts of Christians, viz. that the rest of the nations are *not related* to us—that we do not, *as matter of right*, owe them any regard—that we may innocently neglect them: aye, that it is wrong to pay much attention to them; that we must almost entirely mind ourselves. Alas! ye Christians—was this the mind that was in Christ Jesus, when he passed by and saw us in a perishing condition? and is it thus we regard the nations whom our Father created, and for whom the Saviour died? Do we maintain the infidel opinion, that we are a superior race; and that God did not make of one blood all nations of men, and thus contradict and blaspheme the Bible! Do we still hold the silly opinion that geographical limits, a river, a mountain, or an imaginary line, destroys the brotherhood of the family of man? Do we purpose to set up those partition walls, which our Saviour broke down; and assume the Jewish pride, and arrogate to ourselves the special favour of of heaven, and by the assumption, nurse that pride, instead of remarking God's goodness and our own ingratitude, and misuse of privileges, and unfaithfulness in our stewardship? What is all that the spiritual Christians do, compared with what the carnal votaries of pleasure do? with what the lovers of war do? but (which infinitely surpasses every other consideration) what is it that Christians do for others, compared with what Jesus Christ has done for them!

Many do not like to look at the things of others, lest an acquaintance with the real state others should compel the lookers-on to assist. Not so the ancient patriarch Job. The cause of distress which he knew not, he searched out that he might relieve it. And there are some pious people justify their apathy concerning the inhabitants of the eastern limit of Asia, by saying they perceive no opening; they see no movement. As if the dry bones were to move before they were breathed upon; as if the door were to be opened before any herald of salvation knocked at it; as if our Saviour's redeeming work, and infinitely agonizing labours for us, were subsequent to some movement towards him. By a strange perversion of what is right, men exercise their ingenuity to find out reasons, not always very specious, why they should not do their duty and care for others; rather than why they should do it and comply with the precept. In the church, as well as in the world, many of the precepts of the Bible seem to be considered a dead letter. The bitter-spirited disturbers of the peace of churches, never think that the Saviour's command, to be meek and lowly, is at all binding on them. The lovers of money forget that covetousness is idolatry; and those who could, with heaven's aid, materially assist in the propagation of the Gospel in foreign parts, seem to think that the Saviour's promise—"There is no man that hath forsaken father and mother, or brothers or sisters, or wife or children, or houses or lands, for my sake and the Gospel's, but shall receive manifold more in this life, and in the world to come life everlasting"—means, that no man shall forsake either the one or the other of these ties and good things for the Gospel's sake.

You perceive that my mind and discourse falls much into the duty of Christians to look to the things of other nations and tribes of men; but I by no means intend that we must *neglect* those that are near, and *care only* for those that are remote; though I do maintain, agreeably to the example of Paul and Barnabas, that, when men reject the Gospel, it is right to turn away from them, and address it to others. It will not be fair either to charge me with magnifying that in which I myself happen to be engaged, as every one likes to do. My view of the matter is this, and I think it will prove what I have now asserted. I hold that the whole world is guilty before God—that there is none righteous—no, not one. I maintain that every inhabitant of Britian needs salvation as much as a West-Indian slave, or a Hindoo, or a Chinese; that the hearts of Englishmen are as much at enmity against God, previously to that change which we call conversion, as the hearts of any pagan idolater whatever. It is not here that the difference between evangelized and unevangelized lands really lies: but the difference consists in the quantum of means enjoyed in one region and in the other.

Since Augustine, the first archbishop of Canterbury, obtained a footing in this then pagan land, to what a degree have the means of Christian knowledge increased! It is not possible for your preacher to describe the difference of means enjoyed by this country, and that land from which he has returned for a season. It has taken at least ten centuries to bring you to the state of Gospel privilege in which you are this day; and it is not easy for you to look back and realize the pagan state of the Saxon heptarchy. But I have actually experienced a similar state of moral and religious degradation in yonder eastern hemisphere. The people there are not, in a physical point of view, worse off than you. Their climate is not to them generally insalubrious; they have food and raiment, and sunshine and shower, which contribute to the gladness of the animal spirits—but the Christian church protestant has not, till yesterday, taken any pains to convey to them the glad tidings of salvation. The heathen know, by history and experience, the unsubstantial and unsatisfying nature of all sublunary pursuits; of pleasure, of ambition, of riches, of honours—they feel that they are sinners against conscience which accuses them, but still Satan keeps them in a dark prison; and Christians take little pains to send them the light of Gospel liberty—they remain in darkness, and in bondage; hugging their chains; observing rites which cannot profit; cherishing hopes which must prove fallacious; and dreading evils from every source but the real one—sin against God. There are yonder, who can read Chinese, people equal in number to a fourth of the whole population of the world; and there are not there more than four efficient ministers of the reformed religion, for nearly three hundred millions of human beings. The United Kingdom of Great Britain would be better circumstanced than those regions, as to the attainment of Christian knowledge, were all religious books in the land consumed by fire; the churches and chapels demolished; the colleges and academies overthrown; and the ministers of religion annihilated: for after all this havoc and destruction, there would be, I believe, hundreds of thousands of spiritual Christians possessed of divine knowledge; and willing and able to preserve this knowledge, and to re-edify an apparently ruined Christianity in this land. Whilst yonder Satan sits enthroned, and receives the mistaken homage of millions, under the appearance of an endless variety of demon gods, heroes, and virgins, and saints, and spirits of rivers, and mountains, and hills; and the manes of parents and ancestors. And yonder, lying miracles, and false prophets; and cunning diviners, and astrologers; and ignorant, or self-deceived, or hypocritical priests; and monks, and nuns, and masses of *pagan* origin; and a delusive mummery of unintelligible words, every where abound. And in some cases, where the minds of the educated and thinking men revolt at these vulgar deceits of the devil, and misguided men and women, they rush from the extreme of a gross superstition to atheism and annihilation, and live with no better pursuits, and die with no higher hopes, than the beasts that perish.

Now I know very well that there are some, I fear many, in our own land not better than these; but I likewise know that the means of being better informed, and better circumstanced, are almost universally in the power of every individual in these islands—but they will not come to Christ. However, I still give my vote for the employment of every possible effort to compel them to come to the Saviour, and to persecute them (if they will call it so) with the remonstrances and invitations of the gospel. Still I maintain that it is not consistent with a fair representation of the case, to compare or liken Britain to yonder pagan lands; and it is a pitiable niggardliness of some pious misjudging people, who seem to regret that there are British Christians who look not entirely at their own wants; but also look at and endeavour to supply the wants of others, beyond the political limits of our own dominions. I fear these opinions will appear to some, unjustly censorious —if they be so, it is my mistake, of which I shall be happy to be convinced; and as my remarks refer to opinions which I have seen in books or heard in conversations in general society, they are not in the least degree personal. I close by saying, Oh! remember Jesus—his degradation for us; his painful life; his agony in the garden; his death upon the cross,—and remember the *cause* of these; in none of these did he regard his own things, but the things of others. Learn then of Jesus; let the same mind be in you, that was also in Christ Jesus: and look not every man on his own things, but every man also on the things of others.

To this procedure it may be objected, that many other "peoples," and other tribes of men do not *desire* our aid; but if offered, are more likely to despise it than receive it. This is in many cases true, but their misconduct is not the rule of our duty. How many human beings in this country—(aye, it may be there are many in this assembly,) who neglect the great salvation wrought out by the Son of God! How many are there who, when the Almighty himself gives counsel and reproof, set at nought all his counsel, and will accept of none of his reproof? But that is *their* sin,—for that *they* are accountable. Although many may reject spiritual aid, it is not to be apprehended, if we judge by past experience, that *all* will: but even *if* all were to reject it, still Christians are bound by the command of God to use diligently the means of benefiting others; for if any man have not the benevolent spirit of Christ, he is none of his.

DISCOURSE XVIII.

DELIVERED BEFORE THE LONDON MISSIONARY SOCIETY, IN SURRY CHAPEL, MAY 11, 1825.

INTRODUCTION.

[Fathers and Brethren!

So long ago as 1807, Jan. 31st, I embarked for a distant country, as a Messenger of the Churches, to convey to a people of a strange speech and of a hard language, the Books of Divine Revelation. From that time to the present my attention has been almost entirely devoted to that language, and to accomplish the object for which I was sent; which object, with the aid of my beloved friend and colleague, the late excellent, laborious, and indefatigable Missionary Milne, was effected. But those labours were such as altogether tended to disqualify me to appear in the place which I now occupy; to address a British audience. I remember well that a return to this land was never anticipated by me. At 5, P.M. as the sun was declining in the west, on the 26th of February of the year I have already named, when the ship in which I sailed took her final departure from the British shores, I find from my Journal that I thus wrote—

"This is in all probability (but God alone knows) the closing prospect of a land I shall visit no more. O may the blessing of God rest upon it! the land that gave me birth; the land that till this hour has nourished me; the land of my fathers' sepulchres—a land I esteem most precious, because there, I trust, I was born again; and there the saints in numbers dwell. Happy land! May the light of the Gospel never be removed from thee. The prayers of a departing Missionary are ended. Amen, and Amen."

Afterwards, being removed to a far distant land, about 17,000 miles from Britain, when standing on the sea-shore, in the cool of the evening; or walking solitarily on the beach; often have I cast a wishful look across the ocean—but dared not cherish the hope of revisiting England. However, Providence has led me by a way that I knew not; and I am, by the will of others, placed, this day, in circumstances which I had not anticipated. I therefore crave your indulgence, whilst I deliver the following discourse; and I pray that the blessing of God may rest on my endeavours to state, and to enforce the TRUTH.]

THE KNOWLEDGE OF CHRIST SUPREMELY EXCELLENT.

PHILIPPIANS, III. 8.

"*I count all things loss, for the excellency of the knowledge of Christ Jesus my Lord.*"

IN this passage of sacred writ, the ideas conveyed by St. Paul may be, I conceive, thus paraphrased. Messiah, Jesus, my Lord! He of whom the ancient prophets spake as the Lord's anointed and chosen one;—a Redeemer, Deliverer, and Saviour; who was manifested as Emmanuel, God with us; who came to save his people from their sins; who came down from heaven to give light, and life, and salvation to the world; who having given his life a ransom for many—given himself to be a sacrifice—a sin offering—a propitiation for the sins of men; rose again from the dead, a glorious conqueror of Satan, and the gates of hell; and who hath ascended up on high, in the possession of full power to rule in heaven and in earth, till all his enemies be put under his feet; and till he hath brought to eternal bliss and glory all those, of every tribe, and tongue, and nation, who believe on his name. And his is the only name given among men (the only name proclaimed by divine authority from the skies) by which man can be saved.

Messiah, Jesus, my Lord!—to know him: to win him; to be found in him; redeemed by his death; justified by his righteousness; and sanctified by his Spirit,—is in my estimation of infinite value—there is nothing under heaven to be compared to it. The esteem and regard of my kindred; the consideration of my friends and countrymen;

the rank and privileges of a civil and religious nature, which all men so much value; if denied me because of my devotion to Christ, I willingly forego them.

The ground of hope as to acceptance with God and eternal bliss, which I once fondly cherished; arising from a religious and strictly moral education, and (as far as man is concerned, and the rites and observances of religion referred to,) a blameless life—these I abandon; not desiring to have my own righteousness which is of the law; but that which is through the faith of Christ; the righteousness which is of God by faith.

My bodily ease, and temporal comfort; a sure competence in my native country; the delights of a settled home, and a circle of friends with whom I have grown up from childhood—these, when my Lord's cause requires it, I willingly relinquish. Things that I have heretofore esteemed gain, I now count loss for Christ. "Yea, doubtless, and I count all things but loss, for the excellency of the knowledge of Christ Jesus my Lord." Such, my friends, is St. Paul's language; and this language is not the vapouring boast, or the declamatory harangue of an untried man. For the sake of Jesus he had already suffered the loss of all things. Friends, and kindred, and home and country, and domestic comfort, and personal ease and safety, he had already sacrificed. And he had lost the good opinion of the society amongst whom he lived, and for his devotedness to the crucified Jesus, had subjected himself to the appellations of enthusiast and madman; and had been despised and vilified, and suffered persecution and insult, and endured hunger and thirst, and every privation. For he considered that winning Christ,—obtaining a knowledge of him, more than compensated all.

The knowledge of Christ, it is affirmed, is supremely excellent. And in what then does its excellency consist? A dignified and eminent preacher and prelate of former days has, in a discourse on this text, argued the excellency of this knowledge from the four following topics. The knowledge communicated by Christ, does, in the

1st place, more fully reveal to us the nature of God.

2dly, It gives us a more certain and perfect law for the government of our lives.

3dly, It propounds to us more powerful arguments to persuade men to the obedience of this law than did Judaism or Paganism, and,

Finally, it furnishes us with better motives and considerations to patience and contentedness under the evils and afflictions of this life than they did.

These generalities are true, and good, and important, as far as they go, but they come not up to that *distinct* and *experimental* knowledge of the salvation which is in Christ; which was the object of St. Paul's admiration and esteem. There is a work which Jesus performed, as well as doctrines which he taught; and that sort of knowledge which not only makes us acquainted with Christian principles, but also makes us participators of the benefits of the Saviour's work, is the thing which is of such high value, and to be held in supreme estimation.

It is the saving knowledge of Christ's mediatorial work, by which human beings are delivered from the awful penalties of a violated law; whereby they are delivered from the curse of sin, and the love of sin, and the practice of sin; by which they are restored to peace with God; to peace with conscience; and to peace with their fellow men; as far as *their* tempers and actings can effect that peace.—A knowledge which, in proportion as it is diffused throughout the world, will not only bless individuals and families, but which will unite families, and tribes, and nations in the bonds of peace and of reciprocal love; and will banish strife and injustice, and oppression, and bloodshed, and wars from the face of the earth.

Knowledge of every sort is good; learning and science, which contribute to the rational and useful occupation of the human mind, and which promote the civilization and temporal comfort of man, are to be esteemed—we are not this day the advocates of ignorance: we too say 'encourage education all round the world; especially make man acquainted with the wonders of his Creator's works—lead him if you can through the garden and the forest, and across the ocean, and to the mountains' top, and shew him the hand of God as displayed in the creatures, animate and inanimate, which every where he beholds; and raise his eyes to heaven, to contemplate the sun, and the moon, and the stars, their magnitude and motions, and light and glory.' But, since man is a guilty creature, justly deserving God's wrath and curse—if you carry not to him a knowledge of the salvation which is in Jesus Christ, you have still left him without that which is essential to his happiness; without that which is essential to the transformation of his character. You leave him still in spiritual darkness; you leave him Satan's captive; the slave of selfish or malignant passions—in his heart an enemy to God; and consequently still justly under the curse.

The knowledge of Christ's mediatorial work; the fellowship of his sufferings; the efficacy of his atoning sacrifices when he died for us on the accursed tree; the triumph of his resurrection; the glory of his ascension; and the proclamation of mercy from the Redeemer's throne in heaven, to all kindreds and peoples and tongues, and all classes of rebels and offenders—soften and melt man's previously hard and impenitent heart; and accompanied by the influences of God's Holy Spirit, bring him with weeping and supplication to confess his guilt; to renounce his sins; to renew his allegiance; and commence a career of loyal and affectionate devotedness to God his Saviour, whose love he desires to imitate; whose precepts he studies to obey; whose beneficent spirit he cherishes—inducing him to care not only for his own things, but also for the things of others; and to seek not only his own salvation and happiness, but the salvation and happiness of all mankind; and this leads him to desire, from motives of the purest and most heavenly benevolence, that all the kingdoms of this world should become the kingdoms of our God and of his Christ.

My brethren, are not these the feelings and motives which have brought you together from different parts of the British Isles this morning? Is it not a wish to promulgate to the ends of the earth the knowledge of Christ Jesus our Lord, that fills every breast? and that wish arises from a conviction that the excellency of this knowledge so far exceeds every other attainment, or distinction, or good, that the acquisition of these, and the omission of this, could not be denominated a *gain;* but a mighty *loss*. Yea, doubtless! and ye count all things but loss, for the excellency of the *knowledge* of *Christ Jesus* our Lord.

We have then set before us distinctly the *object* of this assembly; it is not any subject of amusement for the imagination; or merely intellectual gratification; nothing that concerns personal aggrandizement, or family distinction, or party superiority, or national glory;—but an object of greater interest to every regenerated soul than all these united; an object of infinitely greater magnitude than the merely temporal concerns of the whole world; an object that elevates the mind far above, and keeps it clear of, the attractions and antipathies that name or sect, or climate or colour, or tribe or nation, induce. The benignity of the deity, and the love of Christ, bear us along with them, and constrain us to rise superior to self, and to the transitory good that temporalities confer, and the momentary evils that destitution of these can inflict; in order that we may convey to every child of our heavenly Father's world; to every human creature, the saving knowledge of Jesus Christ.

I will here quote to you, in confirmation of this statement the words of the preacher to whom I have already alluded.

"If a man," says he, "by a vast and imperious mind, and a heart as large as the sand upon the sea-shore (as it is said of Solomon) could command all the knowledge of nature and of art, of words and things; could attain to a mastery in all languages, and sound the depths of all arts and sciences; measure the earth and the heavens, and tell the stars; declare their orders and motions; could discourse of the interests of all states; the intrigues of all courts, the reason of all civil laws and constitutions; and could give an account of the history of all ages; could speak of trees from the cedar that is in Lebanon, even unto the hyssop that springs out of the wall; and of beasts also, and of fowls, and of creeping things, and of fishes, and yet should in the mean time be destitute of the knowledge of *God* and *Christ*, and his duty; all this would be but an impertinent vanity and a mere glittering kind of ignorance; and such a man would but be undone with all this knowledge, and with a great deal of wisdom go down to hell."*

But, I would remark, in the second place, the state of the world is greatly diversified; and the intellectual and social condition of the several tribes and nations of men, is greatly varied. If in imagination we go forth from this land, west, and north, and south, and east, we shall find all degrees of intellect, from the ignorant savage who knows not the use of letters, up to the highly cultivated mind, which has been in the possession of literature and of books for nearly forty centuries, and which has possessed the art of printing at least seven hundred years. Where history and poetry occupy the leisure of the affluent; and books, such as they are, may be seen in the hands of the poorest of the people.

And the external condition of the various tribes of men to whom the gospel has not yet been conveyed, is not less dissimilar than their intellectual character. Some are destitute of the useful arts which clothe and lodge human beings; whilst others have possessed for ages garments of the richest stuffs and most curious workmanship, and dwell in luxurious mansions and gorgeous palaces. But still, notwithstanding the literature, and the civilization, and the arts which populous pagan nations possess, these things have not induced them to cast away their dumb idols; any more than the boasted simplicity, and nature, and rudeness of the uncivilized and unlettered tribes of men.

And again, the political institutions of the several nations yet unchristianized differ materially. Some are more open and accessible to what is foreign than others. These varieties of character and condition, will appear necessary to be attended to, when the adaptation of agents, and of means, for promulgating the gospel, is the subject of enquiry.

It may here be expected of the preacher that he should say something of the character and condition of the people

* Tillotson, i. 1.

on the eastern verge of the Asiatic Continent;—amongst whom he has spent so many years of his life, and who are still ignorant of God and of his Christ.

To that people the God of heaven has given an extensive territory, containing large portions of fertile, salubrious, and delightful country; and they possess a knowledge of the useful arts, to a degree which supplies all the necessaries, and most of the luxuries of life. In these respects they require nothing from Europe. They possess also ancient and modern literature in great abundance; and an unlicensed press, and cheap books suited to their taste. With poetry, and music, and elegant compositions; and native ancient classics, and copious histories of their own part of the world; and antiquities, and topographical illustrations; and dramatic compositions, and delineations of men and manners in works of fiction; and tales of battles and of murders; and the tortuous stratagems of protracted and bloody civil wars. With all these, and with mythological legends for the superstitious, the Chinese, and kindred nations, are by the press most abundantly supplied. Nor is their literature destitute of theories of nature; and descriptions of her various productions; and the processes of the pharmacopolist, and the history and practice of medicine.

There is also a large portion of the gentry of China devoted to letters, in order to qualify themselves to fill with intelligence and wisdom the offices of magistracy; and such learning as government has deemed proper for that end, is encouraged and rewarded, either by honorary rank or by actual office.

With Magistrates thus formed, they govern, according to laws written, printed and published amongst the people. And every poor man's house is his castle, which no inferior officer can legally enter without a special warrant from the governor of a province. Throughout the whole of that vast empire there is a system of social order and regularity, in the intercourse of individuals and families, sanctioned either by law or by the etiquette of established usage, which is not exceeded by any nation under heaven.

What then do the Chinese require from Europe?—Not the arts of reading and printing; not merely general education; not what is so much harped on by some philanthropists—civilization:—they require that only which St. Paul deemed supremely excellent, and which it is the sole object of the Missionary Society to communicate—They require, *the knowledge of Christ*. For with all their antiquity, and their literature, and their arts and refinement, they are still infatuated idolaters; they are still given up to what Heaven regards as abominable idolatries and to vile affections, working that which is unseemly. Not liking to retain God in their knowledge, they worship and serve the creature rather than the Creator; they are haters of the true God, are filled with all unrighteousness, fornication and wickedness. With all their civilization, still envy and malice, deceit and falsehood to a boundless extent, pride and boasting: a selfish ungenerous, scarcely honest prudence, and a cold metaphysical inhumanity, are the prevalent characteristics of the people of China.

Their well known backwardness to assist persons in imminent danger of losing their lives by drowning or otherwise; the cruel treatment of domestic slaves and concubines in families;—the tortures both of men and women before conviction, in public courts; and the murder of female infants, connived at, contrary to law; are the proofs I offer of the truth of the latter part of my accusation. Their principles are defective, and hence their vicious practice.

The philosophy of their celebrated ancient sage Confucius, acknowledges no future state of existence; and concerning the duties of man to his Maker presents a complete blank. It presents nothing beyond the grave to the fears or hopes of the human mind, but the praise or censure of posterity. Present expediency is the chief motive of action. Of the great and glorious God who is infinitely above, and distinct from the heavens and the earth, the teaching of Confucius makes no mention: it rises not superior to an obscure recognition of some principle of order in nature, which when violated induces present evil. There is in ancient Chinese philosophy something very similar to the unintelligible numbers of Pythagoras which are introduced into the theory of the universe. Heaven and earth, it is said, assumed, by the operation of some internal principle, their present order, from a previously existing chaotic mass; and a supposed *dual* or twofold energy co-operated in the formation of creatures and of gods—and *heaven* is now the highest power in nature superior to the gods. Even this clod of earth on which we tread, is the second power in nature, and superior to the gods. Heaven earth, gods and men, is the order in which the existencies recognized by the Chinese are often placed: but at other times the gods are excluded, as their existence is, by some of the philosophers considered uncertain; and then *heaven*, *earth*, and *man*, are the three great and coequal powers. This atheistical theory which is at the foundation of the public belief, and influences also the superstitions of the religionists of China, induces in the human mind great pride and impiety, even when superstitious observances are attended to. It is true that in some of the most ancient written documents in China, which Confucius collected and edited, there is a more distinct recognition of the supreme God, than is to be found in any thing that he taught as his own; or that the learned of China, in subsequent ages, have advanced; for I believe it is a fact that man, when left to himself, sinks into, never rises from, Atheism or idolatry; and the written word of God is necessary to bring him back. Exclusive of the system of Confucius, there are, you know, in China, two other systems which make much more use of the gods than his, and which acknowledge a future state of rewards and punishments. These systems enjoin fastings, and prayers, and penances, and masses for the dead; and threaten the wicked with varied punishments, in different hells, in a separate state; or with poverty, or disease, or a brute nature, when they shall be born again into this world.

The doctrines of *Laou-keun* who lived at the same time as Confucius (or Kung-foot-tsze) is mixed with notions which he is supposed to have collected in the western parts of the world: about the æra of Pythagoras. He makes the incomprehensible *Taou*, the eternal *Reason* or *Logos*, the supreme principle: and there are Europeans who suppose that when he says "*One* produced a *Second; Two* produced a *Third;* and *Three* produced all things;" he refers to opinions which he had heard concerning the *Triune* God of the Sacred Scriptures. His followers represent him as having been often incarnate; as a teacher of mankind. They inculcate austerities and abstractions, for the purpose of attenuating the grosser part of human nature, and gradually rising to a sublime, spiritual, and divine state; and they have in different ages devoted themselves much to the visionary pursuits of alchemy, and an attempt to exist without food and without respiration, supposing that the breath could circulate round the system as the blood does; and so respiration would be unnecessary, and man immortal.

These people, as well as the third class of religionists in China, the Foo-too, or Budha sect, which was, at the close of the first century, brought from India to China, believe the transmigration of souls. They both of them have priests and priestesses, who live as the monks and nuns of Europe; and who are licensed by the state; but none of them receive any emoluments from it. The sect of the Learned, who profess to be followers of Confucius, and who fill the offices of government, employs no priests. Fathers, and Magistrates and Princes worship, and do sacrifice in their own proper persons, to the household gods; the district gods; the spirits of rivers and of hills; and the gods of the fire, and the winds and the rain, and the thunder and the earth, and the heavens and the polar star. They worship too the image of Confucius, who never professed to be more than a man, and who even declined the title of Sage, and who never taught the separate existence of the human soul; which doctrine indeed his disciples deny. These Philosophists often laugh at the religionists of their own country, but still observe the rites and superstitions, and worship the idols of the other sects, as well as their own. The governors of provinces, and local magistrates, often visit the Budha temples, and fall prostrate before the cross-legged image of woolly-headed Budha; and subscribe largely for the support of the priests, the repair of the temples, the making of new gods, and the cleaning and ornamenting of old ones. And his Tartar majesty of China frequently confers new titles and honours on the gods of the land. Oh how absurd! Man creates and dignifies the gods that he worships! Alas! my brethren, how long shall the millions of eastern Asia continue to inherit lies, vanities, and things wherein there is no profit? When shall they come from the ends of the earth, as the prophet speaks, and acknowledge their folly, and abandon their idols! I would remark finally, in this part of my discourse, that the priests of China do not instruct the people either in the principles of morality, or the rites of their religion, either in private or in public; and there is no social worship, nor any day of rest, on which to assemble at the temples. Some regard is paid to the new and full moon, after the manner of the Jews; but in China there is no Sabbath. The priests in companies worship the idols morning and evening, and recite prayers to them, and chant incantations, and light up candles, and burn incense. They are also employed to recite prayers for the sick, and say masses for the dead; and some of them, belonging to the sect of *Laou-keun*, attend funerals. In families, in shops, and in boats, where people live, any person that may have leisure, old man or boy, a mother or her daughters, light the matches of incense morning and evening, and place them before the idol, after having made three bows, holding the matches ignited in their hands, joined and held up before the face. Women are discouraged by the Moralists of China from going to the temples, and are told to worship their parents at home, for they are the best gods. When children, or a husband, or a parent, is sick, and death is apprehended, they depute persons to go round to the various idol temples, to intercede with all the gods and goddesses for them; and sometimes devote their children, if they should recover, to the service of the gods, and consequently to perpetual celibacy, as probably Jephthah did his daughter. Others dedicate to the Budha temples a fish or a fowl, or a swine, and afford the means of sustenance till the creature shall die a natural death; it being thought highly meritorious not to destroy animal life.

These, and many other things that I might state to you, all shew the lamentable ignorance of that ancient, populous, civilized, and worldly-wise nation, concerning God and true religion.

Yet the Chinese, like all the philosophists and moralists of antichristian *caste*, go about to establish their own righteousness, and think their virtues will counterbalance their vices. This, indeed, is a feature in which all false religions, and all corruptions of the true religion agree. Impious, rebellious man, all round the world, labours to justify, or to excuse his impiety and rebellion; and not only so, but to put in a claim to merit, on account of his virtues, or of the hardships he has endured, under the government of the ruling powers in nature. I remember the vain boast of an old rich Chinese, who was a notorious liar and debauchee all his life, that on account of his good deeds, some pecuniary charities, the gods must take care of him.

Oh how different is the gospel of Christ from all the self-righteous machinations of philosophers and superstition! and oh, my brethren, what a revolution takes place in the human mind, when it renounces its own imaginary righteousness, and receives with gratitude the righteousness which is of God by faith in Jesus Christ! And this necessary revolution or conversion, not general education; not science, proudly so called; not civilization—can ever effect. But Bible education, revealed religion, the gospel of Jesus Christ, accompanied by the influences of the Holy Spirit, can effect it. And to communicate this gospel; and to pray for these influences, constitute one of the highest duties of every human creature reconciled to God.

But although there be in man a self-righteous, self-justifying spirit, the very endeavour to justify himself shews that there are inward misgivings, and a consciousness of sin and guilt, and some apprehensions and fears. The numerous superstitions whether frivolous or cruel, that prevail in the heathen world reveal the existence of the same conviction.

The passing observer in distant lands, who witnesses the laughing countenances of the young and thoughtless, often pronounces the people happy; and men disaffected to Christian Missions thence argue that such efforts are totally uncalled for But the human heart under convictions of sin, does not usually reveal its anxieties to the giddy throng in busy active life: in yonder lands, as well as in our own, in the season of distress, of sickness, and of approaching or anticipated death, conscience often does its duty strictly, and in a way that alarms the sinner. Hence the rich give of their wealth, and the poor devote their children to idol temples: and the priests are hired to recite prayers and incantations to the dumb idols; and the repetition of masses for the souls of the dead, is procured by surviving relatives. And wardrobes of rich clothing are consumed by fire to be passed into Hades for the use of the deceased there. Even the proud atheistical disciples of Confucius, who in the time of prosperity laugh at the idea of a future state of existence, often have recourse to the very superstitions they despised, to buoy up their sinking spirits, when the king of terrors makes his approach.

We know from heaven that man is guilty; and we know from universal experience that there are periods of life when he feels himself wretched; therefore he requires mercy to pardon, and grace to help, and that mercy and grace, the knowledge of Christ alone can convey. For Messiah was anointed to preach good tidings to the meek; he was sent to bind up the broken hearted; to proclaim liberty to the captives and the opening of the prison to them that were bound. The knowledge of Christ is necessary; and the knowledge of Christ is fitted to relieve the wants, and to remove the miseries of man.

In the third place, then, these two questions arise, *What are the means* to be employed? And *who are the persons*, on whom the obligation rests, to communicate this knowledge to mankind.

That means are to be employed, I am now taking for

granted, in which I am justified by your assembling together this morning, although there have, and still are some persons who think that a miraculous dispensation of divine Providence is necessary, and therefore will take place before the conversion of the remaining unchristianized nations shall be effected. Archbishop Tillotson said—that without some such miraculous gift as that of tongues, there is little or no probability of the conversion of infidel nations,—because of the great difficulty of gaining languages so different from our own.—If means should be attempted by private persons, the undertaking would (he thought) meet with such insuperable obstacles, that it must, in all likelihood, at last fall to the ground. Still he says that he would not discourage any from using their best endeavours to propagate our religion among infidels, and he deems it not improbable that God would extraordinarily countenance such an attempt,—as heaven did the first publication of the gospel. Miraculous aid, the Archbishop argues, is necessary, and therefore *probable*. "I think it still very credible," says he, "that if persons of sincere minds did go to preach the pure Christian religion to infidel nations, that God would still enable such persons to work miracles, without which there would be little or no probability of success."

And notwithstanding this discouraging view of the subject, Tillotson adds, "I do strongly hope that there still remains a great harvest among the Gentiles, and that before the end of all things, the light of the gospel shall be displayed in a glorious manner; not only in those vast empires of *Tartary* and *China*, and *Japan* and *Indostan*, and other great kingdoms of the east, but in the large and dark regions of the new discovered world; for that solemn promise which God made to his Son, 'Ask of me, and I will give the heathen for thine inheritance, and the uttermost parts of the earth for thy possession;' seems to be very far from being yet accomplished: and since this is like to be the work of some ages, the time perhaps is not far off when *it shall* BEGIN. I anticipate not the personal reign of Christ on earth; but the prevalency of the pure Christian religion a thousand years; and since blindness has in part happened to the Jews, until the fulness of the Gentiles be come in,"—the pious Prelate expresses a hope, that the receiving of Israel again into favour, will be life from the dead, or a kind of resurrection to the remainder of the Gentile world. And he closes thus, "Let us pray that *the knowledge of the Lord* may fill the earth, as the waters cover the sea; and that his ways may be known upon earth, and his saving health among all nations." (10 Vol. p. 4454 and 4527.)

It is delightful to see the mind of this great man anticipating the glories of Messiah's universal reign, although we differ from him as to the necessity and probability of miraculous powers being again conferred; at least we are persuaded it is not the duty of Christian churches to stand still, and only pray; but to join to prayer the diligent use of appropriate means to fill the earth with the knowledge of the Lord. For as Tillotson said, "It is no small reproach to the Protestant religion, that, to our unwearied endeavours to promote the interest of trade in foreign parts, there hath not been joined a like zeal and industry for the propagating the Christian religion." When means are assiduously and perseveringly employed, then may the churches look up to heaven for divine aid; "For as the wisdom of God is not wont to do that which is superfluous, so neither to be wanting in that which is necessary."

Now the thing wanted is to fill the earth with a certain knowledge; a knowledge which is supremely excellent, and it follows that the languages of mankind must be known, in order to effect this end. Without language you cannot teach orally; without language you cannot communicate divine knowledge to the reading part of mankind by the press. And it appears questionable up to this very hour, whether attention enough has been paid by the friends of Missions, to the acquisition of the living languages of Pagan nations. What general encouragement is there given in this country to the cultivation of those languages to which Missionary Societies desire to send the gospel? What facilities have been provided to prepare intended Missionaries to different parts of the world, with a knowledge of the languages of the people they were to instruct?

The Bible and Tract Societies have not yet thought it their duty, to encourage, in any direct way, the acquisition of the living languages of mankind, into which the sacred Scriptures and religious Tracts are to be put. At least we are not aware of any particular attention having been paid to this object by the several benevolent societies in our land. We think it competent to the Christians of this great metropolis and the British Empire to organize associated effort for the cultivation of all the living languages of men. The knowledge of all living languages is a *necessary* means towards filling the earth with the knowledge of the Lord; and this means we think practicable, without miraculous aid.

Further, we believe that all the means which might be employed are not yet in operation for providing intended publishers of the gospel, in foreign nations, with *appropriate knowledge* of the people they have to teach. We acknowledge that, in both these cases, much must be done by the Missionary after he arrives at the scene of his labour; but it is also true that much may be done before he quits his native land; and his fitness for leaving it at all, on his proposed service, will be more satisfactorily ascertained, by commencing his appropriate studies here.

Again—Although there is a good deal doing to qualify native Teachers in various heathen countries; we apprehend that the importance of this means is not sufficiently recognized. We think that the benefit of Christian instruction should be thrown open to heathen youths whenever willing to receive it; even before they profess themselves Christians—that Christian knowledge may be by them received, and diffused amongst their kindred and countrymen.

And of similar importance do we reckon the providing means of Christian instruction for heathen females; who may convey the knowledge they receive to the bosom of their families—to their parents, or their husbands, or their children; or their brothers and sisters. "*Go and teach* all nations;" convey the knowledge of Christ to the human understanding through every practicable channel.

For the reading population of mankind let the PRESS

be extensively employed. Knowledge thus conveyed can be scattered more widely than by living teachers. It can penetrate the palaces of kings and governors, as well as the studies of the learned, and the hamlets of the poor; to whom in some lands no foreigner is permitted admission. Knowledge conveyed in this way is more durable than that communicated by the living voice, and is more certain than that of tradition.

And it remains as a witness for God, like the book of the law which Moses wrote, and king Josiah found 800 years after, and by which he was induced to cast down the idols of the land. *Fill the earth with the Bible and Christian books, in all the languages of all the nations, and you will fill the world with the knowledge of Christ.* And then the Holy Spirit's influences will have that on which to operate, and to carry conviction to the hearts of men; and will say, as the voice which spake to St. Augustine did, "Take up and read;" and light will break in on the understanding, doubts will vanish, and decision of character to be on the Lord's side will take place." The great medium of deliverance from sin (says the pious ecclesiastical historian Milner,) always is, the written word of God, testifying of Jesus and of salvation, by putting him on through faith."

Luther you know, a year after he entered the monastery at Erfurt (1506) accidentally (or rather providentially) met with a Latin Bible, and it proved a treasure to him, for the Scriptures were at that time (says the historian) very little known in the world. Yes! fifteen hundred years after the last portion of the sacred Scriptures was given to man, that holy book was very little known in the world. Tell us not therefore that the Bible and Christian books have not illumined the nations with Christian knowledge; the experiment has never been tried. It is now but being attempted. And nearly thirty years labour of the Bible Christians has but supplied seven millions of copies for ten hundred millions of human beings. And it is not enough *to print* the Bibles, they must be distributed and put into men's hands; and if the Bible Societies do not effect this, they do but perform but one half of their work. I preach this day for a Missionary Society: but let not Missionary Societies say, it is ours only to send preachers, we are not a book society. I thought it had been the object of Missionary Societies to send the *knowledge of Christ* abroad among the nations; to fill the earth with that knowledge; and if that end be gained, the end of Missionary Societies is gained, and to gain that end, to carry the knowledge of Christ to the human mind, it is the duty of Missionary Societies to employ *every channel* of conveyance. Books, and schools, and colleges, as well as Preachers—at least so I take it.

Now there are hundreds of millions in eastern Asia, spread over divers countries, who read one and the same language. But they have little other than pagan books to read. Oh what a field of labour is there among the Chinese language nations for the Christian Literati of Europe and of America! Oh when will these literate Christian men exchange their cry—What can I get—for, what can I give! a speech much more befitting the responsible disciples and servants of the Giver of every good. It is we believe practicable for the men of literature and leisure in this country, without quitting their homes, to compose books, for the instruction of those who inhabit Corea or Japan; and to qualify agents to go forth to distribute and to explain them.

I have deferred till the last, the mention of that means of conveying Christian knowledge which is, in the modern sense, called preaching; because I do not think it the fittest means for foreign Missionaries to employ at first, unless they had the miraculous gift of tongues, as the apostles had.

Preaching is admitted to be one of the most efficient modes of instructing the multitude in countries nominally Christianized, where the people recognize attendance on public worship as a duty, or when employed by native teachers, who can attract the attention of their countrymen, by public discourses, delivered wherever they can; but it is *not* the most efficient and most generally applicable means by which a *foreign teacher* can communicate the knowledge of Christ: at least this is my opinion, and I mention it without disrespect to those who esteem it so highly, as to despise all other modes of filling the earth with Christian knowledge. And I think the opposite opinion to that which I have approved, has operated perniciously, by causing despondency and remissness in the use of many means of conveying knowledge, because the favourite one of public preaching has been in some places inapplicable.

I set not up one means against another, but assert that filling the world with the excellent knowledge of Christ, by any means, is obedience to the Saviour's precept, to proclaim or preach the gospel among all nations. It is the *gospel*;—the *knowledge* communicated by Christ, and the knowledge of Christ's mediatorial work, which constitutes the grand instrument of converting and blessing the nations; but the means of conveying that knowledge, or the channel through which the waters of life flow, is a mere circumstance.

Amongst ancient nations public criers, or heralds, or preachers were employed by sovereigns to signify their will or pleasure to their subjects; the work of the herald was to go into all parts of the king's dominions, and solemnly, with a loud voice, and sometimes with the sound of a trumpet, to publish his edicts, and cause the people to know their prince's commands. In this way the year of jubilee was proclaimed, and the phraseology of the New Testament, in reference to preaching or *proclaiming the gospel*, is in allusion to such usages. But that mode of communicating the sovereign will was a mere circumstance. The sovereign's will is still communicated in modern nations, but not in that way. The herald and the trumpet are not essential to effect the end. In civil matters it is now better done in another way; and in religious affairs, if Christ's gospel can be conveyed to man's mind, it is not essential that it be done by a public herald or preacher; it may be done by a written proclamation of divine mercy. However, let preaching, and teaching, and the press be all employed, to fill the earth with the knowledge of Christ.

And, as all innocent means must be used, so endeavours must be made to convey this blessed knowledge to *every place*, to all parts of the habitable globe, whatever difficulties may present themselves. No part should be neglected because difficulties exist, or as it is often said, "The door is shut." Difficulties are always found to give way to pious persevering efforts, and doors now shut must be knocked at that they may be thrown open. A spirit of negligence, and the love of ease always magnifies difficulties, and that has for ages been the case in respect of foreign missions. In the diffusion of light and knowledge there is an active going forth and assailing the empire of darkness and ignorance. They wait not for invitations and openings. The slaves to passion, under the tyranny of vicious habits, ask not for emancipation. In these cases voluntary efforts, however thankless, must be made.

But by whom? Who are the communities or individuals on whom it is incumbent to employ the means of which we have spoken? Is it binding on individuals in the first instance? Must they *volunteer* and apply to the churches; or must the churches listen to the Holy Spirit, saying *Separate me men to go forth to* the heathen? I incline to the latter view of the case; and think that the churches ought to call upon some of their most esteemed and best qualified men to go forth to the heathen. At present I fear the churches cast obstacles in the way of ministers engaging in this work; and I have heard that some blame the Directors for unsettling the minds of ministers, with notions of limited service in pagan lands. Alas! how unlike the first mission to Europe from Asia. Then Paul and Barnabas, two of the first men in the church of Antioch, were deputed to the work, with Mark for their minister; but in modern days, (in the Protestant churches at least) our Pauls and Barnabases have remained at home, and have sent young men, like Mark, quite alone, to the high places of the field.

I really would not mention this, were I not convinced that on this topic there are still erroneous opinions prevailing, which prevent a few of the ablest servants of God engaging in missionary work. Look at the existing practice. The churches of this united kingdom, national and not national, both in the north and in the south, acknowledge that there is a great duty devolving upon them in their collective capacity, to communicate to all nations the knowledge of Christ: And what do they do to carry into effect this object? They form societies and associations, and collect certain sums of money, and wait till persons *volunteer* to be their agents abroad. And it so happens, that few or none of the existing ministers of religion volunteer. And the generous hearts of the youths of our land, although greatly inexperienced and untried as to their aptness to teach, are constrained, since no others offer, to present themselves as candidates. And since these young and inexperienced men are the only ones who offer, the conductors of Missionary Societies are under a necessity of either going without agents, or accepting these. It is my opinion that this state of the case is greatly to be lamented. It has indeed pleased God to bless the labours of some of his servants, notwithstanding their manifold incapacities for the work. And he can give strength to the feeble and wisdom to the young; but still, that will not justify the want of honest zeal in the churches and their ministers.

I beg leave to suggest the converse of this proceeding for the deliberation of Ministers and Laymen in this assembly: *i. e.* that the churches, or the societies acting for the churches, do invite persons, whom they deem qualified, to undertake the ministry abroad for a season; and let young men who have volunteered to be missionaries, first exercise the christian ministry at home; till they shall have acquired an aptness to teach, and till their principles become fixed, and their characters established.

I know life is short, and foreign languages require youth and strength; but an attention to foreign languages may be commenced during the first years of a man's ministry at home. Oh that the churches were less selfish than they are in this case, that there were such a feeling in them, that they would rejoice to part with the most beloved pastor, or the most favourite preacher, when the Saviour's cause in Pagan or Mohammedan lands requires his services! But the churches must collectively, in order to this, attain to a firmer decision of purpose, and a higher tone of feeling on this subject, and stand forward manfully to lay the proposal of foreign service before the men they deem qualified for the work. As long as there is hesitation, and a tremulous delicacy, and a cold prudence on the part of the churches, no wonder individuals are slow to come forward. The Saviour's precept, is we believe, in the first instance, given to the disciples collectively; and in the next place, to every one whose heart may be stirred up by divine influences, to go and teach the nations. Indeed I would that the disciples generally scattered themselves over all parts of our heavenly Father's world, for the purpose of sowing the seeds of Christian knowledge, whilst they pursue their lawful avocations as circumstances may permit; I believe the promise of the Master's presence and aid may be safely confided in. But still I would lay the burthen of this work on the churches collectively; it is for them to do it, and not cast it off themselves on individual enterprize; saying, *we* will *wait* and pray till heaven raise up some superhuman agents to teach the nations.

Where we do not possess absolute certainty, nor express precept, it is not good to be positive. I do not, fathers and brethren, on this subject dogmatize; but, with deference to your experienced minds, shew also my opinion.

Would a few of the most esteemed ministers and laymen in the land, engage in the direct communication of Christian knowledge to Pagan and Mohammedan nations;—give their time and attention to the intellectual and spiritual part of the work, either in this country or abroad, instead of giving it wholly to the external management and the financial resources; I very believe that, as in the time of Moses when the sanctuary was rearing, *the people would bring much more than enough for the service of the work;* till it would be necessary to proclaim throughout the Christian camp, that neither man nor woman should bring any more work for the offering of the Sanctuary.

People of eminence spend their time in speculating about

the qualifications of Missionaries, and working up poetical pictures of an ideal being, and discoursing of hardships and deprivations, and turning the momentary and light afflictions of an Apostle into permanent and lasting evils, till they scare away themselves from the work; all the sober Christian men of the land deem it presumption to come forwards, and the most highly gifted men and ministers in the churches say they are not fit to be Missionaries. I believe that every one who possesses the knowledge of Christ, may and ought to communicate it to others; and see not the mighty difference which some do, between communicating that knowledge in one country and in another.

There are some persons, who feel well disposed to this work, still linger at home, because they receive not some special intimation from Providence: and they say, they "cannot see their way clear." A willing mind to serve in this cause, and the judgment of the churches that a person is fit to serve, appear to me to make the way perfectly clear. One Evangelist has recorded the Saviour's words to this effect, "*Every one*" that forsakes temporal good and earthly connexions, for Christ's sake shall be blessed. And another relates that Jesus, in his reply to the Apostle Peter, who had left all, not merely to be a disciple, but to aid in propagating the gospel—said, *There is no man* that hath left house, or brethren or sisters, or father or mother, or wife or children, or lands for my sake and the gospel's, but he shall receive a hundred fold now in this time, even though persecuted, and in the world to come eternal life. The promise is to "*every one*" who answers the character given; "*no man*" is excluded. It is, however, impossible to suppose that our Lord inculcated that a man should *disregard*, or be *careless about* his kindred. The sense must surely be, that, as in Peter's case, when a man had to go about his master's business for the Gospel's sake, he could not give to his kindred, his personal *presence*. He must separate from them. Every day does it happen that those who serve their country, their king, or any great and public cause, must be absent from their homes and their kindred.

Alas how mean does it appear in the disciples and servants of the Saviour to say, when His cause, the propagation of the blessed Gospel for the salvation of immortal souls, requires their absence from home, I cannot quit my houses or my lands, or my father or mother, or my brother or my sister, or my wife or my children. Does not such conduct shew more love to these than love to Christ? Our Society does not now require everlasting separation from kindred; and therefore, those who may and should, but will not go, are left without excuse.

I shall now close with one idea, on which I feel still more confident, *viz.* that it is the duty of every disciple of Jesus to subordinate his personal and his domestic affairs to the cause of God his Saviour; for as the knowledge of Christ is of supreme value and importance to himself, so the communication of that knowledge to the whole of mankind is an object, which with him ought to rank higher than any other. We are convinced this will really be the case with him who, in the language of our text, counts all things but loss for the excellency of the knowledge of Christ.

But, my Brethren, can we say that in this Christian land, this supreme regard to Christian knowledge is the prevailing feeling of the disciples, even those of them who are accounted most sincere. We fear not. Oh, how active and zealous and laborious are we for the purposes of individual and family aggrandizement! How much trust in our own exertions; how little faith in the Divine promises! Laying up treasures on earth, providing a competence for old age, accumulating fortunes for our children—for these things the different classes of men in our nation, the literary, the mercantile, the civilians, the clergy, are all anxiously labouring. I decry not industry, but I do decry the making of these things our supreme object: I do decry placing these things higher in our estimation, and nearer to our hearts, than the things which concern Messiah's reign, and a world's salvation. The precept which commands us to *seek first* the kingdom of God, and promises that all other necessary things shall be added to us, is applicable here as well as in our individual case. There is a want of consistency between our principles and our practices; for that which we say we deem supremely excellent, infinitely important, and indispensably necessary to human happiness and salvation, we do less, than for many of those objects, which we confess to be very secondary to the knowledge of Christ.

Still, although I do not think that in the Missionary doctrine, or the Missionary practice we have attained, either are already perfect; I do with you, my Christian friends, rejoice in what the Lord hath wrought;—that he has, in these last days stirred up the hearts of His people to this great argument, and has made the feeble band of modern missionaries not altogether useless. But oh, how much yet remains to be effected! The empire of ignorance still how wide! the night of error in many regions of the globe, yet how dark! It is because so much remains to be done, that I have this day spoken, as if nothing had been achieved. I would not that my discourse tended to discourage; or should seemingly approach to querulous ingratitude. But in this cause, my brethren, look not at the things that are behind, but at those things which are before; that ye may press onwards, and ever keep the eye of faith, steadily fixed, "looking to Jesus." My fellow sinners—Remember Jesus; learn of him, and speak of him;—for yourselves attain the knowledge of Christ, and diffuse the knowledge of Him in every direction—in your families, around you in your own neighbourhoods, and let the circle of your united efforts widen and widen till they reach the most distant circumference of the habitable globe. Begin with the knowledge of Christ, and end with the knowledge of Christ. Christ is man's best Friend. He is head over all things to the Church. He is the Dispenser of every blessing, temporal, and spiritual; and all we possess, should be devoted to the service, or sacrificed to the cause, of Jesus Christ. Yea, doubtless, we should count all things but loss, however, in other respects gainful, that would impede our efforts to promote the universal dissemination of the knowledge of Christ Jesus our Lord. The longest life thus spent in any part of God's world, will not only afford satisfaction in our dying moments; but will, I believe, be matter of joy in Heaven, when we shall see Christ, and know Him as he is.

The following Paragraph was written at the Rev. Rowland Hill's house on the morning of the service, but not pronounced from the Pulpit.

But, O ye servants of Jesus! if the reverse of this be your conduct; if attachment to houses and lands, and home and kindred; or the fear of man, or the love of ease, keep us back from the Saviour's work, where labourers are most required; will it not fill us with shame, even if we should be, through infinite mercy, admitted to the realms of bliss? We thank God that he has poured out, in this our day, a spirit of mutual love, and an ardent desire to diffuse the knowledge of Christ to the ends of the earth. But we long to see a still higher degree of affection, and reciprocal confidence, and brotherly love, existing between the evangelists abroad and the churches at home. We think the churches should thrust forth to the most arduous duties some of the men whom they most esteem and love; and not by a spirit of selfishness, hinder the Gospel of Christ. The churches should, I conçeive, *call* men to their Lord's work among the heathen; and so dissipate the doubts of those who cannot see their way clear, and put to shame those who desire an excuse. On the collective feeling and opinion of the churches, much depends, in this great work. *They* must make sacrifices as well as individuals. And when this shall be the case, when all hearts and all hands join in the use of appointed means, a blessing from on high, the Holy Spirit, will be poured out, and the knowledge of Christ fill every region of the habitable globe.

DISCOURSE XIX.

DELIVERED AT THE REV. JOS. FLETCHER'S CHAPEL, STEPNEY, OCTOBER, 1825.

WATCHFULNESS DURING THE LORD'S ABSENCE.

MARK, XIII. 35.

"*Watch, therefore, for ye know not when the master of the house cometh;" or, according to St. Matthew, "what hour your Lord doth come.*"

THE kingdom of heaven, or the administration of Divine Providence, under the Christian dispensation, is compared by our Saviour to the state of a household whose master is absent, having gone a long journey from home. The members of a household, or family, under such circumstances, are very liable to become remiss in the performance of their several and respective duties, and even to fall into gross irregularities. Those who have been left with a deputed authority, as stewards or overseers, often neglect *their* duty; and then children and servants avail themselves of this, to neglect what is incumbent on them; or, it may be, that the superiors mal-treat and oppress the inferior branches of the family. It is, however, supposed in the parable, that the master of the house may return suddenly, and unexpectedly; and on this supposition, should he find his household in disorder, he would certainly punish those who had abused his confidence, and violated their acknowledged duty; or the specific commands which he had, at his departure, given them. Under such circumstances, the best advice that could be given to a family, would be that which is contained in the words of our text, *Watch;* be careful and attentive to your proper work, for ye know not what hour your Lord doth come.

It is generally thought that our Lord, in the discourse addressed to his disciples, in connexion with the sentence which I have read, referred to four events: to the destruction of Jerusalem; to the termination of the then existing state of the Jewish church; to the death of individual men, and to the final judgment of all mankind. Indeed, its application to the general judgment, could be no otherwise appropriate, than by considering the death of each individual as introducing him to that state of existence in which he shall be judged. I will not this day refer to the awful calamities which befel the Jews, when Jerusalem was overthrown by the conquering Romans, in which transactions an immense number of human beings perished; but shall direct my discourse to two general topics: first, *Man's relative situation;* and, secondly, *Man's obligation to watchfulness;* and whilst discoursing on these two leading ideas, I shall consider man both as a *creature* and a *Christian*.

I. Man is not his own maker, nor was the world he inhabits produced by his power; his being is derived, the supply of his wants is from another, and therefore man is not his own master; he may not do what he pleases, either with himself or with what he possesses. Man owes his existence, and the sustentation of his being, to a supreme Lord, who is the great and glorious Creator of the universe. To him man owes life, and breath, and every good. If a fellow-creature, who affords any one the means of daily support, is entitled, by general consent, to a certain portion of service, to be performed with perfect good faith and good will, how much more ought man to acknowledge that the great Creator and Lord of the universe is entitled to his service? But holy Scripture not only represents the relation of the Almighty towards man as that of a sovereign, a king, a lord and master, but also graciously blends with these, the softened, though not less just authority, of a Father, and the gracious and condescending claims of a Saviour. It is useful for us, I conceive, to cherish in our minds the same comprehensive regard to the whole character of the divine Being that Scripture warrants us to do; for by this means we shall have the benefit of motives addressed both to our intellect and to our affections; and an acknowledgment of simple duty will be aided by a sense of gratitude; thus we shall be drawn to the performance of duty by affection and love. Indeed, I do not think it useful to detain our minds in the contemplation of the *relation* between the great Creator and man as an innocent creature, since that relation does not now exist; but rather view man's relation to the divine Being as that relation is revealed by the Saviour. The Saviour, or God in Christ, is now, in relation to human beings, the great Lord of all. It is Jesus who has all power in heaven and in earth; he is our Lord, and it is with him that we have to do, and not with the Almighty, simply as Creator, Preserver, and final Judge. And all persons, whether the as yet impenitent sinner, or the sinner who has repented, returned to God, and been sanctified—all classes of persons should view God our Saviour as their supreme Lord, who has prescribed to every one the work proper for him to perform. For all characters, all ranks, all ages, and all conditions of men and of women, there are appropriate duties, to which the Master hath commanded them to attend. It is not practicable to enter now into a minute specification of those duties in every case. The duty of each will appear from briefly viewing the *relations* in which men stand to God, either

Simply, as *creatures*,
Or as *sinners*,
Or as *saints*.

All are *creatures*, all are *sinners*, but it cannot be said that all are *saints*.

And duties will further appear from an attention to the place which each person holds in the great family or household. Some are entrusted with certain offices, intended to promote the well-being of the whole, such as *princes* and *magistrates*, in the state; *fathers*, and *mothers*, and *teachers*, in families; *bishops*, or *pastors*, and *deacons*, in the church. These should be faithful and wise servants of their Lord, and give to his household their meat in due season. Blessed is the servant whom his Lord, when he cometh, shall find so doing!

But duty is not confined to these rulers of the household; there are also duties binding on those who are under authority, and the younger branches of the great family. Duties owing by the people towards princes and magistrates; by children and scholars, towards parents and teachers, and by members of churches towards their pastors and deacons. And all these relative duties among men should be performed with a supreme regard to the great Lord of all. His will is man's law; and pains should be taken to ascertain his will, according to the means which he may have put in our power; and moreover, the different branches of this great family, or, in other words, the different nations and tribes of men, should kindly communicate whatever they know regarding their Lord's will to each other. Those who, like the Jews and Christians, have had superior means of knowing their Lord's will, were made keepers of the oracles of God, not solely for their own use, but for the benefit of all mankind. It is not less a duty in those who know their Lord's will to instruct others, than it is a duty in the uninformed to exert themselves to ascertain it.

Let us, in this part of our discourse, stop a while to consider the character of the Lord or Master of the household, as made known to us in the inspired history of Divine Providence, which constitutes the records of the family.

In the beginning he reared a magnificent mansion for the accommodation of the family, and stored it with all that could contribute to the happiness and delight of its inmates; and in so doing, displayed his *power* and his *goodness*, both of which are infinite. He was not a hard nor a tyrannical master; the house was munificently supplied, and the service required was honourable, just, and easy; goodness and liberality were conspicuous in this first arrangement. Still, however, there were rules to be observed in the family, and previous intimation was given, that a violation of these would be punished. These rules were, alas! violated, and punishment followed; by which it was manifested, that the Lord was *true* to his word. When he threatened, calmness and *truth* were essentially in what he said; and none could trifle or disobey with impunity. But again, the Lord admitted of a respite, and a mediatorial interference, by which his *mercy* is shewn. *Power, goodness, justice, truth,* and *mercy,* then, are manifestly characteristics of the great Lord. Alas! that the hearts of wicked servants should so often, it is to be feared, conceive of him as *weak, unkind, unjust, untrue,* and *cruel.*

The human family is but a small part of the great Lord's vast domain; but still he exercises constant regard to it, and superintendence over it. He has, in every age, manifested himself to chosen servants, and communicated messages of mercy, and of judgment, by patriarchs and by prophets; and in every land, has often rewarded the humble who sought to know and do his will; and has punished the wicked and rebellious, and those who maltreated their fellow servants. In the fulness of time, He himself appeared, and perfected the great mediatorial work. Since which time he is strikingly likened to "*a man taking a far journey,*" who left his house and gave authority to his servants, and to every man his work, and commanded the porter to watch. Watch ye, therefore: for ye know not when the master of the house cometh, at even, or at midnight, or at the cock crowing, or in the morning; lest coming suddenly he find you sleeping. And what I say unto you, adds the Saviour himself, I say unto all—Watch," (St. Mark xiii. 34.) Observe, the command to *watch* is universal; whether rich or poor, or young or old, all are enjoined to watch; for although absent, his *return* is *certain;* but *when,* is *uncertain;* therefore watch. We have before proved, from the records of the family, that all his words are spoken in truth and righteousness; faithful is he when he promises. It is possible, should he permit, that heaven and earth may pass away; but his word shall never fail. In Providence he comes to call nations and churches to an account for their privileges. He comes also to judge the rulers of the family, emperors, and kings, and great captains; and judges, and magistrates, and ecclesiastical dignitaries; bishops and priests, pastors and deacons, and parents and teachers; as well as the great multitude of human beings who belong to the household. But the *time* of his occasional coming, as well as of his final coming, is *uncertain*; therefore, it is the duty and interest of all *to watch*. This brings me to the

Second leading idea proposed, viz. man's obligation to watchfulness. The original word, employed by the Sacred Penman for *watching*, denotes keeping *awake*, in contradistinction from *sleeping*; to be awake to what is about one, or concerns one, like a person *alive*, in opposition to the inactive state of *death*; and it denotes a being vigilant, heedful, attentive not to omit any duty, or commit any error; and a being on the look out to prevent the approach of any evil or calamity. The Lord, who has gone on a long journey, has left to every man his work; let every man, therefore, be careful and attentive to do it. The Lord hath forewarned the evil servant, who shall say in his heart, "My Lord delayeth his coming, and shall begin to smite his fellow servants, and to eat and drink with the drunken." That the Lord of that servant shall come in a day when he looketh not for him, and in an hour that he is not aware of; and shall cut him asunder, and appoint him his portion with the hypocrites, in a place where there shall be weeping and gnashing of teeth, arising from the terrible agony and hopeless condition of a lost spirit.

We are not called to preach to the great ones of the earth, kings and conquerors, and statesmen and judges; not yet to popes and cardinals, and archimandrites or archbishops; otherwise we could read them a lecture on the awful responsibility which rests upon their souls; and the terrible account which some of them must give for the abuse of power, and the neglect of duty, when the great Lord of the human family shall suddenly appear. We shall not, therefore, dwell on what is peculiar to those in high stations, lest, by so doing, we should omit what is more generally applicable and useful to ourselves.

I would say then to all, watch against *neglecting proper means to know the Lord's will.* Some persons are satisfied with being ignorant of religion; and some even prefer ignorance to knowledge, hoping that ignorance will be an excuse for the omission of duty. And our Lord's saying may seem to justify this presumption, when he remarked, that those who disobeyed, notwithstanding their knowledge, should be beaten with many stripes; whereas, those who disobeyed, *being ignorant of their Lord's will*, should be beaten with few stripes. But this remark can apply only to *unavoidable* ignorance, not to *wilful* ignorance. For wilful ignorance is wilful disobedience: *acquaint* thyself with God and be at peace. *Search* the Scriptures, for they testify of Christ, the Saviour. The fear of the Lord is the beginning of *wisdom; get wisdom*, get understanding; wisdom is the principal thing, therefore get wisdom. Neglect not the means of understanding your relation to God as a creature and as a sinner; and the heaven-revealed way of obtaining, through faith in the Saviour, the pardon of sin. Many, alas! are satisfied with the self-righteous notions which are common to human nature in all countries, instead of searching the Scriptures, and receiving the divine instruction contained therein, concerning the mediatorial arrangement, made by the great Lord himself, planned so as to maintain his own honour, and to secure the pardon of the penitent.

I would earnestly exhort the young to watch against the imbibing of *false opinions* concerning the situation in which they stand as creatures; supposing, as too many do, that they are not responsible; as if he who placed them in his household was not their rightful Lord; or, perhaps, deeming his dominion unjust, his superintendance vague and lax, or his coming uncertain; saying, in the rebellion and infidelity of the heart—"Where is the promise of his coming, for since the fathers fell asleep, all things have continued as they were?" not considering that a thousand years in his sight are as one day. Arouse, my fellow servants, to a due consideration of this awfully important subject! What! shall the Lord find you, at his coming, not only asleep or careless, or actually awake, and disputing the right of his controul; doing all that in you lies, to turn the whole family against their absent Lord? Your case is one of the worst, so long as ye live in this open and avowed rebellion, harbouring opinions and sentiments which go to an entire disownment of the Master's right to rule. Alas! if he find you in this state of mind at his coming, what will be the consequence? With the hypocrites your allotment will not be; but with the proud rebels, who said concerning their just Lord—'We will not have this man to reign over us.' Watchfulness, in the sense of our Lord's words, as we have seen, denotes not only care to ward off external ills, but also a wakeful vigilance against internal disaffection; against a selfish, indolent negligence. Let then, your rational powers be awake and active, and let devout, sincere prayer accompany your watchfulness. Watch and pray—pray and watch. There is a prayerful state of the mind, without the external formalities, which may justly be called a praying without ceasing. Whether you kneel in the closet, or sit in the house, or walk by the way, or stand in the congregation, the heart may, under all these varied circumstances, be lifted to heaven in prayerful attitude.

But the simple duty of acknowledging the justice of our Lord's controul, is a low degree of what is required. When ye have guarded against these fundamentally *false opinions*, which lead to open avowed rebellion and anarchy, you have advanced but a short way. Admitting that ye are professed servants of the Lord, and in words acknowledge his just controul it may be that the thought has arisen in your hearts, "Our Lord delayeth his coming;" and has induced a carelessness about the Lord's work, both with respect to yourselves, and also to others.

On the one hand has arisen the selfish diabolical thought, that "man is not his brother's keeper," as wicked Cain so long ago asserted; and on the other, there may have existed such a degree of self-indulgence, as either unfitted for the Lord's work, or made you careless about executing it. According to the allegorical representation of our Lord, there was, in one case, a neglect of those talents committed to the care of the parties; and there was, in another case, a mal-treatment and tyrannical ill-usage of fellow servants; some considering the Lord as a hard master, and others imagining a long protracted absence would secure impunity; but in all the different cases, there was either *disaffection*, *unfaithfulness*, or *unbelief*. Hast thou but one talent, my brother, and does disaffection to the Lord, and a spirit of pride, prevent thy employing it? Hast thou authority or influence, arising either from station or circumstances, and dost thou abuse these gifts, and render them noxious instead of beneficial, to the church and the world? There is a striking resemblance between the facts of the great subject which we are now discussing, and the common-place case of a domestic servant. An affectionate, faithful, willing servant, will never want an opportunity of exercising his capabilities, whether great or small, in behalf of his Lord; whereas a disaffected, unfaithful, unwilling servant, finds perpetual excuses for being idle, and doing nothing.

These remarks, my brethren, are certainly applicable to all the members of the great household, but they are more especially pointed to those whose duty it is to feed the household; the stewards of the divine mysteries—the office-bearers in the church—those who, instead of being instant in season, and out of season, to exhort and console, to teach, to instruct, and to preach the things concerning their Lord's kingdom, are either sleeping, or feasting, or tyrannising over their fellow servants. For such unfaithful stewards, such wicked servants, there is an especial woe prepared. The hypocrite's portion is theirs, weeping and gnashing of teeth, in the state of future and endless despair.

It appears to me, that the warning, and the commandment, implied in the word *watch*, are addressed to all persons; to those who stand in the relation of mere creatures, by creation and Providence; to those who have become children by the grace of faith, repentance, and adoption; and to those especially, who are rulers of the household. There is scope enough furnished by the subject to address every class of persons—ministers as well as magistrates, to be vigilant in the performance of their respective duties; and to address churches on the necessity of communicating a knowledge of their Lord's will to all the different national branches of the household, scattered over the face of the world; beginning, however, in their own houses, their own neighbourhoods, and their respective countries. But we this day merely glance at these various topics, and I shall now close with noticing the motives to watchfulness which Holy Scripture sanctions. Some of these are addressed to *admiration* of what is excellent, and *gratitude* for what is kind; but more to our fears and to our hopes.

It has been a conceit of proud man, both in the west and in the east, in ancient Rome and in modern China, that either *hope* or *fear* entering into the motive of moral action, is destructive of virtue. But this is a sentiment as opposite as possible to the whole scope of divine revelation; for promises and threatenings, exciting *hopes*, and awakening *fears*, run through the whole of the Sacred Volume from beginning to end. The promises of pardon and of peace, and of a filial relation to God, and eternal bliss, are presented to the hopes of faith and repentance. The servant who has faithfully employed the talents committed to his care, shall be commended by the great Lord of all for having done well, and shall be welcomed to his Lord's joy. But on the faithless, and unbelieving, and hard-hearted, and impenitent, who may have wasted their Lord's goods, or neglected the talents committed to them, shall be tribulation and anguish for ever and ever. And indeed, the most prominent motive addressed by our Lord, in the subject of this day's discourse, to the servants of the household, appeals to their *fears*, viz. the *sudden* and *unexpected* coming of the Master, whilst they are indulging in sleepy slothfulness, or tyrannising over their fellows.

I shall now, my friends, drop the figure or comparison employed by our Saviour, and exhort you to let the possibility of sudden and unexpected death, (which may be considered, to you, the coming of the Lord,) have the weight on your minds which it ought. The old-fashioned distinction between an *habitual* and an *actual* preparation for death, has considerable meaning and propriety. Every person who has not repented, and believed the Gospel, is *habitually, totally unfit to die;* and those who have the fear of God before their eyes, and who have, it is hoped, repented and believed the Gospel; if their faith be not in vigorous exercise, and their obedience unreserved, and their usefulness extensive, as the Providence of God may enable them, they are not in *actual* preparation to meet their Lord. And observe, finally, that the warning and the threatening in the passage before us, are both addressed to those who are denominated *servants,* which may justly cause *those who hold offices* in churches, as well *every member,* to watch heedfully against a deadening spirit of self-security, and the pernicious presumption, that long life will be theirs.

DISCOURSE XX.

BEING AN EXHORTATION, DELIVERED AT THE REV. HENRY BURDER'S, THOMAS'S SQUARE, HACKNEY, AUGUST 18, 1825.

THE CARES OF THIS LIFE MUST NOT BE EXCESSIVE.

LUKE, XXI. 3.

"*Take heed, lest your hearts be overcharged with the cares of this life.*"

ALL the various *conditions* of human life, and all the several *ages* and *characters* of mankind, have their appropriate *cares*; objects of solicitude occupy the mind, and sometimes harass it, which are either to be *attained*, or to be *avoided*. In all *countries* too, this is the case, for man is essentially the same in every part of the world. The *poor* are often anxious about a competent supply of necessaries from day to day, sometimes they are anxious to elevate their condition in society, and labour to become rich. The *rich* are often full of cares to secure their property, or anxious about the manner of investing or of increasing it; for the possession of wealth does not usually destroy the wish to possess more. The *young* are frequently *solicitous* about their future settlement in life, and parents are *anxious* about their children, how to provide for them, and to ensure their respectability and comfort in the world; and there are some parents anxious about the moral and spiritual welfare of their children. The *afflicted* are often mentally distressed about the issue of their afflictions; and the *prosperous* sometimes dread what will be their condition in case of a reverse, or in old age. The *ambitious* are racked with *anxieties* to obtain interest, and patronage, and promotion; and those in high places often dread the probabilities of disgrace. The literary aspirant is full of *care* to obtain distinction, and those who have attained it, feel great anxiety to sustain their character. There are many whose lawful concerns, their agriculture, or manufactures, or commerce, fill their minds with constant carping cares. And there are teachers of literature and science, and ministers of religion, whose minds lose their equanimity by over-anxiety about the performance of their duty, or the temporalities of their charge. *Care* and *anxiety* are not confined to those whose only cry is, What shall we eat or drink, or wherewithal shall we be clothed? Cares and anxieties extend to those persons who are perfectly indifferent to, or most abundantly supplied with these comforts.

Some cares and anxieties seem necessarily forced upon human beings, but the greater number are self-induced; that is, they do not arise from the circumstances in which Providence has placed us, but are brought upon ourselves by our own defects or excesses.

I now come to the question, Are the *cares of this life* sinful? Does Christianity require Christians to be *careless* and *thoughtless* concerning the present life? Must the Christian merchant be careless and indifferent about his affairs? Must the mother take no thought about her children, the children about their parents? Are these expressions of Holy Scripture—"Take *no thought* for to-morrow," "Be careful for nothing"—to be understood, as the words, if taken by themselves, plainly mean?

If to these questions we answer, *Yes*, we make the doctrine of our holy religion of a piece with pagan systems in India and China, which require the good man to quit his kindred, and the business of life, and to become a monk and a beggar. But from this interpretation of Sacred Scripture we are preserved, by looking more diligently into the Holy Book. Interspersed, throughout that volume, there are *general maxims*, and *express precepts*, which *commend* and *require carefulness, industry*, and *assiduity* in all lawful callings. The remark of the wise King, contained in these words—"The hand of the diligent maketh rich," is a divine sanction to diligence. The precept of the Apostle, "Be diligent in business," is to the same effect. "He that careth not for his own, especially for those of his own house, hath denied the faith, and *is worse* than a disbeliever of Christianity."—"He that will not work," either with his hand, or his head, or both; "neither should he eat." These sentiments, you know, are given by the Apostles; therefore we conclude that the Scripture does not warrant, much less exhort to, *idleness, sloth, indifference, carelessness*, or *thoughtlessness* about our well-being in the present state of our existence; but, so far from requiring, actually blames these vices; and calls upon Christians to be *diligent, thoughtful, attentive*, and *prudent;* and actually to labour that they may have a surplus to give to him that needeth.

But it may be said, does not your interpretation make void the Saviour's precept, and the apostolic admonition? We answer, No. The precept and the admonition are directed against *excess* and an *infidel anxiety;* against a degree of care and thought for this life, which leaves no time to care for the life to come; an anxiety about temporalities, which forgets that there is an eternity; and a solicitude about human means, which overlooks an almighty, allwise, and ever benignant Providence.

There is, moreover, a *manner* of speaking in the original languages of Holy Scripture, which, when rendered word for word, affirms absolutely what was only intended comparatively: thus, for example, "He that hateth not his father and his mother, cannot be my disciple." In English, this is a hard saying, and what, in the strict grammatical sense of the words, the human reason cannot assent to; and which, indeed, is entirely opposite to the fifth commandment, "Honour thy father and thy mother." But the language of another evangelist has quite explained the mode of speaking here used, by employing another way of expressing the same sentiment, thus: "He that loveth father or mother *more* than me, is not worthy of me." You see, in the first quoted passage, the Hebrew *idiom* (as grammarians speak) is employed in Greek words, and sounds harsh and revolting. What! (may one say,) the author of Christianity require a person *to hate* his father and mother! The idea shocks us; and often in reading this passage to Chinese, who lay so great a stress, very justly, on filial piety, or the duty of children to parents—have I desired authority to change the *mode* of speaking, to what is the *real* sense, as given in the second quotation, namely, that the Saviour must be loved *more* than father and mother. And even thus modified, it is a hard lesson. How often do children, both sons and daughters say, they would go abroad to publish Christ's Gospel; but their father or their mother will not part with them.

This remark concerning the manner of speaking in the Sacred Writings, applies also to the subject under consideration. "Take *no thought* for to-morrow"—"Be *careful* for nothing"—"I would have you *without carefulness*," and such like expressions, are to be understood of a *thoughtfulness* and *carefulness*, which forget Divine Providence, and disregard all the gracious promises of the Gospel, and the endearing relations in which it hath pleased the Almighty to reveal himself to mankind. And if I were asked to solve this nice question, "How much carefulness about this world is *enough?* and how much carefulness constitutes sin?" one way in which I should answer is—All carefulness that leads the person caring to *rely on* self, and to *forget God*, is sinful. And to the pious Christian, who asked a similar question, I would say—When thy mind is so "*overcharged*" or *oppressed*, with the cares of this life, as to make thee less careful or solicitous about thy heavenly Father's care, it is sin; or whenever a person becomes so "overcharged," so excessively full, or oppressed with the affairs of this life, as to neglect the affairs of another life, it is sin, and a dangerous state of mind.

In the preceding remarks I have, as I believe is the best way, taken the scope and general import of the whole

Scriptures, to ascertain the meaning of particular sentences, or texts, as they are called; but in the present instance, I might avail myself of philological remarks.

Parkhurst, an English Clergyman, who devoted himself to the study of the original Scriptures, both in the Hebrew and Greek languages, says, respecting the word which the English translators render—To *care*, to be *careful*,* to *take thought*, as in these expressions, "Be *careful* for nothing"—Take *no thought* what ye shall eat—"Take *no thought* for the morrow," and so on—Parkhurst says, These, I must confess, have long appeared to me some of the most *unhappy* translations in the whole English Bible; since the text thus rendered, by seeming to enjoin what is plainly inconsistent with the present condition of humanity, are apt to make men less scrupulous in repressing that *anxious solicitude* about worldly things, which is indeed absolutely forbidden to Christians in these very texts." Since the Greek words evidently mean *anxious solicitude*, Parkhurst thinks, that when our translation was made, (which is about 200 years ago,) the terms *careful* and *thoughtful*, had a stronger sense than they now have.

But I will quit these verbal remarks, and ask ye, O Christians, why ye should be *anxiously solicitous?* I will not say about what; but extend it to all your concerns. Why should your mind be oppressed with the anxieties of this life? It is *not necessary*, and it is *dangerous*.

The general providence, and the special promises of God make it *unnecessary*, and the *ingratitude* of disregarding God's providence and his promises, and the being so "overcharged" with temporal concerns and cares, as to forget or neglect eternal things, make it *dangerous*. "Take heed lest that day come upon you unawares."

* Μεριμναω.

T

DISCOURSE XXI.

THE ANTICIPATED END OF THE WORLD SHOULD INDUCE A USEFUL AND PIOUS LIFE.

2 Pet. iii. 11.

Seeing then that all these things shall be dissolved, what manner of persons ought ye to be in all holy conversation and godliness; looking for, and hasting unto (expecting and earnestly desiring) the coming of the day of God.

The Holy Scriptures of the Old and New Testaments differ from all other writings in this particular, as well as in other things; they give a credible history of creation, and of the successive ages of the world, to the end of time, onward to eternity; and many circumstances of these successive ages, now past, were given by anticipation, in prophecies, which have been long ago realized; from which facts we have substantial ground to believe the statements in Holy Writ concerning the future destinies of this world, and the final consummation of all things. And the things declared concerning the future are not put down as mere abstract facts, which are not to influence our hopes and fears, our tempers and conduct, in passing through life; but are declared to us, like the whole of divine revelation, for practical and useful purposes.

The earth, with all its animated beings, the sun, the moon, the distant starry worlds of light; the vast system of the universe, which we behold, presents to contemplative minds, a grand display of the infinite and incomprehensible power, and wisdom, and goodness of God. Even the very small part of his ways, and of his doings that man can survey, fills the mind with admiration and astonishment; and these wonderful works of the Creator, which have existed from time immemorial, and which have observed such amazingly minute exactness in their manifold motions for thousands of years, seem destined to last for ever. The speculations also of philosophers on the progress of society and human improvement, and the perfectibility of man, and the hopes of the benevolent and pious, seem to lead to the same anticipation; or if not, to a settled belief that the world shall remain eternally as it is; at least these things lead to a forgetfulness that "all these worlds shall be dissolved, that the heavens and the earth, which now exist, are, by the word of God, kept in store, reserved unto fire, against the day of judgment, and perdition of ungodly men; when the heavens shall pass away with a great noise, and the elements shall melt with fervent heat, and the earth also, and the works that are therein, shall be burned up."

I take these expressions of Holy Writ, my brethren, in their literal acceptation, and do not think that they refer figuratively to the dissolution of the Jewish dispensation; nor do the new heaven and new earth refer to the introduction of Christianity, nor to the millennial glory and happiness; but I believe the whole refers, as St. Peter expresses, to the antecedent and subsequent circumstances of the final judgment.

I do not know that the Mosaic records of creation teach that in the beginning of the world matter was then first of all called into existence, but only that the present system of the universe was then *formed,* and fashioned as we now behold it: so also St. Peter does not teach that the existing universe will, at the last day, be destroyed and annihilated; but only that it shall be melted down, and remoulded; it shall be burned, and from its ashes shall spring a new heaven and a new earth, wherein dwelleth righteousness, and where righteous persons shall be for ever happy.

T 2

Whether the final conflagration will involve any other than the solar system, to which our earth belongs, is not revealed, and cannot be ascertained; nor is the decision of such a question at all necessary to the practical inferences which St. Peter draws from the general truth in the passage before us. It is indeed said that the heavens shall pass away with a great noise, and the elements shall melt with fervent heat, which certainly indicates a *mighty change*, to a *great extent;* but that which I would have your minds this day fasten upon, is, the assurance that the earth, and all the works that are therein, shall be burnt up. From this simple fact it is easy for every mind to derive many important inferences.

Scoffers may indeed deride the promise of this coming event, and willingly shut their eyes against the most convincing evidence, to the end that they may follow, with the more seeming reason, their own hearts' lusts. But if the world we inhabit was once destroyed by water,—which catastrophe not only tradition asserts, and true history affirms, but the appearances of nature present occular demonstration of:—What may prevent, if it should please God to permit, but that fire, either from the volcanic crucible beneath, and within the bowels of the earth; or the flaming, frightful, erratic comet from without, should ignite, and melt, and liquify the terraqueous globe, and all the works that are therein. Since the words which were spoken before by the holy prophet, concerning Babylon and Nineveh, and Egypt and Tyre, and many other places and circumstances, have been accomplished; and the words of our Lord and Saviour concerning Jerusalem and his church, have been fulfilled; what sense or reason is there in the cry of the profligate or the sceptic; "—Where is the promise of his coming?" Know they not that with him who inhabiteth eternity, "a thousand years are as one day." "The Lord is not slack (or slow) concerning his promise (or his threatening), as some men would count slackness; but is long suffering to usward, not willing that any should perish, but that all should come to repentance."

That death removes man from all earthly good is a fact

daily confirmed to every one by his own observation; and one would think that all the purposes of the monitor, moralist, and religious instructor, would be answered by resting his admonitions on that fact alone. But it is not so; the man excessively immersed in temporal concerns will admit that he cannot remain here for ever; but he must labour for his posterity, and entail his estates to interminable generations, and give his name to his houses or his lands; and for this terrestrial immortality he thinks it reasonable to toil; forgetting all the while that not only shall he soon die, and his posterity die also, but eventually the earth, and all the works that are therein, shall be burned up. The corroding tooth of time itself, does indeed destroy all the works of man; but the last conflagration will most completely annihilate them; and the man who in any degree neglects the concerns of his immortal spirit, for the sake of a perishing world, is in the eye of reason left utterly without excuse.

Seeing, then, my brethren, that we must all, in succession, soon die and leave this world; seeing our posterity also must, in like manner, quit this world; seeing that time will moulder into dust the proudest works of art, and the most magnificent productions of human power; and seeing that the world itself, and all the works that are therein, shall be dissolved and burned up, "*What manner of persons ought ye to be?*"

This question, to be understood and answered aright, must be taken in connexion with other great truths; viz. that the human spirit is imperishable—and man is an accountable creature; both the wicked and the righteous must render an account of the deeds done in the body to the Great Sovereign of the universe. Seeing, then, that our immortal souls shall survive the ruins of the universe, *What manner of persons ought we to be?*

Our text furnishes the answer, which is this:—We professed Christians should, "in the exercise of holy conversation and godliness, be looking for, and hasting unto, the coming of the day of God." By the terms "looking for and hasting unto," the coming of that day, is denoted, *expecting, earnestly desiring*, and *preparing for it.*

It may be objected to the vivid impression of the awful view of the subject before us, that it tends to paralyze all human efforts; and that we shall, like the Millenarians of former days, be led to discontinue works of industry and art, and make ourselves ridiculous. That this is a just inference we deny. The true inference which Scripture and reason draws is, not that man should desist from the duties of his present station, but that he should abound in them, both towards God, and towards man; as the best preparative for that great day. The constant recollection of the great and awful consummation, exhibited by the spirit of prophesy, should operate as *a check on wickedness*, should *wean the affections* greatly from temporal and earthly things, and *ensure to spiritual, eternal, and heavenly things, a due proportion of our time and our study, our anxieties and our cares;* and should make us continually live under the practical influence of this solemn truth—that if we gain the whole world, and lose our own souls, we shall be infinitely the reverse of being profited thereby.

The habitual recognition of the great truth before us, should *prevent covetousness*, worldly-mindedness, the desire of riches; *niggardliness in the cause of God; discontent*, repining; over-valuing worldly things, or the breath of applause—it should prevent *remissness*, procrastination in pious works, the delay of repentance, and the deferring of reproof or exhortation to fellow sinners. And on the other hand, the truth before us should stimulate every disciple of our Saviour, *to abound in the work* of the Lord; *to be assiduous* while it is day; should induce *sobriety*, vigilance, watching, *benevolence, walking with God;* holding fellowship and communion with him, and a constant state of heavenly-mindedness. It is not easy for language to express so intensely in detail the *manner of persons ye ought to be*, as the Apostle's interrogative elicits from the imagination, unaccompanied as it is with any paraphrase.

The facts of the case ought to make your conversation and behaviour more *holy* and more *godly* than I can describe.

I have said that the anticipated end of the world should not induce carelessness about the present life, either in the case of individuals, or families, or nations. Let industry, and intellect, and benevolence, exert themselves to ameliorate and improve the present condition of humanity; but let not the affairs of time, and merely physical comforts, or intellectual luxuries, occupy an undue proportion of our care, and lead us to forget God, and to neglect religion. Since neither our stay in the world is for ever, nor is the world itself everlasting, let us not act as too many do, and give our whole soul to that which is transitory and perishing. Let us give to religious instruction, to the diffusion of Christian knowledge which benefits the never-dying spirit, a degree of importance in our estimation, and in our efforts, which the truth requires.

Let us not be led away by the specious, but superficial and unreal anticipations, of some mistaken philanthropists of our day, who suppose that merely physical knowledge, and the cultivation of natural science, constitute the great business of life, and the remedy for all human ills; whilst God, and the soul, and its eternal welfare, are neglected and forgotten.

We deny, then, that the consideration of the world's end should check human industry and physical improvement; but we admit that it should greatly moderate the importance which they assume, and diminish the supreme attention which many persons claim for them, and give to them. The destiny of an immortal spirit *is* of more importance than the physical improvement in arts and manufactures of a temporary world. We wish now to steer between two opposite extremes; a supremacy claimed by worldly science, and the affairs which concern the material world, on one hand; and a neglect of the body, with a fanatical spiritualism, on the other. We believe that man's duty in time, and his duty in reference to eternity, are perfectly compatible with each other; and he is the only wise and good man, who so passes through the things temporal, as not to lose those that are eternal. On the right hand, or right side of the question, it must be admitted that there have been extravagances and errors; but on the other, there is a large majority of mistaken, misguided, human beings, who give to the least concern the greatest attention; and who pursue the shadows of temporary bliss, whilst they forsake the realities of eternal happiness. Having guarded our doctrine against a plausible objection, which infidelity has alleged not only against this article of our faith, but against the whole Christian system, on the ground of its withdrawing man from the duties and the pleasures of the passing state of existence; we proceed to mention some of its beneficial results, which will appear the more clearly, the more impartially the subject is considered; as indeed is the case, wherever substantial truth is concerned.

The doctrine of the world's end and a final judgment, which in the pages of St. Peter's Second Letter go together, presents a check to wickedness, and is sufficient to make prosperous villany turn pale, with frightful anticipations of the approaching day. When viewed in reference to the great truths of Divine Revelation now brought before us, how absurd and foolish the pursuits of violence, oppression, and injustice, do appear; the gains are positively good for nothing, which injustice and wickedness acquire. The earth, and all the works that are therein, shall be burned up—and the naked spirit of the wicked aggressor must face the impartial tribunal of the Eternal. Here the mightiest conqueror, who, in proud ambition, grasped at the dominion of a world, with the comparatively puny village oppressor, who, by unjust means, added house to house, and field to field, must stand confounded and appalled. Trace wickedness in its progress, from the highest to the lowest, through all its varied forms of injustice and deceit, and impiety and lust, and bring the conscience of the offender in close contact with a burning universe and an omniscient tribunal, and it will have good reason to tremble and feel an astounding check to its progress. In this predicament, the conscience that is not seared as by a hot iron, and callous as the indurated hoof, must feel. The world and all that is therein consumed by fire, and awaiting the imperishable spirit, a state of suffering, acute and lingering as the Indian widow's concremation, to endure for ever! This, O my fellow sinners, is what every impenitent worldling is fast hastening to; and are not such anticipations calculated to be a *check to wickedness?* Oh! who can dwell with devouring fire? who can inhabit everlasting burnings? Is it not incumbent on every ungodly man, either to prove satisfactorily that these dire calamities shall never come upon him, which he cannot do, or betake himself to the divinely revealed mode of averting them, to faith in Jesus, the Almighty Saviour; to repentance, and to a holy conversation, and a life of godliness? In this case remissness and procrastination are big with eternally lamentable consequences. Now is the day of salvation; now is the time to repent and be converted, that sin may be blotted out, and a life of holy conversation and godliness be commenced ere it be too late.

I have thought it right to begin with the lowest class in this congregation; not lowest in worldly temporal circumstances, but lowest in reference to a spiritual preparation and fitness to meet the terrors of the final conflagration. The experienced Christian may feel impatient whilst the preacher is dwelling on these first principles, faith and repentance, but it is wrong to do so. We must divide the word of truth, and apportion it according to the states and circumstances of men; and to awaken the unconcerned, and to change the unconverted, and gather in the scattered sheep, is to me more pleasing work than simply to feed the flock, who should, in the proper use of means, be competent to procure their own food.

But St. Peter, in our text, addresses professed Christians, which authorizes me to turn my exhortation from the young and the inexperienced, who have not as yet submitted to the Saviour's yoke, but who will, I trust, from henceforward do so; that I may address those who have already entered on the Christian journey and conflict, what manner of persons ought *ye* to be in all *holy* behaviour and *godliness!*

The conversation, conduct, or manner of life, incumbent on a Christian, from a great variety of considerations, and particularly from the anticipation of the world's dissolution, is here expressed by "*holiness* and *godliness;*" or in other words, by *purity* and *piety;* a separation from all that is sinful and polluting, and a dedication or devotedness to the service of God. It is not the mere absence of gross vice, not the suppression of bad tempers and spiritual wickedness alone, that is here required, but an eminence in sanctity and devotion which is inculcated. The requirement of the Apostle rises infinitely higher than the mere negation of overt-acts of vice and wickedness, and demands of the Christian a spiritual purity and heavenly aspiration, which shall for ever distinguish him from the sensual and the earthly minded. The man who has regard either to health or to reputation, or to pecuniary prosperity, will never be a profligate debauchee; and therefore a degree of sobriety and industry, which common worldly prudence dictates, is far short of the holiness and godliness which our text requires; so far short, indeed, that they possess not one particle of the principle of true holiness and real piety; for these, at the outset, have a reference to God, but worldly prudence regards only man. Think not that I am decrying moral and benevolent actions; I ask not for the absence or neglect of these, but I ask for something more, and immeasurably superior to these; I require of the human spirit an entire submission, and a total consecration of itself to God. It must be *un-earthly*, it must be *heavenly*, it must be *set apart for God*, it must "*well-worship*" *God*, and must subordinate all affairs to the cause of God.

"The word holiness, when applied to God, signifies the peculiar eminency of the divine nature, whereby it is separated and removed to an infinite distance from moral imperfection, and that which we call sin; that is, there is no such thing as malice, or envy, or hatred, or revenge, or injustice, or falsehood, or unfaithfulness in God; or if there be any other thing that signifies sin, and vice, and moral imperfection, holiness signifies that the divine nature is at an infinite distance from all these, and is possessed of the contrary perfections." And the Almighty requires in his people resemblance to himself in this particular. As he which hath called you is holy, (saith St. Peter,) so be ye holy in all manner of conversation; because it is written, Be ye holy, for I am holy: and without holiness no man shall see the Lord. The import of the word holy will be more clearly seen by attending to the explications given of it in scripture. Thus it is explained by opposition to sin and impurity. "Let us, (says the Apostle,) cleanse ourselves from all filthiness of the flesh and spirit, perfecting holiness in the fear of God." Sometimes, by the negation of sin and defilement; so we find "*holy and without blame*," put together; "*holy and without blemish*," "*holy, harmless and undefiled*." It is true, indeed, this negative notion doth imply something that is positive; it doth not only signify the absence of sin, but a contrariety to it. The absence of sin implies the presence of grace; as, take away crookedness from a thing, and it immediately becomes straight. Whenever we are made holy, every lust and corruption in us is supplanted by the contrary grace.

It is scarcely necessary to remark that the word "*conversation*," in our text and elsewhere in Sacred Scripture, is not confined to the modern and popular sense of speaking or talking, but includes also behaviour, or conduct, or actions. *Holy conversation* requires holiness in thought, word, and deed, and not merely talking religiously or piously; nor, on the other hand, is religious conversation excluded. "Out of the abundance of the heart the mouth speaketh," and there are times in families, and in general society also, when it is right to speak for God, to confess Christ, and to explain or to defend the truth.

The term *godliness*, in our text, and in other parts of Holy Scripture, refers to the respect, reverence, or worship, which man owes to God; and in a preceding paragraph of this discourse, I have used for it the words "*well-worship*," i. e. worship which is sincere, and spiritual, and devout; in contradistinction from that which is insincere; merely bodily service, or careless and remiss in its manner, that which is mere *form* without the *power*. Holiness and godliness include the whole of human duty, the whole law of love towards God and towards man; they include all that tends to human happiness in time, and throughout eternity. Our Lord Jesus Christ, according to his divine power, gives to us all things that pertain to life and godliness, through the knowledge of him that hath called us to glory and virtue. It is thus Simon Peter, a servant and an Apostle of Jesus Christ, speaks to those who with him had obtained like precious faith. Jesus is the source from whence divine influences flow from heaven, to the guilty and corrupted children of men; and from him, in the exercise of faith and prayer, must be sought the things that pertain to spiritual life, holiness, and godliness. And he most graciously "gives the Holy Spirit to them that ask him." He who commences the Christian course, must begin by an *application to Jesus;* and he who hopes to abound in holiness and godliness, must "*abide*" *in Jesus.* "As the branch cannot bear fruit of itself, except it abide in the vine; no more can ye, (says our Saviour,) except ye abide in me."

Having, as I hope, reminded you of the absolute necessity of an *interest in* Jesus, and a *never-ceasing connexion* with Him; I shall now close with enforcing the duty of looking onward to eternity; or, as the words of our text denote, "*Expecting, and earnestly desiring,* the coming of the day of God."

It appears to me that the doctrine of the world's approaching dissolution, because it may have in some instances been abused, is, in the present day, more lost sight of by the Christians of this land, than the Holy Scriptures warrant. Our Saviour, and his Apostles, and the primitive Christians, looked not at the things seen, but at the things not seen (by the carnal eye); for visible things are transitory and temporary, but the unseen realities which faith discerns are eternal. Oh, how rarely, I imagine, can it be affirmed, that Christians in our day, are *expect-*

ing, and *earnestly desiring*, the coming of the day of God, which would so greatly promote an elevated spirit of devotion, and an unearthly spirit of public benevolence. How completely would it tend to eradicate the lust of covetousness, and the aspirings of worldly ambition, if men and Christians were expecting, as they have good reason to expect, the day of God, when the earth, and all the works that are therein, shall be burnt up! Would they then lay up their treasure here, where moth and rust corrupt, and thieves break through and steal; and where the whole is doomed, by the righteous Providence of God, to one general and all-consuming conflagration? Oh! alas for that day, when it shall be said, "Go to now, ye rich men, weep and howl for the miseries that shall come upon you. Your riches are corrupted, and your garments are moth-eaten; your gold and silver is cankered, and the rust of them shall be a witness against you, and shall eat your flesh as it were fire—ye have heaped treasure together for the last days;" injustice, and luxury, and niggardliness in the cause of righteousness, marked your course on earth; and now ye receive the fruit of your own doings.

But it is not to unbelievers that I now address my exhortation, it is to the parents, and children, and kindred, of those who have received precious faith. Endeavour, my brethren, to let the exhortation of the Apostle be reduced to *a practical influence* on your minds. Let your hearts be in heaven, and your expectations and desires have a reference to the last day. In prosperity it will induce you to spend much for God, to give your property to his cause; your time to his cause, your persons, soul, spirit, and body, to his cause; which is, whatever some may think, a reasonable service. And, in adversity, it will induce you to be patient unto the coming of the Lord. Time, and suffering—Oh! how short! Eternity, and enjoyment—Oh! how long! "I reckon that the sufferings of this present time, which are but for a moment, are not worthy to be compared with that exceeding great and eternal weight of glory" which shall be conferred on all God's people; through our Lord and Saviour, Jesus Christ, Amen!

DISCOURSE XXII.

TRUST IN THE MOST HIGH, THE BEST DEFENCE AGAINST FEAR.

PSALM LVI. 2, 3.

"O thou Most High,—what time I am afraid I will trust in Thee."

THESE are the words of one of the most extraordinary men, whose names, from a high antiquity, have descended to us, either in sacred or profane history. In early life he was a simple shepherd, on the hills of Judea. Whilst yet young, his musical talents, under Providence, caused him to be brought to the court of king Saul; from which time he became a warrior, and the leader of a brigand. After being long persecuted, and hunted from place to place by the jealous monarch, he at last himself ascended the throne of Israel; where war, and poetry, and sins, and reverses filled the latter period of his days. David, the beloved son of Jesse, and the sweet singer of Israel, the devout poet of Judea, penned the words of our text.

The commencement of his exaltation was the beginning of a continual series of anxieties and difficulties. His heroic conduct in the affair of the gigantic Goliath, excited against him the envy of his sovereign, who foresaw that the young shepherd, the fair and ruddy minstrel, was destined by Providence to succeed to the throne; and, with a sort of fatuity, he sought to thwart Providence, by attempting the life of David with his own hand; and, subsequently, by sending in pursuit of him detachments of troops. When this persecuted youth had resolved to flee from the face of Saul, and had parted with his beloved and most attached friend, the king's son, he took refuge in Gath, a foreign kingdom, and the native place of the mighty warrior whom he had slain. Here he was recognized by the people, and information against him given to the king, and his person seized and brought before Achish. The history, as given in the First Book of Samuel, states, that when David overheard the accusations against him, made by the servants of Achish, he "was sore afraid." And it was under these circumstances, "when the Philistines took him in Gath," that he composed the ode which, in our collection of Psalms, is numbered as the Fifty-sixth; and which contains these words, "O Thou Most High, what time I am afraid, I will trust in Thee:" or, "In the day of fear I will cling to Thee," as the ivy clings to the oak, or the vine to that which supports it.

Fear is the apprehension of some evil likely to befall us, accompanied with a desire of avoiding it. In prosecuting this subject, I shall arrange my thoughts and remarks under three heads, for the sake of assisting the memories of the young.

In the first place I observe, that *Fears are common to all men,* at one time or another.

Secondly, That *improper and inefficacious means* of removing fear are often resorted to. And, in the

Third place, There is *a true and effectual method of removing fear,* suggested by the text.

I. *Fears* are common to all, and conscious guilt is the origin of *fear.*

As when children have violated the commands of their parents or guardians, a fear of detection and chastisement follows; and when members of human society have broken the just laws of the land or of their own consciences, they are haunted by fears concerning the result;—so all mankind, in consequence of their revolt from God, and disobedience to heaven, are universally liable to fears and apprehensions concerning possible or probable evils. Much suffering and manifold calamities have been induced by sin. Our bodies are liable to numerous diseases, painful and distressing, and to eventual dissolution and death, at which nature usually shudders and shrinks back. There is much injustice and violence in the earth, and there are millions, in various lands, who tremble at the oppressor's frown. A little experience in the world teaches the uncertainty of every thing future, and exhibits many instances of the most afflictive changes, and sad reverses, by which a prosperous family, with an affectionate and powerful protector at its head, is reduced to want, and to widowhood, and to a fatherless or orphan condition.

And there are moral causes of fear, when convictions of sin wound the troubled spirit, and perhaps keep it in a state of dejection for years, or rouse it at once to acute and scarcely tolerable anguish.

But the prevalent defect in human nature is, that it fears the less evil, and is fearless concerning the greater. It is often afraid on account of apprehended natural evils, such as sickness, poverty, man's contempt or scorn; whilst it remains callous as to spiritual evils, unremoved guilt, impending eternal death, and the wrath of God.

The fear of man, how prevalent in our day, both with the pious and the impious. With many pious people, and pious ministers in the land, how much trimming, lest ecclesiastical dignitaries, or those in affluence and authority, should think them righteous over much! And with men, who seem to have no fear of God, how much dread of man's opinion. The unfortunate tradesman or merchant, the proud man in military or other professions, fearless of the displeasure of the Almighty, often rushes headlong on death by self-destruction, because of the fear of disgrace, or the bad opinion of fellow mortals; and those fellow mortals, not the wise and good, but rather the impious and profane. This is one of the instances of fear, which is wholly without a true and justifiable foundation, more so perhaps than the visionary fears of the superstitious, who tremble at the signs of heaven which indicate nothing, or the terrors of those, in many parts of the world, who dread the wrath of dumb idols, which can do no harm. There are, it is manifest, times and occasions of fear, either well or ill grounded, to which, more or less, all human beings are subject, in every period of life.

I was, in the

Second place, to notice some of the improper and inefficacious means resorted to for the removal of fear.

Some endeavour to work up their minds to a proud self-confidence, and a fool-hardy denial that they are afraid; or they boldly, but without reason, affirm that there is no cause of fear. The fear arising from a guilty conscience, and anticipated death and judgment, they attempt to get rid of by adopting the gratuitous assumptions of infidelity, on the one hand; or by trying to forget and disregard the subject for the time being, and so put the evil day afar off.

Many of the well-educated and opulent drown all serious reflection in a whirlpool of giddy, unintermitted amusement, and frivolity; whilst men of business produce the same effect, by immersing themselves in worldly affairs, and schemes and speculations, to increase their wealth, which pursuits and anxieties swallow up all other considerations.

And there are those who confide in their riches, and vainly expect that wealth will ward off every evil, and remove every cause of fear. "The rich man's wealth is his strong city, and as a high wall in his own conceit."

Some bolster up their spirits by the vain imaginations of self-righteousness. They think they have not been very great sinners. And to help out this idea, they cherish partial views of the divine character, forgetting his holiness, truth, and justice, and remembering only that he is merciful.

There are those of our fellow creatures who possess authority, and power, and influence, who seem to forget that they also are under authority, and have as much reason to fear divine justice as the most powerless and feeble of our species. Their confidence in themselves and their power will not stand them in stead, when the day of fear cometh. Neither will it stand in stead those who trust in them, and place their reliance on mere human beings, on an arm of flesh, or the power of princes, or the son of man, in whom there is no stay.

There are, moreover, those in all nations of the world, who depend for help, in the evil hour, on departed men and women, whom human folly and presumption have canonized or deified, and dignified with the names of demons or saints, angels or gods. In what are called Catholic countries, or, in other words, the nations of Europe, of the Latin or Greek Churches, and foreign colonies, where the image-worship of Popery prevails; there, the poor people, and especially the oppressed and weaker sex, the women, are seen in devout prostration before Christian idols dedicated to virgins, or saints, or martyrs;—some deceased human being to whom they vainly seek in the day of fear. And in Pagan lands, whether civilized or uncivilized, as well in India and in China, as in the Islands of the Southern Sea, do our fellow creatures have recourse to imaginary powers for the removal of fear. In China they dread thousands of imaginary aerial noxious influences, to defend themselves from which they resort to charms and incantations, and the endless *et cœtera* of a vain superstition. They trust, as their fathers have done, in lies, vanities, and things wherein there is no profit.

Your better judgment, my Christian friends, is fully convinced that neither self, nor man, nor demons, nor riches, nor power, can furnish a sufficient support to the mind in the day when calamity, and ruined fortunes, and a shattered constitution, and apprehended death, with all their terrors, make their approach. The young and inexperienced, indeed, who have not yet drunk of the cup of adversity, may pass on for a time, insensible of the truth now declared; but a day of fear is coming, in which every refuge of lies will be swept away. It is the preacher's duty to instruct and to warn men, and to plead with God in their behalf, that they may be awakened from every fallacious slumber of false confidence, and to direct them to *the true and efficient means of removing* fear; which topic is the

Third part of our subject.

It has been remarked above, that some of the fears of human beings are visionary and ill-founded, and to remove all these, it is incumbent on us to transfer our fear from unreal objects and minor ills, to real objects of awe and greater evils; that is, to cease to fear man, and to fear God; to discontinue our fear about bodily and temporal ills, so that the infinite concerns of the immortal Spirit, and of eternity, may engross all our anxieties and our cares. Our Saviour says, "fear not them that kill the body, who are not able to kill the soul; but rather fear *Him* who is able to destroy both soul and body in hell." Here, you perceive, we are commanded to transfer our fear from man, who can do us no more harm, at the very worst, than kill the body, which must at all events soon die; and to fear, not future punishment, but HIM who is able to cast body and soul into hell. Fear God, he is the right object of awe, and reverence, and holy dread; of a fear that should be mingled with love and confidence, as our Lord's discourse, in continuation, fully imports, because he meets the objection that the alienated mind of man usually suggests— God cares not for me. The commonest bird of the feathered creation falls not to the ground without God's notice. Nay, the very hairs of the human head are numbered by providence; say not then your heavenly Father cares not for you, for ye are of more value than many sparrows. Heaven does care for the children of men, and the Saviour notices with approbation those who confess him in the presence of his enemies on earth; such shall be confessed before his Father in heaven; and contrarywise, saith the scripture *if we deny him* through fear of man, *he also will deny us.*

We may all of us, my hearers, when we reflect on our fear of man, and the extent to which it prevails over the fear of God, see the wide-spread existence of unbelief in the human heart; and it is an unbelief which refers not to some speculative nice point of divinity, but an unbelief which seems to deny that God *is;* and that He is the Protector and Rewarder of those that diligently seek him. It is a spirit of practical atheism and disavowal of Providence which reigns in the human heart.

"O ye that seek Jehovah, fear not the reproach of mortals, neither be terrified at their revilings, for the moth shall consume them like a garment, and the worm shall devour them like wool; but Jehovah's righteousness shall endure for ever, and his salvation throughout all generations." Hear, again, the language of the Almighty addressed to his believing people. "It is I, even I, that comfort you; who art thou that thou shouldest be afraid of a mortal that shall die, and of the son of man that shall become as grass, and forgettest Jehovah thy Maker, who stretched out the heavens and founded the earth, that thou shouldest every day be in continual fear because of the fury of the oppressor, as if he were just ready to destroy: and where now is the fury of the oppressor? He hasteth on that shall set free the captive, that he may not die in prison, and that his bread may not fail; I am Jehovah thy God." (Isa. li.) These quotations from Holy Writ abundantly confirm what we have above asserted, that the fear of man and distressing anxiety about natural evils, indicate an absence of the fear of God and faith in him.

Not only do the declarations of the prophets and other sacred writers shew that faith in God would prevent the fear of man; but the examples of ancient worthies all tend to confirm the same idea. Noah being warned of God, of things not seen as yet, and believing in God, was moved with fear of God's impending judgments, and no longer feared the ridicule and scoffing of man, but prepared an ark to the saving of his house. By faith Abraham went forth from his kindred and his country, to a strange land whither Providence called him, and was raised above the fear of difficulties and of wants.

By faith Moses declined the worldly honour of being a princess's son, and chose rather to suffer affliction with the people of God, than to enjoy the pleasures of sin for a season, and esteemed the reproach of Christ greater riches than the treasures in Egypt; and he forsook Egypt, *not fearing* the wrath of the king, for he endured, as *seeing him who is invisible*, the time would fail me to tell of the numerous instances, in every age of the world, in which the fear of God, and faith in him, have raised the human mind far superior to the fear of man, and the fear of suffering, or of want and destitution; for neither cruel mockings nor scourgings, nor bonds nor imprisonments, nor being cast out to wander in deserts and in mountains, and in dens and caves of the earth; destitute, afflicted, tormented; nor being stoned or sawn asunder, or slain with the sword, nor fire nor faggot, nor the rack nor the wheel, could overcome the courage and the constancy of those who feared God. Their courage and fortitude were derived from principle, and were not the result of mere physical or animal fearlessness and blind fool-hardiness, but were founded on reasons rational and satisfactory; their courage was inspired by trust in the Most High God, the Creator, the Almighty Governor, and the benignant Father of the universe; or, as they expressed it, " Our help is in the name of the Lord, who made heaven and earth. In the day when occasions of fear arise, whether by land or by sea, whether from man or from any other cause, O thou Most High we will trust in Thee.

O could we instil the fear of God into the hearts of the children of men, how completely should we banish idolatry and superstition, demon-worship and saint-worship, and man-fearing sycophancy and duplicity, from the face of the earth. Then would Christians, and Ministers, and Messengers of the Churches, testify for God and the Saviour's cause, and be witnesses to the truth, and for the truth, with a zeal, and devotedness, and constancy, which would purify professed churches, and assail and subdue the kingdom of Satan, in a manner that would make angels rejoice.

But here I must enter one caveat; these examples of undaunted courage and invincible fortitude refer only to those who possessed that due sense of religion, which the Holy Scriptures call, "*The fear of God;*" the penitent and the reconciled, through the faith of Messiah, who was then to come;—and do not apply, immediately, to those who are *afraid of God*—those whose hearts are either ignorant of his gracious character, or at enmity against him, whose hearts are unsubdued, impenitent, and unbelieving. Let not such minds be induced by Satan to procrastinate or put off the amicable adjustment of so great a concern as God's approbation or disapprobation. All successful opposition to God is utterly impossible: Wo to him that striveth with his Maker! The dominion of the Almighty is infinitely just, and right, and good; equity as well as power are altogether on heaven's side: on rebel man's part is only wickedness and weakness. By obstinate and persevering opposition to God, ultimate and eternal ruin is inevitable. Here is a true cause of fear; ills arising from man, or from the common afflictions of life of a temporal kind, are absolutely as nothing compared with this. But, unhappily, this is too commonly the very case, on account of which no fear is felt; or if occasionally fear of the final result do cross the mind, recourse is not had to the true way of removing it, but some of the fallacious and futile expedients suggested by the great deceiver of men are resorted to. Either youth, or firm health, or a future intended repentance, or the reasonings of scepticism and infidelity, are resorted to. And day after day, and year after year passes on, and death arrives; and, it is to be feared many perish in their sins, because they will not acquaint themselves with, and yield to the striving of God's Holy Spirit; or submit to the Saviour, and trust in him, and be at peace.

However, we must not omit granting that there may be doubts in the minds of some persons, who are not desirous of daring, nor of forgetting the Almighty, whether or not they may be allowed to trust in him, until they make themselves more worthy of his acceptance; and there are some teachers of religion who would exhort such doubting persons to make themselves deserving of divine mercy, and then tell them they have nothing to fear. In both these cases we believe there is an ignorance and a misapprehension of the revelation of mercy contained in the Holy Scripture. With the Lord there is mercy, that he may be *feared*, and with him is plenteous redemption. He is *ready* to forgive; his own arm hath brought salvation; he spared not his own Son, but gave him up to the death for us all; while we were yet sinners Christ died for us. Believe these declarations from heaven; trust in the great salvation, and thou shalt be saved. The moment thy heart relents, believes, submits, obeys heaven's call;—mercy is thine, and Heaven will help thee to come out from the rebel camp, and from thy sinful companions, and sinful propensities and practices. Look not to self for a worthiness, or a meritorious cause, whereby to deserve mercy; but look to Emmanuel for free unmerited mercy, and for salvation from thy sins, and thy fears of his displeasure.

The passages of Holy Scripture are very many which call upon all the inhabitants of the earth to cherish a religious and *filial fear* of, and trust in God: I will read in your hearing a few of them: thus, "Let all the earth *fear* the Lord; let all the inhabitants of the world stand in awe of him." "The Lord looketh from heaven, he beholdeth all the sons of men; from the place of his habitation he looketh upon all the inhabitants of the earth." "His eye is upon them that *fear* him, upon them that hope in his mercy." "Blessed is the man that *trusteth* in Him." "*Trust* ye in the Lord for ever, for in the Lord Jehovah is everlasting strength." "Hast thou not known, hast thou not heard, that the everlasting God, the Lord, the Creator of the ends of the earth, fainteth not, neither is weary, nor is there any searching of his understanding. He giveth power to the faint, and to them that have no might he increaseth strength; even the youths shall faint and be weary, and the young men shall utterly fall; but they that *wait* upon the Lord shall renew their strength; they shall mount up as with the wings of eagles; they shall run and not be weary; they shall walk and not faint." Again,

"Thus saith the Lord, Cursed be the man that *trusteth* in man, and maketh flesh his arm, and whose heart departeth from Jehovah: for he shall be like the heath in the desert, and shall not see when good cometh, but shall inhabit the parched places in the wilderness, in a salt land, not inhabited."—But

"Blessed is the man that *trusteth* in the Lord, and whose hope the Lord is: for he shall be as a tree planted by the waters, and that spreadeth out her roots by the river, and shall not see when heat cometh; but her leaf shall be green, and shall not be careful in the year of drought, neither shall cease from yielding fruit."

"Wo to the rebellious children, saith the Lord, that take counsel, but not of me." "Wo to them that *stay* on horses, and *trust* in chariots, because they are many, and in horsemen because they are very strong; whilst they look not to the Holy One of Israel, neither seek Jehovah. But powerful armies are *men*, and not *God;* and their horses flesh, and not spirit. When Jehovah shall stretch out his hand, both he that helpeth shall fall, and he that is holpen shall fall down, and they shall fail together. Return, O ye children of men, to the living God, from whom ye have so deeply revolted; and this day cast away, each one his idols of silver and idols of gold; the sin which their own hands have made."

"Be wise, now, therefore, O ye kings; be instructed ye judges of the earth; serve the Lord with *fear*, and rejoice before him with *trembling;* reverence, (kiss) the Son, the Chosen One, Messiah; lest he be angry, and ye perish in your evil way, when his wrath is kindled but a little. Blessed are all they that put their *trust* in Him."

"O *fear* the Lord, ye his saints, for there is no want to them that fear him; they that fear the Lord shall not be destitute of any good." "The Lord redeemeth the soul of his servants, and none of them that *trust* in him shall be desolate." "Whoso *trusteth* in the Lord, happy is he." Christians, "Cast all your care upon him, for he careth for you."

Thus, my brethren, I have quoted largely from inspired witnesses—from Kings, and Priests, and Prophets, and Apostles, by whom the Almighty spake to man; distinctly setting before you, the divine permission for frail, sinful, human creatures to *trust in God* when fear cometh; and whilst doing this, you will have perceived very clearly, that it is a sin not to do so; that to trust in self, or in creatures, or in silver or gold, is not only useless but wicked; is a spiritual idolatry, perhaps not less offensive to heaven, than bowing down to stocks and stones.

I might, in discoursing on this subject, dwell at length on the glorious perfections of the Most High God, to whom we should cling in the day when fear cometh. His omnipotence, by which he created and controls the universe; every creature, from the highest angel to the meanest insect; every element of the physical world, in all their most minute and most tremendous combinations; the storms and tempests of the atmosphere, the raging of the sea, the volcanic fire, and the trembling earthquake; plague and pestilence, the devouring sword and pale famine—all wait on his Almighty behest. And to this omnipotent power is joined omniscience, omnipresence, infinite wisdom, inflexible justice, inviolable truth, boundless goodness and mercy. We presume not to think that we can describe adequately the incomprehensible God; but, my fellow-men, these are some of the perfections of the High God, who commands our reverence, and requires our trust: and he is in Christ reconciling the world to himself.

"In all troubles and adversities then, of what kind soever, under all afflictions that may befal us, of loss or pain, of poverty or sickness, of reproach or persecution for righteousness' sake; and under the most fearful apprehensions of danger and distress, to all human appearance inevitably threatening us, in our persons and private concernments, or with relation to the public peace and tranquillity, or to that which ought to be infinitely dearer to us than all these, the great concernments of our souls, and of all eternity; when we have no hope any where else, no visible means of help and redress; when we are almost in despair of avoiding the danger, and warding off the blow that is made at us; when ruin and destruction seem just to have overtaken us, and are ready to devour us with open mouth, and swallow us up; when we are reduced to the greatest extremity and distress that can be imagined; in all calamities that may befal us; in life and in death, in our greatest fears and troubles, let us ease our hearts, by reposing ourselves on God in Christ, in confidence of his support and deliverence, of his care and providence, to prevent and divert the evils we fear; or of his gracious help to bear us up under them, and of his mercy and goodness to deliver us from them when he sees best." "Help us, O Thou Most High! in the day when fear cometh, to put our trust in, and cling to Thee!"

"Finally, let us so trust God as to use every prudent and lawful means for our security and preservation from evil: and, at the same time, never employ any unlawful means for our ease and preservation, or rescue from the evils which we fear, or lie under: for we may rest assured, that God is never more concerned to appear for us, than when, out of conscience of our duty to him, we are contented rather to suffer than work our deliverance by undue means. Let us 'commit ourselves to him in well doing, as unto a faithful Creator:' and do nothing, no, not for the cause of religion, which is contrary to the plain rules and precepts of it."

I ought not to close without one word more of exhortation to those doubting, anxious spirits, who *fear* that their sins are too great, or too many, or too long persevered in, to obtain pardon; and who at times have a *fearful* looking for of judgment. Of all *fears*, visionary or real, this is the most frightful and awful. In this state of mind, procrastination or delay removes us not from the cause of fear, but every day is bringing us nearer to the thing *feared*—the judgment seat of Christ.

To this apprehension nothing can bring relief but the

glad tidings of complete justification, or remission of sin, and full acquittal in the sight of God, on account of the righteousness and merits of the Redeemer and Surety, received by an act of faith, which is commonly called, the blessed Gospel doctrine of Justification by faith: "Believe in the Lord Jesus Christ and thou shalt be saved!" The "*fearful*" are the "*unbelieving*," against whom a wo is denounced in the Book of Revelation. He who hung upon the cross, and endured the penalty of divine justice instead of a guilty world, is exalted a Prince and a Saviour to give repentance and remission of sins; *He* died for the ungodly—to *save sinners* was the very end of his mediatorial work. If thou *desirest* salvation from sin and its future punishment, *fear* not, only believe." Sinners that come to Jesus for salvation, he will "in no wise cast out." He is *able* to save to the uttermost, and he is *willing;* what occasion then has a sincerely repentant and returning sinner to fear? Again do I say, agreeably to the Scriptures, O thou anxious doubting penitent, only believe in Jesus, and fear not either his willingness or his power to save thee. In the day that thou art in fear, O thou feeble Christian, cling to Emmanuel; God with us—Jehovah Jesus. Amen!

DISCOURSE XXIII.

BEING A MISSIONARY ADDRESS, DELIVERED AT THE REV. H. F. BURDER'S CHAPEL, ST. THOMAS'S SQUARE, HACKNEY, DECEMBER 5, 1825.

THE LORD CHRIST'S COMMAND TO CHRISTIANIZE ALL NATIONS,

GROUNDED ON

The πασα ἐξουσια, "complete authority," possessed by Him in heaven and on earth.

MATT. XXVIII. 18—20.

Και προσελθων ὁ Ιησους ελαλησεν αυτοις, λεγων· εδοθη μοι πασα εξουσια εν ουρανω και επι γης. Πορευθεντες (ουν) μαθητευσατε παντα τα εθνη, βαπτιζοντες—Διδασκοντες, &c.

"*And (Jesus) came unto them and said, Given unto me is* all power in heaven,* and on earth; *go ye therefore, and* disciple *all nations;* baptizing *them, and* teaching *them, to observe whatsoever I have commanded you.*"

IN the midst of the ignorance, error, and perversity of judgment which prevail throughout the world, were a man to decline adopting a course of action for himself, till all his neighbours, acquaintances, and friends agreed in recommending one to him, he is not likely ever to come to a decision.

Men are individually accountable to a supreme authority for their actions, and therefore they must act for

* "I am he that liveth, and was dead; and behold I am alive forevermore, Amen: and have the keys of the unseen world and of death." Rev. i. 18. (See Howe's discourse on the Redeemer's Dominion over the Invisible World.)

themselves. The real disciples of Jesus, in becoming such, think for themselves, and in their subsequent career must act for themselves, without ever expecting that their principles and conduct will always meet with the approbation of the non-discipled. Having once seen it right to become the followers of Jesus, we must be guided by his example and his precepts.

There is an evil spirit who rules in the hearts of the disobedient, and he is the god of this world.

To oppose him and subvert his control, Jesus was manifested, and he has erected a standard, surmounted by the cross, on which he died for the redemption of the world, and around it every true Christian is commanded to rally. Not a physical, but a moral and spiritual conflict, is that to which every Christian is called.

However, I dwell not on the figure; the weapons of our warfare are not carnal; we are prepared not to shed the blood of others, but to sacrifice our own as witnesses for the truth. I mention these things briefly to intimate, that a life of ease and unassailed tranquillity ought not to be expected by any genuine disciple. Satan, and the world, and evil propensities, will not leave him in peace; he must defend himself, and that sometimes in bitter conflict; and it is his duty to go forth aggressively against the empire of Satan, of ignorance, of superstition, and of vice.

It is his, however, not to destroy, but to carry aloft into the rebel camp, a proclamation of mercy from the supreme Ruler of the universe.

"I (says the divine Saviour) *have all power* in heaven and on earth; *go* ye *therefore* and proclaim the glad tidings of mercy to every human creature." This did the first Disciples and the Apostles of our Lord, to the extent of their means; and this, more or less, have all their true successors done up to the present day; and this is still the doing of what, in common parlance, is called, "*The Missionary enterprize.*"

Emmanuel appeared not to destroy men's lives, but to save them. The tyrant oppressor, and artful deceiver of men, is he against whom war is declared; to the deluded children of men, who have joined the arch-rebel, mercy, and mercy alone is intended. But some of these rebel men avowedly oppose the messengers of peace from Zion's King, and others of them, under the cover of professed friendship, do actually take part with the enemy.

There are some professed Christians who would have a truce proclaimed, and terms of peace and amity adopted with idolatry, superstition, and crime; and to secure their end they scruple not to assert many things which assume the shape of untruths concerning the passive virtues, or the noble sentiments, or the simplicity and innocence of the idol devotees; or of the malignant followers of the false prophet. They affirm, what indeed no man of sense ever denied, that an impious profligate idolater, is just as good as an impious profligate Christian, so called. We deem not, that an enemy to God and to Christ among the Christians of Europe, is better than an enemy to God and to Christ among the Pagans of Asia, or of any other part of the world. All such, in every part of the world, say to themselves, *peace, peace,* when there is no peace. Submission to mercy is required of all, and that alone will be availing. Specious glosses cannot deceive the heart-searching God, nor can false representations of the character of distant nations long maintain their ground among men.

The innocent Hindoo Brahmin, regarded and exhibited by some enemies of Christian Missions as worthy of admiration, is now declared by the fashionable * oracles of the day, as "wearing a garb of hypocrisy to maintain his influence among the people, whilst he is, in reality, selfish and vicious. And the meek Hindoo, it is said, when excited, is relentless in his anger and cowardly in his revenge; and for gain's sake unites meanness and duplicity that cannot be exceeded." †

Oh! who can tell the quantum of tyranny and slavery, of oppression and injustice, of cruelty and suffering, of

* News of Literature and Fashion.

† Pandurang Hari, or Memoirs of a Hindoo, 1825.

sensuality and impiety, that prevail in the dark places of the earth. And in our own land how much pride and selfishness, avarice and covetousness, earthly-mindedness and ungodliness exist. Hence it is that some false brethren laugh to scorn our feeble efforts, and just the reverse of the former objectors, argue, that so much is to be done that we can effect nothing. But none of these things need move us, whilst we act in obedience to Him who has all power in heaven and on earth, and who bids us go and proclaim the Gospel. There are not wanting those who admit the premises, in this instance, viz. that our Lord has all power in heaven and on earth, but who draw an inference different from that which our Saviour has stated; they say 'the Divine Being must work a miracle to convert the nations, and Christians need not go and preach the Gospel.' And from this cause it is, that the divinely appointed means, the dissemination of Gospel truth, has been so much neglected.

In none of the churches of this country, whether those established and endowed by Government in England and in Scotland, or those who Secede or Dissent from them, is there, in their *Constitution* or collective capacity, any provision made, either of men or of means, to obey the exalted Saviour's command. Three hundred years have elapsed since the Reformation in Europe, and not more than three tens have elapsed since this precept was materially attended to. We have indeed heard much of a venerable Society of longer standing, for Promoting Christian Knowledge; but neither its existence, nor the novel Missionary Societies, invalidate what has now been said; that neither the National churches, nor the Congregational churches, *have, in their Constitution,* made any provision, either of men or of means, for obeying the Saviour's injunction, to *disciple* all nations, and teach them whatsoever he commanded. Their provisions, so far as we can understand them, are only for the farther instruction of those already discipled in their own country; nothing is contemplated by the Hierarchy of the English church, nor by the Assembled Ministers of the Scotch church, nor by the Independent Pastors of Congregational churches, for going and discipling other nations.

This is left to what is called individual "*charity*,"* or liberality, or benevolence.

* The eleemosynary character which, in many minds, still attaches to the Missionary enterprise, is, probably, one reason for keeping able ministers and superior men from the work. The ministers of religion at home, whether of the Presbyterian, Episcopal, or Congregational *Churches*, whether their income be great or small, are considered to have a full right thereto; and such allowance for the maintenance of themselves and families, is not considered an alms. They are not reproached with subsisting by the "pence of the poor," as we have heard faithful Missionaries reproached, even by Ministers eminent in the Churches.

Another thing is, that the relation between a Pastor and his Flock is so much more consolatory to a poor Minister, than a connexion with Pagans abroad, or the Secretary of a Society at home. And the place which the poor Minister holds among his Brethren or Co-Presbyters, or in the Hierarchy, is much more congenial to the ordinary feelings of a man, than the condition of a Missionary, who is under the absolute direction of a Society, or its Committee, from whose councils the whole Missionary class is generally excluded; or if perhaps admitted, only by courtesy, not by right; and, consequently, Missionaries are ruled and judged of by men who know not the heart of a Missionary, nor (most of them) the heart of a stranger in a strange land, having never quitted their maternal fire side. These, probably, are the real causes which prevent able ministers not "*seeing their way clear*," as the phrase is, to go forth and extend the boundaries of the church. For it is manifestly not merely distance from home, nor climate, that hinders men from going. Bishops, and Arch-deacons, and Chaplains, both for the East and West Indies, and Ultra Ganges India, and Superintendents, and Commissioners, can be procured from men already trained to the ministry. Whereas all the Protestant Societies have, generally, to accept of Missionaries from inexperienced, uneducated youths, whose intentions we believe are usually most sincere, but whose Missionary resolutions have often been formed in the time of their privacy and ignorance, and do not stand the test of enlarged knowledge and intercourse with mankind. Moreover they are, when going abroad, unknown to the Christians at home, and do not carry out with them to distant lands either their respect, their affections, or their confidence. The prayers offered up, even at meetings expressly for Missionaries, usually consist of topics so general, as to betray very little knowledge of, and interest about, their specific and individual circumstances or distresses.

It is argued, that in this country comfort and usefulness are greatly connected: a man striving against the well known evils of penury, and the apprehensions of debt, cannot so vigorously exert himself in any cause, as he would do with a mind unembarrassed on these accounts. At home, among Christians and his personal friends, this is the case with a minister; how much more must such circumstances prey upon a father's

And there are some pastors of churches, who reason in a way on this subject, which would for ever prevent

mind in a foreign land, among enemies to the cross, and without friends on the spot, and who, perhaps, left home ere he had formed friends, or lived long enough to survive them; finally turned over to an official Secretary, whose face he never saw, and to a new race of Directors and Committee-men, who are *individually irresponsible;* and who, notwithstanding their personal piety, are liable to all the headlessness, and heartlessness, and inconstancy of popular Assemblies, or Meetings of Voluntary Societies; where the services being gratuitous, attention to affairs is more matter of convenience than of conscience, and a neglect of duty involves neither pecuniary loss nor personal disgrace. If every member of a Committee or Board were charged with neglect or misrule, every member would throw the blame from himself, by saying, "It was not I who did it; it was the Committee, or the Board;" which is just as satisfactory to the aggrieved, as the child's excuse, that *nobody* did it. And in these evasions every man is safe, since the meetings are private or secret. Ministers of experience who know mankind, since they have no special and individual call from heaven, will not relinquish a certain degree of usefulness and support for themselves and families among friends and at home, for probable usefulness, with probable destitution in a foreign land. It is true, that their faith and zeal cannot be highly praised; but since there is some reason on their side, and ordinary means only can be employed by Christian churches for the propagation of the Gospel; it is, perhaps, too much to expect the indifference to personal and domestic consequences, which many still look for in Missionaries; and whether or not the "pence of the poor," and the guineas of the rich, are not estimated at too high a value, when they are thought more of than the usefulness, and health, and life, of a pious minister abroad. The illiberal system, both in resources and treatment, procures only inexperienced men. Some of these men turn out ill, and disgust the Direction, and destroy confidence in the home management; and the illiberality increases. And so one evil engenders another. A more liberal system, and lower expectations as to "super-human" qualifications, would procure higher degrees of experience and talent; these would increase confidence, and confidence would increase affection and energy, both at home and abroad; and the churches would acquit themselves, having used the means which God put into their power.

In the history of the church, it is notorious that affluence and power have generally been abused, instead of being employed usefully by Ecclesiastics; and in consequence of this, there are opulent disciples, possessing pious minds, who think that poverty is the only security for the principles of the ministers of religion. And there are both ministers and laymen, who think that a "*voluntary poverty*" is essential to the character of a Missionary. Now it is admitted, that he who serves at

X

attention to the Saviour's command. They say, "Souls are of equal value every where: there are plenty of pagans and of unconverted souls in this country; and whilst these

the altar for the sake only of a "living" is evidently unfit to serve; and he who would desert his Apostolic work among the heathen, because of poverty and hardships, is also unfit for his office. But these cases are different from a minister, with a competence and usefulness, relinquishing both for an eleemosynary subsistence, which may, from its scantiness, occasion constant anxiety, injure his health, or destroy his life; and at last terminate in his leaving a fatherless family without friends in a Pagan land. If any man wills to do so, I think he does well in the sight of his Saviour, and God our Saviour will honour great trust in himself; but whether the churches do well, in laying such a burden on men's shoulders, when they can prevent it, is a different question. There are spiritual disciples who give thousands to their children, and leave tens or hundreds of thousands to their posterity, who grudge the minister, or the missionary, the least surplus beyond the bare daily necessaries of life.

As to "*voluntary* poverty." Poverty is like slavery, and neither of them is to be *chosen*, although both may be endured. Vows of poverty, and vows of celibacy,* are, by the Holy Scriptures, alike uncalled for; but when, in the course of Providence, these, like other evils, are inevitable, without a deviation from duty, they must be submitted to with meekness and cheerfulness. "I know, (says St. Paul,) both how to be *abased* and how *to abound;* every where and in all things I am instructed, both *to be full,* and to *be hungry;* both *to abound* and to *suffer need:* St. Paul did not *prefer* poverty.

There is some danger by hazarding these remarks, and others that may occur in this volume, of giving offence to some good men; and of being charged with "wordly" notions, unworthy of the self-denying principles becoming a Missionary. But "I speak not in respect of (personal) want, for I have learned (by past experience) in whatsoever state I am, therewith to be content;" and having, by the Divine help, served a long campaign, bivouacked on the field of battle, I do not much dread the epithet of coward, nor of "carpet" Missionary, and similar accusations, from men who never quitted home service. The opinions I give forth may be erroneous, but I believe them correct, and conscientiously state them, in this land of free discussion, with no other end than to promote *The Truth.*

* The great heretyke Luther, with all his discyples, deprave, and utterly condemne, all maner of religyons, except, onely (as they call hit,) the religyon of Christe. *Religion* is made and standeth in the three essencial vowes, obedience, *wilful povertie,* and chastitie (or celibacy). For these thre ben the substantiall partes of *religyon*" (Pype of Perfection; an Apology for Monachism. 1532.)

are unconverted and unsaved, what is the use of going into other nations. Home is dear to us. English souls are as valuable as Hindoo souls. If I can save five souls a year here, I shall be more useful here than some of the Missionaries, who have laboured twenty years, without perhaps saving one soul, or but one or two."

To this mode of speaking I am really at a loss what to say. It seems pious, but I fear it is impious sophistry, virtually impugning the wisdom and goodness of the Saviour's command, to make known his salvation to all nations. I conceive the Saviour's declared intentions and wishes must be the rule to individual disciples and churches. And whilst there are *many nations* to whom Christ's salvation has not been proclaimed; the reasoning which has been exhibited is impertinent and irrelevant. Oh! man, who art thou that arguest against thy Saviour? He says, "Go and *disciple* all nations"—but thou sayest, "No: we will stay till all the souls in this nation are converted." Here I might ask, on what system of theology is the opinion grounded, that such will ever be the case with respect to any one nation? Would that this were the case! but many men will not come to Christ, that they may be saved. Broad is the road that leads to destruction, and multitudes persist in travelling onward in it. Ye ministers of religion, let the Saviour's command weigh more with you than such reasonings as have been now set before you.

The Chinese occasionally call Christianity the "*European religion*," and our Saviour is, in the Imperial Dictionary, called "*The Saviour of the West*;" and there are those in Europe who seem to *think*, or at least to *act*, the same as the Pagans. It is the *Roman* world, the *European* world; the *civilized* world, (so called by Europeans,) which occupies the attention and the cares of Christendom. Our learning must be European learning, our languages must be the ancient Pagan languages of Europe; and the distant reports of Greek and Latin writers are more regarded than the records, (more probably true,) of Asiatic historians.

I shall, no doubt, be told that some efforts to evangelize the nations, have been made in various quarters of the world, which, in a very qualified sense, I admit; but oh, how disproportionate to the requirements of that precept to which I have this evening called your attention!

Not only have Protestant efforts been vastly deficient; but even a mental recognition of the duty has been rare. Some years ago I looked over half a dozen Commentators on the motto of this evening's address; and found that they either passed over the great commandment to evangelize the nations, without notice, or slurred it over with a sentence or two, whilst pages were spent in arguing the time and manner of water baptism.

The difficulties which exist to impede the prosecution of this work, are many and great. The love of sin in the human heart; the worldly-mindedness of earthly principalities and powers, the pride of science, and the gates of hell, are all in league against the servants of Jesus in this enterprize.

In this Christianized land, notwithstanding a partial triumph of religion, since the days of avowed French Atheism and infidelity, many are the enemies of the cross, in all ranks of the community; from the most powerless and ignorant peasant, up to the most learned and dignified courtier at the foot of the throne, are they to be found; among the merchants, and the lawyers, and the statesmen, notwithstanding all the "cant" of philosophy, philanthropy, and liberalism, there are in all places not a few covert enemies of the cross of Christ.

And in some other nations, the obstacles to the discipling of men are a thousand-fold increased. Ignorance and prejudice, and malignity and enmity against God, exhibited sometimes by the populace, and sometimes by priests, or by politicians, all stand in hostile array against the banners of the cross, and turn a deaf ear, and dart a look of scorn at the envoys of Heaven's mercy to a guilty world. But, notwithstanding all these difficulties, greater is he that is for us, than all they that can be against us.

Jesus has "all power in heaven and on earth," therefore, says the heavenly mandate, "Go and disciple the nations."

If this* suffice not, Oh ye ministers and Christians, to sanction, and to stimulate, and to encourage your going, I have done; my arguments are exhausted. If required obedience to the Almighty Saviour will not operate on ministers and churches, I know not "*by what methods*," nor "*by what topics to excite them to Missionary exertions*."

I might indeed urge, that *the love of our neighbour* requires Missionary efforts. O my fellow Christian, how dost thou value the salvation of thy soul; and how dost thou esteem the benevolence of that man, or those men, who first introduced Christianity to Britain? for after the lapse of many hundreds of years, gratitude from the millions of British Christians, even of this day, is still due to them. Wert thou on an island of the Southern Sea, or on the continent of Asia, without the knowledge of Christ; and couldest by any possibility know its value as thou now dost; what wouldest thou think of that man who could say, an English soul was as valuable as thy soul; and because there were Englishmen unconverted, he would not go and proclaim the King's mercy to thee!

I might urge on you this night the *love of God*, which requires the ministers of the sanctuary to be zealous and valiant for the truth. Among many of the nations, error and wickedness, and the worship of demons, which rob God of his glory, universally prevail. Ought not zeal for the divine glory, to rouse ministers and Christians to Missionary efforts?

But I rest not this duty on our notions of propriety, or expediency, or usefulness; I rest it solely on this, *it is the*

* "Now there were in the Church that was at Antioch certain *Prophets* and *Teachers*, as Barnabas," &c.—from these the Holy Ghost said, "Separate me Barnabas and Saul,"—for a Mission throughout Europe. Such is the example furnished by Holy Scripture. Is there any precedent in Holy Writ for sending (except as Helpers) on a foreign Christian Mission *inexperienced* young men, who have never exercised the ministry.

will of God. And say not, Oh ye rebellious priests and people of Israel, "Thy will be done," and then fancy ye have done your duty. It is *his* will that Christian Churches use the means. "Go and disciple all nations; go and proclaim the Gospel to every creature." But, says the objector and caviller, would you have us all go and leave our own country and our own homes, and we pastors go and leave our flocks? No, my brethren, I require no such thing, Heaven requires it not. England's king has many affairs in foreign lands, commercial, and political, and martial; and it would be England's disgrace, if she could find no able and enlightened men and veteran servants to engage in these important missions. And Zion's King has important affairs in all lands; embassies of pardoning mercy to the guilty, of peace to the bitterest enemies; of salvation to perishing sinners, of conflict with the powers of darkness, where Satan and idols are enthroned; and it is the disgrace of our Zion that she sends not some of the ablest, and wisest, and holiest of her servants.

What our Saviour taught, and did, and suffered on earth, was for the benefit of all nations. And it is his revealed will that the glad tidings of salvation should be proclaimed to *all nations.*

Therefore every disciple, whether private Christian or Minister of the word, at home or abroad, should regard the Lord's will as the rule of his thinking and acting on this subject. He should have solemn soul-communings with the Divine Being on this part of duty; and answer conscientiously to Him, taking that deep interest in the affairs of the kingdom, and making those personal and domestic sacrifices for its welfare, which true unfeigned loyalty to Zion's King demands.

It is incumbent on those who exhort the congregations of God's people, to urge the general duty, leaving the particular application to each individual's conscience in the sight of God. No one has a right to interfere with or judge another man's conscience. As for example, beneficence is a duty binding on every Christian; but no one can prescribe to another how much time, or how much property, he shall spend in doing good. So also to use efforts to disciple or evangelize all nations, is a manifest duty; but no one has a right to prescribe to another the degree of effort, either as to personal service, appropriation of time or of property, to be employed by the said individual. That is a sacred matter between God and his own conscience. But this much may be said, supposing no ostentation or hypocrisy, these efforts will always be in proportion to each disciple's love to the Master; or each subject's loyalty to the king. They that love much will use great exertions; they that love the Saviour little will do little to serve and honour him, or to effectuate his declared intentions. In such cold-hearted cases, every duty, personal, or domestic, or imaginary, will be thought paramount to this duty; every claim will be preferred to the claims of Jesus, and the enlargement of his kingdom.

But worldly comfort is not the chief end of man. To glorify God is the highest end of human existence; and whoever makes this his sincere and supreme aim, will receive, from Divine Providence blessing the use of means, either a greater or a less supply of food and raiment and domestic comfort.

If we be indeed "God's people," and "Christ's disciples," the hallowing of our heavenly Father's name and the coming of his kingdom should be *the business of our lives.* "Seek *first* the *interests of the kingdom,* and all other things shall be added, that Heaven deems necessary for you." First be ye interested in the kingdom, and then seek its interest; let these objects have precedence of all others. Christian fathers, and mothers, and children, should all make common cause in this work.

O ye Christians! do ye really believe that God our Saviour, Zion's King, Emmanuel our Redeemer, lives and reigns in heaven, and now marks either your zeal and loyalty, or your heartlessness and disaffection? If so, let that work upon your fears and hopes. Do you believe that his humiliation, his agony and bloody sweat, his cross and passion, and his cruel death, were all endured for you, that you might not perish everlastingly? If so, let that work upon your gratitude. And know ye not that ye are not your own? God requires your services on earth, this is your reasonable service, your duty.

And what is your life? It is but for a moment! And what are ye on earth? Strangers and pilgrims! And what is before you? Death and judgment and an awful eternity; bliss everlasting, or, oh terrible reverse! expulsion from the gates of Paradise, and an eternal dwelling in darkness with demons and hypocrites.

Oh let fear and hope, and gratitude and duty, and common-sense, all conspire to induce, in families and in churches, a ceaseless spirit of devotedness and personal sacrifice for the promotion of Zion's kingdom on earth, as it is in heaven.

Ye fathers and mothers, and sons and daughters, love King Jesus; give him your hearts! cheerfully obey him! in your families sing his praises, devote to him your dearest relatives, your fortunes, and your lives.

If there be any truth in the Bible, if our Christianity be not all selfishness and hypocrisy, this devotedness were a chivalry at once rational and glorious. Away with those shameful complainings, which insinuate that too much is done for the King's cause. Away with those unbelieving anxieties, which belie the divine promises, and which virtually deny that those who honour God he will honour; and which assert that the seed of them who serve Him may be neglected by Providence.

O spirit of God, that convincest of sin, and of righteousness, and of judgment, convince the families and the churches of this land of their past neglect; and breathe into their souls a spirit of holy zeal and entire devotion to the Saviour's cause among men!

DISCOURSE XXIV.

COMPOSED FOR AN EVENING LECTURE AT ST. THOMAS'S SQUARE, HACKNEY, JANUARY 1, 1826.

MAN IN THIS WORLD IS NOT BY RIGHT, BUT BY DIVINE PERMISSION, A TEMPORARY RESIDENT.

1 CHRON. XXIX. 15.

"*For we are strangers before thee, and sojourners, as were all our fathers: our days on earth are as a shadow, and there is none abiding.*" (Heb. *expectation.*) *No hope of abiding.* (Boothroyd.)

In order to a right understanding of these words, it will be proper for us to review briefly the circumstances under which they were uttered. It is common to man in every country to feel occasionally disatisfied with life, and to give utterance to complaints concerning its troubles and its brevity. Such views of human nature are not peculiar to those who possess a divine revelation. Under the pressure of poverty, or amidst the pains of sickness, when the fond hopes of prosperity are blighted, when reverses take place in the evening of life, and the winter of old age comes upon a man, and his summer friends forsake him; and when, for by-gone kindness, he receives ungrateful returns; or, perhaps, his own kindred, or his own children rise up against him, or neglect and despise him—under any or all of these, I say, it is a common thing for man, in every part of the world, and in all ages, to utter querulous complaints about the vanity and the shortness of life. Ancient and modern Pagans, Jews, Turks, and Infidels, as well as Christians, have uttered such lamentations. But there is no reason to believe that these bewailings indicate a spirit of piety; for they may exist where there is no knowledge of God, no desire to be acquainted with his ways, no submission, no resignation, no repentance, no obedience, no worship; they do indeed more frequently indicate obduracy of heart, impenitence, and discontentedness. I shall not then merely moralize about the hardships attendant on man in his journey through life, the uncertainty of prosperous circumstances, the inevitable ills to which he is liable, and the manifold difficulties and disgusts which he must often experience in his passage to the grave. These topics are true and important, but they come not up to the Scriptural and Christian view of the case. We will then at once advert to the meaning of our text. There is a passage in the Book of Leviticus, (xxv. 23.) which throws much light on the phrase " strangers and sojourners." It is there said of the possessions of the several Jewish tribes, " The land shall not be sold for ever, for *the land is mine,* (saith Jehovah.) *Ye are strangers and sojourners* with me." Here the allusion is not to the *difficulties* of a journey, or to the *discomfort* of a lodging, but to the *right of possession.* The whole earth belongs to Jehovah; man is a stranger and a sojourner on it, and resident but for a short period, and has no just cause to assign why he should be allowed to remain. This is the sense which best suits the scope of the paragraph in which the words of our text are found.

The connexion is this. King David, having attained "a good old age," chose to settle two very important affairs before his death—the succession to the throne, and the erection of a temple to Jehovah. For these purposes the Jewish Monarch " assembled all the princes of Israel, the princes of the tribes, and the captains of the companies, and the captains over thousands and over hundreds; and the officers and mighty men, and valiant men at Jerusalem."

In the presence of this large assembly of the chiefs and

states of Judea, the aged monarch "stood up upon his feet," (Chron. xxviii. 2.) and addressed them as his "brethren" and his "people;" first concerning the *house* which was to be a resting-place for the ark of the covenant of the Lord, and next concerning his son, whom Jehovah had chosen to sit upon the throne of the kingdom.

As the temple, or "palace," to be built, "was not for man, but for the Lord God," King David made provision from the national resources of gold, and silver, and brass, and iron, and precious stones, and marble; and from his own proper good, or private fortune, he gave of gold and silver to the amount of twenty millions of pounds sterling; and the princes, or chiefs of tribes, contributed nearly as much.

On that high day of liberal donation the people rejoiced that their hearts were disposed to offer willingly to this good work of the Lord; and David the king also rejoiced with great joy. To which joyous sentiments and feelings his lips gave utterance in a devout solemn prayer, or humble address to the Divine Being, of which the words of our text form a part. The topics of that prayer are these:—*first*, in the style of adoration, an allusion is made to the Divine Sovereignty; the greatness, the power, the glory, the victory, and the majesty belong to God. Heaven and earth are his: His is the universal kingdom; and He is exalted head above all.

In the *second* place, God is acknowledged to be the giver of every good. Riches and honour come of him; it is his hand that makes great, and gives strength unto all.

Then, in the *third* place, are ascriptions of praise and of blessing to God's glorious name, who liveth for ever and ever.

Next are confessions of obligation for all the riches and the store that were possessed; for the givers of all this wealth were only "*strangers* and *sojourners* on earth"—their days were few and transitory, ever onward moving as a fleeting shadow—their property and possessions were not their own—from God it was that all their treasure came, and to his service, as was most meet, they resigned it.

King David closed his prayer by interceding for his son; and desiring that these sentiments might be kept for ever fixed on the imaginations of the thoughts of the hearts of his people.

From this analysis of the context, it appears to me, that God's people being called "*strangers* and *sojourners*," has not, in this instance, a reference to *trials* or *difficulties* by the way; but is intended to intimate, that man in this life has *no right* to assume a lordship over what is granted, nor any ground to hope for a permanent possession. Our dwelling on earth, with all its accommodations or comforts, whether many or few, are held by the merciful grant of a higher authority, and we have no just cause to claim here a lasting inheritance; for we are "strangers and sojourners, as all our fathers were." In this acknowledgment there is religion and piety, and a feeling totally different from the cynical murmurings and infidel complainings of a discontented rebellious mind. This Scriptural view of the subject brings us into contact with the Divine Being as a great, and glorious, and rightful sovereign; and leads us onward to the awfully sublime realities of the eternity which lies beyond this shadowy fleeting life. As the sun *moves* onward in his daily course, the dark shadow of intervening opaque bodies flung across the plain *also moves*—*constantly*, although *imperceptibly*, till the cause of sunshine and of shadow is lost in the undistinguishing blackness of night. The Jewish Commentators say, "Man's life resembles the shadow of a bird flying." But, perhaps, the allusion is not so much to denote the *rapidity* with which our days flee away, as their *certain*, although slow *progression*, gliding onward *irresistibly* to a close. Man's sojourn on earth is not by right, but by permission; and only for a limited period, which no earthly power can protract, any more than it could arrest the sun in its course, or stop the *constantly-moving* shadow, caused by the light's rays being intercepted.

In prosecuting this discourse, I shall *assert two general principles*, and *draw some practical inferences* from them as we proceed.

The *First* proposition is this,

The Lord God is man's rightful and beneficent Sovereign; and

The *Second* is, that man's sojourn on earth shall inevitably terminate.

These may seem, to many persons here present, very common-place truisms; but, nevertheless, they lie at the foundation of many very important duties, which are little regarded by all of us, and totally neglected by not a few.

It is not necessary to attempt a formal proof, that the great and incomprehensible Being who created the universe, and gave existence to human creatures, *has a right* to rule over the world that he made, and the nations and individuals whom he has placed upon it. The abundant supply of all that could contribute to the delight and happiness of man, in his originally innocent condition, exhibits clearly the divine benignity. The tender mercies of God, are indeed exercised towards all his works; but towards man, so far as we know, he has exercised goodness and mercy to a degree that is unparalleled in the whole history of divine operations. He created man in his own image, possessing knowledge, and holiness, and happiness; and to restore sinning man, he spared not his own Son, but gave him up to the death for us all. As King David, in the devout prayer from which our text is taken, acknowledged "both riches and honour, and all good things come from God, and that he is exalted as head above all; and reigns over all;" so we know that he has granted to guilty man an "unspeakable gift," far transcending in value the whole material universe.

In his providence also, although he sometimes arises to punish terribly the wicked; yet, Oh how much long-suffering and patience does he manifest; not willing that any should perish, but that all should come to repentance. Ye know, my brethren, the tender language of the Prophet, speaking in the name of the Lord, "Turn ye, turn ye, why will ye die? As I live (saith the Lord) I have no pleasure in the death of the wicked."

In the whole of the divine character, as Creator, Preserver, and Saviour, the Lord is gloriously manifested to be a rightful and beneficent sovereign. And this being the case, I would that I could, on this occasion, lastingly impress this truth on the imaginations of the thoughts of the hearts of this assembly. Beginning at the youngest, I would pass upwards to the oldest, and suggest to self-examination the solemn question, whether or not the relationship of a creature, of an accountable and a guilty creature, has heretofore been, by every mind, fully recognised? Alas! (if we may judge by our own hearts, and by the conduct of the millions around us) how few seem to remember that they are *not* their own masters; that what they possess, of bodily powers, of intellectual faculties, of riches or of honours, are *not* their own; that they are but *strangers* and *sojourners* on earth, and these things are only entrusted to them for a season, and entrusted for use, not for irresponsible abuse.

Oh how descriptive is that passage in the Psalmist, where the wicked are represented as saying, "Our tongue is our own—who is Lord over us?" The young men and women say, "Our strength and our time are our own—who is Lord over us?" The rich say, "Our wealth is our own, and we will consume it on our lusts—who is Lord over us?" The men in high stations, civil and ecclesiastical, say, "Our authority and influence are our own—who is Lord over us?"

Oh deluded human beings, know ye not, that whether as creatures or as Christians, ye are *not* your own, but your Maker, your Preserver, your Redeemer is your *rightful Lord*, is your beneficent Sovereign; and to acknowledge him, to submit to him, to devote yourselves, soul, spirit, and body to him, is your reasonable service. Ye are *strangers* on earth; the place of your residence is his, his is the air you breathe; his are all the accommodations ye possess, and ye *sojourn* but for a while; to him soon you must render an account.

We infer then, from this principle, that it is your *duty* to cherish,

1. A spirit of *dependence.* It is the duty of creatures and of Christians to acknowledge continually, and to feel unceasingly, their dependence on God. It is, I fear, impracticable, when addressing a mixed congregation, to suit one's discourse to every age and every condition of the hearers, and to every grade of knowledge and experience possessed by them. This is, I fear, an insuperable defect in pulpit instruction. The attainments, and ages, and characters of the congregations are so different, and the impatience of the better-informed is so great, if the less-informed be attended to, that the preacher too frequently is unintelligible to one half of his audience. Hence the necessity and utility of domestic instruction, and of ministerial catechizing of children, and religious conversations with youths; and of all the varied modes which Christian benevolence can suggest for the inter-communication of scriptural knowledge; not merely of the dry detail of catechetical facts, but of principles and their application to daily practice. However, I return from this digression to say, that I ardently desire to lead every individual in this assembly to a dutiful and daily recognition of his dependence on God. Children in helpless infancy are dependent upon their parents. Every man, less or more, is dependent on his neighbours; all ranks are dependent reciprocally on each other; the poor on the opulent rich, and the rich on the labouring poor; the people on the rulers* for personal and domestic security, and the rulers on the people, for the means of carrying on government. And if men be so dependent on each other, how much more is man dependent on God. The word "independent," although a favourite term, with individuals and communities, is a term more congenial to the pride of the human heart, than to either Scripture or reason; but when applied to a creature in reference to his Creator, it is blasphemous. Independent! on him we depend for every breath we draw, every pulse that beats. If he withhold

* A Chinese once told me he was very grateful for the government of the Tartar Monarch: peace and security, under any government, were so much preferable to anarchy.

his support, that instant our life becomes extinct. As creatures, it is in him we live, and move, and have our being; and as Christians we are like branches, dependent on the true vine for life and growth; cut off from thence, we die and perish. Beside, to affect independence incurs guilt. Shall a child be independent of his parent, a servant of his master, a subject of his sovereign, a creature of his Maker? Our moral sense, and our innate perception of right and wrong, rise up against these propositions. Pride and assumed independence are the radical sins of human beings; they sever man at once from duty and from bliss. Every where, however, there are persons, both among the young and among the aged, the poor and the rich, the ignorant and the learned, the governed and the governors, who impiously demand, as king Pharoah did—who Jehovah is, that they should hearken to him? and who the Lord is, that they should obey him? Oh how unreasonable! Oh what temerity! Oh how awful the ultimate consequences! Oh ye young persons who hear me, I am anxious for you, that ye would deeply consider, and devoutly acknowledge, your dependence on God, who is your rightful and beneficent Sovereign, for ye are only *strangers* and *sojourners* on the earth.

2. From our state of dependence on the great Sovereign of the Universe, we infer, in the second place, the reasonableness of *obedience*. It is manifest that during man's sojourn on earth, he is left to obey or disobey without *immediate* reward or punishment. But to the degree that his mind is *enlightened* in the *knowledge* of his Lord's will, his disobedience makes his conscience less or more uneasy, and his life unhappy. And hence there are wicked servants, who imagine that *voluntary ignorance* of the Lord's will may excuse disobedience. But how futile is this imagination: for is it not the duty of a servant to use every proper means to ascertain his master's will? not to do so is already an act of disobedience. And, further, it is the duty of every good servant to inform, to the utmost of his power, his fellow-servants of the master's will. Some object to Christian Missions, on the fallacious sup-

position, that by enlightening other nations in the knowledge of the will of God, we shall make their condemnation the greater. But it is our *duty* to communicate to our fellow-residents in this transitory world, whatever we know of our Lord's will, and it is their duty to receive it; and instead of serving them, by keeping them in ignorance, as the supposition presumptuously and impiously supposes, we shall only, by so doing, involve ourselves in the guilt of disobedience, disloyalty, and inhumanity; for our Lord's will is full of mercy and of kindness to all his creatures. To seek to know his will, and yield entire obedience to the whole of it, is our most reasonable service, and the only way to be happy.

3. A third inference that we draw is, that during our sojourn on earth, *contentment* with the allotments of our gracious Lord is incumbent on us. A proper sense of his goodness and his wisdom, viewed in connexion with our own sinfulness and ignorance, will invariably lead to a spirit of contentment; not only when our concerns are prosperous, but likewise in adversity.

4. And again, in the fourth place, allied to this contentment is *resignation;* when our afflictions are more than *we* think conducive to our good. There are beautiful examples of this becoming temper of mind recorded in Holy Writ. You remember the exclamation of one who was greatly afflicted, "It is the Lord, (said he,) let him do what seemeth him good." And another, whilst greatly distressed, cried, "Though he slay me, yet will I trust in him." Oh how suitable and exalted were their conceptions of the goodness and the wisdom of God. These experienced holy men *resigned* to God, with devout confidence, their case and their cause during the few and evil days of their earthly pilgrimage. Oh how unbecoming are the murmurings of discontent, and the aspirings of a never-satisfied ambition to be rich, or to be distinguished among men. Happy they, who from holding intercourse with Heaven, are contented in obscurity and poverty, and resigned in the midst of an afflicted sojourn on earth! But when we reflect how the great Lord of all has provided

for this world's sojourners, a vast supply of all that conduces to comfort and delight; and for sinful creatures has furnished all the glorious blessings of the everlasting Gospel; we ask not only for a spirit of dependence, obedience, contentment, and resignation, but also of

5. *Gratitude*, which is our fifth particular. The unholy, the proud, the disobedient, the discontented, the rebellious murmurers and complainers, are also ungrateful and unthankful. The mind that is convinced of its own demerits, will, in the midst of the most afflictive circumstances, see abundant reason for gratitude, to God. Humility and thankfulness, pride and ingratitude, go together. Blessed are the poor in spirit and the grateful; but the proud and thankless sinner God knoweth afar off. You perceive, my young friends, that most of these inferences, which I draw from our condition on earth, being that of strangers and sojourners, refer to the *duties which are exercised in the mind or heart;* for unless our hearts be right with God, we are altogether wrong. The Lord looks directly at the heart. If in the heart there be a humble sense of our dependence on Him; awe and reverence, and devout admiration and contentment, and resignation and gratitude, for all that He is to us, and has done for us, as our Creator, Preserver, and Redeemer, happy are we! Then will our actions and external behaviour be in obedience to his holy, and righteous, and merciful commandments.

6. And, we mention, as a sixth inference, that we sojourners on earth ought to enter cheerfully and zealously into a *co-operation with* the declared intentions or designs of our great Lord, both with regard to ourselves, and to our fellow inhabitants of the world. He is the great Benefactor of all; and it has pleased him to constitute some persons a sort of stewards in the great family. The possession of justly acquired power or affluence, or superior talents, is given for the good of the whole company of sojourners, and not for the sake only of the individual possessors. To *do good* and *to communicate*, is a precept binding on all, to the extent of their means; and of course it applies both to body and to mind, to the whole man;

not only to food and clothing, and medicine for the sick; but also to education, to moral culture, and to religious instruction. There is a class of secularized and materialized professors of Christianity, who will admit the duty of doing good to men's bodies, but would neglect their minds. And there are professed philanthropists, who would teach to the young, physical science, and carry to other nations civilization; that is, they would teach them to weigh and to measure, and to mould pieces of wood, or of stone, or of metal; and to analyze or to compound the various material elements of our earthly residence; and to build comfortable houses, and plant elegant gardens, in this land of our temporary sojourn; but concerning the great Lord and Sovereign of this our abode for a season; of his will and pleasure concerning us; of our obligations and duty to him; of the everlasting dwelling to which we must soon remove; and of the necessary preparation for it, they would teach nothing. They would cast into the shade, or exclude altogether, these greatest and most important parts of human affairs; or, with hypocritical expressions of piety, would profess to leave these matters to the miraculous interference of the great Lord himself. But if they leave the greater concernments of man to the miraculous interference of Providence, why not act on their own principle in the less affairs of human beings? Cannot He (to adopt their mode of reasoning) who miraculously interferes for the spiritual and immortal interests of men, also miraculously interfere for their bodily and temporal interests? Why then plough or sow, or spin or weave, or establish literary schools or mechanics' institutions, or scientific colleges? Leave each individual to himself; no doubt Providence will take care of him. If the reasoning be conclusive in the one case, I see not why it should be inconclusive in the other. But in the latter case, you perceive it is absurd; and not less absurd is it in the former. The truth, I fear, really is, that it is only a pretext, made by a mind that is disaffected to the great Lord himself, or doubts his existence, or hates his moral government, and would have men live as atheists in the world.

O ye Christians—ye loyal subjects of Zion's King—ye true worshippers of the God of the Bible; who is the great Lord of our present, and of our eternal residence—and who declared it to be his will, that Christ's gospel should be proclaimed and taught to every creature—be it your study to co-operate in this divinely benevolent work! And among other motives, the

Second division of our discourse, which is, that

II. *Man's sojourn on earth shall inevitably terminate,* furnishes not the least. Man is here a *stranger*, a *sojourner*, a *guest*, a *traveller*, a *pilgrim*. The Christian pilgrim is going indeed to a *holy-place,* but not on earth. Here he abides not. This description of the life of man implies *another state of existence;* the belief of which, as you are well aware, is not peculiar to Christianity, or to revealed religion. The belief of a separate state of existence, different from our earthly one, is found not only among the Mohammedans, who may have derived it from the Christian religion; but it is also found among the savage tribes of America, and the old civilized nations of Asia. There are, however, in different countries, individuals and sects who deny it. There is nothing about it in the books left to the eastern world by the Chinese moralist Confucius; and many of his followers deny it. But, on the other hand, a great majority of the Chinese not only believe that we human beings shall exist after our bodies die, but also that we existed in another state before we were born into this world; and on *their* supposition we are, in a very striking manner, only "*strangers* and *sojourners,*" on earth. There is, perhaps, no absurdity in this notion; but we can only say, it wants evidence, and God's inspired servants, who wrote our Holy Scriptures, have not taught it in the Bible. We therefore reject it, as we do every other theory or supposition, which, however plausible, has no proof. But the glimmerings and anticipations of the human mind, in reference to *a future state,* are abundantly confirmed and put beyond all doubt by the revelation of Him who came down from heaven, to give his life for the redemption of the world;—He has brought life and immortality to light by the Gospel. Some persons have said that the Jews did not look for a future state; and an English Bishop of the last century, (Warburton), wrote a book, on the supposition that the Jews did not expect an hereafter. But the ancient Patriarchs, and king David, when they confessed that they were "*strangers and sojourners" on earth; "declare plainly,"* as St. Paul observes, in his letter to the Hebrews, that they *looked for another country;* and truly, if their minds referred, when they made such a declaration, to the country from which they came out, they might have had opportunity to have returned; but now they desire a "*better country,"*—" that is a heavenly." If St. Paul understood the old Testament, it is manifest the Bishop was wrong.

Since, then, mankind generally, in all ages and in all nations, in the old world of Asia, and the new world of America, have believed in a future state, and the same is confirmed by the sacred writings of the Jews and of the Christians, is it wise, my young friends, to let the bold assertions of here and there a profligate infidel, or an irreligious cold-hearted sceptic, have any weight on your min ds?

A very few *deny* an hereafter; many *wish* there were none; and still more *live* as if there were none: and even those who are "*looking" for a future state,* alas! too frequently seem to forget that their sojourn here shall inevitably *soon terminate.* This appears, even among the most devout Christians, by their being too much distressed about the ills and discomforts of their present abode, and from an undue anxiety to secure earthly comforts. And of this inconsistency the aged, who have nearly finished their course, are often more guilty than the young. This state of mind is full of distrust in the gracious Lord and Master, who has in times past provided for them: it meets, indeed, with some excuse in the prevailing vice of selfish mortals—

neglect of the infirm and the aged—of which, alas! Christian communities are not guiltless. But this apology amounts not to a justification. If we trust God our Saviour with our immortal happiness, shall we not confide in him, for what is requisite during our temporary sojourn? But I would observe by the way, that the doctrine of laying up treasures in heaven, instead of hoarding them on earth, does not suppose idleness, or carelessness, or extravagance; but still requires industry, and economy, and care, that we may give pecuniary aid to him that needeth, when he is sick or in prison; in helpless childhood or in feeble old age; or that we may instruct those that are ignorant of the blessed Gospel. We should be industrious, that we may contribute to the general good during our sojourn here. We should give to the really poor, (but not foster idleness and vice,) and we should teach the unwillingly ignorant, and in this way lend to and serve the Lord; ever remembering, that all things come of him, both riches and honour, and also talent and strength; and it is of his own that we give to him:—As the Jewish Commentators rendered the prayer of our text, "We only return to Thee what thine own hand hath blessed us withal." And as the ancient Christians said, at the place of presenting offerings, (τα σα απο των σων) Ours is a gift of "*Thine own things, from thine own people.*"

Now, my brethren, since our sojourn on earth shall soon terminate, and its termination is not annihilation, or the destruction of our being; but a removal to another and an eternal state, either happy or unhappy, according to our spiritual character and behaviour in the present life, it follows that a due anxiety and effort to avoid the unhappy eternity, and attain the blissful one, is the greatest and most reasonable concern of every human being. Oh let not Satan darken your minds, my fellow sinners, on this great question! He may display to you all the kingdoms of the world, and the glory and the pomp of them; or fascinate your imaginations with voluptuous dreams of pleasure and delight, or urge you on to the pursuits of a never-satiated avarice, with anticipations of the independence, and comfort, and security of fortune and affluence, aiming all the time to make you forget or neglect the coming eternity. But, oh fools that we are, and slow of heart to believe *the truth*. We are but sojourners here, and have no right to stay, no real property in the goods we accumulate; we build houses for others to inhabit, we hoard riches for others to squander, we enlarge our barns and stock them with supplies for many years, (every one to the extent that he can,) and after wearisome days and nights of misplaced toil, ere we have sat down to enjoy, the rightful owner, having warned and exercised long patience with us, bids us at once remove. Preparation for eternity was, at the commencement of our course, enjoined upon us; we despised the commandment, and neglected the admonition, and now further respite is impossible. Thus are the men of ambition, of sensuality, and of avarice, driven away in their wickedness. Oh that every individual who now hears me, of every age and of every condition, children and servants, and young and aged, and poor and rich, would, as in the sight of God, look solemnly and distinctly at a coming eternity, so as to retain throughout this year, and the rest of life, vivid and uniformly abiding impressions of its infinitely important concernments;—then should we see a rational and devout preparation for it. I alarm you not with declamation about sudden and unexpected death, events, however, very common; but I would fix your attention on its *shadow-like*, *slow* and *noiseless*, and *certain* and *inevitable* approach.

"Every beating pulse you tell
Leaves but the number less."

What earthly power can arrest the sun in his course, or stay the dial gnomon's shadow, as it silently and imperceptibly moves? None! and equally powerless are all human efforts to protract man's *sojourn* on earth, beyond the period of God's good pleasure.

Prepare then, oh *sojourner!* to quit at thy Lord's bidding! Prepare then, oh thou moral criminal, to meet thy Judge! Prepare, oh Christian, to meet thy Saviour!

Under these various circumstances ye know what preparation is requisite. It is not so necessary on this occasion, I imagine, to teach you what is right, as to stir you up to do it. Hast thou heretofore forgotten God, and lived without Christ? Repent and be converted. Didst thou once ascend the mount of faith and hope, and hast now slidden back to a lower state of heavenly aspiration? to thee also would I say, Repent, and do thy first works.

When we look within our own breasts, and around us in the world, how lamentably prevalent is a worldly spirit! One periodical religious pamphlet of the high church (Christian Remembrancer) for the last month, has indeed complained that "a religious ferment" is rather too much gone forth among the people; but, alas, how *still* is *this* fermentation, compared with the *fermentation of worldly aggrandizement!* I push not the doctrine of our text to any extravagant and impracticable degree, but only ask, for such a course of acting and thinking, as common sense requires, from the facts laid down and proved every day, by ocular demonstration, viz. that here on earth there is none abiding; and added to that, an eternal existence, a heaven of happiness, or a hell of misery, lie before us. We must come to an honest application of our Christian principles, if we would live as it becomes the Gospel.*

* Oh what lamentable ignorance, misbelief, forgetfulness of God, and fear of man, must exist in the many unhappy cases of suicide that take place, in every part of the world, and not least in this highly enlightened country. Shame, and revenge, and peevish discontent, have more influence than the natural fear of death, and than the fear of God, with persons of all ranks, of either sex, and of all ages. Some at the outset of their sojourn, and others when it must be near its close, impiously and presumptuously hurry themselves into eternity, instead of waiting the dismissal of their rightful Sovereign. God grant that a better understanding of man's condition and duty, may every day increase, and so prevent such melancholy occurrences. And would to God that human governments would cease to be so lavish of men's lives for crimes which concern only property. Ah, how seemingly hypocritical, for our legislators to pray God to have mercy on those to whom their laws, in pecuniary matters, will shew no mercy. What a contradiction between such doings and the Lord's prayer, "Forgive us, as we forgive." Holy Scripture, indeed, commands that "He who sheddeth man's blood, by

Finally, ye who have believed in Jesus, remember that he has gone to prepare mansions for you in his Father's house. Oh repine not at the afflictions which ye may be called to endure in this land, wherein ye are strangers and pilgrims. Be not impatient; be not like the Budhist of China, and the pleasure-sated, wearied, profligate of Europe, to call your existence a curse. Rather up and be active to do all the good possible here. Opportunities to do and to suffer for Jesus, will soon be over. Work therefore while it is day, and rejoice in hope of the glory of God, when ye shall attain to your eternal abode in heaven.

"O God of Bethel! by whose hand
Thy people still are fed;
Who through this weary pilgrimage
Hast all our fathers fed;
Our vows, our pray'rs we now present
Before thy throne of grace:
God of our fathers! be the God
Of their succeeding race.

Thro' each perplexing path of life
Our wand'ring footsteps guide;
Give us each day our daily bread,
And raiment fit provide.
O spread thy cov'ring wings around,
Till all our wand'rings cease,
And at our Father's lov'd abode
Our souls arrive in peace.

Such blessings from thy gracious hand
Our humble pray'rs implore;
And thou shalt be our chosen God,
And portion evermore."

man shall his blood be shed." But beyond this we doubt the right of any earthly power to shorten man's sojourn on earth, or to remove a fellow creature into eternity before the Sovereign Lord himself shall be pleased to do it.

DISCOURSE XXV.

DELIVERED IN 1806, BEFORE GOING TO CHINA.

The Manuscript was preserved by an Old Friend.—The place *where this Discourse was preached, like many other occurrences of that period, has totally escaped from the memory of the writer.*

SOURCES OF CONSOLATION TO THE BELIEVER.

JOHN XIV. 1—3.

"Let not your heart be troubled: ye believe in God, believe also in me. In my Father's house are many mansions: if it were not so, I would have told you. I go to prepare a place for you. And if I go and prepare a place for you, I will come again, and receive you unto myself; that where I am, there ye may be also."

It is my desire this day, my brethren, to bring to your recollection some of the consolations of the Gospel. I have chosen, as the foundation of my discourse, a portion of our Lord's consolatory address to his disciples, ere he left the world and went to the Father.

We are all by nature children of wrath, and we do well to recollect it—the depraved children of our apostate first parents, and as such, exposed to the deserved punishment of the Great and Righteous Supreme.

Such being our condition, it is a great mercy that the vials of wrath are not, ere now, poured out upon us. Thanks be to God for our respite from punishment! But, Christians, our state is not merely a state of respite from punishment. No: through Jesus Christ our Lord, we have received the atonement—have passed from death to life. But yet we are not delivered from temporal evils. Our God has wisely and graciously appointed to every one his period of residence in this state of trial. Ye are exposed to outward afflictions and various troubles, in common with other men; but, in the midst of these, we can address to you, what we cannot address to them—in the words of our Lord Jesus, we say, "Let not your heart be troubled: ye believe in God, believe also in me. In my Father's house are many mansions: if it were not so, I would have told you. I go to prepare a place for you; and if I go and prepare a place for you, I will come again, and receive you to myself; that where I am, there ye may be also."

You are familiar with the occasion on which these words were spoken; and we shall not occupy your time in going over it, but shall, with humility, examine for your comfort the sources of consolation which our Lord here suggests to his disconsolate disciples, and which are calculated to bear up your minds under any trial, and make you, through the whole of life, happy Christians.

The sources of consolation which our Lord suggests, are these five. Confidence in himself—Mansions in his Father's house—His presence there now—His second coming—and, our everlasting abode with him.

The Lord grant that your souls may be edified and comforted, whilst I speak, and you muse, on our dear Redeemer's words.

First, then, have confidence in Christ Jesus. "Let not your heart be troubled," said he, "ye believe in God, believe also in me." You believe in God who laid the foundation of the earth, who stretched abroad the heavens, who holdeth the sea in the hollow of his hand, and who taketh up the isles as a very little thing; whose arm is omnipotent, whose understanding is infinite, who is the governor among the nations;—believe also in me. Believe what I have said concerning myself, what the Father has testified concerning me, and what the works that I do bear witness of. I told you that I came forth from God. The Father testified, saying, "This is my beloved Son, in whom

I am well pleased, hear ye him." And if ye believe not these, believe my works.

My Christian brethren, tell me, can ye gather consolation from a belief in God, simply considered, when you remember your own sinfulness. I wish you not to form frightful ideas of God, or in your imaginations to make him a cruel tyrant. But say, when you form the *most lovely* ideas of God, (which are the true ones,) and when you keep in sight your own wickedness and impurity, say if ye can gather consolation. It is impossible. Unless you rob God of his perfections, and make him like yourselves, it is impossible! The highest that we can obtain will be a painful uncertainty. It will only be, at its highest, a peradventure—who can tell but what God may have mercy and spare us. Yours is not a painful uncertainty, if you believe in Jesus Christ as Mediator betwixt God and man. When conscience told thee the truth, my brother, that God was incensed against thee, that everlasting destruction awaited thee—what couldst thou have done? what could have eased thy troubled breast, hadst thou not discovered, hadst thou not believed that Jesus was a daysman betwixt thee and offended Deity? Is it not the faith of this that now restores peace to thy conscience when troubled by sin? Cherish the belief. Dwell with delight upon the person, the work, the relations, and the fulness of Jesus.

And who is Jesus? Is he a great and good man? He is more than man—he is more than angel—he is more than super-angelic spirit—he is the Son of God. When the Father bringeth his first begotten into the world, he saith, "Let all the angels of God worship him." He maketh his angels ministers, and his spirits a flaming fire; but to the Son he saith, Thy throne, O God, is for ever and ever; a sceptre of righteousness is the sceptre of thy kingdom: of old hast thou laid the foundation of the earth, and the heavens are the work of thy hands. Jesus is over all, God blessed for ever.

And what has Jesus done?—What has Jesus done! Though he was in the form of God, and thought it not robbery to be equal with God, yet for us he humbled himself: took upon him the form of a servant, and was made in the likeness of sinful flesh, and became obedient to death, even the death of the cross. He cheerfully gave himself a sacrifice for us. He was made a curse for us, that he might redeem us from the curse of the law. He bore for us what was equivalent to everlasting perdition.

I have not mentioned that he revealed to men fully the law of God—that he brought life and immortality to light; for my mind was led away to the great work of making atonement for our trangressions. For what would it have availed to have made known to us the law of God, if it only showed to us more clearly our crimes and our guilt? What would the knowledge of immortality have availed, if we were to have been immortally miserable? But Jesus died that we might live. And what are his relations to us? He is our Surety; he is our Shepherd to feed us, and to lead and guide us; he is our elder Brother; by faith in him, we are received into the family of God: Yea, we are bone of his bone, and flesh of his flesh.

And what is his fulness? His fulness is inexhaustible. In him there is a fulness of power, of wisdom, of goodness, of grace, but I enumerate them not; the Book of Inspiration has said more than the mind of man can conceive of his fulness; for in him dwelleth all the fulness of the Godhead bodily.

Wherefore consider, my Christian brother, the relations in which Jesus stands to thy soul. Who he is, what he has done, and the fulness that is treasured up in him. I say, consider it, and believe it, and say if there be reason for your heart to be troubled.

Is there not in the faith of Jesus enough to raise our minds far above, as far as the heavens are above the earth, and to make us move as undisturbed as the celestial orbs amidst all the convulsions that rend the solid world. Let us pass on to the

Second thought that is suggested for our consolations. Our Saviour says, In my Father's house are many mansions. I wish you, my brethren, to realize what is your state whilst in this world, viz. That of strangers and pilgrims. I wish you to look forward, and to gather your consolations from your future prospects. But look not to any thing on this side the grave. Lift up the eye of faith, and look beyond the gloomy vale, and tell me if you do not perceive the heavenly palaces. It is the new Jerusalem, it is the temple of our God, it is our Father's house. Yes, *our Father's house!* We claim God as our Father, and he is not ashamed to call us children, seeing he hath prepared for us a city and dwellings that are worthy of himself. Our present dwellings, my brethren, are in the dust; we are the inhabitants of our earthly house. We meditate, sometimes, with considerable anxiety, the day when these bodies shall be assimilated to the clods of the valley. From time to time we are called to lament the ruined fabric of our near and dear relatives. But why, my brethren! why should we look forward with anxiety to our own dissolution, or mourn the dissolution of the earthly dwelling of our friends in Jesus? We know that when this earthly house of our tabernacle is dissolved, there is a building of God, an house not made with hands, eternal in the heavens. Reflect on its properties. It is a building of God, from which he has excluded sin and the curse, which effected the ruin of the house we now inhabit. It is not made with hands, an expression that denotes its excellence, as being far above the power of the creature. Let the most skilful workman select the choicest materials, the most delightful situation, and give to his building all the charms that nature or art can furnish, or fancy herself could ever paint, thou, my Christian brother, hast a mansion that infinitely excels in thy Father's house, and unlike the mansions built by feeble man, it is eternal. Where now are the temples and cities that once boasted immortality? Where is ancient Nineveh? Babylon the great, is fallen, is fallen! Where is golden Thebes, her ivory palace, her hundred gates? they are buried in their own ruins, and not only so, *sed etiam perire ruinæ*, but even their very ruins perish. We have heard their names, but can with difficulty ascertain the spot where they stood. But why do I mention these, though the wonder of the world and the pride of nations; for the world itself shall pass away, and no place be found for it. Nature herself shall yield her dying groans, and all the things that are therein shall be burnt up; but the abodes of the Redeemed of the Lord are eternal in the heavens.

But say you, what assurance have we of these things? If it had not been so, said Jesus, who is the true and faithful witness, I would have told you.—And what security have we of entering into those blessed mansions? This leads us to the

Third source of consolation which we mentioned, viz. our Lord's presence there now. He is our forerunner, and has for us entered into the possession of the heavenly inheritance. It is our Lord's design to bring many sons to glory. As our surety, he has put himself in our stead and borne our sins, that he might ransom us from hell; and by his resurrection and ascension to glory he prepares the way for all his followers. There would be no admission there but for Jesus. Say not, but will Jesus remember the low estate of his servants? O when shall we cease to doubt of the love of Jesus! How much proof do you ask of his most ardent affection? Did he leave the bosom of his father—for us give himself to shame and spitting—to scourging and crucifixion; and can we imagine that he now forgets us?—No, no, Christians, you are engraven on the palms of his hands,—you are ever before him. Honour the Lord by leaning much upon him, expecting much from him. Realize then, my Christian brethren, your interest in Jesus; realize the work in which he is engaged for you, worthless creatures; and the believing consideration of it will dispel every gloom, and afford a most powerful argument for the exhortation—"Let not your heart be troubled."

But will Jesus return when those mansions are prepared? Yes; the words of our Lord are, "I will come again;" and this is the

Fourth source of consolation which we mention—our Lord's second coming. Now in his absence he has sent the Holy Spirit, the Comforter, to abide with us.—You feel, I trust, though you cannot explain, his happy influences; but still you look forward, and hasten to the coming of the day of our Lord Jesus Christ. *When* he will come he has not told us; but he says, "Lo! I come quickly." —He will come at the hour of our death, previous to which the time may be but very short. I do not mention five, or ten, or twenty years, which will most assuredly bring *many* of us to death and to the house appointed for all living;—but I mention a hundred years, which will bring us *all* to death, and introduce us to our Lord.

But we stop not here: direct your prospect onward still to the great and notable day of the Lord, when he shall come in flaming fire in his glory—in the glory of the Father and all the holy angels with him; and by his all-creating voice, that spoke the universe into existence, shall rouse thy dust from the slumbers of death, and transform thy body; and in the audience of an assembled world shall bid thee welcome to his Father's house, and to those mansions which were prepared for thee from the foundation of the world.

But are we sure that Jesus will come again? where is the promise of his coming? for since the fathers slept, all things continued as they were. My young brother, suffer not Satan to whisper into thine ear such an insinuation. The Lord is not slack concerning his promise, as some men count slackness, but is long-suffering to usward, not willing that any should perish, but that all should come to repentance. Know ye not that a thousand years are with the Lord as one day, and one day is as a thousand years? You have seen the promises of Jesus fulfilled in other instances, and these furnish a rational evidence that this also shall be fulfilled in its time. But what shall succeed my Lord's coming? shall I see him whom my soul loveth for a short time, and again be separated from him? No;—he will receive us to himself, that where he is, there we may be also; we shall be ever with the Lord. And this is the

Fifth and last source of consolation offered in our text.

In this distant land we for a short time ascend the mount to converse with God in his ordinances, as I trust ye this day did in a peculiar manner at his holy table; but soon we must again descend into the world, and engage in its cares and pursuits. But when we have seen the temple of God above, and entered into the possession of those mansions in our Father's house, we shall go no more out. Jesus says, "Father, I will that those whom thou hast given me may be with me where I am, that they may behold my glory." We behold his glory now, but it is through a glass darkly; whereas then we shall see him face to face, and know even as also we are known. The object will be the same, but the perceptive faculty will be infinitely improved, and with steady eye we shall behold the glories of God and of the Lamb; enlarged discoveries of the love and grace of God in the person of the Son; which have been gradually unfolded to us, and exercised on our behalf to the day of our admission into glory, will fill our astonished souls with gratitude ineffable, and our tongues with never-ceasing praises. O with what delight shall we "sit on every heavenly hill," and talk of our Saviour's love to us, poor sinful mortals. The only matter of debate will be, who owes most to sovereign grace. With joy unfelt by angels, we shall join the ransomed millions round the throne, and sing the hymn of endless praise to Him who loved us and washed us from our sins in his blood, and made us kings and priests to God. O thrice happy state of all who believe in Jesus Christ! all the perfections of God are on your side; on the dissolution of the body there are mansions in heaven to receive you—Jesus is now preparing for your reception—Jesus will come and receive you to himself, that where he is, there shall you be also, and be ever with the Lord. Amen! So let it be! The Saviour says,

Let not your heart with anxious thought
Be troubled or dismay'd,
But trust in Providence divine,
And trust my gracious aid.

I to my Father's house return,
There numerous mansions stand,
And glory manifold abounds
Thro' all the happy land.

I go your entrance to secure
And your abode prepare;
Regions unknown are safe to you
When I, your friend, am there.

Thence will I come when ages close,
To take you home with me:
There shall we meet to part no more,
And still together be.

DISCOURSE XXVI.

DELIVERED AT THE REV. J. CLAYTON, JUNIOR'S, CHAPEL, FEB. 26, 1826.

THE POWER OF CHRIST RESTING ON HIS PEOPLE AND SERVANTS, THE ONLY TRUE CAUSE OF GLORYING.

2 COR. xii. 9.

"*Most gladly therefore will I rather* glory *in my* infirmities, *that the* power *of Christ may* rest *upon me.*"

"IT is recorded of the Apostle Paul, (I determine not how truly,) that he was of low stature, crooked and bald; some add that he had an impediment in his speech, that his voice was shrill and unpleasant, and his delivery ungraceful." (Scott, in loco.) He himself tells us, in a paragraph of his second epistle to the Corinthians, that his enemies represented his letters as indeed weighty and powerful; but his bodily presence as weak, and his speech contemptible. This accusation was probably exaggerated, but still, had he been a man of commanding appearance, and had he excelled in the eloquence of the day, they would not have brought against him such an accusation.

The *infirmity* which he calls a "thorn in the flesh," and "a messenger of Satan sent to buffet him," some have considered to arise from his "personal defects, of which he was conscious, and which gave his enemies, especially the false apostles, a colour of reviling and derid-

z 2

ing him." But it cannot be supposed, without apparent absurdity, that St. Paul would pray for the removal of *bodily defects*, which could not be brought about without a miraculous interposition of Almighty power. Beside, his bodily defects of low stature, and so forth, had been with him through life; they were not *given* or *sent* at any particular period, nor could they be removed.

The Apostle, by employing figurative language on the subject of the *infirmity*, which occasioned him so much uneasiness, has cast a veil over it, which no industry of commentators or others has ever been able to remove. Nor is it at all of consequence to the complete understanding of the Apostle's reasoning. The circumstances of the case are these: St. Paul had been highly favoured, and treated as a man greatly beloved in the heavenly world. Jesus had in a special and unexampled manner appeared to him in the glory of his exalted human nature, with an effulgence exceeding that of the sun shining in its strength; and he was, at a subsequent period, "caught up to the third heaven," to the paradise of God, where he was blessed with visions and revelations of the Lord; and "heard unspeakable words," which it is not possible for a man to utter, in the language of mortals.

But St. Paul had still to reside a little longer on earth among his fellow-men, and was liable, as other men are, to be unduly elated by the privileges conferred upon him; to prevent which it pleased God his Saviour to permit him to be assaulted by the enemy of man, in the form of some temptation or infirmity, calculated to humble him in his own estimation, and perhaps also to lower him in the esteem of others.

To have this "thorn," which galled and annoyed him, removed, he was very anxious, and besought *the Lord* thrice, that it might depart from him. But his prayer was not granted: what he desired was not conceded. Instead of removing his infirmity, the Lord said unto him, "*My* grace is sufficient for thee; for *my* strength is made perfect in weakness." Paul was satisfied, and formed the resolution, contained in the words of our text—"Most gladly, therefore, will I *rather glory* in my *infirmities*, that the *power of Christ* may *rest* upon me."

You perceive St. Paul prayed to a person he styles *the Lord;* that *same Lord* replied to his prayer; and the *Lord* who was prayed to, and answered, was the *Lord Christ*. The Lord said, "*My grace*" shall be with thee, and "*my strength*" shall support thee; and these the Apostle calls the "*Power of Christ.*" Christ Jesus is therefore the object of prayer, and consequently truly God. By this *power* resting upon him must be understood its being always present with him, to assist and sustain him in the time of need.

Having thus briefly traced the *occasion* and *import* of the words of our text, I shall deduce from them a few practical inferences. And,

First, Infirmities, temptations, and anxieties, have been the lot of the most eminent servants of God; of inspired Apostles, as well as of ordinary ministers and private Christians; for so general, in all places, and in every age, have been the pernicious effects of man's first apostacy; it has involved all mankind. Although the renewing influences of God's Holy Spirit produce an extensively beneficial change upon the human soul, sanctification has still to progress through the whole of life, and is, we believe, never perfected whilst man remains on earth. The idea of sinless perfection whilst here below, is not a doctrine, we apprehend, according to the Scriptures; and the idea of entire rest on the Christian's part, or a complete cessation of hostilities on the part of Satan, the world, and corrupt nature, derives no proof either from Scripture or experience.

But it would appear from the promise made to the Apostle Paul, that some conscious weakness or inability for the performance of his great and important duties, was that which depressed him, or caused him anxiety. If he surveyed the power of spiritual enemies, and the hostility of earthly authorities, with the inveterate prejudices and corrupt usages which prevailed among the mass of mankind, he might naturally desire to have arrayed on the side of the

Christian cause, more apparent sanction from Heaven, and a more visible demonstration of strength to support its interests. Whether a tendency to distrust, to unbelief, and secret misgivings as to the truth and final issue of this cause, constituted "the thorn" which galled him; or whether it was a temptation to some corporeal sin, to which he alluded, we cannot tell. But all these, in the experience of eminently good men, have been, in every age, as "messengers of Satan" sent to buffet them: and God has been pleased to cause the facts to be recorded in Holy Scripture for the consolation of those who may, in different ages, be similarly tried.

I remark, secondly, that as St. Paul desired and prayed for a complete deliverance from that infirmity, temptation, or trial which harassed him; so do most Christians, in similar circumstances, desire to be completely delivered from temptation: it is a common wish, but it does not seem to be a suitable or proper one; and when granted, it seldom proves a season of soul prosperity. Man's weak mind is soon elated. The love of ease to an undue degree is inherent in depraved nature. The desire to attain a supposed sufficiency in self is ever at work in the human mind. In the carnal mind it refers to worldly possessions; and in the spiritual mind, it refers to spiritual gifts. Hence most men, instead of a suitable and daily reliance upon Divine Providence, labour and toil to be rich; and are discontented, and thankless, and fretful, if they succeed not in obtaining what they call an independence; and spiritually minded men are importunate to be delivered from temptations and trials, instead of pleading for divine help to resist them, and looking continually to the power of Christ to sustain their souls and give them the victory.

Men who, like St. Paul, are called to difficult duties, are prone to look too much to self, and to desire to be made independent of heaven. Thus, Moses and Jeremiah objected to undertake the duties assigned them, till each received from the Great Lord a severe rebuke. If God bid thee go and speak to thy fellow creatures, and to deliver to them a message from him, why object to do so from thy want of eloquence: for who made man's mouth? Look to the Almighty for help, and go thou to perform his bidding. It is not a good spirit that induces a child, or a servant, to refuse to do what a father, or a master requires, on the plea of inability, and the want of sufficient means. It implies a direct charge of a defect of knowledge or wisdom in the person who gives the command; and also a distrust of being sufficiently attended to and supported. And it indicates a lack of cheerful, willing devotedness in the person who receives the command. How opposite was the impulse of Isaiah's good feeling, when he heard the question put by the *Triune Jehovah*, "Who will go for *us*?" How prompt was his answer, although but a minute ago lamenting his unworthiness! Being blessed by a seraphic touch, communicating a purifying and ardent zeal to his lips, as if inflamed by a living burning coal from off God's altar, he instantly cried out, "Here am I; send me."

Oh, my brethren this ready mind, this willing cheerful devotedness, is what we should possess in all the duties God calls us to, whether in private or in public; whether in the Ministry at home or the Ministry abroad. We should possess a cheerful alacrity to serve, and a God-honouring confidence in His goodness and faithfulness and power.

For I remark, in the *third* place, The Lord would have his people cherish a daily and an hourly dependance on himself. It is safest and best for them. Man in his original condition, when innocent, and stronger than he is now in his guilty and fallen estate, should still, as a creature, have cherished a spirit of humble and constant dependence on his Creator. Or if we consider that man was then entrusted with more than he is now; and that from the temptation of a proud desire to be independent he failed to secure and preserve the innocence he possessed; we see the reason why the restored spirit of man must be *united* to Jesus; and that it is in Him only the strength of every believer resides. He is the HEAD of that body, which is spiritually called the *Church*;

the *members* of which are known certainly only to himself. He is the *vine*, and believers are the *branches*.

But can a hand live when severed from the body; or can it move and act without influence from the head? Can a branch grow and bear fruit when cut off from the vine? Is the dependence only annual, or is it not daily, and hourly, and momentary? Still simple and obvious as this truth is, there is perhaps no truth which, judging by the practice of God's people in every age, they have sooner disregarded and seemingly forgotten. In the season of weakness and in the hour of adversity, they cleave to the Lord; but in the day of supposed strength, and in the time of prosperity, they forget him. They become, as the Bible represents them, like high-fed animals, turbulent, and vicious. "Jeshurun waxed fat and kicked."

I dare say, in the history of your own lives, there are not a few here present, who can remember seasons in which they have been (like St. Paul, but with much less reason) exalted above measure; and who subsequently would acknowledge that it was good for them that they were afflicted and humbled—it was good for them that they were reminded of their own weakness, and were made to cease from man; to relinquish dependence on princes, or the son of man, in whom there is no stay. Ah, how many have there been, who have really felt, as a celebrated cardinal expressed himself, "Had I served my God as faithfully as I have served my king, he would not have forsaken me in my old age." In his temporal prosperity, he forgot his God, and in his adversity he repented; and it may be returned with acceptance—God alone knows.

But the fact serves the purpose of our main argument, that it is good to be afflicted, and be made to know our frailty and weakness.

And hence we observe, in the *fourth* place, Divine Wisdom sees fit in mercy, to allow of temptations, trials, and persecutions, or infirmities; sinless infirmities, if you please; and also temptations to sin, in thought, word, and deed. The type of the Christian life, contained in the events of God's chosen people, the posterity of Jacob, commonly called the children of Israel, represents very fully the character of real Christians, and the manner of God's dealing with them. They are not, from a state of bondage, darkness, and sorrow, *at once* transplanted into a paradise of rest and enjoyment; but are brought through a dreary wilderness, and to a land good in itself, but, for the possession of every foot of which they are compelled to fight. Possession is the result of danger and conflict, and the death of some. We must, my brethren, through much tribulation enter into the kingdom. My young brother, who art entering on the Christian course and the Christian warfare, thinkest thou, all at once, to gain the ascendancy over thy evil propensities? There is not, my brother, reason, if we judge by the experience of those who have preceded thee, to expect it. The enemy of God, who is still allowed an existence in the universe, will not so readily desist from whatever may be in his power to harm thee. The influence of corrupt nature, and the effects of habit, are not so easily overcome—thy resolutions made to-day and broken to-morrow, do not so readily attain a fixed and determined character. There is no period, my brother, on this side the grave, at which a Christian can say, "My warfare is accomplished," much less at the beginning of his career. This representation is, we believe, the fact; and being by Heaven's permission, it is therefore wise and good. No doubt God could make the earth bring forth spontaneously all that is necessary for man, without his effort or labour. But it was not done even in Paradise. No doubt Heaven could perfect the Christian life, and complete the Christian character at once; but it is not done. We therefore infer, that industry and effort are better, both for the natural and spiritual man, than ease and indulgence: and hence also God is pleased to permit infirmities, temptations, trials, and persecutions, during the whole of a Christian's sojourn on earth.

Is the Christian then abandoned and unsupported? left single-handed to withstand the assaults of the devil, the world, and the flesh? O, no! There is a voice from heaven, speaking audibly to his anxious spirit, and that voice comes from the *Lord Christ*, saying,

"*Sufficient* for thee is MY *grace*; for MY *power* is in (thy) weakness *perfected*."

This supplies a *fifth* topic, to which I respectfully solicit your attention. And we must here stop for a moment to attend to the Person speaking. At the commencement of our discourse, we adverted to the fact, that the *Lord Christ*, who gave the promise, *was the Person* to whom the *Apostle prayed*. To remove the "*infirmity*," or weakness, or temptation, which St. Paul spoke of metaphorically, as a *thorn in the flesh*, he thrice, in solemn prayer, *besought the Lord*. But the *Being* who is prayed to, must, according to the Christian Scripture, be the true God. Angels, who are of a higher nature than human creatures, in Holy Scripture, refuse to be worshipped; and they direct mistaken mortals, that worship must not be offered to them, but to God. Our text is one of many passages contained in Holy Writ, from which light incidentally falls upon the *great and fundamentally important question of our Lord's real character*. That is, his two-fold character—very God, and very man. St. Paul speaks of the *Man* Christ Jesus, and St. Paul prays to the *Lord* Christ. Did St. Paul then worship a mere man? or a superhuman being? or, did he worship God? Admitting that Christianity is true, and that St. Paul understood and practised it; if he worshipped either *man* or *angel*, we see no difference in this respect, between Christianity and the hero or demon worship of China, or of any other part of the world; and their worship also, on this supposition, must be proper. But if, when he worshipped the "Lord Christ," the *object* of his worship was not similar to objects of worship in the pagan world, but was God; then the Lord Christ *is* God. This, my brethren, as you well know, is the *fact* of Divine Revelation: of the *nature* or *mode* of God's existence, and *how* the divine and human natures are united, we know nothing. But, as is perfectly *reasonable*, we human creatures, (even if our nature were of a higher order than it is, and possessed all the intelligence of innocence and perfection) must believe implicitly the testimony of our *Creator* concerning himself. From Revelation we know that *Jesus* is *Emmanuel*, which being interpreted from the Hebrew into the English tongue, means, "God with us." The Saviour is styled, "God manifest in the flesh," or in human nature. It is written, that, "Christ Jesus, being in the form of God, was made in the likeness of men." The evident scope and import of the Bible is, that *Jesus Christ*, the Saviour of the world, is *God-man*: that in the Person of Christ, we behold *Deity-incarnate*. And, according to the Scriptures, it is equally evident that the Person of Christ, with the Father and the Holy Spirit, constitute *One Jehovah*. For most clearly do the Sacred Writings declare the doctrine, that the Father is God, the Son is God, and the Holy Ghost is God; yet there are not three Gods, but ONE *only; and He is the living and true God*. The Jehovah, or God of the Bible, is ONE—Father, Son, and Holy Spirit, and whichever term be used, the import still is, that this *Three-one* Jehovah is the only true and proper object of worship. In the practice of mankind, there is nothing more usual than to speak of the same person under different relations, and our Saviour, the Lord Christ, is, throughout the New Testament, also spoken of in this variety of manner. In the language of our text he is evidently spoken of in relation to his divine nature; for, most apparent is it, that the *grace* or *favour* promised to St. Paul, is not the grace or favour either of *man* or of *angel*, or super-angelic being, but the grace or favour of the Divinity. Alas, what consolation could it afford to be told by a human being, "*My* grace is sufficient for thee; for *my* strength is made perfect in weakness." If Jesus were a mere man, as some in our day assert, (and we fear *blasphemously*,) why should not the Apostle Paul as well trust in himself, as trust in the Prophet Jesus; and glory in his own Apostolic power, as glory in the power of Christ? According to the heterodox opinions of Arius and of Socinus, O what a meagre, miserable, system is Christianity! and how discordant the various precepts and declarations of the Bible. In places unnumbered, we have idolatry denounced, and curses heaped on the head of him who shall trust in an arm of flesh; whilst, in the passage before us, we have St. Paul, the chief of the Apostles, (supposing Socinianism true,) praying to a creature—a mere human being.

But according to the orthodox creed—the twofold nature of Christ, and the Trinity-in-Unity—Holy Scripture is all plain, perspicuous, and consistent. The consolations that are in Christ are *divine* consolations, the promise of *his favour*, and the presence of *his power*, secure to the Christian in the time of his infirmity or weakness, the gracious regards of *infinite benevolence*, and the unwearied support of an *Almighty arm*. Here we see sense, and significance, and propriety, and wisdom, in St. Paul's determination to glory in the power of Christ resting on him; but, on the other supposition, neither common sense nor common propriety are at all discernible. Glorying in a deceased fellow-creature's power resting upon him! How utterly incredible! If this be well, they also do well who remove their confidence from God, and trust in living fellow mortals, or glory in their own wisdom, power, or skill. But "thus saith the Lord, (he whose name is Jehovah,) Let not the wise man glory in his wisdom, neither let the mighty glory in his might; let not the rich man glory in his riches; but let him that glorieth, glory in this, that he understandeth and knoweth me—that I am the Lord, which exercise loving-kindness, judgment, and righteousness in the earth: for in these things I delight, saith the Lord." Well, but, Jesus Christ promises to exercise "loving-kindness, judgement, and righteousness, in the earth," therefore the *Lord Christ* is the true *Jehovah*.

One disposed to cavil may object, "I have misrepresented St. Paul: he says, he will "glory in his infirmities;" but does *not* say, he will "glory in the power of Christ." In answer to this, I reply, True, St. Paul says he will "glory in his infirmities," but it is not in the infirmities themselves that he gloried, for he anxiously desired to have them removed. He gloried in their proving an *occasion* for *Christ's power* to rest upon him; and, therefore, manifestly it was *that power* which was the object of his glorying. He was no longer mortified and distressed about those things which proved the means of so glorious a result.

Having good reason then to conclude that the promise of the Lord Christ is the promise of the true and proper object of worship, that is, of One possessing all the attributes and perfections of Diety—self-existence, eternity, omnipresence, omniscience, omnipotence, incomprehensibleness; also wisdom, goodness, justice, mercy, holiness, and truth, all in an infinite degree; we may see clearly the value of his promises. Oh how rich the consolation to be derived from—oh how rational the confidence to be reposed in, a promise of Jehovah-Jesus! whose deep and intense interest in the happiness of man has been so wonderfully displayed. For he took not on him the nature of angels, but of the children of Abraham—the nature of man. For man's sake he condescended to be born into our world, to sustain the form of a servant; to bear poverty, insult, agony, and death, even the death of the cross—the slow and ignominous death of the accursed tree!

But it may be objected, the promise I refer to was made to Paul, not to us. An answer to this brings us to a *sixth* topic of discourse.

It is true, that there are, in Holy Scripture, specific promises on some subjects, made to particular individuals; and we believe it is equally true, that there are very many precious promises made, not to particular individuals, but to all who sustain a given character; as for example, to those who fear God, who trust in him, who believe in Jesus, who are humble, and pure, and peaceable; and, further, some of those promises made to individuals, may safely be applied to all, who resemble the characters of the individuals to whom the promise was originally made.

The case before us, we apprehended, comes under this class; all who, like St. Paul, are conscious of their infirmities, lament them, and pray to God either for deliverance or help—either for a removal of the temptation, or a way to be opened to escape from it—may consider the Saviour's promise as justly applicable to themselves. For seeing that no polluted, guilty, helpless, miserable, perishing creature of the human race, that comes to Jesus craving eternal salvation, shall in any wise be rejected: it is not supposable that any feeble, tempted, harassed disciple, who relinquishes self-confidence, and trusts in him, shall not receive mercy to pardon, and grace to help. For his "grace is sufficient" for the necessities of countless millions of souls; and his strength is exhibited as perfect and complete, in supporting and assisting every faithful servant, however weak.

We see, then, what is our duty. It is, not to be anxious and solicitous to possess high talents, eminent gifts, great resources, splendid establishments; for these of themselves will be unavailing; but it ought to be our anxiety and our solicitude, that the "power of Christ" may *rest* upon our souls, our Churches, our Ministers and our Missionaries,—our home Pastors and our Apostolic Evangelists. (I speak of their *office*, not of their *persons; the office is Apostolic*, whatever the character of some who fill it may be.)

However, this is rather beside my main object—it is not any office, nor any person, that can produce the effect desired; it is the Saviour's "power" *resting* (as our English translators have it) on the agents of the work. There is great emphasis on the word *rest*. It is not a casual visit, not a momentary stay. It is (as some would render it) an "entering in, and taking possessing of the soul;" a "taking entire possession of, and *dwelling* in." For the word has an allusion to a tent in which a person *dwells*, or which *overshadows* and *protects* him. And this last idea is that adopted in the Syriac, Italian, and English translations; all expressing a wish that the Divine power of the Lord Christ should "*overshadow*," "rest upon," be permanently *placed over*, and *protect* or defend him who is weak, and conscious of his own infirmities.

Now, then, if they would follow the example of Paul, how should disciples regard their infirmities? With repining and discontent? With envious feelings towards more highly gifted persons? No! But with humility, and submission, and thankfulness, and even with a hyperbolical or ultra feeling of satisfaction, or of glorying; knowing that the Saviour's power is most likely to be present with the *weakest* of his servants—the *lambs* of his flock; and the strength derived from his *overshadowing power*, is a better defence, a more efficient auxiliary, than the inherent strength of the strongest. "If I must needs glory, (says St. Paul,) I will glory of the things which concern my *infirmities*." And the word *infirmity* is of very extensive application; it denotes *weakness*, *sickness*, bodily frailty, poverty, or indigence; a being *destitute of authority*, *dignity*, or *power*—a condition in man's eyes *contemptible*; and also *sufferings*, or afflictions, and persecutions. But had he not explained himself, as in the words of our text, how inexplicable would his assertions have remained; as it is, he is perfectly intelligible: and no where does he make a secret of his imperfections. "Ye know," says he to the Galatians, "how through *infirmity of the flesh*, (i. e. bodily infirmity,) I preached the gospel unto you at the first, and my temptation (or affliction) which was in my flesh (a Jewish expression for body,) ye despised not nor rejected." So far indeed from making a secret of his infirmities, or of repining and discontentedly grieving about them, he asserts, that in consequence of the Lord's gracious promise, *he took pleasure in them*. His words are these, "That the power of Christ may rest upon me, I take pleasure in infirmities, in reproaches, in necessities, in persecutions, in distresses, for *Christ's sake*; for when I am weak, then am I strong."

In this passage you perceive he gives all the latitude of meaning to the word "infirmity," which we just now noticed; "reproaches, necessities, persecutions, distresses," are all included; but it must be at the same time observed, that they were endured for "*Christ's sake*;" which leads us to this conclusion, that, although the gracious promise of the Saviour's over-shadowing power, and all-sufficient grace, is fairly extended to every humble believer, under all circumstances, there is a *special* reference to private Christians and to public servants, who suffer for *righteousness' sake*.

I take pleasure in infirmities, in reproaches, in distresses, for *Christ's sake.* How extraordinary the language! How intense the devotion to Christ's cause! How completely superior to all distrust of the Saviour's aid! The idea evidently is, the more we suffer with him, and for him, the more secure and certain are we of his constant and almighty aid. This is indeed throughout the doctrine of the Scriptures. "As thy day is, so shall thy strength be."—"For, as our sufferings on account of Christ abound, so our consolation also aboundeth by Christ."—"Blessed are they that are persecuted for righteousness' sake, for their's is the kingdom of heaven."—"Blessed are ye when men shall revile you, and persecute you, and shall say all manner of evil against you falsely, for my sake; rejoice and be exceeding glad, for great is your reward in heaven; for so persecuted they the prophets which were before you." There is, in all these passages of God's Word, the same principle pervading them; viz. that the *faithful and devoted servant,* however great his infirmity, however few his talents, however small his success; if he do but labour and suffer in his Lord's cause, he shall be recognised, supported, honoured, and rewarded. When Heaven looks on mortal efforts, it is not the high talent alone, not the lofty perfectionist, but the sincere and devoted servant, who is honoured with approbation and divine protection. Most Christians have had the proofs and exemplifications of this, in their own experience. It has not been the most highly gifted, but the most sincerely devoted, on whom the Saviour's power has most conspicuously rested. It was, we believe, a view of the case, similar to that which has now been taken, which induced St. Paul to declare, that if he must needs glory he would glory in his infirmities.

Observe, *finally,* the encouragement which is afforded by this subject to engage in the Saviour's cause. To the young disciple, whose often violated resolutions dispirit, and depress, and discourage from adventuring onward in the Christian warfare, I would suggest, that however necessary the use of means to avoid temptation, and to resis-

evil, certainly is; still it is not less necessary to look beyond and above oneself to the Divine Saviour, and place our entire confidence and only hope of success absolutely in his *power* resting on us; ye know He has said, "Without me ye can do nothing. Can the branch bear fruit of itself, except it abide in the vine? No more can ye, except ye abide in me." But, on the other hand, he also says to those who are dicouraged, on account of their weaknesses and infirmities, "My grace is sufficient for you, for my strength is made perfect in weakness." Let not then your heart fail you, nor your hands hang down in remissness and inactivity; but take courage and press onward, looking to Jesus, whose over-shadowing protection, and whose ever-present power, constitute such a stimulus and defence, as shall ensure to the feeblest Christian an ultimate and complete victory over all his enemies.

To all sincere and devoted Ministers of the Word, Home Pastors and Foreign Evangelists, this subject affords the greatest encouragement. We sometimes have seen the necessary qualifications of Ministers and Missionaries drawn in such a high style of natural and intellectual, as well as moral and religious perfection, that I am sure no modest man could ever deem himself at all fitted for the service of his Lord. But the Master himself has not thus stated the case; Paul has not so stated it. The Apostles of our Lord have not led us to suppose that they were men exempt from the passions and the infirmities, and the wants and the imperfections of other men. As if it came by their own wisdom, or power, or goodness, that they "made men whole," converted many thousands, and radicated Christianity in the world. They too had strifes and contentions among themselves and with their fellow-disciples; and whatever painters may represent on the canvass, or orators declaim from the rostrum, there is no reason to believe that the great Apostle of the Gentiles either possessed a fine person, or a powerful voice; but there is reason to believe, from his own testimony, as well as from tradition, that he had unprepossessing bodily defects, and was, according to the taste of the times, an inferior public speaker. Oh no! it was not a commanding gentlemanly* person, nor a smooth and graceful oratory, nor the absence of human imperfection in temper and conduct, that converted the nations. The vessels which bore the Gospel "*Treasure*" were not vessels of gold or silver, or precious stones, but "earthen vessels," that the excellent and soul-transforming *power* should manifestly appear to be of God, and not of man. It was the "*Lord working with them,*"—it was the divine "*power of Christ*" resting on them, which caused the primitive Evangelists always to triumph and spread the savour of Christian knowledge in every place.

The false Apostles were those who *preached themselves*, exhibited their fine persons and their fine speeches, and practised a dishonest secret craftiness, and handled the word of God deceitfully, and by specious glosses, to please man's taste, corrupted it.

But the true Apostles set up no claim to external accomplishments; St. Paul does not deny the truth of the allegation of his adversaries, that *his bodily presence was* WEAK, *and his speech contemptible.* "But (says he), though *I be rude in speech,* yet not in knowledge." "We preach not ourselves, but Christ the Lord; as of sincerity, as of God in the sight of God, speak we in Christ."

I infer, therefore, my brethren, that every one who possesses ad ue *knowledge* of Christ's Gospel, unfeigned *love* to the Saviour, a sincere *desire to glorify Jehovah,* by receiving himself, and bearing to others the glorious Gospel of God, is justified in his endeavours to do so, and to hope that the Saviour's power will rest on him, whatever or how many soever his personal infirmities may be.

In accordance with these principles, my brethren, your preacher ventured at first to undertake the work of an evangelist; on the same principles he has hitherto persevered in it, and those alone are the principles which still encourage him to go forward in the work. Pray for

* Some Patrons of Missions, in distant parts of the world, have requested to have "gentlemenly" Missionaries sent to them.

him that he may very gladly glory in infirmities, and may take pleasure in reproaches, in necessities, in persecutions, and in distresses for Christ's sake; and that the power of Christ, in all his journeyings, may overshadow him and perpetually *rest* upon him.

Finally, brethren, farewell! Glory not in the supposed "*dignity* of human nature," but "glory in Christ." "Be perfect, (i. e. complete as a Christian church,) be of good comfort, be of one mind, live in peace; and the God of love and peace shall be with you."

"Let me hear my Saviour say,
'Strength shall be equal to thy day,'
Then I rejoice in deep distress,
Leaning on all-sufficient Grace.

I glory in infirmity,
That Christ's own power may rest on me;
When I am weak, then am I strong,
Grace is my shield, and Christ my song."

HINTS

ON THE

MEANS REQUISITE TO PROMOTE CHRISTIAN KNOWLEDGE THROUGHOUT THE WORLD.

ON TEACHING ALL NATIONS.

" *Then the eleven disciples went away into a mountain, and Jesus came and spake unto them saying, ' All power is given unto me in heaven and in earth: go ye therefore and* (μαθητευσατε παντα τα εθνη) *teach, or disciple, all nations, baptizing them in the name of the Father and of the Son and of the Holy Ghost;* (διδασκοντες) teaching *them to observe all things, whatsoever I have commanded you: and lo! I am with you alway, even unto the end of the world."*—Matt. xxviii. 18—20.

TO BRITISH CHRISTIANS.

That it is the duty of the disciples of Jesus to teach the Christian religion to the whole world, is a principle that has been felt and acted on in the United Kingdom, within a few years past, more than at any former period. But that the duty is felt by the churches, to the degree which it ought, cannot yet be affirmed; nor has the *Christian* intellect of this land as yet engaged in the performance of the acknowledged duty, in a manner that is at all suitable to the disciples of that Master whose claims are admitted to be divine. The spirit of persecution, which has so much disgraced our common humanity, even under the Christian name, gave occasion to a strong feeling, in the minds of many, against all interference in matters of religious belief. The history of past ages in Christendom, affords a reason of the most convincing character against the application of physical force, or pains and penalties, in matters of religious belief; but no history furnishes aught against the use of intellectual weapons: such as a lucid exhibition of truth; or even a contest for the truth, conducted by the pen and the press. There is a conflict going on in the world between truth and error, virtue and vice, piety and irreligion, the cause of the "God of heaven," and of the "spirit of this world." It is a moral conflict—a conflict of mind,—a conflict of free agents in a rebellious world. Heaven chooses so to consider it; for were it a conflict of power, there is an arm that could crush the wicked, and not stay till mercy reasoned with them.

Jesus Christ the Son of God was manifested, that he might destroy the works of the devil. He did this by the sacrifice of himself; and by teaching those truths which arise out of that great transaction, and are contained in the Gospel; and he has made it the duty of his disciples to follow up the design, by teaching to others all those things which he taught to them. To diffuse Christian knowledge is the duty of all Christ's disciples, to the extent of their capabilities; and this must be done in the way which times and circumstances may direct, in different periods, and in different places.

In the apostolic age there existed no press; and, therefore, to convey knowledge to the multitude by printed papers or books, was not practicable; and oral teaching was of necessity the only method that could be employed; for manuscript letters, and books, could not be multiplied rapidly, and unexpensively enough to scatter them amongst the mass of mankind. And there are now regions where the people cannot read, and there, of course, the living voice alone can be the medium of conveying knowledge. The habits of various people also render different methods of conveying knowledge to the mind less or more applicable to them. In China, and the surrounding countries, where no Sabbath is observed, people will not leave their work and their secular avocations to listen to a preacher; but they will individually, or in groups, read, at their leisure, and in their own house, a tract or a book which interests them. They read it, and converse about it; or dispute or approve, or mock and ridicule it, and excite the attention of the family and of the neighbourhood, to the things stated in the book, or tract; and the leaven spreads, perhaps more widely and durably than when the same truths are communicated by the living voice, for then the sounds pass away, and their meaning is forgotten.

To a reading people the press is, to say the least, as efficient a method of conveying Christian knowledge, as the system of oral lecture; and in many parts of the world it is more easily employed. A few living teachers, aided by the press, can convey knowledge as widely as many times the number of living teachers, without it. Christian books form the ground-work of domestic native instruction, and of schools, and can be referred to again and again, and year after year, and generation after generation.

Christian books can be carried round the world, and from region to region, and find their way into kingdoms, and the houses of the opulent, and the palaces of governors, and of monarchs, where no living teacher can obtain access. Were there a due degree of attention paid, by Christian scholars and Christian patrons, to the living languages of mankind, it is perhaps practicable to prepare Christian books for Pagan lands, without the writers quitting the metropolis of the United Kingdom. And were efforts made to cultivate the several principal languages of the world, Christian teachers might be qualified for the work of Christian tuition before they quitted British shores. The complaint of Missionaries, from the celebrated Brainerd's day, down to the Birman Missionary, Mr. Judson, has been, that they were for a long period but ill qualified to teach Christianity, from not being thoroughly versed in the language, and mythology, and false theories of the heathen; and in such learning as the heathen possessed. There is not, even up to this hour, a combination of Christian intellect to assail the false theories with which the deluded votaries of idolatry and superstition are fortified. Individual zeal and solitary efforts are not to be checked nor despised, but in such a cause they should not certainly be rested in; when the *Christian* talent of this United Kingdom can with ease afford that a considerable portion should be turned exclusively into the channel of associated efforts, to transfuse the Gospel of God our Saviour into all the living languages of mankind.

To propose the study of all the living languages of mankind, appears to some persons, on the first mention of it, as altogether Utopian. But if acquisition of these languages be Utopian, the hope of "teaching all nations" the things which Jesus has commanded must also be so; unless some miraculous change shall take place; for without language it is not possible to teach.

That it is *possible* to associate so much Christian talent in this land, as to cultivate all the known languages of mankind, cannot be doubted; the question can only be whether or not the object to be gained is worth the expenditure of time and money; whether these languages, when acquired, can be applied in such a manner, as to subserve the final object. That the object, viz. the spiritual illumination of mankind, is one which all sincere disciples of Jesus will acknowledge to be worthy of the greatest possible effort; and that it can be applied with considerable effect, may be anticipated from several considerations.

(1.) Amongst the reading population of mankind, a supply of suitable Christian books can be prepared, without the risk and expense of the writers taking long voyages, and residing in climates to them insalubrious.

(2.) Missionaries may be prepared for actual service, and enter on their work as soon as they arrive in pagan countries, and so escape that tedious, and often injurious labour, which they must undergo, where, in hot climates, the helps of acquiring languages are not supplied.

(3.) Candidates for missionary labours, who cannot acquire pagan languages, will be prevented going abroad, and so the expense of their long voyages, and their useless services, be saved.

The teachers and students of the various living languages of mankind, would, in this country, form a central body of efficient co-operators, in matters spiritual and intellectual, to whom, from every quarter of the world, missionaries could send information, and from whom that information could again radiate forth in every direction.

In addition to the European resident linguists, native scholars, from pagan countries, could be added, for some of the principal languages, which would make the apparatus more complete.

The principle that it is right, and a duty to use means to convey the knowledge of divine revelation to all mankind, is adopted by the Missionary and Bible Societies; but language is indispensable to the use of means of any kind, and, therefore, if the end be not Utopian, the first and essential step in the operation cannot be so.

The question turns chiefly on the method of acquiring pagan languages; whether the agents shall be sent into pagan lands, to acquire, as individuals, the languages as they can, or whether there shall be associated efforts made at home, to facilitate the acquisition of the languages.

That association is strength and power, is acknowledged as a general truth; and why it should not be so in this case does not appear. Human efforts, by God's blessing, have carried human beings all round the world, and made mankind, as to general intercourse, nearly like one family; and were the attention of a benevolent public turned to the uniting the world by a society of universal philologists, the way would be opened for the going forth of revealed truth in every direction, and the temporal, as well as spiritual good of the human species be promoted.

Some pious people argue, that the Saviour's precept is "*Go,*" and that persons must be "*sent,*" and that "*preaching* is *the* divinely appointed method. And the Missionaries Hall and Newell have insisted on this view of the subject, and required of the churches 30,000 Missionaries.

The fondness of our revered English translators for the word *Preach*, induced them, as Dr. Campbell has shewn, to translate *six different* Greek words, in the Acts of the Apostles, by the one English word "*preach;*" and hence, there is, in the English Testament, more "preaching" than in the Greek. One man sitting in a carriage with another, and speaking about Jesus, they have called "*preaching*." The *disciples*, when scattered abroad, went every where, and *talked about* the Saviour, and the occurrences at Jerusalem; and this proceeding our translators have called *preaching*; and Greek words, that denote reasoning, arguing, and *spreading a report*, they have called *preaching*: and it is in the minds of some modern Christians, that a pulpit, and pews, and a church, or a chapel, are essential to preaching.

Now, that *such preaching* is not at all essential to Christianity, nay, is in fact no part of it, but is a *circumstance* that arose from the previous habits of the people of the Roman empire, is probably the truth. It is my opinion, that conveying the proclamation of Divine mercy to the human mind, by any means, whether by schools, colleges, the press, or the pulpit, is, virtually "*proclaiming*" the *Gospel*, and obeying the Divine Precept. A pertinacious adherence to a single word, instead of gathering the spirit and sense of a proposition from all the words employed on a given subject, never leads to a true understanding of it. And were St. Matthew's phraseology adhered to, which might be plausibly done, since he has given the fullest statement of our Lord's last precept, it would go to exclude preaching; for St. Matthew has used only the words, "To *disciple* and to *teach*." There is no *preaching* mentioned by St. Matthew.

Messrs. Hall and Newell argue, that "there is no instance on record, of a nation being evangelized by the Bible, without the preaching of the Gospel." To this it is only necessary to ask, "Where was the experiment ever made?" It was never made, and never will. The Bible has been the instrument of converting many individuals, and they have talked about the Saviour, and so preached the Gospel. How was Moses *preached* every Sabbath-day? the answer is, *by being read** in the synagogue.

* "In following the course and order of yeeres, wee find the yeere of our Lord 1450 to be famous and memorable, for the *divine and mira-*

The truth is, that in all the nations which have been evangelized, all the various means of domestic instruction, the perusal of writings or books, the public discourse or oral lecture, the charity school and the college, have all contributed to scatter the seed of the word in the human heart, and produce the harvest which is witnessed. We also want to "*send*" forth some living agents; and would have a portion of the most eminently qualified men the churches possess to "*go*," and when they can, we desire that they should "*preach*:" but, to preach, not to say *eloquently*, but even *intelligibly*, in some pagan languages, is more than many pious men are qualified to do. If the conduct of the Apostles be referred to, and it be said that they did not employ the press, it will prove nothing; since, as we before observed, they had no press to employ. But as they exhorted the people, who had Bibles, to read their *MS. Scriptures*, and wrote letters, which were to be read, they recognised the principle, that letters, and the art of reading, are to be employed in the diffusion of Christianity. And if it be right to use these means at all, it will be right to employ them as extensively as possible. But those who desire to see the press, that mighty instru-

culous invention of printing."—"Without all doubt God himselfe was the ordainer and disposer of printing, no otherwise than he was of the gift of tongues, and that for a similar purpose. And well may this gift of printing be resembled to the gift of tongues."—"Hereby tongues are knowne, knowledge groweth, judgement encreaseth, bookes are dispersed, the Scripture is seen, the doctours be read, stories be opened, times compared, truth discerned, falsehood detected, as with finger pointed, and all through the benefit of printing. Wherefore I suppose, that either the Pope must abolish printing, or else, doubtlesse, printing will abolish him. Instead of John Huss and other, *God hath opened the press to* PREACH, whose voice the Pope is never able to stop with all the puissance of his triple crowne. By this printing, as by the gift of tongues, and as by the singular organe of the Holy Ghost, the doctrine of the Gospell soundeth to all nations and countries under heaven: and what God revealeth to one man, is dispersed to many; and what is known to one man is open to all. What the Pope hath lost since *printing and the press began to* PREACH, let him cast his counters. First, when Erasmus wrote, and Frobenius printed, what a blow thereby was given to all friers and monkes in the world!" &c.—(*Fox's Acts and Monuments.*)

ment of scattering opinions over the world, more employed by Christians, never mean that it should tie people's tongues, and that Christians should not speak about the good news to others, and preach either to individuals, like Philip to the Eunuch, or to families, from house to house, or to assembled thousands, whenever they can collect them, and are able to discourse to them.

Since the time of the invention of printing, in China and Europe, it has been employed chiefly for the dissemination of pagan notions and false philosophy; and how efficiently does it support these. The god of this world; the diabolical usurper, who opposeth himself to the rightful dominion of the Almighty, sustains his cause in various regions, by the use of the press, without any other preachers than "profane talkers." Now is it supposable that heaven has limited the servants of truth to oral lecture; and discountenanced what has become, in the progress of the world, the most efficient method of conveying right opinions to the understandings of the whole reading portion of mankind. Alas! that the children of this world should be so much wiser, and so much more ready to avail themselves of the growing facilities to disseminate wrong opinions, than the children of light do to propagate right ones.

If it be admitted that the press should be more employed for the dissemination of Christian opinions amongst the reading portion of mankind, it will appear evident that the cultivation of the living languages of mankind, in this country, could be made available to the diffusion of Christian knowledge, without it being necessary that all the students should go abroad; and, by consequence, the utility of a Society for the introduction of all the living languages of mankind will appear.

Could Missionaries be in this country qualified for their work, previously to going abroad; could they be permitted to go abroad to some regions for a limited time, and to return if they chose; and could they, on their return, be still useful in the same department of Christian labour, viz. communicating Christian truth to certain regions of the world; a new aspect would be given to Missionary operations, which would greatly increase the number of agents, and open a door for a class of labourers at present excluded. Were the home department of co-operation originated and supported with vigour, Missionaries, whose want of health compelled them to return, could be still usefully employed in reference to the same object which they pursued abroad. Native converts from foreign countries, who should visit England, would be received in this country by those who were fully competent to hold intercourse with them, and instruct them in whatever they might require, without loss of time.

It is within the capability of a few Christians to make an experiment of the practicability of this mode of proceeding at home, by attending to some of the principal languages of Asia, the Chinese, Sanscrit, Malayan, &c. Should the plan succeed, it may be gradually extended, till it embraces the whole world. It would, however, be a more satisfactory trial, if the several churches or *Missionary Societies* would unite their efforts in making the experiment on a large scale. And as the peculiarities of theological sentiment are not to be introduced, but only that instruction in language and modern pagan opinions, which are necessary to all Missionaries, to enable them to publish divine truth, and to refute error, there does not seem any reason why all Societies, which desire the diffusion of Christian knowledge, should not co-operate.

The utility of those persons, who have civil duties in India to perform, first studying the language in this country, has been proved at the Honourable Company's Home College, where young men are initiated by European Professors in the languages of the East, previously to their going abroad. Professor Lee's example and opinion, also, are both in favour of the practicability of the projected measure.

It may be objected to the whole of what is here proposed, that it is an endeavour to introduce a new æra of Missions made easy, and to dispense with the primitive spirit of devotedness and personal sacrifice which should distinguish the servants of Christ. In answer to which, a distinction between those difficulties which are inherent in the work, and those which are of man's making will be sufficient. For example, that a Missionary should, on going to a pagan region, abandon his native country for life, has long been the prevailing opinion; but neither apostolic example, nor the precepts of the New Testament, require any such thing. For man to make the service more difficult than Heaven and its own nature have made it, savours of the same superstitious spirit as the self-imposed austerities of pagan devotees. To remove the impositions of the man of sin—celibacy, vows of poverty, and so forth, might have been called, in Luther's days, a making of Christianity easy; but all judicious Christians now agree, that it was only removing a human yoke, by which removal Christianity was greatly benefited: so also, as to the case in hand; if Christian Missions can be freed from an implied vow of poverty and perpetual exile, and similar difficulties of man's imposing, although doing so may be stigmatized as a worldly policy, to remove the cross, it will be, in truth, only removing the impositions of a self-righteous will-worship. A worldly, money-making, covetous spirit, is utterly unchristian, whether found in Messengers of the Churches, or Pastors, or People. A dependence on abstract education, learning, and means, instead of a dependance on the simple unadorned Gospel of our Saviour, and the energies of the Divine Spirit, is not the thing that we advocate. But we do advocate the diligent employment of proper means to convey Christian knowledge to men's minds all round the world; and the removal of every impediment that Holy Scripture will allow to many persons engaging in this work.

The world is, under God, one vast empire; or, as the Chinese Sages say, it is but "one family;" and whether a Christian teacher be employed in one province of this empire, or in reference to this, or to another department of the great family, cannot make such a mighty difference in the rules applicable to these teachers, and the means to fit them for their work, and which they should employ, as some persons would suppose.

In the early history of the Church, the writings and apologies of the Christian Fathers were of great efficacy; and at the Reformation, the press was productive of the greatest good. Also in the present day its effect is of the utmost service to the Christian cause. If we would have it operate on mankind, the study of all the living languages on earth must be more encouraged. Archbishop Tillotson thought that a miraculous gift of tongues was necessary for the universal propagation of the Gospel, and being necessary, would be granted; (Vol. x. p. 4454 and 4527.) but till human industry has done its utmost, it is not fair to assert the necessity of miraculous aid. Would not a Society in London to encourage the study of all living languages, for the purpose of communicating Christian knowledge to all nations, be a means very likely to further greatly the universal dissemination of Christian truth? Would it not be a most important means of preparing the Messengers of the Churches to fulfil the Saviour's last command to his disciples, " Go and teach all nations?"

With a view to the formation of such a Society,* these thoughts are respectfully submitted to the public who take an interest in the propagation of the Gospel.

* The "*Language Institution*, in Aid of the Propagation of Christianity," established in Bartlett's Buildings, carries into effect a part of these suggestions. It still requires, as an integral part of the Institution, a Literary Committee, to call periodical meetings of pious Literati, versed in ancient and in modern languages, for the purpose of extending information, and exciting interest about the less cultivated languages of mankind.

PROPOSAL

FOR

BETTERING THE MORALS AND CONDITION OF SAILORS IN CHINA.

As the spiritual condition of seamen in China, referred to in the following Paper, yet remains unattended to by the zealous Christians of England and America, the document is here inserted, to keep alive the subject, in the hope that by the blessing of Divine Providence, something may eventually be done in that distant land for the Sailor's welfare.

TO THE PUBLIC.

Canton, December 1, 1822.

The General Plan given in the following Proposal being approved of by some individuals to whom the manuscript has been shown, it is now printed, to make the subject more extensively known, that its merits or demerits, practicability, or impracticability, may be conversed about, and more distinctly ascertained. Dr. Morrison will be happy to receive the written opinions, or suggestions of any Gentleman who is resident in, or who frequents China, on either or both of the subjects proposed, for the benefit of any Committee, who may hereafter meet to deliberate and report thereon.

PROPOSAL.

Canton, China, September 25th, 1822.

At Whampoa, the anchorage of European ships which frequent China, there are annually from fifteen to twenty large Indiamen, and between twenty and forty smaller vessels from the United States. The crews of those ships make collectively from two to three thousand men, all of whom speak the English language; and therefore, under the operation of liberal and Christian sentiments, any benevolent efforts for the good of these men, whilst in China, may include both nations.

The assistance that Sailors in China require, is medical attendance for many of them; and for all of them instruction concerning their duties as moral and religious beings. Medical assistance is provided for all the Indiamen, and for some of the American ships, and therefore it only remains to be enquired whether the mode of communicating that assistance may not be improved, so as to make the condition of the sick and healthy men better; and the fatigue of the medical attendants less: that is, whether a FLOATING HOSPITAL, to which the sick men may be removed from their own ships, away from the noise and bustle occasioned by unloading, and other duties daily going on; and what is perhaps of the first importance, in some complaints, (arising as it is supposed from the local circumstances of a particular ship) removing the Hospital to a more healthy part of the river. In case of infectious diseases also, the Floating Hospital would remove the sick men from those still in health.

Moreover, ships do arrive frequently, (i. e. English India ships as well as Americans) and occasionally the vessels of other nations, without any medical person on board, and sometimes without any such person at Whampoa: in those cases the FLOATING HOSPITAL, always having a medical man belonging to it, would afford such relief as every humane mind would be happy to avail itself of; and humanly speaking, many lives might be saved. And when death did occur, the rites of sepulture could perhaps be more decently attended to by those persons belonging to the FLOATING HOSPITAL than is practicable amidst the hurry of a ship's duty.

However, much is done for the seamen's health, and his bodily comfort; and but little, or nothing for the improvement of his mind. In some ships, it is true prayers are read, which is so far well; but prayers are not for the instruction of the ignorant; but are the language of a person already instructed, addressed to the Deity; and hence it happens that hearing prayers, but seldom reforms individuals. Without, however, discussing this question, the fact is, that the thousands of seamen, who in the course of a year stay a shorter or longer time at Whampoa, and many of whom die there (Note 1st), neither have prayers nor any kind of religious instruction: and hence the Sunday only gives them leisure to get intoxicated and quarrel with the Chinese. A Floating Chapel (Note 2), with sermons twice a day, would furnish the means of rational occupation, and of religious and moral instruction to as many of the seamen as chose to avail themselves of it; many of whom would no doubt gladly do so, if a pious zealous Preacher addressed them. The benefits arising from such an Institution would not only apply to the individual sailors whose minds were improved; but from the more moral and orderly behaviour of the sailors, which would in all probability follow, the interests of all who trade in China would be subserved, and the respectability of foreigners, in the eyes of the Chinese, would be promoted.

The Floating Hospital, and the Floating Chapel, being perfectly unconnected with the natives, and the sailors not having to go on shore when frequenting either, no opposition can be anticipated from the Chinese Government, nor any interruption to Divine Service, from the curiosity, or insolence of the populace.

The only objection to the Plan appears to be the probable expense of the vessels employed; and of the persons who shall perform the necessary duties.

At London on the Thames (Note 3), at Liverpool, and at Leith, and other places, the Floating Chapel has been adopted, and been found to meet the wishes of sailors, and to be useful to them. At London a Floating Hospital has been commenced, and met with the approbation of His Majesty's Government, and many persons of distinction in the country.

The expense for the Hospital would arise chiefly from

the vessel employed; for it may be hoped that the medical gentleman belonging to the fleet would arrange a plan by which they could attend the Hospital by turns, and so have indeed more leisure than when attending each his own ship. The expenditure of medicines would not be more in one case than the other: and those ships which were unsupplied with a surgeon, could not object to pay a sum of money, as they now do, for the visits of the Surgeons of other ships.

The Chapel would of course be an entirely new source of expense, as no means have heretofore been used by the English or Americans, for the moral and religious instruction of their seamen in China. Some of the continental nations, who formerly frequented China, had schoolmasters and chaplains on board.

Whether Chinese chop-boats could be fitted up to answer the purposes intended, and other details of the subject, could be ascertained by a Committee of Gentlemen; well affected to the general objects.

The Honourable Company's Chapel in Canton is not of use to the sailors, for they are not allowed to visit Canton, excepting as boat's crews;* and the few that happen to be in Canton on Sundays, never attend the Chapel; probably under an idea that it is not intended for them but for gentlemen. If they were disposed to go, it could not contain many.†

P.S. December 1st.—On the 2d of November, the room fitted up as a Chapel at Canton was burnt down.

* The sailors, in former times, had perfect liberty to go to Canton in large numbers; but they so frequently disgraced themselves and their country, by drunkenness, and became so often involved in serious affrays and homicides, it was found necessary to confine them much to the ships.

† On Sunday, the 10th of November, 1822, a *Bethel* flag, prepared by Mr. Oliphant, a pious American Gentleman of the Presbyterian Church at New York, was hoisted at Whampoa, at the mast-head of the ship *Pacific*, of *Philadelphia*, belonging to Mr. Ralston, a veteran foreign Director of the London Missionary Society; and a sermon was preached on deck to an attentive congregation, from a passage in the Prophet Ezekiel, "They caused my name to be blasphemed among the heathen," &c.

NOTE.—I. Captain W. of the Honourable Company's Service, thinks the average number of deaths at Whampoa, amongst the English Sailors, annually is one hundred; others think the average between one and two hundred. In the season 1820-21, a single Company's ship lost THIRTY men.

II. Instead of a vessel fitted up on purpose for a Chapel, the deck of any ship in the harbour, may at first be borrowed on a Sunday morning, and if there were service twice a day, the deck of another ship, in a different part of the river be employed in the afternoon. It is presumed that there would always be found Commanders who would be perfectly willing to subject themselves to the slight inconvenience which this arrangement would occasion, for the sake of at least making a fair trial to improve the morals of the seamen.

III. "The Port of London Society for promoting Religion among Seamen," was instituted in 1818. The East India Company subscribed to it £100. Prince Leopold attended the Second Anniversary, in May 1820.

(Highmore's View of Charitable Institutions.)

B B 2

TRACT,

ADDRESSED TO SAILORS.

China, September 22, 1822.

British Sailors! Men born in Christian lands!—In consequence of your being now far off from your native islands, and from your kindred, and sojourning for awhile on the borders of a proud pagan nation, I address you as a fellow-countryman and as a friend. I desire to appeal to your understandings and to your good feelings. I desire to promote your personal respectability, the honour of our country, and your happiness, both in this life, and in that eternal state of existence, which God our Saviour has assured us will come after the death of the body. Your circumstances as to your kindred at home are no doubt very various; some of you have fathers and mothers yet alive, who are anxious about their sons, exposed as they deem to the perils of the ocean; scorched by the hot rays of a vertical sun; and in danger of being seduced by bad company to impiety, to drunkenness, or to debauchery; other men and lads are fatherless or motherless, and alas! friendless: others again, it may be, are the only support of an aged mother, of a sister, or of a wife and family. I address you as a man who knows the feelings of a son, of a father, of a husband, and of a friend; and I hope on the perusal of this paper you will cherish all the kindest recollections of your homes and your kindred; that serious reflections may gain the readier access to your understandings and your hearts.

Sailors! you know that, in reference to fighting his country's foes, the gallant Nelson said, "England expects every man to do his duty." This was nobly said in the day of battle, and it is not less true in the *time of peace*; England expects, and I will add, Heaven expects, every man to do his duty. Now every man has certain duties to perform to *himself*, to his *kindred* and *country*, to *mankind* generally, and to his *God* and *Saviour*. And what is man? Man is a creature composed of a body and of a soul: in his body (the flesh, and blood, and bones,) man resembles the beasts; but in his soul, a spiritual thinking substance, he resembles the angels; when the body dies, the soul dies not, but passes to an invisible eternal state. Man is a creature accountable for his thoughts, his words, and his actions to Almighty God, the Maker and Preserver of the Universe, which is composed of the sun, the moon, and the stars; the earth, and all that are on it; the ocean, and all the creatures that are in it. Every man therefore should remember daily that he is not allowed to do as he pleases; but he must do what reason, and conscience, and God's declared will require him to do. When God Almighty made the first man, he taught him to know his will perfectly; and all nations, the Chinese and other heathen nations, have retained to this day some part of this knowledge; and any man may, from studying God's works and God's providence, infer, to a considerable extent, the will of God; but God's will is most fully made known in the books written by Moses and the Jewish Prophets; and by the Apostles and other Disciples of Jesus Christ our Saviour; for those men, out of mercy to all mankind, were taught by God Almighty, what was his will, and what he required of men, and what were his plans of mercy towards men. Now then, Reason, and Conscience, and the Bible must be your guides, and you ought to think and read; and also take the advice of well-intentioned men, who may have had more time to think and to read than you have had. It is on this supposition, that I, although not born with a silver spoon in my mouth, may have had more time and more favourable opportunities than some of you, that I take upon me to volunteer my advice.

Your duty to yourselves requires you to take due care

both of your body and of your soul. You must work to obtain an honest supply of food and raiment; and that, if possible, you may have an overplus to help your kindred, some of whom may be old, or sick, or helpless. If a man merely eats, and drinks, and works, and sleeps, and never thinks about his family, or of improving his own mind, or of promoting the welfare of his immortal spirit, he lives as if he were all body, and not better than the beasts: and further, if a man exerts his mind as well as labours with his hands, only to pamper his animal appetites, he makes his soul, which is the spiritual, noble, and angelic part of his nature, a slave to the brutal part, the animal body, and so, in many cases, becomes worse than a beast; or, as some old writers say, such a man is "half brute and half devil." A good man uses his reason and religion to regulate his animal appetites, because God has forbidden excess and irregularity, and because the unrestricted indulgence of appetite and lust is injurious to man's health; wastes the property which should enable him to do good to his kindred or to the sick and distressed; for excess and irregularity are generally injurious to other people, either by the withdrawment of some good, or by the infliction of some positive evil.

Those of you who have performed several voyages to China, know very well, that annually many men belonging to the fleet die at Whampoa; sometimes by the usual course of God's providence, without any direct cause induced by themselves, and in this case they are blameless; but also sometimes in consequence of diseases brought on by drunkenness and lewdness before coming to China; or by indulgence in the same vices whilst in China. Now although it is sometimes said "such a man is only his own enemy, he hurts nobody but himself;" this is not quite true. If he have parents or sisters to take care for him, and he for them, he injures them by bringing on his own death, he grieves their hearts, and perhaps brings down a parent's grey head with sorrow to the grave. Besides, the drunkard often injures others by his quarrelling and fighting: and the whoremonger either reduces a poor and much-to-be-pitied woman to the most degraded state possible in this life, and to the most hopeless for the life to come; or he assists in perpetuating that unhappy state. Let every man feel for a poor prostitute, as he would if his own mother or his sister were in that state. It is not true that drunkenness and debauchery injure only a man's self: however, if it were true, still every man, (a sailor as well as any other man,) should in duty to himself avoid making his mind the servant or slave of the merely brutal part of his person; and should employ reason and religion to regulate his appetites. All a man's duties to himself and to others, are moreover sanctioned by the approbation of God, and a violation of those duties is followed by his displeasure. Providence has attached, as an usual consequence, disease and penury to intemperance and lewdness; and the Bible says, "for these things' sake the wrath of God cometh on the children of disobedience."

In China the British Sailor too commonly misuses the leisure of the Sunday; and on liberty days abandons himself to the grossest, and most unrestrained indulgence of his beastly appetites; even when on duty at Canton, he sometimes allows himself to get drunk in Hog-lane; and in so doing, not only injures his health, but exposes his person, his country, and his religion to the scorn of the Pagan Chinese; and he, in common with every unjust, covetous, avaricious, lying, drunken, debauched European, in Pagan countries, causes God our Saviour to be blasphemed amongst the heathen; such men, whatever their station, or whatever their cloth, not only neglect their own salvation; but also hinder the salvation of others. These are awful views of the subject, and not alone applicable to sailors in China.

But to return,—British Sailors! it is allowed on all hands that you possess courage and generosity; that you can fight hard, when your commander bids; and that you will jump overboard at the risk of your own lives to save a person drowning: still war and danger are evils; you do not wish an eternal continuance of strife and of hurricanes. What is your character in peace! I will tell you; you are accused in the British Parliament, and in the English newspapers, and in the conversation of some gentlemen, of being ungrateful, turbulent, and riotous; and of getting drunk, and of quarrelling, and fighting, and sometimes of causing the death of the natives; and by such conduct, in China particularly, of occasioning an immense loss of property to your employers, by involving them, through your misconduct, in discussions with the Chinese Government, to prevent your being tortured and strangled unjustly in cases of accidental homicide. The Chinese law will not excuse a man who kills another in a fight, because the other man struck him first, or insulted him by words or looks. The English law does not allow of slight pretexts for killing a man; and the Chinese law is more strict than the English law is. If therefore you get drunk, or put yourselves in a passion, and fight and kill a native, you will not only be censured by your countrymen, but your own life may be sacrificed, should the facts be proved against you; for nobody should screen a murderer. The sailors of other countries are commended as more reasonable and better behaved than you are; and even the Chinamen are preferred before you, as an orderly sober people. Now, as a man, and a man bred up in a Christian land, every sailor in the Chinese fleet should *reflect*, and see how far these accusations are true in reference to himself; and if his conduct has heretofore given just occasion for these censures, let him resolve to alter his conduct. Let him think of his home, of his kindred, of his country, and of his Saviour, and no longer by his misconduct cause injurious reflections to be thrown on them. And let him think of his duty to himself; that he has a soul to be saved, as well as a body to be fed and clothed; and let him resolve to be true to her who is, or whom he intends (if Heaven will) to make his wife. Thus with God's help, a general reformation in the conduct and character of British Seamen who frequent China will take place, and the shameful excesses of liberty-days will be discontinued.

I might here reason with seamen on their duties to mankind generally, to Hindoos and to Chinese, to Malays or to any other people,—to act justly and kindly, and to *behave peaceably;* for all these men are (as the Lord's Prayer implies) God's creatures, nay, God's children; hence these words which begin the Prayer, and which may be used by all men, "*Our Father* which art in heaven," and so on. All nations, it is true, are not the same in character, any more than all the sons of a family are the same in temper and conduct. Some sons are dutiful, others are undutiful; some are clever fellows, others are great blockheads; still they should in a family be *all kind to each other.* These members of the human family, the *rascally* Chinamen, as they are sometimes called, are shrewd fellows; and I am sorry to say, they too often take in the honest-hearted British Sailor. They sell him bad poisonous grog or spirits, and they pretend to be friends till he is drunk, and then they rob him of his money. These fellows should be *shunned* and guarded against. All Chinese are not so bad. They have both good and bad men amongst them. But all of them, even when saucy, are not worth fighting with. A British seaman's courage is well known; he need not show it in fighting with the Chinamen, but he should try to be quite as sober, and as well behaved as the best of these people are: and he should not allow himself to be taken aback by a spirit-drinking breeze, whilst the bad Chinamen are sipping tea with a final intention of coolly robbing poor Jack's pockets. This simplicity of the Sailor is what every body blames; and those who most love and admire a True British Tar, still weep over his too frequent thoughtlessness and folly.

Wishing you, Men and Lads, health and every good, and I say it very seriously, Peace with God, by repentance and faith in the merits of our Saviour; for then you will study to "live a godly, righteous, and sober life," wherever you go.

I remain,

Your's sincerely,

AMICUS.

SAILOR'S PRAYER.

Written in the Atlantic Ocean, on board the Ship Mexico.

Guide us, O! thou great Jehovah,
Wanderers on the mighty deep;
From the storm and raging tempest
Deign our floating bark to keep;
Lord of Heaven!
Bid the breeze propitious blow.

Be our safe guard thro' the night-watch,
And our guardian all the day,
To our destin'd port in safety,
Give us fleet and gladsome way;
Strong Deliv'rer!
Be thou still our strength and shield.

And when life's short voyage is over,
In the haven of the blest,
May we, guided by thy Spirit,
Find an everlasting rest;
Father hear us!
For the great Redeemer's sake.

A

BRIEF INQUIRY

INTO

WHAT MAY REASONABLY BE EXPECTED OF

(αποστολοι εκκλησιων)

"MESSENGERS OR APOSTLES OF THE CHURCHES,"

TO UNEVANGELIZED NATIONS.*

1.—"The great principles of moral science require every individual first to *study and practice virtue himself*, and then to *communicate the knowledge and practice of virtue to others*."—(CONFUCIUS.)

2.—"Touching the preferment of the *contemplative*, or *active* life—Christianity decideth it against Aristotle." For contemplation, which should be finished in itself, without casting beams on society, assuredly (Christian) divinity knoweth it not."

"There is formed in every thing a double nature of good: the one, as every thing, is *a total in itself*; the other, as it is a part or *member of a greater body*, whereof the latter is in a degree the greater and the worthier, because it tendeth to the conservation of a more general form. Therefore we see the iron in particular sympathy moveth to the loadstone, but yet, if it exceed a certain quantity,

* The English Version renders
Αποστολος—*Apostle* and *Messenger*;
Εκκλησια—*Assembly* and *Church*;
Υπηρετης—*Minister*, *Officer* and *Servant*;
Διακονος—*Minister*; and *Deacon* and *Servant*.
This, in my opinion, is a defect, because it does not afford the English Reader an opportunity of judging for himself of the use of these and such-like epithets. Jesus himself is called "*The Apostle*" of our profession. The difference between the *Twelve Apostles*, and other *Messengers*, did not consist in, nor is it marked by, the term employed to designate them, but in the Person sending, and in the qualifications he bestowed upon them. The immediate "*Apostles of Christ*," and the "*Apostles of Churches*," either in the primitive or any subsequent age, hold very different offices in degree, although similar in kind, for both carry God's message of mercy to perishing sinners.

it forsaketh the affection to the loadstone, and, *like a good patriot*, moveth to the earth, which is the region and country of massy bodies; so may we go forward and see that water and massy bodies move to the centre of the earth; but rather than to suffer a divulsion in the continuance of nature, they will move upwards from the centre of the earth, forsaking their duty to the earth, in regard of their *duty to the world*.—But it may be truly affirmed, that there never was any philosophy, religion, or other discipline, which did so plainly and highly *exalt the good that is communicative, and depress the good which is private and particular*, as the holy (Christian) faith; well declaring, that it was the same God that gave the Christian law to men, who gave those laws of nature to inanimate creatures that we spake of before."—(BACON.)

3.—" Christianity never expects that men will, of their own accord, originate that movement by which they are to come in contact with the faith of the Gospel; and therefore, instead of waiting till they shall move towards the Gospel, it has been provided from the first that the Gospel shall move towards them.

" It is no where supposed that the demand for Christianity is spontaneously, and, in the first instance, to arise among those who are not Christians; but it is laid upon those who are Christians, to go abroad, and, if possible, to awaken out of their spiritual lethargy those who are fast asleep in that worldliness which they love, and from which, without some external application; there is no rational prospect of ever arousing them."—(CHALMERS.)

4.—" The Lord Christ, having ascended up far above all heavens, gave some Apostles, some Prophets, some Evangelists, and some Pastors and Teachers."—" God hath set in the church gifts of healing, helps, governments, diversities of tongues," &c.—(ST. PAUL.)

5.—" *Prophets* may denote such as *possessed the word of knowledge* as well as the gift of prophecy."—(BOOTHROYD.)

6.—" The office of *Apostles* is acknowledged, on all hands, long since to have terminated.

" Of *Prophets* it is only necessary to observe, that their office must terminate, of course, when inspiration terminates.

" *Evangelists* are universally acknowledged to have been *extraordinary officers*, and to have ceased in a very early period of the church.

" There remain then only *Pastors* and *Teachers*—but the same person was Pastor and Teacher.

" We are (thus) come to *one class of permanent Ecclesiastical officers*, viz. that which is known by the word *Pastors*."—(DWIGHT.)

7.—Thus it is that some men get rid of a variety of officers, *i. e.* of a *diversity* of *Labourers* and *Helpers* in the church, in order to suit their own local wants, or their modern systems, by assuming and exaggerating the " *extraordinary*" character and circumstances of the primitive church; just as some others in our day get rid of primitive *doctrines* and *duties* on the same plea."—(MORRISON.)

8.—" All our long conversation on the subject of religion ended in nothing. My friend was convinced he was right; and all the texts I produced were, according to him, *applicable only to the times of the Apostles*."—(MARTYN.)

9.—" *Evangelists*:—Under this name they are to be understood whom the Apostles used as their attendants, in performing their office; because they were not sufficient for every thing. Of this kind were Timothy, Titus, Silvanus, Apollos, whom Paul joined with himself in the inscription of the epistles, yet so as to call himself alone an Apostle: this office, therefore, was only temporary."—(BEZA.)

The opinion of this venerable Reformer, in *the last clause*, seems not well founded. The office of " Evangelists," in the primitive times, was in most respects similar to that of Missionaries in subsequent times. They were preachers of the Gospel without full apostolical authority and without any stated charge; going among the heathen to found churches, visiting the churches already planted, &c. —*When zeal for propagating the Gospel subsided, this office sunk into disuse; and thus, for ages, the heathen have been in a great measure neglected*: and it seems to have been one GRAND DEFECT at the Reformation, that no part of the funds, which had been appropriated to religious purposes, was reserved for the special object of supporting *Evangelists* to the heathen world.—The office of *Evangelist must revive along* with the spirit of evangelizing the nations."—(SCOTT.)

10.—" Those employed in preaching the Gospel to those who had not yet received it, the Scripture calls Evangelists."—(HAMMOND.)

11.—" The motives that ought to determine a man to dedicate himself to the ministering in the church, are a zeal for promoting the glory of God, for raising the honour of the Christian religion, for the making it to be better understood, and more submitted to. He that loves it, and feels the excellency of it in himself, that has a due sense of God's goodness in it to mankind, and that is entirely possessed with that, will feel a zeal within himself, for communicating that to others; that so the only true God, and Jesus Christ whom he has sent, may be more universally glorified and served by his creatures. And when to this he has added a concern for the souls of men, a tenderness for them, a zeal to rescue them from endless misery, and a desire to put them in the way to everlasting happiness; and from these motives, feels in himself a desire to dedicate his life and labours to those ends; and in order to them, studies to understand the Scriptures, and more particularly the New Testament, that from thence he may form a true notion of this holy religion, and so be an able minister of it: this man, *and this only man*, so moved and so qualified, can in truth, and with a good conscience, answer, that *he trusts he is inwardly moved by the Holy Ghost*."—(BISHOP BURNET.)

12. . . . . "Much remains
To conquer still; peace hath her victories
No less renowned than warr."
(MILTON, *May* 1682, *on a proposal for the propagation of the Gospel.)*

"Heretofore, in the first Evangelic times, (and it were happy for Christendom if it were so again,) Ministers of the Gospel were by nothing else distinguished from other Christians, but by their *spiritual knowledge and* SANCTITY *of life.*"

1. THERE are some professing Christians, of whom we have recently heard, who still argue that Christian Missions should be deferred, till the Almighty shall be pleased to grant *miraculous powers* to the men who shall be sent to heathen nations. But the communication of Christian knowledge to a fellow creature, is within the compass of man's ordinary powers; and therefore the reason for desiring miraculous gifts does not appear. The earth, by culture, accompanied by heaven's showers and sunshine, brings forth grain for the sustenance of man; and therefore no one asks for a miraculous production of the earth's fruits. The knowledge of Christian principles, like other knowledge, may be communicated by human industry; and when watered by heavenly influences from God's Holy Spirit, be made productive of holiness and virtue. We therefore deem it impious to be idle, and pretend to wait for miraculous powers.

2. Some advocates for Missions contend, that a renunciation of all assistance from regularly organized bodies of Christians, of a pecuniary nature, is essential to the character of a modern Missionary; and till such devotees can be obtained, the Churches must be contented to wait and pray, &c That men who can prosecute a Mission to teach Christianity to unenlightened nations, free of all charge to the Churches, or the Heathen, are perfectly justified in so doing, there can be no doubt. But it is denied that the Churches should inactively wait, and only pray for Providence to raise up such persons. We argue this on

the principle, that, to *neglect human means*, which God has put in our power, for the effecting of any good, and *to pray* that heaven may be pleased to effectuate that good *without means*, is impious hypocrisy and mockery. Man has no right to look for extraordinary help from Heaven, till he has "exhausted human efforts." In a devout spirit of humble dependence on God, first, *Tsin jin leih*, "exert-to-the-utmost man's strength," and then it is justifiable to cast one's-self on the Almighty arm for extraordinary aid, if God be pleased to grant it.

The rational spirit of Christian Protestantism always does this now in all cases; as for instance, in the midst of tempests and shipwrecks, instead of remaining motionless, as some do, under a belief of Mahommedan fatalism, or cursing and beating their gods or saints, as do image-worshippers, of Pagan or of Christian name, British seamen never abandon the use of means.

The principle that it is man's duty to use all just means in his power, for the promotion of spiritual as well as temporal good, before he expects or prays for extraordinary interpositions of Providence, is but now being applied to Christian Missions. There has been, since the late revival of Missionary zeal, too much looking for "*super-human*" agents; men that should not require instruction; men without human passions, and above human wants and human infirmities; and there has been too much anticipation that Providence would interfere extraordinarily or miraculously, ere ever man had put forth the strength and energy already entrusted to him.

In a spirit of devoteeism all the Christian self-tormentors, the monks of Alet, who made a merit of stinging their hands with nettles, and the flagellantes, who scourged themselves with whips, are far outdone by the self-torturing devotees of India, and other parts of the world. Austerities may excite admiration from the ignorant, and serve the purpose of self-righteous, self-deifying mortals; but they communicate no knowledge; they lead not men to God and to the Saviour; they have been in every age of the world assumed as a cloak for secret impiety and licentiousness, or have been the lamentable vagaries of weak and mistaken minds. I know I now tread on dangerous ground, and the opposite extreme has not been less ruinous to all that is estimable and good in the character of man. But I advocate not either extreme. Prosperity I know is dangerous as well as adversity, and self-indulgence is a more frequent vice than an excess of self-mortification. Still there is a medium line of moral rectitude and Christian wisdom, equally remote from each extreme, and it is for that medium I now contend.

Having put the case negatively, I will now state it positively. I think some theorists on the Missionary character, have worked it up to an utterly unattainable degree of ideal perfection. I choose a simpler and more practicable view.

3. A messenger of the Churches should then, I conceive, generally speaking, possess the same qualifications as a Minister of religion at home. Whilst the enemies of Missions ask for miraculous powers, some of the professed friends have maintained that an absence of all talent and acquirement does not disqualify a person; and that any body who has piety, will do for a Missionary, but not for a Minister. If a difference be argued for, I think the higher qualifications are required for the Missionary work.*

* I have heard it suggested among Protestant Dissenters, that their *weakest Ministers*, who can be of little service in Europe, are very proper for Missionaries." (And I have heard the same sentiment expressed by Missionary Directors, in 1825.) "Under shelter of the opinion that men of the best talents should be kept at home, we shall give too much encouragement to that self-complacency which cleaves to such men, and grant them a dismission from the service, which they will be glad to avail themselves of. But I cannot believe those Gentlemen think soberly of themselves, as they ought to do, who suppose they are too great, or too considerable to engage in Missions." (Up to the present time I have still heard it maintained, that the most highly gifted and best instructed Ministers of religion ought to be retained at home, and take the advice given to King David, "Thou art *better than ten thousand of us*; therefore now it is better that thou succour us out of the city.")

"As a man of no learning myself, I cannot but feel it a little contemptuous for me and my poor brethren, to be shoved with so much good

However, the Missionary should doubtless possess *Christian knowledge and real personal piety*. Without prescribing what his soul-experience of the "terrors of the Lord," and the "joy of believing" in Jesus should be, he ought not to be unacquainted with spiritual exercises of the heart, connected with, or antecedent or consequent to, the conversion of the soul, or its being turned from darkness to light, and from Satan to God. He must be an experienced Christian.* God usually makes the most holy men the medium of spiritual blessings to others.

He should possess some skill in languages; a rather critical knowledge of Holy Scripture, and of the evidences of revealed religion; a knowledge of the history of the

will into the hottest front of the battle, by men who are fitter for the work, but who claim that very fitness as the apology for sitting still; pleading their literature, and popular elocution, as a discharge from the war." (Melville Horne.)

"Among other calumnies which were circulated against the founders of the Missionary Society, was the ungenerous imputation, that they were ready to transport their brethren to uncongenial climates, to labour amongst savage and heathen nations, whilst they continued to enjoy the delights of home. This reproach was as untrue as it was unkind, for Dr. Bogue and others requested of the East India Company permission to go to India, and were refused. (*Cong. Mag. Feb.* 1826.)

Some have gone to be temporary Superintendents and Commissioners; but, query? Did any of the Founders or Directors ever actually *go to be Missionaries?* Have they not all "continued to enjoy the delights of home?" They *have transported others*, but *never gone themselves*. Where then is the calumny or the untruth?

* "In the qualification of a Missionary we must enquire not only into the *sincerity* of his *piety*, but also into the *power* of it. We should injure many by questioning their piety, who are not yet possessed of that vigourous and steadfast faith, that joyous hope, and that fervent love, which are absolutely necessary to support a man under all the sacrifices, dangers, hardships, and discouragements of a Missionary warfare. *The tree that is green, flourishing, and fruitful, while standing in a rich soil, and sheltered by a surrounding wood, might wither and die, or be torn up by its roots, if removed to a heath, and standing alone exposed to the tempest.*" "A tolerable strength and maturity of religion, will therefore be as needful as the sincerity of it." "His Missionary zeal should not have been lately kindled, but such as having burned for years promises to continue in its heat." (Melville Horne.)

church and of the world. He should have enlarged views of human nature, in contradistinction from strong sectarian or national prejudices. English, or American, or French, or even European prejudices should not be allowed to influence strongly his mind. He should not have a zeal for his national usages, which form no part of Christian practice. A Christian Missionary from England is not sent to India or any other part of the world to introduce English customs, but Christ's Gospel. He should not be shocked nor irritated by the innocent usages of other nations, which happen to differ from his own. A Missionary's views of Providence, and the gracious care of God extended to all parts of his world, should elevate his mind above the Swiss disease of extravagant love of country. A notion which some people possess, that there is nothing good or comfortable out of England, that all God's works, every where, are inferior and to be despised, in comparison with what he hath done for England, may be called patriotism; but it is a notion that is unjust, and of an impious tendency, and is unworthy of a Christian Missionary.

He should have enlarged views of human governments, and not be a stickler for or against any form into which circumstances may have moulded the system of national rule, or even of Ecclesiastical Government. There is no reason why he should not have his own opinions on such subjects, but he should not be a keen politician, nor a high man for his own *sect*-ion or "branch" of the universal Church, whether Greek, Latin, or Protestant."* He should have "a single eye" to the glory of God and the good of men; a simplicity of intention that appears above board. He should not be an intriguing Ecclesiastic, nor of a grovelling plebeian mind, that would flatter the rich and powerful to obtain secular interest. He must carry the principle of unlimited toleration to the ends of the earth—that *man* is *not* accountable to man, but *is* accountable to

* "You greatly prevaricate (or err) if you are more zealously intent to promote Independency than Christianity; Presbytery than Christianity; Prelacy than Christianity." (Howe.)

God "*onely*" for his religious opinions. If he could, he must not induce the state to make up his lack of persuasion and spiritual industry by penal statutes.

5. He should possess an aptness to teach, and affectionate *zeal* to do good to men in every way, but especially by proclaiming to them the blessed Gospel of our Lord Jesus Christ, and by teaching them all that our Saviour commanded. A fierce zeal, a melancholy austerity, and a restless, fretting, irritability of feeling,* and an eccentric, odd temper—although these may possibly be connected with true piety, are still all so many blemishes in a Missionary. A well-meaning, obstinate wrong-headedness, may appear to a sincere young man decision of character and Christian courage; but under such a persuasion he may rather "hinder" than "further" the Gospel among the Heathen.

6. He should be a man of prayer, and hold daily and hourly communion with God—a holy man.† He should enter on his work as the servant of Him who has all power in heaven and on earth; and with the same feeling and intention, he must go onward in it. He must look above and beyond the Churches, up to God and to his Saviour. If man forsakes him, he must not forsake the work. If he be neglected by Missionary Societies, or their Secretaries, and his office be merely praised and pitied, rather than really esteemed,‡ he must not abandon it in disgust. He must *lead*, and not *follow* in this great enterprise.

* The two most lauded Protestant Missionaries, Brainerd and Martyn, justly esteemed for their general excellencies, were not, however, the one in his suicidal austerities, and the other in his sensitive irritability, to be imitated.

† "The moral weight of the clergy, [and of every minister of religion at home or abroad,] arises above all, under the divine blessing, *from the holiness of their lives*. It was in part the personal holiness of our Lord, as contrasted with the hypocrisy of the Scribes, which enabled him to speak as one having authority. And had the enemies of St. Paul found aught to object against the purity of his life, he would not have been brought before four successive tribunals, to defend himself merely from the frivolous charge of being a ringleader of the sect of the Nazarenes." (Sumner.)

‡ In the Quarterly Theological Review, (Dec. 1825,) which is con-

7. With his mind thus fortified by an immediate reference to, and constant dependence on heaven, he will

ducted in a mild but partial spirit of criticism, there are some remarks on a book of the late learned Missionary Printer, Mr. Ward, entitled, "Reflections," &c. The reviewer has expressed the sentiment, which, in Discourse XV. page 195, we suspected was generally prevalent, viz. "That the Missionary work is still, by the churches, deemed, in comparison of the Ministry at home, a low service."

The Reviewer sneers at Mr. Ward for asserting that our Saviour appeared in Judea as an "*humble itinerant*," and as "*the Missionary* from heaven."

This sneer is countenanced by applying to the case Dr. Johnson's remark, in his life of Milton, that every man's particular profession, acquires in his own mind an undue degree of importance. This is, no doubt, true; but it applies equally to Authors, Reviewers, Parish Priests, and Bishops, as well as to Missionaries. There may be a bias in the Reviewer, as great as in the Missionary. What then are the facts? Can it be denied by any Christian, that the blessed Jesus appeared in Judea in the form of a "*servant going about*" doing good, or as an "*humble itinerant* teacher,"* unsanctioned and disallowed by the priesthood of the land.

Bishop Heber, the Reviewer remarks, took his leave of the Christian Knowledge Society with a "graceful modesty," describing himself as "*their Missionary* to Calcutta." By this it is supposed the Bishop did not mean to *magnify his office*, but the opposite. Now, for Bishop Heber we have the highest possible respect, and sincerely believe him to be a Bishop of an Apostolic spirit; but if Bp. Heber thought, as the Reviewer seems to do, that being a Bishop over a few thousands of European Christians in India, was a *higher office* than being a "Messenger of Christian Churches" to millions of Pagans, we differ both from the Bishop and the Reviewer: and this opinion we form, not from a desire to magnify our office, but *to do justice to an office* still in very low estimation, not only among the "Great Clerks" of National Churches, but also among the Pastors, or preaching Bishops, of Congregational Churches both in England and Scotland. To be plain, we consider the venerable Missionary Carey to have filled, during his residence in India, as high a station under the Government of Providence, as the Lord Bishop of Calcutta, whose office, and the importance of whose duties, we have no wish to depreciate.

* It is true our blessed Saviour appeared in Judea as the *Messiah*, but still the question returns, Did Messiah appear as a dignitary of the Jewish church, or as an "humble itinerant teacher?"

persevere.* No man who puts his hand to this plough does well to look back and desert it, without some apparent and just cause. But when such cause does occur, a Missionary may return with honour to his native land. That he should bind himself to perpetual exile, and to expatriate his children, is a superstitious requirement of man's imposing.

8. He should "endure hardness as a good soldier of Jesus Christ." To complain of difficulties inseparably connected with the work, is unworthy of him.† And he should have the determination of a good soldier, rather to die in conflict, than desert or compromise his cause. But this soldier-like feeling and resolution, to fight till death, striving to dispossess spiritual enemies, does not make him insensible of the neglect of his fellow Christians;‡ nor are

* "If *success* be demanded, it is replied, *that* is not the inquiry of Him "of whom are all things," either in this world or in that which is to come. With Him the question is this, What has been *aimed* at, what has been *intended* in singleness of heart?" (*Martyn's Memoirs.*)

"Success may be viewed two ways; as to the actual preparation of means for the extensive diffusion of knowledge, and as to the actual turning of many to righteousness. The former kind of success has in some measure attended the Ultra-Gangetic Missions; for the latter we greatly long, and earnestly pray." (Milne.)

† "The conservation of duty to the public (and to his Saviour) ought to be more precious than the conservation of life and being; according to that memorable speech of Pompeius Magnus, when being in commission of purveyance for a famine at Rome, and being dissuaded with great vehemency and instance by his friends about him, that he should *not hazard himself to sea* in an extremity of weather, he said only to them, '*Necesse est ut eam, non ut vivam;*' It is necessary that I should go, not that I should live." (Bacon.)

‡ "The People of the *Universal Church* comprise *all nations—whose conversion it is the duty of all men to promote to the utmost of their power.*"

"With regard to the remuneration to be allotted to the *Ministers of the Universal Church*, as well as to those of *particular religious communities*, it must be allowed that a certain recompence is both reasonable in itself, and sanctioned by the law of God, and the declarations of Christ and his Apostle, *The workman is worthy of his meat. Who goeth a warfare at any time at his own charges? Let him that is taught in the word, communicate unto him that teacheth in all good things—let the elders that*

the Churches, who constitute the Commissariat Department at home, justified in gratuitously adding, by their

rule well, &c. Hence it is lawful and equitable, and the ordinance of God himself, *that they which preach the Gospel, should live of the Gospel.* It is, however, more desirable for examples' sake, and for the preventing of offence or suspicion, as well as more noble and honourable in itself, and conducive to our more complete glorifying God, *to render an unpaid service to the church;* in this, as well as in all other instances, and, after the example of our Lord, *to minister and serve gratuitously. Even as the Son of man came not to be ministered unto, but to minister. Freely ye have received, freely give. Remember the words of the Lord Jesus, how he said, It is more blessed to give than to receive.* Paul proposed the same to the imitation of ministers in general, and recommended it by his example. *Ye yourselves know, that these hands have ministered unto my necessities, and to them that were with me: I have showed you in all things, how that so labouring, ye ought to support the weak. Yourselves know how ye ought to follow us; for we behaved not ourselves disorderly among you; neither did we eat any man's bread for nought; but wrought with labour and travail night and day, that we might not be chargeable to any of you: not because we have not power, but to make ourselves an example unto you to follow us. I have used none of these things; neither have I written these things that it should be so done unto me; for it were better for me to die, than that any man should make my glorying void: what is my reward then? verily, that when I preach the Gospel, I may make the Gospel of Christ without charge, that I abuse not my power in the Gospel. When I was present with you, and wanted, I was chargeable to no man. . . . . In all things I have kept myself from being burthensome unto you, and so will I keep myself. No man shall stop me of this boasting. What I do, that I will do, that I may cut off occasion from them that desire occasion, that wherein they glory, they may be found even as we are. Behold the third time I am ready to come unto you, and I will not be burthensome to you; for I seek not yours, but you; for the children ought not to lay up for the parents, but the parents for the children. Did I make gain of you by any of them whom I sent unto you? Did Titus make a gain of you? Walked we not in the same spirit? We do all things, dearly beloved, for your edifying.* And if at any time extreme necessity compelled him to accept the voluntary aid of the churches, such constraint was so grievous to him, that he accuses himself as if he were guilty of robbery. *I robbed other churches, taking wages of them, to do you service.*"

"Pecuniary considerations ought by no means to enter into our motives for preaching the Gospel. *Thy money perish with thee, because thou hast thought that the gift of God may be purchased with money.*" If it be a crime to purchase the Gospel, what must it be to sell it? How then, ask the Ministers, are we to live? How ought they to live, but as the

parsimony or neglect, to the sufferings of the soldier in the field. Still, if they do carelessly add to his sufferings, the good Missionary will, nevertheless, remain at his post, as long as ever the banner of the cross continues to be unfurled.*

9. A Missionary should be a man of good temper,† tender feeling, and active benevolence, bearing much and long with enemies and young converts; in meekness instructing those that oppose themselves; not a stern,

Prophets lived of old? On their own private resources, by the exercise of some calling, by honest industry, after the example of the Prophets, who accounted it no disgrace to hew their own wood, and build their own houses;—of (our blessed Saviour Jesus) Christ, who (some suppose) wrought with his own hands as a carpenter." (MILTON.)

Of the *lawfulness* of Christian Missionaries and Ministers following some secular profession for a livelihood, whilst they teach the great truths of Christianity to others, whether in Christianized or Pagan countries, I have no doubt; but the general *practicability* of it in modern times, is not so apparent. In this, as in other cases, the work will be best done by a division of labour. (MORRISON.)

"If, however, such self-denial be thought too arduous for the Ministers of the present day, they will most nearly approach to it, when, relying on the providence of God who called them, they shall look for the necessary support of life, not from the edicts of the civil power, (nor from the fixed stipends or salaries of Missionary Societies,) but from the spontaneous good-will and liberality of the Church, in requital of their voluntary service." (MILTON.)

"Bishop Mant justifies the union of the magisterial character and that of an instructor of youth, as '*secular occupations*' consistent with the functions of a clergyman." (*Christian Remembrancer, Feb.* 1826.)

The Minister of religion "desecrates his high calling, when he considers it in the light of a commercial transaction, in which a bargain is struck for a certain return of services, upon the payment of a certain price." (SUMNER.)

* We should almost doubt the propriety of this martial imagery, were it not sanctioned by Apostolic example, lest we should be supposed the advocates of war. For the Missionary should be the *Herald of peace*, not only between a guilty conscience and high heaven, but also of peace on earth among men. (MORRISON.)

† Some young English Missionaries are far inferior to Asiatic Pagans, in command of temper, in a knowledge of human nature, and of the rights of others to respectful treatment, however erroneous their creed may be. (MORRISON.)

bitter, metaphysical doctrinalist. He should ever be ready to do good to all men, to the evil and unthankful, as well as to the household of faith. If he have it in his power to communicate pecuniary aid to the distressed, he will not confine it to those who profess to become Christians, but extend it liberally to all human beings who are in the midst of suffering. Some persons, to avoid the possibility of encouraging hypocrisy, would have Missionaries studiously avoid bestowing any charity. But then, in this case, the heathen mock his discourses on benevolence, for he is never seen to practise it. The straitened circumstances of Missionaries generally, whose allowances are often scarcely adequate to support their own families, place pecuniary charities out of their power. The late Dr. Milne felt much this difficulty, and sent home a request to have small sums placed at the disposal of Missionaries, to be expended by them in relieving cases of distress among the heathen. But however desirable this may be, it is possible, without silver or gold, to exhibit kindness and benevolence of heart and conduct, in various nameless ways.

10. The Missionaries should not cherish high notions of priestly* power and privilege, but should introduce

* Seeing it is now generally admitted that the choice of a nation can constitute rightful magistrates, and a rightful dynasty of kings, (who are also "*ministers of God*" for good,) it seems inconsistent to reason, that the choice of a Christian assembly, or church, consisting of "faithful men," cannot constitute a rightful Pastor or Bishop. The kings of England, since the "*glorious revolution*," acknowledge that their right to reign is derived from the choice of the people; but the Bishops of the English Church still cling to a supposed divine right, derived mysteriously by a disputed, uninterrupted succession from the Apostles, through the Bishops or Popes of Rome; deeming this a better title than the election of Christian congregations. And some of the advocates of this system still scoff at those whom they call "self-created," and "self-constituted" teachers. The Presbyterian Church of Scotland too, and the Secession Church, are not less staunch in requiring, as by divine right, the communication of their authority to teachers of Christianity, and the same leaven seems working among Dissenters and Methodists. But if Bishop Burnet was correct in considering an experimental knowledge of Christianity, and an ardent desire to communicate it to others, as a being

a system of mutual instruction, to bear as extensively as possible on the facts, principles, and duties of Christianity.

"*moved by the Holy Ghost*" to undertake the ministry, surely any believer whatever, *provided with the requisite knowledge and piety*, is competent to teach Christianity. *Knowledge* of any science *constitutes a right* to teach it, and why the communication of Christian science should be fettered by any other conditions, is not easy to apprehend.* It is true, incompetent persons may assume to teach; and it is equally true, incompetent persons may be regularly appointed to teach. There is no system without its defects or abuses. Unless the disciples of Jesus, "scattered abroad" throughout the United Kingdom, and all nations of the world, exert themselves, and exhort their fellow-creatures to "know the Lord," we see no adequate means for the universal diffusion of Christian knowledge. The Pagans of China teach, that it is the duty of every man, not only to study virtue for himself, but also to communicate it to others, with all the knowledge and experience he may acquire; if he perform only the first part of this duty, and omit the latter, he sins against the light of nature; whereas many of the Christian priesthood of Europe discourage every effort to communicate Christian knowledge by any other persons than themselves; and some avow that they would rather have persons ignorant of Christian doctrine, than that a layman should teach it. A Dutch merchant in China wrote prayers, and distributed them amongst the poor Catholics resident in Macao, for doing which he was summoned before the Bishop, and reprimanded. The Bishop told him, that although the prayers were good, it was irregular and improper for any but a Clergyman to write and circulate them.

The Ecclesiastics of Europe, who have had it in their power to influence the legislatures of different countries, instead of encouraging, have procured the *prohibition of private assemblies* of Christians for *mutual instruction* and *devotional exercises*. The prevention of seditious meetings has been the plea; but the utmost charity cannot help suspecting other motives, arising from selfishness and the lust of power; motives, indeed, similar to those that originated the Brahminical caste in Asia. Under such circumstances, no one can be surprised at the ignorance of Christian doctrine, and the hostility to it which still prevails in all the nations of Europe; for Ecclesiastics have usurped the keeping of the key of knowledge, and have, in a large majority of instances, (it is to be feared,) neither entered themselves, nor suffered others to enter. The Archimandrites, and Cardinals, and Bishops,

* "The Romanists reproach the Protestants, that their Ministers have no Mission, as not being authorized in their ministry, either by an uninterrupted succession from the Apostles, or by miracles, or by any extraordinary proof of a vocation. Many among us deny any other Mission necessary for the ministry, than the talents necessary to discharge it."

Every new disciple should be, to the extent of his capabilities, a new Missionary. No native convert should be taught to live only for himself. In this way, under the fostering care of the Great Shepherd, Christian truth will spread itself in all lands, and the vocation of Missionary eventually cease.

> "And they shall not teach any more
> Every man his neighbour, and every man his brother,
> Saying, 'Know ye Jehovah,'
> *For they shall all know* ME,
> From the least of them unto the greatest of them,
> Saith Jehovah——"
>
> *(Jeremiah.)*

CONCLUSION.

The preceding thoughts on the qualifications of Missionaries are presented to the reader, not as a complete essay on the subject, but as touching on the leading points, which the writer, from his own experience, considers applicable to the present times.

The qualifications of each Missionary, natural or ac-

and Presbyters, and other Rulers of national churches, who, by envying the Lord's people, being prophets, and interfering to prevent their prophesying or teaching, *hinder* the Gospel, instead of *furthering* it, have reason to anticipate a terrible account at the day of judgment.

Since the human mind is substantially the same in all ages and countries, and by it the patriarchal and the Jewish revelations were corrupted, it is not matter of surprise that the Christian revelation should also be neglected or perverted, and corrupted by those who should teach it.* And, therefore, as in great monarchies, there are appointments which proceed, not through the usual channels, but immediately from the throne, so the Divine Providence seems sometimes to overlook the constituted authorities on earth, and Himself bring forwards unsanctioned individuals to reform and bless mankind. Such was the Reformer Luther, and many others.

* "As the Church of *Jerusalem*, *Alexandria*, and *Antioch*, have erred, so also the Church of *Rome* hath erred, not only in their living and manner of ceremonies, but also in matters of faith."

(Articles of Religion.)

quired, should be suited to the people he has to instruct. For the old civilized nations of Asia, a degree of literary attainment may be suitable, which is not required in Africa or the South Seas. And in the same Mission, it will be most efficient when it consists of various gifts and qualifications. To require perfection, or high excellence, in many departments, from the same individual, is to expect more than the experience of mankind warrants.* Preachers, Teachers, Writers, Catechists, School Masters

* "I can do nothing to any purpose at speaking the language myself."—"To ride about, frequently in order to procure collections for the school, &c. &c. leave me little for application to the study of the Indian languages. And when I add to this, the time that is necessarily consumed upon my Journals, I must say I have little to spare for other business."—"I have been obliged to labour twelve and thirteen hours in a day, till my spirits have been extremely wasted, and my life almost spent, to get these writings accomplished. I cannot possibly gain two hours in a week for reading or any other studies. Frequently when I attempt to redeem time, by sparing it out of my sleeping hours, I am by that means thrown under bodily indisposition, and rendered fit for nothing." (BRAINERD.)

How lamentable that a man of Brainerd's spirit and zeal should have time and health consumed in riding about to procure collections and in *writing journals, instead of* learning the language of the Heathen! (MORRISON.)

"Tues. Dec. 11. Felt very poorly in body, being much tired and worn out the last night."

"12. Was again very weak, endeavoured to spend the day in fasting and prayer; I was much disordered when I arose, but having determined to spend the day in this manner, I attempted it." "The sins I most lamented were pride and wandering thoughts, the former of these excited me to think of writing, or preaching, or converting Heathen, or *performing some* other *great work*, that my name might live, when I should be dead."

"16. Was overwhelmed with dejection, that I knew not how to live; I longed for death exceedingly." (BRAINERD.)

In *these* expériences of Brainerd, it is lamentable to see how much *Christlessness* there is. They are recorded, we hope, not for the imitation of Missionaries, but as a caution. He says, "My soul was in anguish and ready to drop into despair, to find so much of that cursed temper—Pride." Yes! that "cursed temper" is, we fear, too much mingled with the best services of the best of men. (MORRISON.)

and School Mistresses; Principals and Assistants, united in one Mission, centrically situated, are more likely to communicate, to a wide circumference, extensively and effectually, Christian knowledge, than a Mission composed of Preachers only.

Those Christian Societies who make each member of a Mission, whether experienced or inexperienced, whether judicious or injudicious, whether of twenty years or a day's standing, totally independent of each other; and who from principle reject all authority or control, among the foreign agents themselves, may perhaps elicit more individual effort than is the case where a contrary system is adopted; but they produce not that co-operation, harmony, and general effect which the others do; because the individual efforts are liable to be eccentric and extravagant, conflicting rather than co-operating with each other. A Moravian Missionary Community, with a mild paternal system of episcopal order and subordination, or a control of "Elders,"* is a more pleasing and edifying spectacle, and perhaps a more efficient agency, than several independent isolated individual Missionaries, without any system of order and co-operation; where not even length of service, nor grey hairs, are allowed any weight; where the "*younger*" do not "submit themselves to the *elder*," but "wrest" the next clause of St. Peter's admonition, so as to make him (by their interpretation) immediately contradict himself, and also the whole scope of the inspired writers, by saying, "Be subject one to another;" as if it meant that all distinctions of age and experience should be confounded, and the precept just uttered be reversed, and that the "elder must submit to the younger."

At home, independent pastors who may be young and injudicious, are kept in their place, and in order, by the common sense of a large body of Pastors, Deacons, and Churches; but in distant lands that check is removed,

* Since the "young," in due time, become "elders," this mode of rule is not to be confounded with an aristocratic oligarchy.

and when, abroad, unhappily a want of humility and sense of propriety do occur, there is, on the Independent system, no authority nor Christian community to repress them; and since old experienced servants may not always think it for the good of the service to submit, even to a majority of young and inexperienced ones, disunion occurs, and merely individual effort is presented to the enemy, instead of a close and well directed phalanx, continuously filled up by new men, as disaster or death may thin the ranks.*

I am greatly in favour of Missionary communities,† with a diversity of talent and acquirement, of age and of sex, not even excluding lay brethren,‡ for the superinten-

* "In Missionary establishments the greatest care should be taken in giving to every man his proper department, and in preserving a general co-operation in all their efforts. Each Missionary should guard against pertinacity of opinion, and the encouraging of those habits of fastidious delicacy which grow upon men, who are accustomed in all things to consult only their private feelings. Unless we can resolve on this sacrifice we are not qualified to act in Missions." (MELVILLE HORNE.)

† "For as we have many members in one body, and all members have not the same office: so we being many, are one body in Christ, and every one members one of another: having then gifts differing according to the grace that is given to us, whether prophesy, let us prophesy according to the proportion of faith; or ministry, let us wait on our ministering: or he that teacheth, on teaching: or he that exhorteth, on exhortation: he that giveth, let him do it with simplicity; he that ruleth, with diligence; he that sheweth mercy, with cheerfulness. Let love be without dissimulation. Abhor that which is evil; cleave to that which is good. Be kindly affectioned one to another with brotherly love; in honour preferring one another." (PAUL.)

‡ "To procure a large supply of Missionaries, I propose that an equal number of pious lay brethren should be employed in every Mission, as school-masters, transcribers, exhorters, and to assist in all the emergencies of the Mission, to which Missionaries may not be able to give attention The young and inexperienced would derive instruction and support from their elder brethren, and after a few years trial they might be promoted to the honourable station of Missionaries. Such an establishment would be the best seminary of education for Missions, and with occasional helps from Europe, be sufficient for all demands." (MELVILLE HORNE.)

dence of secular affairs, and perhaps by industry for the sustenance of the Mission; whilst all persons of the community co-operate to promote Christian knowledge, and all its temporal affairs are made subservient to the propagation of the Gospel. Not, however, to such a degree as to interfere with private property; but so as to destroy all selfishness and individualism; presenting not dislocated members, but a *Body* complete and efficient, either for support, or defence, or useful and benevolent exertion.

ON THE

QUALIFICATIONS AND DUTIES

OF

DIRECTORS OR MANAGING COMMITTEES

OF

Missionary Societies.

"In these (Missionary) Associations, I wish those Ministers to come forward whose character and services give them most respectability; and having once engaged, I would have the *Association* to be actuated by *a true spirit* of Missions. They should be zealous, active, indefatigable. Any Minister who is not warmly affected to Missions, should be excluded from the acting Committee. What these Gentlemen are, their Missions will be." (Melville Horne.)

A modern Missionary Society has not any exact exemplar in Holy Scripture, nor does it resemble in its nature any Political or Commercial Association; and therefore the rules and usages which suit these, will not necessarily suit it. If, indeed, they be inconsiderately applied, they may injure it. As for example, the assumption that a Missionary Society resembles a Commercial Association, may introduce a relative distinction between the Subscribers, the Managing Committee, (by some not very happily, perhaps, called Directors,) and the foreign Evangelists, subversive entirely of the *Christian relation* and *spirit of love* which ought to pervade all who are connected a Missionary Society. The first principle of Com- Association is individual temporal advantage; the ınnciple of Missionary Association is the spiritual . eternal welfare of others. The foreign Agents of Commercial Societies engage in the service for their own private emolument, and properly stand in the relation of servants; the foreign Ministers of Missionary Societies engage, without reward, to carry into effect the benevolent designs of associated Christians, and subscribe to the cause their personal services. They are then Fellow-labourers with the Subscribers and their Managing Representatives at home. As disciples of our Lord Jesus Christ, all are equal at the time of their association; and a spirit of devotion to *the* MASTER, of reciprocal affection to each other, and of good will to men, constitute the only proper impulse to their association, and the only principle on which they should ever continue to act. There is no period at which this equality should cease. They have no affairs to keep secret from each other; no separate or private ends to promote. They do not stand in the relation of master and servant, employer and employed. They should all have but one end; they should *meet in one common council.* Mutual confidence, esteem, and affection, are essential to the well-being of the association: nay, are essential to the maintenance of its Christian character.

In secular Associations, the dissevering tendencies of reciprocal jealousies will be overcome by the impulse of private interest; but in a benevolent Association, where there is, in fact, no private interest to serve, mutual jealousies and distrust are ruinous to the whole concern. The subscription of *personal service* from a man whom the Association does not esteem, and in whom it cannot confide, had better not be accepted; and the *Committee-services* of a narrow-minded, money-loving pietist had better not be requested. When the Missionary Class are treated as mere *Employés,* or hirelings, good men will not join them, and they will gradually become mere mercenaries and there will be complaints of domination and niggardliness on the one hand, and of rebellion and extravagance on the other; and the spirit of piety will decay, and the *love of Christ, which is the soul of Missions*, will wax cold—an evil in this enterprize, of much more magnitude than the diminution of funds, or any other which affects not the vital principle.

1. A Director should, we conceive, be like a Missionary, a man of unfeigned piety, conversant with intellectual, spiritual, and eternal realities. A worldly or secularized, merely mercantile mind, that places literary, moral, and religious considerations far behind in the back ground, whilst pecuniary matters are exalted to the chief place and to the highest influence, is unfit for directing the affairs of a Religious Society; because the moral apparatus of well-qualified Ministers, Teachers, and Preachers; Books, Schools, Colleges, and Chapels, will be kept out of the service, for the sake of pecuniary savings.

2. A Director should, like a Missionary, be a devoted disciple of the Lord Jesus. His doings as a Director should be considered as done to the Lord, and not to man. If he look no higher than serving "the public," and consider his gratuitous service as what may either be done or left undone, he is not fit for a Director.

3. He should not consider himself as a Lord over (God's) *heritage* (των κληρων), i. e. (as some would say,) the "Clerks or Clergy;" but as an example to the whole Christian flock; and as a *Father* or a *Brother* to his fellow-servants in distant lands. If they are prosperous and successful, he will no doubt rejoice with them; this is easy: but also if they be unprosperous, and unsuccessful, he will sympathize with them; and if they backslide, he will mourn over them with true sorrow, as a father or a brother would do. If they write unwise letters, recording petty strifes, &c. (for who is wise at all times,) he will reprove and admonish, but not scorn them.

The devout men and women in the land, who supply the funds of Missionary Societies, cherish, no doubt, the kindest possible feelings to good Missionaries; but these kind feelings must generally be communicated by proxy, through Directors and official Secretaries of Societies. And a good Director or Secretary, who has the "*true spirit of Missions*," will, from the impulse of his own love and zeal, even outdo the requirements of the pious contributors to the cause. The Churches and pious Friends of Missions, could never mean that Directors or Managing Committees should be Masters over the Foreign Evangelists, but Fellow-helpers to the Truth; a representative medium between the Christian Public and the Foreign Agents; an important and indispensable link in the chain of operations.

4. A man who does not view the welfare of the *Universal Church*, or the *conversion of heathen nations* to the faith of Christ, a greater object than the local welfare of his own branch or section of the church, is not well fitted for a Missionary Director. He who is more anxious to retain talent for the sake of Independency or Episcopacy in Scotland, or Presbyterianism in England, than to employ it for the sake of the heathen world—or who thinks it wrong to request an eminent Minister of a particular congregation, to remove and serve the cause of the *Universal Church*—does not appear to possess the *true spirit* of Missions. He has far *too low an idea* of the *service* which he is called upon to superintend, to provide for it *well-qualified Agents*, which, after all, constitute its real and its only "dignity." For a Society, however rich, or a National Establishment, however affluent, are, in reference to Christianity, but like the scaffolding employed to rear a magnificent temple. They have neither dignity nor worth in themselves. They are only useful so far as they subserve the end. If the time, and attention, and property, given to rear the temple, be spent on ornamenting the scaffolding, instead of employing good materials, with able and efficient labourers to raise the building, it is very apparent that the time, and attention, and property have all been mis-spent. The Home Management of foreign Missions, is but as the external scaffolding. Christian Labourers, in distant lands, are those alone who can there rear the temple of truth to

Jehovah. Therefore, whilst a good Missionary will be thankful for all the help afforded him, a good Director will rejoice, for the ***Temple's*** sake, to afford every possible facility to him who actually labours at it; and all ought to remember, that "except the Lord build the House they labour in vain that build it."

5. He who would wish to be a good Director, should not undertake too many offices in benevolent Societies. In London benevolent men are generally called upon for more sacrifice of time than their private affairs will admit of; and when they consent to hold many offices, they are liable to do justice to none. Let there be a division of labour. I have known a party of persons enter a committee room an hour and a half after the appointed time of meeting, and interrupt the business by an excessive haste to conclude it, because they had to attend three public meetings on the same evening. In that case they could not do justice to any, and had better have staid away with their half hour of time from that meeting which required four hours to perform the duty of it. A good Director of Missions should be "*warmly affected*," *enthusiastic* in their behalf; so as cheerfully to devote to them the time requisite.

6. A good Director will inform himself as fully as possible of the circumstances of each Mission; the character of the people among whom it labours, the persons who constitute it, their wants, their difficulties, their sufferings, their sorrows, and their joys. He is not a man who merely desires the end, whilst he neglects the ordinary and requisite means.

7. *He who directs well, is worthy of great honour,* both from his fellow Christians, and from the Missionaries; and he will, no doubt, receive eventually the approbation of his Saviour. The most sincere and purest motives must have influenced the leading men, in the late revival of Missions, to bear them onward, in attending to the duties of their office. Their reward has been in their work; the Saviour's glory, and the eternal happiness of kindred spirits, have, we believe, been ever pre-

sent to their minds. Such men boast not of their services to the public, nor regret the discomfort to which those services must often have subjected them. Nor have their families any real cause to regret the time taken from their society, and devoted to the general interests of the Redeemer's kingdom; for, "If any man *serve me*, (said the blessed Jesus,) him will my Father honour."

A PARTING WORD

TO

PROTESTANT MISSIONARIES.

My fellow servants—In the preceding pages I have advocated, not your individual cause, or my own, but have stated opinions which I think of importance to the propagation of the Gospel. These opinions are the result of my experience, and I offer them only as views of the Missionary cause, which appear to me correct. It is notorious that some of our number, during the last thirty years, have deserted, and others have done injury to the sacred cause; and that in former times Missionaries from the Latin Church, under the famous congregation for the propagation of the faith, the Priests of Foreign Missions, during the seventeenth and eighteenth centuries, appear in Asia to have laboured almost in vain.

The Congregation, or Society, founded by Gregory XV. 1622, was enriched with ample revenues; a vast number of Missionaries; books of foreign and domestic languages; seminaries for Christian and Pagan youths, charitable establishments for the relief of the persecuted, &c. But after the labours of two centuries, beyond the limits of Europe, a large portion of the world still remains Pagan or Mohammedan; and in Europe, the ancient and the reformed churches are, according to credible witnesses, greatly degenerated. "The religious orders that made the greatest figure in these Missions, were the Jesuits, the Dominicans, the Franciscans and the Capuchins, who, though concerned in one common cause, agreed nevertheless very ill among themselves; accusing each other of the want of zeal in the service of Christ, and of corrupting the purity of the Christian doctrine to promote their ambitious purposes."

It is said of these Missionaries, that they perpetually employed the arts of adulation, and the seductions of bribery, to insinuate themselves into the friendship and protection of men in power, that they were deeply involved in the cabals of courts, and the intrigues of politicians, &c. In what relates to the propagation of the Gospel in foreign parts, much more confidence was placed in the austere sobriety, poverty, industry, and patience of the Capuchins and Carmelites, than in the opulence, artifice, genius, and fortitude of the disciples of Loyola. It is asserted that the Jesuits persuaded the Indians and Chinese, that there was a great conformity between their ancient theology and the new religion they were exhorted to embrace. "*The protection of men in power was the great object they principally aimed at, as the surest method of establishing their authority, and extending their influence.* And hence they studied all the arts that could render them agreeable or useful to great men; hence *their application to mathematics, physic, poetry; to the theory of painting, sculpture, architecture, and the other elegant arts; and hence their perseverance in studying men and manners, the interests of princes, and the affairs of the world, in order to prepare them for giving counsel in critical situations, and suggesting expedients in perlexing and complicated cases.* It would be endless to enumerate *all the circumstances that have been complained of in* the proceeding of the Jesuits." Such is the report of ecclesiastical historians, but I am of opinion that the Catholic Missionaries, with all their faults, have been greatly calumniated.

One class of the Catholic Missionaries in Asia, adopted (it is said) the system of a "wilfull povertie," &c. the other class appeared as "men of the world," but both failed. There are modern patrons of Missions, who possess authority in foreign colonies, who write home for "gentlemanly Missionaries," who shall attend to the "higher classes" of natives, instead of *preaching the Gospel to the poor.* Now it is my humble opinion, that all plots, whether for duping the ignorant, or flattering the learned; courting the populace, or cringing to the great, should, by Missionaries, be totally abandoned. Kindness to inferiors, and respect for superiors in society, must always be cherished; whilst towards both, the Missionary's great object should be the exhibition of CHRIST'S Gospel;—I mention this *Blessed Name* with the greatest reverence, although it be unaccompanied by any adjunct.—The spiritual Christians, both at home and abroad, have, I fear, too much regard in this day to the patronage of the powerful. Alas! many men at the Head of Governments and of Churches, and among the Counsellors of Monarchs, have as much need of being what our blessed Saviour calls, "γεννηθῃ," (*renatus*, or born again) as the Pagans of China, or of India. It is utterly a mistake that by man's efforts merely, or by human learning, or the influence of Rulers, the glorious Gospel can be propagated. God our Saviour must be honoured, and the Holy Spirit continually referred to, by never-ceasing reliance, and ever-constant humble prayer. We should *use* the best means, but *trust* only in the Almighty arm. "Not by might, nor power, but BY MY Spirit, saith Jehovah," shall the conversion of the world be effected. The means to be employed consist, no doubt, of a simple, sincere, and lucid declaration, and reiterated inculcation of the glorious Gospel of the blessed God; with the constant practice of tempers and conduct becoming the children of God, and teachers of the religion of Jesus. Thus occupied, may we be found, when death shall summon us to appear before God in judgment. Amen!

We, my brethren, I conceive, should be exceedingly grateful to God, that he has inclined the hearts of his people, in the United Kingdom, to afford us means of a pecuniary nature, and some of us education, without which we could not have carried into effect the pious desires of our hearts. We should esteem them, and love them, for their co-operation in our Saviour's cause. And, O, how careful should we be not to give them just cause of grief and discouragement. They have often had much cause for regret and sorrow, respecting some who seemed to run well for a time, but who have subsequently wasted their strength in strifes which eventually ate up the spirit of Christian piety and zeal. Differences of opinion among Missionaries should be, in a kind spirit, settled on the spot; and not sent home in angry letters, to grieve and dishearten the Churches.

From the unavoidable character of popular Societies, they can never, I fear, supply the place of Kindred, and Friends, and Home; and a Missionary must generally submit to be without the natural supports to his mind, which these things afford. I believe, however, that in some Societies there might be less of the *frigid manner of mere counting-house business;* and more *affectionate attention* to the solace of a disconsolate Missionary's mind, than is usually the case. But should we not remember, that it is expected of us to look to Heaven, and gather our consolations from the Gospel of Christ? I do not think that, because we dedicate ourselves to the naturally uninviting office of Missionaries, we have lost our rights, either as men or as Christians; but if the world thinks it may scoff at us, and the Churches look upon us as a sort of devotees, who have voluntarily abandoned our place amongst them, we must bear these things, and still go onward with our work. If, by God's help, we remain faithful, there are bright prospects before us. These hasty thoughts are not, my Brethren, brought before you as any thing new; but as the opinions of a fellow-servant, to be preserved on record, and to appear whenever evidence on these subjects shall be adduced. Farewell!

TO

COLLECTORS AND CONTRIBUTORS

TO THE

CAUSE OF CHRISTIAN MISSIONS.

Friends and Fellow Servants,

I ADDRESS you as Members of the Universal* Church of God, as sanctified in Christ Jesus, as those that call upon the name of Christ Jesus our Lord.

You and the Missionaries are under equal obligations to our Divine Redeemer, and should equally have a regard to the accomplishment of what he has commanded in all the labours of Christian philanthropy. The Missionary work may, perhaps, more than the Home ministry, with scriptural propriety, be compared to a warfare. Missionaries are the soldiers who go forth to assail, under the banners of the cross, Satan's usurped dominion over our fellow creatures. It is a just and necessary war, not against our fellow men, but against the powers of darkness, to deliver enslaved sinners from the devil's despotism. Enemies may scoff at a " church militant," but the sneer is superficial. We use the phrase in a moral and spiritual sense; and wo to the church, when in this sense she shall lose her martial character. Alas, that she has so often sunk this character, and instead of resisting with the weapons of truth and Christian fortitude the lovers of sanguinary war, and fighting manfully against satanic usurpation in every land, she has supinely and traitorously associated herself with the enemies of Zion's King!

Missionaries, we have said, are the *soldiers* in this warfare; " But who goeth a warfare at any time on his own charges?"

* *Catholic* has been assumed exclusively by the Romanists, and therefore there is a difficulty in using it.

E E

It is not practicable for him to provide the transport ships, the equipment, the military stores, the commissariat, supplies, and also to fight his country's battles. It devolves on the Christian community to supply these;—to supply liberally an adequate number of men;—a competent provision of all the necessary *materiel* for carrying on the war with vigour, and a steady perseverance, till a glorious peace be established, by the complete overthrow of Satan's kingdom. There are *spiritual* supplies, to communicate which is beyond your power: they must come from the "Captain of Salvation." But there are *physical* supplies, to raise which devolves on you. And in a qualified sense, these, constitute the "sinews" of this war. Your department, therefore, is one of high importance to the success of the cause. In proportion as you fulfil or neglect your duty, the Christian army will be weakly or ably manned and officered; will pine and die through fatigue and want in distant lands; or go onward with spirit and vigour in their benevolent conflict.

I hope you will be more and more convinced that your department of the King's service is a *duty*, not a "*charity*:" And whatever is done to aid the brave men who fear not the worldly man's scorn, nor the oppressor's frown, nor exile, nor dangers, nor death, in His service, *deserve* all the support that it is possible for you to afford them.

Women are renowned for loyalty to their King and attachment to their Country's defenders; and in the Church also, since the day they appeared at the foot of the cross, and at the sepulchre of Jesus, they have maintained their character for efficient aid to "The Good Cause." To them we look to fan the flame of missionary zeal in their husbands', and brothers', and lovers' breasts; and to instil the "True Spirit of Missions" into their children's docile minds.

FINALLY,

To all the subjects of Zion's King, throughout the British Isles, and the rest of Christendom, I would suggest certain arrangements, such as they may see fit, to bring the concerns of Foreign Missions more efficiently into the domestic and social circle; that *Families* may sympathise more completely with the circumstances of solitary Missionaries, or new formed churches abroad.

It has occurred to me, that zealous Christians, in the same neighbourhood, might with great advantage meet occasionally, without any of the formalities of an association, to inform themselves fully concerning foreign churches and missionary stations generally; whilst the members of each association, attach themselves to one or two missions, for the purpose of interesting themselves especially in their behalf; and writing out an occasional letter of Christian sympathy or congratulation, in the united names of the persons so assembling. An autograph communication from a faithful soldier in the field, in return, would interest the hearts of the disciples more than a printed despatch ever can. All the Missionaries I have known have felt the want of private expressions of Christian sympathy, and tokens of friendship, in contradistinction from merely official correspondence. Friendship and love are, of all human supports, the most powerful to the heart of man. Adieu!

THE END.

Dennett, Printer, Leather, Lane London.

Zeitfracht Medien GmbH
Ferdinand-Jühlke-Straße 7
99095 Erfurt, Deutschland
produktsicherheit@kolibri360.de